Aligning Enterprise, System, and Software Architectures

Ivan Mistrík
Independent Consultant, Germany

Antony Tang
Swinburne University of Technology, Australia

Rami Bahsoon
University of Birmingham, UK

Judith A. Stafford
Tufts University, USA

Managing Director:	Lindsay Johnston
Editorial Director:	Joel Gamon
Book Production Manager:	Jennifer Romanchak
Publishing Systems Analyst:	Adrienne Freeland
Development Editor:	Myla Merkel
Assistant Acquisitions Editor:	Kayla Wolfe
Typesetter:	Alyson Zerbe
Cover Design:	Nick Newcomer

Published in the United States of America by
Business Science Reference (an imprint of IGI Global)
701 E. Chocolate Avenue
Hershey PA 17033
Tel: 717-533-8845
Fax: 717-533-8661
E-mail: cust@igi-global.com
Web site: http://www.igi-global.com

Library of Congress Cataloging-in-Publication Data

Aligning enterprise, system, and software architectures / Ivan Mistrik ... [et al.], editors.
     p. cm.
  Includes bibliographical references and index.
  Summary: "This book covers both theoretical approaches and practical solutions in the processes for aligning enterprise, systems, and software architectures"--Provided by publisher.
  ISBN 978-1-4666-2199-2 (hardcover) -- ISBN 978-1-4666-2200-5 (ebook) -- ISBN 978-1-4666-2201-2 (print & perpetual access) 1. Management information systems. 2. Business enterprises--Computer networks. 3. Information technology--Management. 4. Software architecture. I. Mistrík, Ivan.
  HD30.213.A45 2013
  658.4'038011--dc23
                        2012026463

British Cataloguing in Publication Data
A Cataloguing in Publication record for this book is available from the British Library.

List of Reviewers

Fernando Alcántara, *Indra, Spain*
Charlie Alfred, *Foliage, Inc., USA*
Nour Ali, *University of Limerick, Ireland*
Rain Ali, *University of Trento, Italy*
Thomas Alspaugh, *Georgetown University, USA*
Hazeline Asuncion, *University of Washington, Bothell, USA*
Jakob Axelsson, *Mälardalen University, Sweden*
Stefanie Betz, *University of Karlsruhe, Germany*
Rafael Capilla, *Universidad Rey Juan Carlos Madrid, Spain*
Christine Choppy, *LIPN (Universit Paris13), France*
Lawrence Chung, *University of Texas at Dallas, USA*
Viktor Clerc, *inspearit, The Netherlands*
Chris Cooper-Bland, *Endava Ltd, UK*
Félix Cuadrado, *Polytechnic University of Madrid, Spain*
Juan C. Dueñas, *Universidad Politécnica de Madrid, Spain*
Veli-Pekka Eloranta, *Tampere University of Technology, Finland*
Funmilade Faniyi, *University of Birmingham, UK*
Rodrigo Garcia-Carmona, *Universidad Politécnica de Madrid, Spain*
John Grundy, *Swinburne University of Technology, Australia*
Mark Harman, *University College London, UK*
Maritta Heisel, *University of Duisburg-Essen, Germany*
Suresh Kamath, *MetLife Inc., USA*
Kai Koskimies, *Tampere University of Technology, Finland*
Soo Ling Lim, *University College London, UK*
Ruth Malan, *Bredemeyer Consulting, USA*
Myla Merkel, *IGI Global, USA*
Christoph Miksovic, *IBM, Switzerland*
Thenalapadi S. Mohan, *Infosys Technologies Ltd, Bangalore, India*
Irene Moser, *Swinburne University of Technology, Australia*
Gerrit Muller, *Buskerud University College, Norway*
Manuel Noguera, *Universidad de Granada, Spain*
Andreas Oberweis, *Karlsruhe Institute of Technology, Germany*

Table of Contents

Section 1
Architecture Alignment - Theories

Section 4
Industrial Case Studies and Practices

Detailed Table of Contents

Section 1
Architecture Alignment - Theories

Chapter 1
  Eoin Woods, Artechra, UK
  Nick Rozanski, Artechra, UK

The architect takes a high-profile role in many IT departments today. In fact, it can be quite difficult in some organizations to find a senior member of IT technical staff whose job title does not include the word "architect." However there is little consensus in the academic community or amongst practitioners as to the responsibilities of the many different types of architect we encounter – or indeed, what they should even be called. In this chapter, the authors propose a simple, widely applicable taxonomy of architects, namely enterprise architects, application architects, and infrastructure architects. The authors define distinguishing characteristics, their responsibilities, the stakeholders with whom they engage, and the tools and techniques they use. The chapter shows how this taxonomy can be applied to most, if not all, practicing architects in the information systems domain, and explains how it helps us understand how such architects work together to help deliver the organization's business goals.

Chapter 2

Khrystyna Nordheimer, University of Mannheim, Germany

Stefan Seedorf, University of Mannheim, Germany

Christian Thum, University of Mannheim, Germany

Although the early phases in software development are important to project success, there are only a few lightweight tools for the integrated management of core software entities. Especially, small and medium-sized enterprises (SME) often lack knowledge and resources to use complex development environments. In this chapter, the authors present a wiki-based approach which allows multiple stakeholders to develop a shared understanding of business elements as well as software design elements. Business processes, requirements, and the architectural design are documented and modeled in a common wiki platform, which provides the foundation for semantic traceability. This allows users to react to changes and track down affected elements on both sides. Finally, the wiki platform supports real-time collaborative modeling of process and design models natively integrated into the Web browser.

Chapter 3

Jakob Axelsson, Swedish Institute of Computer Science (SICS), Sweden &

Mälardalen University, Sweden

Many industries rely heavily on embedded software and systems to maximize business value in their products. These systems are very complex, and the architecture is important to control the complexity and make development efficient. There are often also connections between the embedded system and the different lifecycle processes, and hence, to the enterprise systems supporting those processes. It is rare to start from scratch when developing new products, and instead, these companies evolve their products over time, which means that architecting needs to be evolutionary. This chapter describes what such an evolutionary architecting process can look like based on observations from industry, and how the process can be continuously improved using a maturity model. It is also presented how the embedded system relates to different elements of the enterprise architecture.

Chapter 4

Thomas A. Alspaugh, University of California Irvine, USA

Hazeline U. Asuncion, University of Washington Bothell, USA

Walt Scacchi, University of California Irvine, USA

A substantial number of enterprises and independent software vendors are adopting a strategy in which software-intensive systems are developed with an open architecture (OA) that may contain open source software (OSS) components or components with open APIs. The emerging challenge is to realize the benefits of openness when components are subject to different copyright or property licenses. In this chapter, the authors identify key properties of OSS licenses, present a license analysis scheme to identify license conflicts arising from composed software elements, and apply it to provide guidance for software architectural design choices whose goal is to enable specific licensed component configurations. The scheme has been implemented in an operational environment and demonstrates a practical, automated solution to the problem of determining overall rights and obligations for alternative OAs as a technique for aligning such architectures with enterprise strategies supporting open systems.

Section 2
Crossing Enterprise, System, and Software Architecture Boundaries

Mobile devices create new opportunities for companies. However, innovative applications can cause challenges for software and system architecture. In this chapter, the authors describe a trap to fall into when starting a promising mobile application in a shortsighted way. When the application gets popular and successful, diversity of mobile platforms increases. Many users have an almost emotional relationship to their own smartphone or platform and may not be willing to change it. In order to make the mobile application available to more users, a company may be tempted to add a "simple" extension to accommodate other platforms. Thus, the diversity in devices leads to diversity in distributed object technologies and with it to problems in complexity and compatibility. The authors describe an approach that counters this problem with RESTful services. They use the ConTexter system for illustrating experiences with the problem and for evaluating a proposed solution. The chapter shows the key issues the authors had to solve while migrating ConTexter to a RESTful platform.

Chapter 6

The authors provide a method to systematically develop enterprise application architectures from problem descriptions. From these descriptions, they derive two kinds of specifications: a behavioral specification describes how the automated business process is carried out. It can be expressed using activity or sequence diagrams. A structural specification describes the classes to be implemented and the operations they provide. The structural specification is created in three steps. All the diagrams are expressed in UML.

Large software projects have many stakeholders. In order for the resulting software system and architecture to be aligned with the enterprise and stakeholder needs, key stakeholders must be adequately consulted and involved in the project. This work proposes the use of genetic algorithms to identify key stakeholders and their actual influence in requirements elicitation, given the stakeholders' requirements and the actual set of requirements implemented in the project. The proposed method is applied to a large real-world software project. Results show that search is able to identify key stakeholders accurately. Results also indicate that many different good solutions exist. This implies that a stakeholder has the potential to play a key role in requirements elicitation, depending on which other stakeholders are already involved. This work demonstrates the true complexity of requirements elicitation – all stakeholders should be consulted, but not all of them should be treated as key stakeholders, even if they appear to be significant based on their role in the domain.

Section 3
Architecture Processes, Tools, and Techniques

Chapter 8

Stefanie Betz, Karlsruhe Institute of Technology, Germany

Andreas Oberweis, Karlsruhe Institute of Technology, Germany

Alexander Eckert, FZI Research Center for Information Technologies, Germany

Erik Burger, Karlsruhe Institute of Technology, Germany

Ralf Reussner, Karlsruhe Institute of Technology, Germany

Ralf Trunko, FZI Research Center for Information Technologies, Germany

The lifecycles of business processes and business software interact with each other since business software is used to support business processes, and requirements on business software are derived from business processes. By integrating these lifecycles, it is possible to test if the business software meets the process-based requirements as well as to identify which impacts changes of the software product have on the business process. In this chapter, the authors give an introduction into these interdependencies. Foundations of lifecycle management, business process modeling, and performance engineering are presented, followed by the description of a framework for an integrated lifecycle management for business processes and business software. This framework is based on business process simulation and software performance prediction. The evaluation of the framework is described by applying it to an example of use and the results are discussed. The chapter closes with a conclusion and an outlook on future work.

Chapter 9

Gerrit Muller, Buskerud University College, Norway

The IT industry is suffering from severe budget overruns and ill-performing IT services. Some of the problems that have caused IT project disasters could have been anticipated in the early project phases and mitigated in the project follow-up by modeling the system context and the software design. This chapter shows how to make models of varied views and at varied levels of abstraction to guide software design choices. Models of the enterprise provide understanding of the objectives. Models of the specification provide understanding of system performance and behavior. Models of the design provide understanding of design choices, such as the allocation of functions, resource usage, selection of mechanisms for communication, instantiation, synchronization, security, exception handling, and many more aspects. High-level models are simple models with the primary goal to support understanding, analysis, communication, and decision making. The models have various complementary representations and formats, e.g. visual diagrams, mathematical formulas, and quantitative information and graphs. Model-driven and model-based engineering approaches focus mostly on artifacts to analyze and synthesize software and hardware. High-level models complement model driven approaches by linking the system context to more detailed design decisions. High-level modeling as discussed in this chapter is based on research performed in industrial settings; the so-called industry-as-laboratory approach.

Chapter 10

Olaf Zimmermann, IBM Research GmbH, Switzerland & ABB Corporate Research, Switzerland
Christoph Miksovic, IBM Research GmbH, Switzerland

Contemporary enterprise architecture frameworks excel at inventorying as-is and at specifying to-be
architecture landscapes; they also help enterprise architects to establish governance processes and architectural principles. Solution architects, however, expect mature frameworks not only to express such
fundamental design constraints, but also to provide concrete and tangible guidance how to comply with
framework building blocks, processes, and principles – a route planner is needed in addition to maps of
destinations. In this chapter, the authors show how to extend an existing enterprise architecture framework
with decision guidance models that capture architectural decisions recurring in a particular domain. Such
guidance models codify architectural knowledge by recommending proven patterns, technologies, and
products; architectural principles are represented as decision drivers. Owned by enterprise architects but
populated and consumed by solution architects, guidance models are living artifacts (reusable assets)
that realize a lightweight knowledge exchange between the two communities – and provide the desired
route planners for architectural analysis, synthesis, and evaluation.

Chapter 11

Suresh Kamath, MetLife Inc., USA

The development of an IT strategy and ensuring that it is the best possible one for business is a key
problem many organizations face. This problem is that of linking business architecture to IT architecture
in general and application architecture specifically. Without this linkage it is difficult to manage the
changes needed by the business and maximize the benefits from the information technology (IT) investments. Linking the two domains requires defining the two architectures using a "common language."
While the application architecture domain has developed tools and processes to define and represent the
architecture, the business architecture domain, however, lacks such processes and tools to be useful for
linking of the two. The chapter addresses several questions dealing with the linking of the business and
the application architectures. The author proposes to use category theory related constructs and notions
to represent the business and information architecture and the linkages.

Section 4
Industrial Case Studies and Practices

Chapter 12

Veli-Pekka Eloranta, Tampere University of Technology, Finland
Kai Koskimies, Tampere University of Technology, Finland

This chapter is based on the results of a survey carried out in 11 IT companies in Finland in Fall 2010. In
this survey, the existing practices regarding software architecting work in agile enterprises using Scrum are
mapped out. Four main practices to cope with software architecture in Scrum are identified and analyzed.
The adoption of these practices is discussed in relation with the characteristics of the teams and project
types. Further, the interaction of these practices and Scrum patterns is analyzed. The results indicate
that most of the found practices are in conflict with Scrum. The analyzed relationships between Scrum
patterns and the identified architecture practices help to understand how software architecture work is
aligned with Scrum in real life, as well as the problems of the practices from the Scrum point of view.

Historically, architecture has been about the structure of the solution, focused on the components that make up a system and the connectors which enable their coordinated interaction. Given this solution focus, systems, enterprise, and software architecture evolved in different directions. During the past 15+ years, architectural theory and practice have been undergoing a gradual, but significant, shift in focus. Five trends which highlight this shift are: decision rationale, challenges vs. requirements, systems-of-systems, contextual analysis, and design cognition. Each of these trends facilitates a necessary shift from the architecture of the solution to the architecture of the problem. In addition to enabling a clearer link between the problem and solution, these trends also help to unify systems, enterprise, and software architecture by providing a common foundation for collaboration on complex problems.

Chapter 14

In this chapter, the authors motivate the need for a systematic approach to cloud adoption from the risk perspective. The enormous potential of cloud computing for improved and cost-effective service delivery for commercial and academic purposes has generated unprecedented interest in its adoption. However, a potential cloud user faces numerous risks regarding service requirements, cost implications of failure, and uncertainty about cloud providers' ability to meet service level agreements. Hence, the authors consider two perspectives of a case study to identify risks associated with cloud adoption. They propose a risk management framework based on the principle of GORE (Goal-Oriented Requirements Engineering). In this approach, they liken risks to obstacles encountered while realising cloud user goals, therefore proposing cloud-specific obstacle resolution tactics for mitigating identified risks. The proposed framework shows benefits by providing a principled engineering approach to cloud adoption and empowering stakeholders with tactics for resolving risks when adopting the cloud.

Foreword

Since the late 1980's, architecture research has emerged as the principled study of the large-scale structures of systems. From its roots in qualitative descriptions of empirically observed useful system organizations, architecture has matured to encompass broad explorations of notations, tools, and analysis techniques. Whereas initially the research area interpreted practice, it now offers concrete guidance for complex design and development. It has made the transition from basic research to an essential element of design and construction.

So began a retrospective paper that Mary Shaw and I wrote for *IEEE Software* entitled "The Golden Age of Software Architecture" (Shaw & Clements, 2006). I took the liberty of removing six instances of the word "software" and one "system," and I think the result makes a suitable beginning for this book.

There are countless examples like this. Notations, tools, analysis, methods, languages, papers, case studies, and more, each created within one architectural "genre" (software, system, enterprise) could be easily generalized to embrace the other two.

Are all of these kinds of architecture the same? That's the wrong question to ask. The right question is "Does it pay to consider the similarities among these kinds of architectures, or does it pay to concentrate on their differences?" I think the answer is easy: "Examine the similarities!"

I have been thinking and writing about software architecture for, on some days, longer than I like to remember. It has been fun watching the field grow up. In the early days, we spent most of our time teaching and writing about what was meant by this new (for us) term "architecture," and why anybody would want to devote time and resources in creating one, and what you could do with it after you had.

In those days, so much energy was spent on definitions, and on advocating *my* definition over *your* definition. This is symptomatic of a field in its early days. In the 1980s you could bring any object-oriented meeting to its knees by raising your hand, putting on your best innocent face, and asking, "What's an object?" The resulting debate was guaranteed to de-rail the meeting's agenda.

Architecture, like the O-O community, got past that. These days, neither they nor we have a single crisp universal definition of our central term, and yet we are not paralyzed because of that. We make progress. We communicate effectively. We build better systems. It's as though all the competing definitions form a scatterplot in a concept space, and what we mean lives in the neighborhood of the centroid, and that's good enough.

In fact, this "useful ambiguity" may help us as we try to merge the different kinds of architectures. We are already used to making allowances for the fact that what *you* mean by architecture is not precisely what *I* mean by architecture, but it is close enough that we can communicate and use the concept to our mutual engineering advantage as we build systems (of whatever type). So it's a small marginal effort, then, to admit that *your* kind of architecture is not the same as *my* kind, but we can still find common ground.

Maturing fields stop looking inward at some point and start looking outward, to see how they relate to the world they live in. I think a sad consequence of this early inward perspective for software is that software architecture still is not able to express its constructs in ways that seamlessly and unambiguously translate to the ways that implementers express theirs. This more than anything else leads to architectures that by dictate or by benign neglect become irrelevant after the first code release. But maybe we'll learn from others. Do enterprise architects know how to bridge that gap? Do system architects?

And so we've started looking around, and this book is a wonderful and unmistakable sign of that.

The enterprise and system architects I talk to are looking around, too, and to my surprise and delight, many of them see the work we've done in software architecture as something they can put to good use. We have done a good job methodizing ways to evaluate our architectures, and to express the goals that our architectures need to satisfy. We have bodies of guidance (over and above notations) for capturing our architectures in way that stakeholders can see their needs met, and (oh, yes) an excellent grasp of who our stakeholders are and how to capture what they need. We have a rich body of knowledge comprising architectural solutions for a staggering collection of hard problems, and have thought a lot about effective ways to capture, catalog, and disseminate that knowledge.

The title of this book speaks of aligning these three kinds of architectures, but what I think it means is "aligning those aspects of these three kinds of architectures that aren't *already* aligned, because a lot of them are." I grant you that's a lousy book title. But the reason that it's an interesting topic is because there's so much already shared in common, and the goal is to push that commonality harder, to nurture it and make it grow.

I played a small role in creating the Architectural Tradeoff Analysis Method (ATAM), for methodically analyzing and evaluating a software architecture for its suitability vis-à-vis a set of functional and quality attribute goals for it. The ATAM was created for use squarely in the genre of software, and yet we soon began to realize that its fundamental principles and many of its specific techniques are "genre-agnostic." If you want to evaluate an architecture – any architecture – for suitability, it doesn't take a genius to realize that you need to compare it against its stated goals. That means you have to know how to state them. For software architecture, we express those goals as quality attribute scenarios (very short structured stories of stakeholders interactions that depict how well – how fast, how securely, how reliably, etc. – the system reacts). Scenarios are very general, and work just fine for system and enterprise concerns as well (although the quality attributes of interest may differ). If you want to state the goals, you have to collect them, which means you have to know who owns them or can express them. That leads you to stakeholders. In the ATAM our results comprise risks and non-risks that we discover by running scenarios (prioritized by their importance to the salient stakeholders) against the architecture. There is nothing software-specific about that.

The kinds of architecture – what I call genres – don't bring different governance principles to the table, just different concerns. One aspect of aligning the genres, then, is to try to discover as many of these common principles as we can.

In 2008, the U.S. Army – a very large consumer of all of these kinds of architectures – engaged the Software Engineering Institute to arrange and hold a workshop on exactly this topic (Bergey, 2008). In addition to the three genres of architecture treated by this book, the Army workshop added system-of-systems (DUSD, 2008) architectures as well, for good measure. The workshop's goals included clarifying the relationships among these different genres, and exploring and identifying areas of commonality and difference. Some two dozen people from the Army, their contractors, and government R&D labs participated.

Here are some statements that emerged from the workshop. Each of these statements was made about the architecture of a particular genre, but as I did in the opening paragraph, I've "sanitized" them by removing the genre name or replacing it with "#". No matter which genre you consider your "native" one, see if you disagree with any of them:

- # architecture is the process of translating business vision and strategy into effective # change by creating, communicating and improving the key requirements, principles, and models that describe the #'s future state and enable its evolution.
- The scope of the # architecture includes the people, processes, information and technology of the #, and their relationships to one another and to the external environment.
- Architects compose holistic solutions that address the business challenges of the # and support the governance needed to implement them (Lapkin, 2008).
- # architecture is an ongoing process.
- # architecture must provide holistic solutions.
- # architects work for the client and with the builder; thus, architects generate requirements as much as receive requirements.
- # architects develop information in all of the views needed to make the client's decision.
- # architects write an architecture description as a consequence of the information developed to support the decision.
- # architecture is an early life-cycle artifact and perfectly poised to serve as an early life-cycle risk mitigation vehicle.
- # architecture is an abstraction of a #.
- # architecture defines the properties of elements.
- #'s can and do have many structures; these constitute its architecture.
- Every # has an architecture.
- One of # architecture's most important roles is to be the primary carrier of quality at-tributes.
- # architecture is the bridge between business and mission goals and a #.
- Quality attribute requirements drive the # architecture design.
- # architecture drives # development throughout the life cycle.
- # architecture must be central to # development activities.

Can you find one you didn't like or rings false for the genre you work in? I can't. This suggests that these genres have a great deal in common, which probably matches our intuition all along. And it also suggests that if we continue to look, we'll continue to find more commonality – another reason to be happy that this book has come along.

A workshop being a place where people work, the participants were asked to form groups (one per genre) to answer, among other things, "What are the major activities involved in each genre?" The working groups came up with dozens of activities. Speaking as a long-time proponent and teacher of the practice of *software* architecture, I can tell you that I certainly wish that I'd thought of several of the things that came out of the *other* (that is, the non-software) working groups, such as "crafting an incremental integration strategy." Yes, we do get around to teaching that in software architecture classes, but I was delighted to see it achieve first-class status in one of other genres.

Every one of the captured activities fell neatly into one of the following four buckets:

1. Understanding goals, context, and requirements.
2. Creating, evaluating, and documenting architecture.
3. Managing the architecture post-creation.
4. Assisting in post-architecture activities.

This commonality suggests that the alignment of these genres is already well under way. All is not solved, of course, and there are many hard problems remaining, as the chapters you are about to read attest. My own list of critical research areas includes these:

- Finding a common architectural ontology (concept set) among the genres that could lead to a documentation or specification language that applies very well, even if not perfectly well, to architectures in each genre.
- Finding a common ontology for the "implementation" phase of each genre, and finding a mapping to the elements of the first ontology. This could give us a path towards bridging the language gap between architects and downstream engineers.
- Finding a common concept set for evaluating architectures in any genre. Using a method like the ATAM as a starting point, this set could be seeded with concepts such as "stakeholder," "scenarios," "prioritized scenario," "quality attributes," "architectural risk," "architectural non-risk," "architectural tradeoff," and more. All of these seem genre-generic.

This work lets us all become intellectual citizens of a larger world, and not just our own parochial regions. When we work in our own genre, I hope that we all can pause to reflect how our work could (if we just thought about it for a bit) apply and thereby contribute to the other genres as well. With this work, all of us have gained whole new communities that we can now call colleagues. Let's help each other.

Paul Clements
BigLever Software, Inc, USA

REFERENCES

Bergey, J., Blanchette, S., Clements, P., Gagliardi, M., Wojcik, R., Wood, W., & Klein, J. (2009, March). *U.S. Army Workshop on Exploring Enterprise, System of Systems, System, and Software Architectures.* (Technical report CMU/SEI-2009-TR-008, March 2009).

Lapkin, A., Allega, P., Burke, B., et al. (2008, August 12). *Gartner clarifies the definition of the term enterprise architecture* (Gartner ID #G00156559).

Office of the Deputy Under Secretary of Defense for Acquisition and Technology (ODUSD). (2008). *Systems and software engineering: Systems engineering guide for systems of systems*, Version 1.0. Washington, DC: Author. Retrieved from http://www.acq.osd.mil/sse/docs/SE-Guide-for-SoS.pdf

Shaw, M., & Clements, P. (2006). The golden age of software architecture. *IEEE Software, 23*(2), 31–19.

Paul Clements *is the Vice President of Customer Success at BigLever Software, Inc., where he works to spread the adoption of systems and software product line engineering. Prior to this, he was a senior member of the technical staff at Carnegie Mellon University's Software Engineering Institute, where he worked for 17 years leading or co-leading projects in software product line engineering and software architecture documentation and analysis. Clements is the co-author of three practitioner-oriented books about software architecture: "Software Architecture in Practice" (1998, second edition 2003), "Evaluating Software Architectures: Methods and Case Studies" (2001), and "Documenting Software Architectures: View and Beyond" (2002, second edition 2010). He also co-wrote "Software Product Lines: Practices and Patterns" (2001), and was co-author and editor of "Constructing Superior Software" (1999). In addition, Clements has also authored dozens of papers in software engineering reflecting his long-standing interest in the design and specification of challenging software systems. In 2005 and 2006 he spent a year as a visiting faculty member at the Indian Institute of Technology in Mumbai. He was a founding member of the IFIP WG2.10 Working Group on Software Architecture. He received a B.S. in Mathematical Sciences in 1977, and a M.S. in Computer Science in 1980, both from the University of North Carolina at Chapel Hill. He received a Ph.D. in Computer Sciences from the University of Texas at Austin in 1994.*

Preface

In this publishing project we are editing a book titled Aligning Enterprise, System, and Software Architecture (AESSA). The main goal of this book is to outline some of the current thinking on the processes and practices for aligning enterprise, system, and software architectures. These three architecture areas have many commonalities and they often overlap in practice. There are many gray areas in which the expertise of more than one of these architectures are required in the planning and design of a system.

This book brings together representative views of recent research and practice in the area of aligning enterprise, system, and software architectures. Practicing software engineers, software architects, all researchers advancing our understanding and support for the aligning enterprise, system, and software architectures, and all students wishing to gain a deeper appreciation of underpinning theories, issues and practices within this domain will benefit from this book.

INTRODUCTION

It is imperative that the architecting process be intertwined and interleaved with requirements and architectures: much of the requirements communicate stakeholders' and the enterprise technical, business, environmental and strategic concerns. These concerns need to be realized and accommodated by the architecture of the software system. Architecting software systems is process that crosscuts business, technical and strategic concerns. In today's world of rapidly changing information technology, organizations, and market places, requirements tend also to change, and in ways that affect the stability of the architecture. The landscape for managing the co-evolution of requirements and architectures is becoming more complex; as a result, it is becoming a trend to describe various architectural views relating to the enterprise, software and systems perspectives. Such as an approach is believed to cater for "modularity," "separation of concerns," and manage complexity through "decomposition"; it follows the trend towards heterogeneity in reasoning and assist in development and evolution of long-lived complex software systems. However, reconciling these views and managing their evolution is a problem. For example, it is challenging to prioritize these views, weight their importance and trace their concerns to relevant stakeholders and software artefacts. It is also challenging to manage the conflicts arising from inconsistencies in reconciling these views and co-evolving the views with the associated artefacts (and as the requirements change). Current architectural practices, however, do not provide a support for traceability from the requirements specification to the architectural description related to these views (e.g., which and (how) requirement(s) in the requirements specification an individual architectural element relate to and satisfy and vice versa). Maintaining traceability "links" between these views is necessary for managing the change, the co-evolution of both the requirements and the architecture, confining the change, understanding the change impact on both the structure and the other requirements, providing a support for automated reasoning about a change at a high level of abstraction. Further, such traceability "links" make it easier to preserve the enterprise strategy, the acquired knowledge of the team, the architectural knowledge through guided documentation. For example, this may then minimize the impact of personnel losses and may allow the enterprise to make changes in the software system without damaging the architectural integrity (and making the software system un-evolvable).

WHAT ARE ENTERPRISE, SYSTEM, AND SOFTWARE ARCHITECTURES?

Enterprise, System, and Software architectures play a critical role in developing software-intensive complex systems. However, the scope and focuses of each type of architecture design is different but overlapping. Enterprise architecture is a complete expression of the enterprise; it describes the alignment of business processes with IT, the composition of software systems and subsystems, and their relationships with the external environment, and the guiding principles for the design and evolution of an enterprise. Enterprise architecture acts as collaboration platform between aspects of business planning such as goals, visions, strategies and governance principles; aspects of business operations such as business terms; organization structures, processes and data; aspects of automation such as information systems and databases; and the enabling technological infrastructure of the business such as computers, operating systems and networks.

System architecture is defined as a formal description of a system, or a detailed plan of the system at component level to guide its implementation. It is also the structure of components, their interrelationships, and the principles and guidelines governing their design and evolution over time. System architecture comprises the design of both software and hardware systems, design issues arising from such a system architecture design often concern both systems.

As the field of Software Architecture enters its third decade of formal study it finds itself moving from its traditional focus on software structures to the more general notion of software architecture as the set of design decisions made to ensure the software requirements will be met. Consistent with this view is the trend toward focusing software architecture documentation on supporting stakeholders in understanding how the software solution satisfies their concerns. These stakeholder concerns can be viewed roughly along two axes: concerns related to the software itself and concerns about how the software relates to other systems with which it interacts. Over the last decade it has been widely recognized and accepted that architectural decisions must take into consideration not only the functions the software is expected to perform but also the quality attributes associated with the functions. In recent years the community has come to consensus that quality concerns related to security, performance, reliability, maintainability, etc. cannot be ensured unless they are considered and their realization mechanisms properly documented from the outset, and they cannot be coded in during development. In the next decade we will see increasing focus on the second of our two axes: how systems software relates to the software of systems with which it interacts. Thus there will be increasing collaboration between those concerned with software architecture and those concerned with system and enterprise architectures.

As business processes are supported and realized by software systems, the design of software and systems in turn can pose constraints and generate requirements for the former. The interrelationships between the three areas of architecture designs are intricate and interdependent. The current practice of treating the three architectures separately cannot work as Business-IT alignment remains a major issue. This issue is partially a result of not having alignments between the three architectural practices. For instance, the contradictions in the scoping, feasibility, budget and schedule between enterprise architecture and software architecture are often experienced in practice when the two architecture planning are misaligned.

BOOK OVERVIEW

We have divided this book into four parts, with a general editorial chapter providing a more detailed review of the domain of aligning enterprise, system, and software architectures.

Section 1: Architecture Alignment - Theories

The goal of Section 1 is to clarify the relationships among different kinds of architectures, explore and identify areas of commonalities and differences, and discuss the role of various approaches in helping to capture these architectures.

The four chapters in this section deal with: relationships between enterprise, applications, and infrastructure architects; using semantic Wiki for tracing process and requirements knowledge in enterprise: evolutionary architecting of embedded systems; relating software licenses, open source components, and open architectures.

In recent years, a rapid emergence of the role of the technology architect has been seen. However the lack of widely accepted definitions for the responsibilities of different types of architect can cause quite a lot of confusion between them, often reducing their effectiveness. Chapter 1, by Rozanski and Woods, helps to remedy this situation by identifying the defining characteristics that all architects share and defining a simple taxonomy of architects that can be used to classify the many varied jobs that technology architects perform (enterprise architects, application architects and infrastructure architects). The authors examine the responsibilities of each group and the interactions that should be expected between them. This analysis helps to define each type of architect more clearly so helps to define the relationship between enterprise, system and software architects.

Small and medium enterprises (SME) lack knowledge and resources for managing traceability links between requirements, processes, system, and software architecture. Wiki systems are widely used for documentation, but currently too limited in functionality to be applicable for these purposes. Based on SME case studies Seedorf, Nordheimer, and Thum describe in chapter 2 a solution for the lightweight modeling, documentation, and traceability of business processes, requirements, and software components. The wiki-based solution is realized as an extension to the Semantic Media Wiki software. Practical cases demonstrate how SMEs can benefit from the suggested approach.

Many industries rely heavily on embedded software and systems to maximize business value in their systems. These products are very complex and the architecture is important to control this complexity and make development efficient. It is rare that these companies start from scratch when developing new products, and instead they evolve their products over time, which means that the architecting needs to be evolutionary, and that this evolutionary architecting becomes a central business process. In chapter 3, Axelsson describes what such an evolutionary architecting process can look like based on our observations from industry. He also discusses how the process can be continuously improved using a maturity model and through process optimizations using lean principles. A special concern is to find a balance between short-term and long-term considerations, and in this, strategic refactoring plays an essential role which is further elaborated, together with a description of analysis methods that can be used to ensure business value over time.

The central problem Alspaugh, Asuncion, and Scacchi examine and explain in chapter 4 is to identify principles of software architecture and software licenses that facilitate or inhibit success of an enterprise open architecture (OA) strategy when an enterprise develops large systems by composing open source software together with other non-open software components through open APIs. This is the knowledge we seek to develop and deliver. Without such knowledge, it is unlikely that an OA that is clean, robust, transparent, and extensible can be readily produced that aligns strategy, system architecture, and software together. Such an outcome results in an enterprise not knowing what its license obligations are, thus requiring expensive legal consultation for uncertain technical guidance, or the enterprise becoming subject to legal liabilities for license infringement. On a broader scale, this chapter seeks to explore and answer the following kinds of research questions:

- What license applies to an OA system composed with components with different licenses?
- How do alternative OSS licenses facilitate or inhibit the development of OA systems?
- How should software license constraints be specified so it is possible to automatically determine the overall set of rights and obligations associated with a configured software system architecture?

This chapter may help establish a foundation for how to analyze and evaluate dependencies that might arise when seeking to develop software systems that embody an OA when different types of software components or software licenses are being considered for integration into an overall system configuration. Simple examples involving software systems commonly found in different enterprise subject to different licenses are included.

Section 2: Crossing Enterprise, System, and Software Architecture Boundaries

It is imperative that the architecting process is intertwined and interleaved between requirements and architectures: much of the requirements communicate stakeholders' and the enterprise technical, business, environmental and strategic concerns. These concerns need to be realized and accommodated by the architecture of the software system.

The four chapters in this section provide insights into following topics: using RESTful architecture to tackle software diversity in mobile web systems; enterprise applications; using genetic algorithms to search for key stakeholders; seamless coherence in security issues across enterprise, system, and software architectures.

Mobile devices create new opportunities for companies. Innovative applications can cause challenges for software and system architecture and have an impact on business. In Chapter 5, Wehrmaker and Schneider describe an anti pattern of short-sighted propagation. A new and risky application is explored using a single technology to start with. When the system spreads throughout the enterprise, diversity of mobile platforms increases. The initially simple architecture gets messed up by "simple" extensions to accommodate other platforms. This leads to decreasing performance and maintainability. Their proposed solution approach is based on the REST paradigm. As a road to a better system, software, and enterprise architecture, they propose a migration process and explain its key steps to an extensible and forward-looking application.

In Chapter 6, Choppy, Hatebur, Heisel, and Reggio provide a method, which allows one to systematically develop enterprise application architectures from problem descriptions. For enterprise applications, they have developed a specialized enterprise application problem frame (pattern). The authors describe the requirements through problem diagrams that are instances of the enterprise application frame and of other problem frames. Based on the problem diagrams, they systematically develop enterprise system architecture. For this, they consider technical requirements, for example that some functionality should be implemented on another computer (e.g., remote databases). They introduce coordinator components, considering the formal descriptions of the business model, and facade components. Their method not only provides detailed methodological guidance for developers, but also validation conditions to find semantic errors early in the development process.

Large software projects have many stakeholders. In order for the resulting software system to be aligned with the enterprise and stakeholder needs, key stakeholders must be adequately consulted and involved in the project. Chapter 7 by Soo Ling Lim, Angelo Susi, and Mark Harmon proposes the use of genetic algorithms to identify key stakeholders and their actual influence in requirements elicitation, given the stakeholders' requirements and the actual set of requirements implemented in the project. The proposed method is applied to a large real-world software project. Results show that search is able to identify key stakeholders accurately. Results also indicate that many different good solutions exist. This implies that a stakeholder has the potential to play a key role in requirements elicitation, depending on which other stakeholders are already involved. This chapter demonstrates the true complexity of requirements elicitation – all stakeholders should be consulted, but not all of them should be treated as key stakeholders, even if they appear to be significant based on their role in the domain.

Section 3: Architecture Processes, Tools, and Techniques

A good architecture is realized through the application of solid processes and carried out using appropriate tools and techniques. Development of these supporting technologies has been an increasingly active area of research over the past two decades and current thinking suggests that the use of models as a part of documentation is fundamental to communication of the architecture to others for such purposes as education of various stakeholders, architecture assessment to ensure the systems built to it will meet the project's quality as well as functional goals, and as the embodiment of architectural decisions. In Section 3 of the book we present 4 chapters describing new techniques presented with supporting examples and case studies describing application of the processes, tools, and techniques in practice.

Betz, Burger, Eckart, Oberweis, Reussner, and Trunko discuss the importance of understanding dependencies among business process and business software lifecycles in Chapter 8. They present a framework based on business simulations and predictions that improves overall management of the organization.

In Chapter 9, Muller describes a technique for capturing various abstractions of architecture as models for which the relationships among the models are mapped in a way that allows the models to be used together to gain insight into the project plan as a part of the larger enterprise.

In Chapter 10, Zimmermann and Miksovic present a lightweight technique for capturing architectural knowledge in a way that will preserve decisions that recur in a domain along with their rationale. Their technique extends enterprise architecture frameworks with guidance models to support the exchange of knowledge about known problems and solutions between enterprise and solution architects.

Taken together these chapters give insights as to the importance of understanding and modelling interdependencies among various artifacts and processes and present solutions to help organizations deal with human and technology based complexities inherent to any project involving software. In Chapter 11, Kamath discusses the importance for understanding the relationships among business, information technology, and application architectures as these three facets of an organization, though usually created and managed as if they are isolated, are highly related to each other and indeed generally suffer from crucial interdependencies. Kamath presents an approach using Category Theory to link these architectures in such a way as to highlight interdependencies in a way that increases an organizations ability to evolve based on sound decision-making that promotes agility in all facets of operation.

Section 4: Industrial Case Studies and Practices

Section 4 contains three chapters looking at a variety of industrial cases and practices. The chapters in this section present practical approaches and cases. Chapter 12 analyzes architecture practice in an agile environment; chapter 13 focuses on the software architecture of the problem; chapter 14 describes using obstacles and goals to guide adoption of cloud computing;

Chapter 12 is a review of the results of a survey carried out in twelve IT companies in Finland. In this survey, Eloranta and Koskimies mapped out existing practices regarding software architecting work in agile enterprises, and analyze their benefits and problems. They found correlations with the agility degree of the enterprise and those practices. They studied the Scrum process as the reference work management framework to explore the relationship of agility (in the form of Scrum) and the process of architecting. They found that some architecture practices are problematic and are in conflict with using Scrum. The study indicates that possible management risks arising from conflicts between the new Scrum patterns and the adopted way of architecture work need to be managed.

Enterprise, Systems, and Software Architecture share many commonalities and many of their concerns overlap, but they also have marked differences in focus and approach. Each solves problems for different stakeholders, uses different technologies, and employs different practices. The specialization on their respective solutions has made it difficult to transfer methods and knowledge across a broad range of topics. One way to align these topics is to shift the focus from solution to problem domains. In Chapter 13, Alfred suggests using context and challenge constructs for modeling a problem domain. A context represents a set of perceptions, desired outcomes and priorities of like-minded decision makers. Challenges are significant risks or obstacles within a context which must be overcome to deliver value. From this perspective, much of what separates Enterprise, Systems, and Software architecture are their respective focus on solution concerns.

- Enterprise Architects focus on issues such as security, fault tolerance, availability, and system integration.
- Systems Architects focus on issues such as electro-mechanical control, real-time scheduling, product line opportunities, safety and fault handling.
- Software Architects focus on GUI's, business logic, workflow, databases, and non functional requirements in software.

The different stakeholders that enterprise architects, systems architects and software architects interact with each have their environments, their expectations, and their constraints. The modeling of a problem domain provides a means of aligning these stakeholders' concerns.

Chapter 14 motivates the need for a systematic approach for cloud adoption, aligning the enterprise goals and its architecture with cloud systems architectures. This chapter suggests use goals and obstacles for identifying, managing, and mitigating risks in the cloud adoption process. Zardari, Faniyi, and Bahsoon propose an architecture-centric risk management framework (CloudMit) for systematically identifying risks and possible mitigating strategies, using architecture-level security risks as an example.

Ivan Mistrík
Independent Consultant, Germany

Antony Tang
Swinburne University of Technology, Australia

Rami Bahsoon
University of Birmingham, UK

Judith A. Stafford
Tufts University, USA

Acknowledgment

The editors would like to sincerely thank the many authors who contributed their works to this collection. The international team of anonymous reviewers gave detailed feedback on early versions of chapters and helped us to improve both the presentation and accessibility of the work. Finally, we would like to thank the IGI Global management and editorial teams for the opportunity to produce this unique collection of articles covering the very wide range of areas related to aligning enterprise, system, and software architectures.

Editorial Chapter

Ivan Mistrik
Independent Consultant, Germany

Antony Tang
Swinburne University of Technology, Australia

Rami Bahsoon
University of Birmingham, UK

Judith A. Stafford
Tufts University, USA

ABSTRACT

Architects (of any kind) need to understand the system, its environment, its stakeholders, their concerns, and the solution approach. The solution approach varies across different kinds of architecture. In software architecture, the solution approach is software-oriented. For system architecture, the solution approach is hardware- and platform-oriented. For enterprise architecture, the solution approach is people- and business-oriented. The goal of this introductory chapter is to clarify the relationships among different kinds of architecture, explore and identify areas of commonalities and difference, and to discuss the current challenges and future directions in aligning these architectures.

WHAT ARE ENTERPRISE, SYSTEM, AND SOFTWARE ARCHITECTURE?

When we use the term architecture, we mean that architecture as a product resulting from an application of the science of architecting to a system or other entity of interest.

Enterprise, System, and Software architectures play a critical role in developing software-intensive complex systems. However, the scope and focuses of each type of architecture design is different but overlapping. Enterprise architecture is a complete expression of the enterprise; it describes the alignment of business processes with IT, the composition of software systems and subsystems, and their relationships with the external environment, and the guiding principles for the design and evolution of an enterprise (Giachetti, 2010). Enterprise architecture acts as collaboration platform between aspects of business planning such as goals, visions, strategies and governance principles; aspects of business operations such as business terms, organization structures, processes and data; aspects of automation such as information systems and databases; and the enabling technological infrastructure of the business such as computers, operating systems and networks (ISO/IEC, 2010).

System architecture is defined as a formal description of a system, or a detailed plan of the system at component level to guide its implementation (The Open Group, 2009). It is also the structure of components, their interrelationships, and the principles and guidelines governing their design and evolution over time. System architecture comprises the design of both software and hardware systems, design issues arising from such a system architecture design often concern both systems.

As the field of Software architecture enters its third decade of formal study it finds itself moving from its traditional focus on software structures to the more general notion of software architecture as the set of design decisions made to ensure the software requirements will be met. Consistent with this view is the trend toward focusing software architecture documentation on supporting stakeholders in understanding how the software solution satisfies their concerns. These stakeholder concerns can be viewed roughly along two axes: concerns related to the software itself and concerns about how the software relates to other systems with which it interacts. Over the last decade it has been widely recognized and accepted that architectural decisions must take into consideration not only the functions the software is expected to perform but also the quality attributes associated with the functions. In recent years the community has come to consensus that quality concerns related to security, performance, reliability, maintainability, etc. cannot be ensured unless they are considered and their realization mechanisms properly documented from the outset, and they cannot be coded in during development.

In the next decade we will see increasing focus on the second of our two axes: how systems software relates to the software of systems with which it interacts to support the quality requirements. Similarly, how software and systems can be architected to provide the flexibility and quick responses to market changes that are required by enterprises. Thus there will be increasing collaboration between those concerned with software architecture and those concerned with system and enterprise architectures.

The following definition seems equally applicable to enterprise, systems, software and other aggregations of interest:

Architecture: The fundamental organization of a system embodied in its components, their relationships to each other, and to the environment, and the principles guiding its design and evolution (ISO/IEC, 2010).

The key ideas in the IEEE 1471 and ISO/IEC42010:2010 definition are these:

- Architecture embodies the fundamental concepts about a system, including its components, their relationships and governing principles.
- Architecture recognizes the role and influence on an architecture of the environment in which a system is embedded.
- Architecture is not merely about the static arrangement of a system parts but its evolution and principles governing that evolution.

All three architecture disciplines have been maturing over the past decades. Enterprise architecture has been evolving around the premise of aligning business processes with IT. It deals with the business management levels for planning purposes. Plans and designs are then translated into systems and software designs. Many methodologies and frameworks have been used in the industry: IEEE 1471 (IEEE, 2000) was first approved in 2000. Other frameworks address system and/or enterprise concerns, such as GERAM (IFIP-IFAC Task Force, 1999) and ISO 15704 (ISO, 2000), Zachman Framework (J. Zachman, 1987; J Zachman, 1997), the US DoD Architecture Framework (Department of Defense, 2007) and related frameworks such as MODAF (Ministry of Defence (UK), 2012) and TOGAF (The Open Group, 2009). On the other hand, system and software architectures view setting requirements as an important part of the architecturally significant decision making process (de Boer et al., 2007). Architects in each field have different processes and methods for carrying out design and implementation. To date, these processes and practices are not seamless across the different levels of architecture design, and the integration in theory and practice is still a challenge.

We need to improve our current understanding of the relationship between the types of architecture, their related artifacts, their processes and the systems supporting their associated reasoning process. There is a disjoint between different types of architectures (enterprise, system, software) due to misunderstandings across the boundaries between architects. The rather simplistic view of segregating a development process into enterprise, system and software architectures cannot solve the issues in complex system development. An alignment of these architecture design processes is imminent to improve the current practice.

WHAT IS ALIGNING ENTERPRISE, SYSTEM, AND SOFTWARE ARCHITECTURE?

As business processes are supported and realized by software systems, the design of software and systems in turn can pose constraints and generate new requirements. The interrelationships between the three areas of architecture designs are intricate and interdependent. The current practice of treating the three architectures separately cannot work as Business-IT alignment remains a major

issue (Luftman, Papp, & Brier, 1999). This issue is partially a result of misalignments between the three architectural practices. For instance, the contradictions in the scoping, feasibility, budget and schedule between enterprise architecture and software architecture are often experienced in practice when the two architecture planning are misaligned.

One of the reasons for the gap between enterprise, system, and software architecture, is that there have not been sufficient considerations of the commonality between them. Not only does each community have its own paradigm (metamodel, languages, methods etc.), they also publish their research results and experiences in different forums (conferences, journals, books), duplicating their efforts and results.

The last decade provides a rich set of architecture-related standards, motivated both by recognized practices and a hope that standards can effectively improve practice. There is a need for more structured and systematic treatment of the relationships between the three kinds of architectures.

From the industrial perspective, we observe that practitioners in the field deem the knowledge linking an enterprise to its architectures as a core knowhow, and invest major efforts in keeping track of the relations between enterprise, system, and architectural elements. For instance, software and enterprise architects regard business goals and their relation to architectural decisions as core information to be maintained for architecting. Although key business processes drive decision making for IT projects, organizations continue to experience major problems when the information aligning business processes and technical architectures is missing.

At various conferences/workshops and in several research projects many issues in enterprise (EA), system (SA), and software (SWA) architectures have been explored. Methodologies and approaches for defining, improving and aligning the three types of architecture activities have been suggested. From these studies, e.g., (Bergey et al., 2009; WICSA/ECSA, 2009) a number of key questions have emerged:

- *What are the major activities involved in each kind of architecture?* Any architecture is motivated by a set of stakeholders, a set of concerns, a set of mandatory "architecturally significant requirements," and a "vision" (something to use to make tradeoffs, to say how systems might evolve). These frame what the architect does to produce asset of viewpoints and instantiate them to show the architecture meets the concerns and complies with the vision. So the activities could be articulated as the following: understanding goals, context, and requirements; creating, evaluating, and documenting architecture; managing the architecture post-creation; and assisting in post-architecture activities.

- *What is the boundary between the different kinds of architecture?* The boundaries of the kinds can be understood in terms of the concerns of stakeholders for each kind of architecture. Questions to be asked when moving from one kind of architecture to another are: What stakeholders should be involved in each type of architecture? What are the common concerns of these stakeholders and how do their interests shift? What new concerns arise or are reinterpreted?

- *What common activities exist for each type of architecture (e.g., specification, evaluation)?* There are some basic activities that any kind of architecting would take (Emery & Hilliard, 2009). Some of these activities include defining the problem, understanding the context and environment in which problem and solution are situated, and working the problem within those bounds

in terms of requirements analysis and specification, solution modeling and explorations. (Hofmeister et al., 2007) discuss a generic process for Software Architecting, aside from some terminology, there is no reason to believe the archetype would not work for other kinds, or architecting in general.

- *How do we capture and represent architecture in each kind?* The workshop on architecture genres (Bergey, et al., 2009) has summarized its findings on the documentation issue as follows:
  - **Enterprise Architect:** No 'one size fits all' no *de facto* standard.
  - **System Architect:** Usual approaches include block diagrams, use cases, context diagrams and versions of the DoDAF; value and objective models; and prototyping, simulation and analysis reports.
  - **Software Architect:** Standard approaches include Kruchten's 4+1 Views approach (Kruchten, 1995), SEI's Views and Beyond approach (Clements et al., 2002), ANSI/IEEE Std 1471-2000 approach (IEEE, 2000).

- *How can architectural frameworks be used?* There seems to be a clear consensus (WICSA/ECSA, 2009) that architectural frameworks, e.g., TOGAF (The Open Group, 2009), GERAM (IFIP-IFAC Task Force, 1999), DODAF (Department of Defense, 2007), are helpful in some areas, but are neither necessary nor sufficient to capture a high-quality rendition of architecture in any kind.

The following sections explore the means how to partially resolve the main issues in aligning enterprise, system, and software architectures.

ARCHITECTURE ALIGNMENT

Architects (of any kind) need to understand the system, its environment, its stakeholders, their concerns, and the solution approach. The solution approach varies across kinds. In software architecture, the solution approach is software-oriented. For system architecture, the solution approach is hardware- and platform-oriented. For enterprise architecture, the solution approach is people- and business-oriented.

To capture the relationships among the kinds graphically, we suggest that simple class diagram. For example, the diagram would show that all types of architecture are influenced by stakeholders' needs and concerns. It would show that system architecture heavily influences software architecture, that system architecture influences enterprise architecture in the case of acknowledged EA, and so forth.

Consequently we decided to use a normal association relationship between the entities in a UML class diagram, shown in Figure 1.

Stakeholders of a system include management, users and the technical people who design and implement the systems. These stakeholders contribute to the three kinds of architecture in one way or another. Their interactions with the architecture design are iterative in nature: a user may need to change her requirements if technology constrains what can be achieved, or an architect may need to reconsider a design if new non-functional requirements arise. Architects in each of the architectural areas also influence each other's decisions. For instance, software architects designing for software reliability needs the design support of system architects; enterprise architects designing for system integration requires software and system architects to align and synchronize their designs.

CROSSING ENTERPRISE, SYSTEM, AND SOFTWARE ARCHITECTURE BOUNDARIES

It is imperative that the architecting process is intertwined and interleaved between requirements and architectures: much of the requirements communicate stakeholders' and the enterprise technical, business, environmental and strategic concerns. These concerns need to be realized and accommodated by the architecture of the software system. Architecting software systems is process, which crosscuts business, technical and strategic concerns. In today's world of rapidly changing information technology, organizations, and marketplaces, the requirements tend also to

Figure 1. Relating enterprise, software and systems architectures

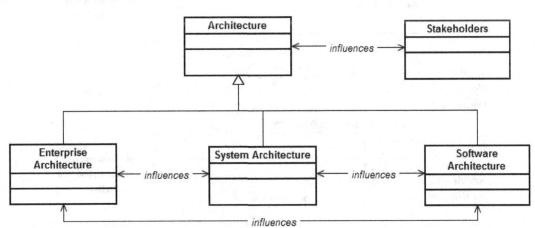

change, and in ways that affect the stability of the architecture.

The landscape for managing the co-evolution of requirements and architectures is becoming more complex; as a result, it is becoming a trend to describe various architectural views relating to the enterprise, software and systems perspectives. Such as an approach is believed to cater for "modularity," "separation of concerns" and manage complexity through "decomposition"; it follows the trend towards heterogeneity in reasoning and assist in development and evolution of long-lived complex software systems. However, reconciling these views and managing their evolution is a problem. For example, it is challenging to prioritize these views, weight their importance and trace their concerns to relevant stakeholders and software artifacts. It is also challenging to manage the conflicts arising from inconsistencies in reconciling these views and co-evolving the views with the associated artifacts (and as the requirements change).

Current architectural practices, however, do not provide full support for traceability from the requirements specification to the architectural description related to these views (e.g., which and (how) requirement(s) in the requirements specification an individual architectural element relate to and satisfy and vice versa). Maintaining traceability "links" between these views is necessary for managing the change, the co-evolution of both the requirements and the architecture, confining the change, understanding the change impact on both the structure and the other requirements, providing a support for automated reasoning about a change at a high level of abstraction. Further, such traceability "links" make it easier to preserve the enterprise strategy, the acquired knowledge of the team, the architectural knowledge through guided documentation. For example, this may then minimize the impact of personnel losses and may allow the enterprise to make changes in the software system without damaging the architectural integrity (and making the software system un-evolvable, Figure 2).

Figure 2. Architecting for enterprise, software, and systems goals

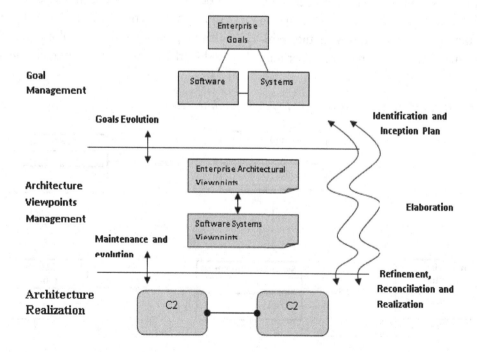

We envision that the architecting process tends to follow an intertwined and interleaved phases encompassing iterative phases of inceptions, refinements and realisations spanning enterprise, software and systems goals and their associated viewpoints. In practice, the realisation is often distilled into an "implementable" architecture and associated architectural knowledge. Relating the architecture to various architectural viewpoints and associated architectural knowledge (through the architecture viewpoints management) enforces traceability and provide primitives for managing changes and evolution (through the Goal Management layer).

ARCHITECTURE PROCESSES, TOOLS, AND TECHNIQUES

The process of architecting can be through of as a translation of system requirements into a solution with consideration for additional constraints that may be imposed by the enterprise. This translation process does not happen as a specific, well-defined phase during system development but rather is ongoing as negotiations among stakeholders take place and vision of the system is refined and evolved. Throughout these activities the architecture is a central reference for stakeholders at all levels. Given the central role of architecture throughout the planning, development, and maintenance phases of a system's life it is critical that it be a faithful representation of the current state of the system.

Much progress has been made over the past two decades and some consensus has been achieved as to what to capture, how it should be modelled, and what will constitute good documentation. Architecture description languages have been developed that provide support for describing the components and connectors of a system as well as describing both static and behaviour related properties associated with, or required of, these architectural elements (Feiler, Gluch, & Hudak,

2006; Magee, Dulay, Eisenbach, & Kramer, 1995; Object Management Group, 2003). Standards for architecture documentation have been defined (ISO/IEC, 2010), and templates have been provided that support just in time capturing of that information (Clements et al., 2002).

The process of capturing and maintaining architectural information is on-going as it will be the primary carrier of architectural decisions, which as we have note previously must be traceable to enterprise-wide elements, artifacts, and concerns. Not only must the relationships among architectural artefacts be identified and maintained but also their mappings to other elements in the enterprise. It is not possible for any manual process to support flexibility on this scale thus tools support must be provided to manage the architectural models as well as other supporting documentation and linkage. Automation is critical to this process and support tools must be integrated with other tools that support the enterprise (Figure 3).

INDUSTRIAL PRACTICES

Enterprise, Systems, and Software Architecture share many commonalities and many of their concerns overlap, but they also have marked differences in their focuses and their approaches. Presently in the IT industry, it is common to see each architecture discipline solving problems for some specific stakeholders, they use different technologies and employ different practices. The focus on their respective solutions has made each them inward looking. Alignment of these topics is to shift the focus from the solution domain to problem domain, and to be able to communicate goals and design problems across the architecture disciplines.

In recent years, researchers have started to emphasize design decisions and knowledge management as core elements of architectural design. All architectural solutions are the results of design decisions, but how do these decisions come about

Figure 3. Traceability of architecture elements, artifacts, and concerns

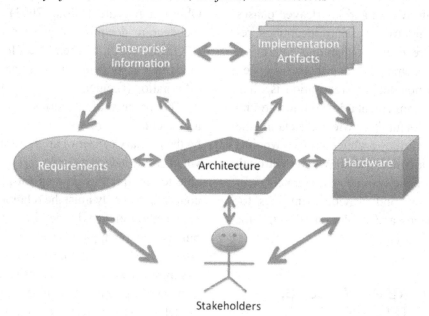

and how are the decisions justified? Avgeriou et al. (Avgeriou, Kruchten, Lago, Grisham, & Perry, 2007) suggest that identifying design issues and design concerns are central to rationalizing a solution. Tang et al. (Tang, Liang, Clerc, & Vliet, 2011) not only support the notion of design problem as a key element in architecture design, they outline that architecture design problems and solutions should co-evolve. The goals and the design problems are not all known up-front when architecture design activities begin. Many of the design problems are discovered during design. The process of architecture design can be problem-driven if one does not understand the problem domain very well or it can be solution driven if the solutions the problems are well-known to the architects, it is usually both.

The communication of the design contexts, design problems and potential solutions across different architecture disciplines is an essential part of bridging the knowledge gap between them. As architecture design decisions often have wide ranging implications to different parts of the business and technical architectures, these impli-

cations, mostly often issues, cannot be detected easily without communicating knowledge from another perspective. Architects from the three architectural disciplines can bring about such a broader perspective with wider coverage of the different stakeholders' views (Figure 4).

Figure 4. Co-evolving architecture design problems and solutions

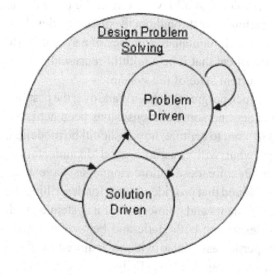

CURRENT CHALLENGES AND FUTURE DIRECTIONS

System and Software architecture are defined as "the fundamental organization of a system, embodied in its components, their relationships to each other and the environment, and the principles governing its design and evolution" (ISO/IEC, 2010). Bass and co-authors (Bass, Clements, & Kazman, 2003) describes architecture as a description of system structures, its properties and a set of early design decisions. Some important and common properties are quality attributes of a system. The description of a system structure and its properties are not and cannot be definitive, they can be subject to interpretation by different people and under different circumstances. What is structural to an architect may be considered as implementation details to another architect. What is an important property to one architect may be considered as obvious to another.

The authors in this book have explored many issues in enterprise, system and software architectures. Methodologies and approaches for defining, improving and aligning the three types of architecture activities have been suggested. From these studies, a number of challenges have emerged:

- Clements has argued that it is useful to have some ambiguities of different kinds of architecture. This concept is further explored by Woods and Rozanski in which the roles of architects might be a focal point. An architect must determine the extent, in terms of system scope as well as the problem-solution domain, to which his/her role lies. Making an appropriate situated-decision given the ambiguity of architecture boundaries requires a sound judgment.
- Axelsson describes the architecting process and the maturity model of embedded systems. One of the challenges suggested is how to synchronize architectures at the enterprise, software and system levels during their evolution. Zimmermann and Miksovic also describe evolution in terms of the architecture guidance model. They describe the challenge of reusing a guidance model to extended projects. The original guidance and principles may no longer be applicable in the new situation.
- Muller models architectures in a hierarchy. He suggests that the heterogeneity, uncertainties and complexity of real-world architectures post challenges to practical architecting.
- Alfred describes architecture challenge in terms of the architecture of problems. He argues that the essential issue is problem identification. It is all too common for practitioners to apply analogous solutions that are unfit to the problem. When architectural decisions are made under these circumstances, they become difficult to change.

The chapters in this book have provided some insights to address these challenges. Though there are similarities between architectures, situations also vary from system to system. An observation is that there are always ambiguities and challenges in architectural design. No single method can address that. We rely on architects to apply the right principles, the right guidelines, and making the right decisions.

FUTURE RESEARCH DIRECTIONS BEYOND THIS BOOK

We reflect on some challenges and future directions, which future research into enterprise, software and system architectures should consider. We explicate our focus on change management, through maintaining, managing and evolving traceability across various artifacts. We also motivate the need for future research in change impact analysis and associated suites explicating the interconnection between these artifacts.

Change Management: Traceability of Requirements to the Software, System, and Enterprise Architectures

An important outcome of the initial development of the software system is the knowledge that the development team acquires the knowledge of the application domain, user requirements, role of the application in the business process, solutions and algorithms, data formats, strength and weakness of the architecture, and operating environment. From inception to evolution, Software, system, and enterprise architectures depend on this knowledge. Such knowledge is crucial prerequisite for the co-evolution of the three artifacts. In particular, these architectures and the team knowledge make evolution and co-evolution possible. These artifacts, to a great extent, allow making changes in the large-scale and complex software systems possible without damaging the integrity of the architecture. Once one or the other architecture disappears and following a similar argument to that of (Bennet & Rajlich, 2000), the system will be difficult to evolve and enters the stage of servicing (also referred to as maturity by Lehman) (Bennet & Rajlich, 2000). At the servicing stage, only small tactical changes would be possible. For the business and the enterprise, the software is likely to be no longer a core product and the cost-benefit of the change becomes marginal. Quoting from Bennet and Rajlich (2000): "There is a positive feedback between the loss of software architecture coherence and the loss of software knowledge." Less coherent architectures requires more extensive knowledge in order to evolve the system of the given architecture. However, if the knowledge necessary for evolution is lost, the changes in the software will lead to faster deterioration of the architecture. Very often on software projects, the loss of knowledge is triggered by loss in key personnel and the project slips into the servicing stage (Bennet & Rajlich, 2000),. Hence, planning for evolution and stable software architectures urges the need for traceability techniques, which traces requirements and their evolution back and forth into the software, system and enterprise architecture; such traceability is believed to aid evolution, co-evolution of various artifacts and tend to "preserve" the team knowledge.

Davis (1993) gives the earliest definition of traceability. Davis defines traceability as "the ability to describe and follow (track) the lifetime of an artifact, in both a forward and a backward direction, i.e., from its origin to development and vice versa" (Davis, 1993). Gotel & Finkelstein (1995) have preserved the spirit of Davis's definition of traceability. They, however, have scoped the definition on tracing a requirement through its "life." The requirement life covers periods of a requirement origin, development and specification, deployment, use, and on-going refinement. They have defined requirements traceability as "the ability to describe and follow the life of a requirement in both a forwards and backwards direction (i.e., from its origins, through its development and specification, to its subsequent deployment and use, and through periods of on-going refinement and iteration in any of these phases)." (Gotel & Finkelstein, 1995) have particularly discussed the importance of tracing requirements back to their source. These sources might be people, other requirements, documents, or standards.

Traceability is important for modeling dependencies among software objects and for managing the change across software artifacts. Traceability information records the dependencies between requirements and the sources of these requirements, dependencies between requirements themselves, and dependencies between requirements and the system implementation (Kotonya & Sommerville, 1998). Advances in software-development environments and repository technology have enabled software engineers to trace the change in software using traceability techniques. According to (Gotel and Finkelstein, 1995), these techniques span a variety of approaches ranging from cross-referencing schemes (e.g., cross-referencing schemes, based on some form of tagging, numbering, indexing, traceability matrices, and matrix sequences), through document-centered techniques (e.g., Templates, hypertext, and integration documents), to more elaborate structure-centered techniques (e.g., assumption-based truth maintenance networks, constraint networks, axiomatic, key phrase, relational dependencies and/or social networks).

We define requirements to architecture traceability as the ability to describe the "life" of a requirement through the requirements engineering phase to the architecture phase, including systems, software and enterprise architectures, in both forwards and backwards. Forwards demonstrates which (and how) architectural element(s) satisfy an individual requirement in the requirements specification. Backwards demonstrates which requirement(s) in the requirements specification an individual architectural element relate to and satisfy. Current architectural practices, however, do not provide a support for traceability from the requirements specification to various architectural descriptions related to systems, software and enterprise (i.e., which and (how) requirement(s) in the requirements specification an individual architectural element relate to and satisfy and vise versa). Maintaining traceability "links" is necessary for managing the change, the co-evolution of both the requirements and the architecture artifacts, confining the change, understanding the change impact on both the structure and the other requirements, providing a support for automated reasoning about a change at a high level of abstraction. Further, such traceability "links" make it easier to preserve the acquired knowledge of the team through guided documentation. This may then minimize the impact of personnel losses,

and may allow the enterprise to make changes in the software system without damaging the architectural integrity and making the software system unevolvable.

Change Impact Analysis Crosscutting System, Enterprise, and Software Architectures

Although change impact analysis techniques are widely used at lower levels of abstractions (e.g., code levels) and on a relatively abstract levels (e.g., classes in O.O. paradigms), little effort has been done on the architectural level (i.e., architectural impact analysis). Formal notations for representing and analyzing architectural designs generically referred to as Architectural Description Languages (ADLs) have provided new opportunities for architectural analyses (Garlan 2000). Examples of such analyses includes system consistency checking (Allen & Garlan, 1994; Luckham et al., 1995), and conformance to constraints imposed by an architectural style (Abowd et al., 1993).

Notable effort using dependency analysis on the architectural level includes the "chaining" technique suggested by Stafford and Wolf (2001). The technique is analogous in concept and application to program slicing. In chaining, dependence relationships that exist in an architectural specification are referred to as links. Links connect elements of the specification that are directly related. The links produce a chain of dependencies that can be followed during analysis. The technique focuses the analysis on components and their interconnections. A component may have a set of input and output ports (which correspond to the component's interface). These ports may have been connected to one another to form a particular architectural configuration. Communication between components is accomplished by sending events to the component's ports. Stafford and Wolf (2001) supports the approach with an analysis tool, Aladdin. Aladdin accepts an architectural specification as input. A variety of computations can be then performed. The computations include unconnected component identification, change impact analysis (i.e., which components will be affected by an architectural change), and event dependence analysis (i.e., which components can send the following event to this port). These computations start at a particular component and/or port. Forward and/or backward chaining are then performed to discover related components. Forward and backward chaining is analogous in concept to forward and backward walk in the dataflow slicing. The applicability of this technique is demonstrated on small-scale architectures and could be extended to address current architectural development paradigms. For example, how such a concept could be refined to perform what-if analysis on large-scale software architectures describing enterprise, system and software? This is necessary for reasoning about how the change could impact the commonality, variability, cross-cutting concerns and their interdependence across various artifacts. These techniques could be then complemented by analysis tools, which could facilitate automated reasoning and provide a basis for what-if analyses to manage the change across instances of the core architecture. Understanding how the change could then ripple across different architecture artifacts might be feasible. These techniques could be complemented by automated reasoning to manage evolution and co-evolution of systems, software and enterprise architectures. When combined with traceability links, the combination could provide a comprehensive framework for managing the change and guiding evolution.

REFERENCES

Abowd, G., Allen, R., & Garlan, D. (1993). Using style to understand descriptions of software architecture. In *Proceedings of Foundations of Software Engineering* (pp. 9–20). ACM Press.

Abowd, G., Bass, L., Clements, P., Kazman, R., Northrop, L., & Zaremski, A. (1996). *Recommended best industrial practice for software architecture evaluation (CMU/SEI-96-TR-025)*. Software Engineering Institute, Carnegie Mellon University.

Allen, R., & Garlan, D. (1994). Formalizing architectural connection. In *Proceedings of the 14th International Conference on Software Engineering*, (pp. 71-80). ACM Press.

Avgeriou, P., Kruchten, P., Lago, P., Grisham, P., & Perry, D. (2007). Architectural knowledge and rationale – Issues, trends, challenges. *ACM SIGSOFT Software Engineering Notes, 32*, 41–46.

Bass, L., Clements, P., & Kazman, R. (2003). *Software architecture in practice* (2nd ed.). Boston, MA: Addison Wesley.

Belady, L. A., & Lehman, M. M. (1976). A model of large program development. *IBM Systems Journal, 15*(3), 225–252.

Bennet, K., & Rajilich, V. (2000). Software maintenance and evolution: A roadmap. In Finkelstein, A. (Ed.), *The future of software engineering* (pp. 73–90). ACM Press.

Bergey, J., Blanchette, S., Clements, P., Gagliardi, M., Wojzik, R., Wood, W., et al. (2009). *U.S. Army Workshop on Exploring Enterprise, System of Systems, System, and Software Architectures*.

Clements, P., Bachmann, F., Bass, L., Garlan, D., Ivers, J., & Little, R. (2002). *Documenting software architectures: Views and beyond*. Boston, MA: Addison Wesley.

Davis, A. (1993). *Software requirements: Objects, functions and states*. Englewood Cliffs, NJ: Prentice-Hall.

de Boer, R. C., Farenhorst, R., Lago, P., van Vliet, H., Clerc, V., & Jansen, A. (2007). *Architectural knowledge: Getting to the core*. Paper presented at the 3rd International Conference on the Quality of Software Architectures (QoSA).

Department of Defense. (2007). *Department of Defense architecture framework version 1.5 - Vol 1 to Vol 3*. Retrieved 15th January, 2008, from www.defenselink.mil/cio-nii/docs/DoDAF_Volume_I.pdf

Emery, D., & Hilliard, R. (2009, 14-17 September). *Every architecture description needs a framework: Expressing architecture frameworks using ISO/IEC 42010*. Paper presented at the Joint Working IEEE/IFIP Conference on Software Architecture, 2009 & European Conference on Software Architecture, WICSA/ECSA 2009.

Feiler, P. H., Gluch, D. P., & Hudak, J. J. (2006). *The architecture analysis & design language (AADL): An introduction. Carneigie-Mellon University*. Software Engineering Institute.

Giachetti, R. E. (2010). *Design of enterprise systems: Theory, architecture, and methods*. Taylor & Francis Group.

Gotel, O., & Finkelstein, A. (1995). Contribution structures. In *The Third Proceedings of the Requirements Engineering Symposium*, (pp. 169-178). York, UK: IEEE CS Press.

Hofmeister, C., Kruchten, P., Nord, R. L., Obbink, J. H., Ran, A., & America, P. (2007). A general model of software architecture design derived from five industrial approaches. *Journal of Systems and Software, 80*(1), 106–126.

IEEE. (2000). *IEEE recommended practice for architecture description of software-intensive system (IEEE Std 1471-2000)*. IEEE Computer Society.

IFIP-IFAC Task Force. (1999). *GERAM: Generalized enterprise reference architecture and methodology*. IFIP-IFAC Task Force on Architectures for Enterprise Integration March Version 1.6.3 (March).

ISO. (2000). Industrial automation systems -- Requirements for enterprise-reference architectures and methodologies. *ISO, 15704*, 2000.

ISO/IEC. (2010). *ISO/IEC 42010:2010 Systems and software engineering - Architecture description*.

Kruchten, P. (1995). The 4+1 view model of architecture. *IEEE Software, 12*(6), 42–50.

Luckham, D. C., Augustin, L., Kenney, J., Vera, J., Bryan, M., & Mann, W. (1995). Specification analysis of system architecture using Rapide. *IEEE Transactions on Software Engineering, 21*(4), 366–355.

Luftman, J., Papp, R., & Brier, T. (1999). Enablers and inhibitors of business-IT alignment. *Communications of the AIS, 1*(3), 1–32.

Magee, J., Dulay, N., Eisenbach, S., & Kramer, J. (1995). Specifying distributed software architectures. In Schäfer, W., & Botella, P. (Eds.), *Software Engineering — ESEC '95 (Vol. 989*, pp. 137–153). Berlin, Germany: Springer.

Ministry of Defence (UK). (2012). *MOD architecture framework (MODAF)*. Retrieved from http://www.mod.uk/DefenceInternet/AboutDefence/WhatWeDo/InformationManagement/MAF/

Object Management Group. (2003). *UML 2 superstructure final adopted specification*.

Stafford, J. A., & Wolf, A. W. (2001). Architecture-level dependence analysis for software system. *International Journal of Software Engineering and Knowledge Engineering, 11*(4), 431–453.

Tang, A., Liang, P., Clerc, V., & Vliet, H. v. (2011). Supporting co-evolving architectural requirements and design through traceability and reasoning. In Avgeriou, P., Lago, P., Grundy, J., & Mistrik, I. (Eds.), *Relating software requiremens and software architecture*.

The Open Group. (2009). *The open group architecture framework* (v8.1.1. enterprise edition). Retrieved 21 February 2012, from http://www.opengroup.org/togaf/ WICSA/ECSA. (2009). *Workshop on Exploring Enterprise, System of Systems, System, and Software Architectures*.

Zachman, J. (1987). A framework for information architecture. *IBM Systems Journal, 38*(2&3).

Zachman, J. (1997). *Concepts of the framework for enterprise architecture*. Retrieved 2 July, 2004, from http://members.ozemail.com.au/~visible/papers/zachman3.htm#Article

Section 1
Architecture Alignment – Theories

Chapter 1
Relating Enterprise, Application, and Infrastructure Architects

Eoin Woods
Artechra, UK

Nick Rozanski
Artechra, UK

ABSTRACT

The architect takes a high-profile role in many IT departments today. In fact, it can be quite difficult in some organizations to find a senior member of IT technical staff whose job title does not include the word "architect." However there is little consensus in the academic community or amongst practitioners as to the responsibilities of the many different types of architect we encounter – or indeed, what they should even be called. In this chapter, the authors propose a simple, widely applicable taxonomy of architects, namely enterprise architects, application architects, and infrastructure architects. The authors define distinguishing characteristics, their responsibilities, the stakeholders with whom they engage, and the tools and techniques they use. The chapter shows how this taxonomy can be applied to most, if not all, practicing architects in the information systems domain, and explains how it helps us understand how such architects work together to help deliver the organization's business goals.

INTRODUCTION

In recent years we have seen the role of the IT architect take a much higher profile in enterprise computing. In fact, today it can be quite difficult to find a senior member of IT technical staff who is not referred to in some way by the title "architect," for example an "enterprise architect," an "integration architect" or a "Unix architect."

However the lack of widely accepted definitions of the responsibilities of the different types of architect causes quite a lot of confusion.

In this article, we attempt to remedy this state of affairs. We believe that there are some defining characteristics that all architects share, and that it is possible to identify a small set of architecture roles into which all of the different architecture jobs can be placed and which can be used as a

DOI: 10.4018/978-1-4666-2199-2.ch001

test for a role actually being an architecture role (rather than that of, say, a technical expert).

Our taxonomy of architects comprises the enterprise architect, the application architect and the infrastructure architect. We characterize and classify these groups in terms of two specific aspects of their jobs: the breadth of focus that they need (e.g. the number of systems they are interested in) and the mix of domain and technology knowledge that the job requires.

RELATED WORK

When we started thinking about the relationships between the various sorts of IT architect, we tried to find existing approaches for classifying the blizzard of job titles in this field. However, although there are plenty of references to the various job titles in formal and online literature, we found relatively few attempts to discuss how the different roles related to each other.

What we did find were a number of classification schemes used in career development or certification programs (namely those from IASA, IBM, CapGemini and the Open Group) and a number of discussions of the responsibilities of software architects specifically.

As part of its attempt to establish and formalize a profession of software architecture, the International Association of Software Architects (IASA) defines five distinct specializations (IASA, 2011) within software (or IT) architecture, namely enterprise architecture, software architecture, infrastructure architecture, information architecture and business architecture. IASA defines these roles as follows.

- **Enterprise Architecture:** Describes the terminology, the composition of enterprise components, and their relationships with the external environment, and the guiding principles for the requirement, design, and evolution of an enterprise.

- **Software Architecture:** The set of structures needed to reason about the system, which is comprised of software elements, relations among them, and properties of both.

- **Infrastructure Architecture:** Describes the structure and behavior of the technology infrastructure of an enterprise, solution or system. It covers the client and server nodes of the hardware configuration, the infrastructure applications that run on them, the infrastructure services they offer to applications, the protocols and networks that connect applications and nodes. It addresses issues such as performance and resilience, storage and backup.

- **Information Architecture:** The art of expressing a model or concept of information used in activities that require explicit details of complex systems. Among these activities are library systems, Content Management Systems, web development, user interactions, database development, programming, technical writing, enterprise architecture, and critical system software design

- **Business Architecture:** A part of an enterprise architecture related to architectural organization of business, and the documents and diagrams that describe that architectural organization.

Interestingly, one local chapter of IASA, IASA Sweden, independently looked at the same question of specialization within software architecture (Akenine, 2008) and identified a slightly different set of roles, namely enterprise architecture, business architecture, application architecture and software architecture.

IBM defines IT architecture as one of the career development professions within the company (Yi Qun, 2009) and again identifies a number of specializations within it, namely enterprise architecture, application architecture, information architecture, infrastructure architecture, integration architecture and operations architecture. These specializations naturally reflect the type of work in which most of IBM's architects are involved.

- **Enterprise Architecture:** Concerned with the definition of a high level enterprise-wide IT Architecture focusing on the mapping of IT capabilities to business needs.
- **Application Architecture:** Concerned with the design of applications required to automate business processes and resolve business issues.
- **Information Architecture:** Focused on the elements required to structure the information and data aspects of solutions and also required to design, build, test, install, operate and maintain the system of solution information.
- **Infrastructure Architecture:** Concerned with the design of infrastructures including servers, storage, workstations, middleware, non- application software, networks, and physical facilities that support the applications and business processes required by the client.
- **Integration Architecture:** Focused on the design of solutions which enable existing applications, packaged software offerings, networks, and systems to work together within an enterprise or among enterprises.
- **Operations Architecture:** Focused on defining plans, strategies and architectures for the installation, operation, migration and management of complex information systems

Cap Gemini's IAF (Integrated Architecture Framework) (van't Wout, 2010) defines the following types of architecture:

- **Enterprise Architecture:** Supports enterprise wide decision making and planning, and shapes the enterprise landscape.

- **Domain Architecture:** Supports business unit level decision making and planning, and shapes the domain landscape.
- **Solution Architecture:** Provides architectural guidance to programs and projects (that is projects or large programs of work which are involved with the design, installation, commissioning and integration software systems – usually packaged solutions – to provide an entire functional solution for an organization, rather than just a piece of software or a standalone system);
- **Software Architecture:** Provides architectural guidance to software development (that is the process of developing a bespoke system, service or major reusable component from scratch, rather than installing and integrating an existing large scale reusable application, such as a CRM system).

There have also been a number of attempts to characterize the work of the software architect (an "application architect" in our classification), such as (Fowler, 2003), (Vickers, 2004) and (Kruchten, 2008). All of these descriptions focus on the single role of an architect creating a single system, rather than the relationship of software architects to other types of architect. All three references stress the architect as a technical leader, with a system wide view, working in or closely alongside the software development team(s) and providing requirements and context to the development team and communicating with those outside the development organization who need to understand the system being built. This aligns very closely with our experience of software architecture.

Finally, the book (Taylor, Medvidovic & Dashofy, 2010) also briefly discusses the role of the software architect (in largely the same terms as the three references above) and also mentions the relationship between software architects and other related roles such as systems engineers and requirements engineers. This discussion appears to relate to the systems engineering domain though, whereas our classification is aimed squarely at enterprise systems development.

MOTIVATION FOR OUR WORK

In our careers as consultants and employees, the authors of this chapter have worked as architects and with architects in tens of organizations across a number of industries including banking, insurance, financial asset management, law enforcement, retail and high technology. In these roles we have frequently needed to cooperate with many other architects and so, to allow productive cooperation, it has been important to understand the focus, scope and competence of each. The problem we have often faced is someone introducing themselves using one of the many of architect titles that are in common use, but this not helping to define the key characteristics of their role.

That said, it's clear that in each organizational context, these various job titles are meaningful and clear, describing the various environment specific nuances of the particular jobs within a particular organization. It's when working across organizations that the job titles cause problems.

When we considered this situation, it seemed to be a fruitless exercise to try to create a complicated and intricate system of architectural job classifications. People wouldn't be able to remember its subtleties and would probably confuse different aspects of it. And in any case, we would never be able to capture all of the details of the variety of architecture jobs that exist in the industry today.

Instead, we realized that what we needed was a clear and very simple classification of architects that divided them into broad groups according to their main concerns and which could be clearly defined using a couple of straightforward rules that would be common to all organizations. This would be enough to allow the existing jobs to be mapped to these simple classifications but would provide enough precision to allow architects to

quickly understand what each other's primary focus would be.

We started off by trying to find an existing standard classification to use; we had no particular desire to create another, and we assumed that this was a common problem. So we were expecting to find that industry organizations would already have defined suitable classifications. However, we found a number of problems when we tried to use the existing classifications that we found in the industry:

- Several of the more comprehensive classifications are proprietary (e.g. IBM's and CAP Gemini's) and so information about them is not freely available.
- The existing classifications don't relate easily to each other (for example it's not clear where IBM's Infrastructure Architecture would fit in CAP Gemini's classifications).
- There do not appear to be clear principles to allow a new architectural job to be mapped to the roles within the classification systems and so it is not clear how to classify responsibilities as belonging to specific roles. For example, Infrastructure and Operations architecture in IBM's classification and Enterprise Architecture and Information Architecture in IASA's classification appear to have a strong relationship between them, if not a direct overlap in the concerns that they address.

These difficulties with the existing sets of classifications led us to consider how we would categorize IT architects and we came to the conclusion that in our experience, the primary concerns of an architect are driven by their scope (single system or organization wide) and their focus (the problem domain or the technology domain). When we considered these two dimensions, we rapidly converged on the three roles we define here, and found that all of the architectural roles we were aware of could be mapped cleanly into these three groups and that the groups seem to form very coherent collections of roles with a lot of common interests.

THE ROLE OF THE ARCHITECT

The role of IT architect has grown slowly to take its current position in enterprise computing. The first references to the idea of software architecture emerged at the now famous NATO conference on software engineering in 1969. However the idea of a software or IT architect did not become widespread until the 1990s, when it became more common to hear of people described as "architects," and the first mainstream publications talking about architecture were published, such as the IEEE Software special issue on software architecture in 1995 (IEEE, 1995). Since then, awareness and understanding of the role has accelerated, to the point where today you can find architects in almost any enterprise with a significant IT capability.

However, while today architects appear to be in every organization, and there is some similarity in what they call themselves, there is still widespread confusion over what IT architecture is, what IT architects do (or should do) and what types of IT architect exist. In this article, we hope to answer some of these questions, by clearly defining the different roles that IT architects play, the focus of each, and the activities that they typically perform.

While there are different types of IT architects, there is a core set of characteristics that they all share. We have found these to be as follows:

- **Design-Centric Work:** Architecture is a design centric activity, although different architects are responsible for designing different types of artifact. However, designing something, be it a system, an infrastructure, a process or a service is core to the activity of being an architect.

- **Stakeholder Focus:** Being an architect involves a lot of focus on stakeholders, much more so than more traditional technical and design oriented jobs. This is because a key part of the architect's role is to bring clarity and consensus to problems that are often poorly understood or poorly communicated by the different stakeholders.

- **A Focus on System-Wide Concerns:** Rather than focusing on the detailed design of one particular element of a system or problem, architecture inherently involves taking a broad view and focusing on the overall organization, the common design aspects shared across it and the overall qualities of the artifact being designed.

- **Balancing Concerns:** Architectural design tends to involve searching for an acceptable solution amongst a range of possible options, which meet the concerns of different stakeholders to a different degree. It is often a case of achieving the least bad option, given stakeholder needs and biases, rather than the optimal engineering solution (which is usually the goal for more detailed or bounded design contexts).

- **Leadership:** Most architecture jobs involve some sort of technical leadership, even if this isn't through a traditional line-management relationship. Architects usually need to define standards, norms and direction for their specialist area within their organizations, and ensure that they are adhered to.

- **Managing Uncertainty:** Architects are usually involved at the very earliest stages of software development projects, when ideas are hazy, priorities and requirements are ill-defined and the overall goal may not yet be known. Architects need to keep this under control, to encourage creativity and inspiration but also to focus stakeholders on reaching consensus on what needs to be done.

Looking for these characteristics in someone's work helps us to identify that they are performing "architecture" work, even if their job title may not reveal this.

This leads us to naturally consider what we mean by *architecture* in this context. When defining architecture in its most general form, we follow ISO Standard 42010 (ISO, 2007) and define it as the set of design decision which define the essence and core characteristics of the system, or more formally "the fundamental conception of a system in its environment embodied in elements, their relationships to each other and to the environment, and principles guiding system design and evolution."

This definition naturally leads us to require a definition of a *system*, which is the artifact which requires an architecture and which the architect is concerned with designing. Our scope here is information systems development, but different architects design different types of information system and so our definition is somewhat generic. It's quite similar to definitions used by the SEI and others (Ellison & Moore, 2003), and is that a system is the combination of hardware, software and human activity that supports one or more functions within an organization, such as management, operations or decision-making. So the concept of a system can span an organization-wide set of applications that automate an entire-business process through a generic service that provides a facility used by other systems, to an individual small information system that automates one part of a department's work.

So if architects simply design systems, then why do we need to consider different types of architect? The reason for this is that while the idea of creating an architecture is quite simple, creating an effective architecture for a system requires a great deal of specialist domain knowledge and experience. The systems that require architecture work will vary greatly between different

environments, and even in a defined domain, such as enterprise information systems, there are significant differences between the architecture required for different systems within the domain. It is also often important to have different types of architect cooperate in order to achieve a successful outcome, so understanding the role of each and the relationships between them is an important factor in achieving this.

A CLASSIFICATION FOR ARCHITECTS

Having held a number of architectural roles ourselves, and observed architects at work in many other organizations, we have found that architects fall into one of three broad groups: enterprise architect, application architect and infrastructure architect. These three groups encompass all of the architectural roles that we have seen in practice.

To help explain the differences between these roles, we classify them along two axes, namely their business/technology focus (the extent to which they focus on the problem domain as opposed to the solution domain), and the breadth of their architectural portfolio (the number of systems that they have architectural responsibility for).

Some architects focus primarily on the business of the organization that they work for (the problem domain) being experts on one or more aspects of the business that they are helping to automate. Other architects focus primarily on the technology used to solve business problems (the solution domain), and are experts in one or more broad technology areas, such as messaging, networking, user interface development or data storage and retrieval.

Some architects need to find a balance between these two areas, as their role involves understanding some aspect of the problem domain to allow them to automate it, but also understanding the technology of the solution domain well enough to be involved in the detailed design and implementation of the solutions they create.

When considering the breadth dimension, some architects are responsible for a large number of systems (possibly all of the applications in the organization), but at a necessarily shallow level, whereas other architects are responsible for a single application, but at a very deep level of involvement. We also find that the number of systems that an architect is responsible for determines the time horizon and abstraction level that she works at. Architects that work across many systems tend to have a longer term, more abstract focus than those architects responsible for a small number of systems, who are involved in shorter term single-system change and many more of the details of how a system works and is operated. We illustrate our architectural classification in the informal diagram in Figure 1.

DEFINITIONS

An enterprise architect is responsible for defining the capabilities, functional components, information assets and systems required to support the activities of a business unit or of the whole organization. The knowledge that she needs to perform her job is a blend of domain and technology knowledge, and is often biased towards broad domain knowledge.

Common organizational synonyms for enterprise architect include functional architect, business architect, strategic or strategy architect, domain architect and stream architect.

An application architect is someone who focuses on a small number of systems (often only one or two) and is the design authority for those systems, their capabilities and their internal structure. The knowledge she needs is a balanced blend of technology and domain knowledge, combining deep practical knowledge of the technologies needed to build and run her systems, with enough

Figure 1. Classification of architectural roles

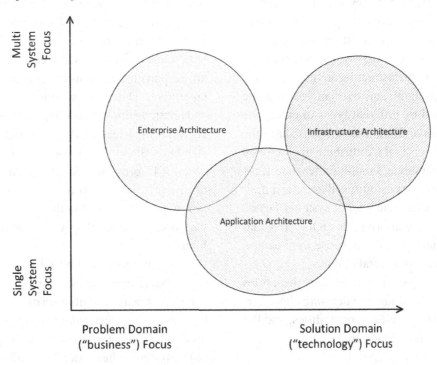

detailed domain knowledge to ensure that her systems effectively meet business needs.

Common synonyms for application architect include software architect, solutions architect, application architect, systems architect and technical architect.

An infrastructure architect is someone who, like an enterprise architect, has a scope ranging over many systems, probably all of those in an organization, but where the knowledge she needs to perform her job is nearly all specific technology knowledge, with a limited amount of domain knowledge being required.

Common organizational synonyms for infrastructure architect include technical architect (again), technology architect, and specialist job titles such as database architect, middleware architect, network architect or storage architect.

It is worth noting that our definition of Enterprise Architect also encompasses a couple of commonly used architectural titles, namely Information Architect (or Data Architect) and Business Architect. This is not to say that these are not valid types of architect in some environments, but rather that we have found that they are best classified as sub-specializations of enterprise architecture rather than distinct classifications in their own right (just as storage or network architecture are specializations of infrastructure architecture). We have observed significant overlap between the work performed by different types of enterprise architect but have found that they all share the key characteristics that we attribute to enterprise architecture, namely a domain rather than technical focus and responsibilities that extend their influence over a large number of systems. Hence we decided to unite information architecture and business architecture with enterprise architecture, rather than trying to separate them.

In the following sections we explore these roles more deeply, by defining the defining characteristics of each role, their responsibilities, and the methods and tools that are used.

ENTERPRISE ARCHITECTS

Defining Characteristics

The enterprise architect has a primary focus on the problem domain (i.e. the business) rather than the solution domain (i.e. the technology) and is responsible for some aspect of the organization's enterprise architecture which, based on the MIT CISR's definition (Weill, 2007), we would define as the set of principles, standards and blueprints for the organization's business processes and IT infrastructure, that reflect the integration and standardization requirements of the company's operating model. As such, enterprise architects create a functional model of the whole enterprise, and map this model onto the physical systems that implement these functions (sometimes referred to as a "system landscape model"), but are not directly involved in the development of application systems or the implementation of the infrastructure platform (which are the domains of the application and infrastructure architects, respectively).

Enterprise architects are primarily interested in what IT needs to provide to the business in order to support its needs, and aligning the provision of IT to the direction and needs of the business is a core focus. That said, some enterprise architects are responsible for purely functional aspects of enterprise architecture, such as the responsibilities and relationships between applications, while others have more technical responsibilities, such as standards, direction or governance over particular types of IT provision (such as data management or enterprise network provision). So, as suggested in Figure 1, even within this role, there is some variation in the problem versus solution domain focus.

The enterprise architect has a cross-system focus, being interested in how all of the systems in the organization combine in order to provide the business with its technology needs. This results in the role being centered around the responsibilities of the systems, their interfaces and how they are integrated, rather than in their internal workings. She often has a role in overseeing major decisions relating to individual systems (an activity usually referred to as "governance"), but rarely gets involved in the details of how they are constructed.

The enterprise architect necessarily has a long-term, quite strategic, view of IT provision in the organization, not being involved in the day-to-day running and improvement of the production systems. Her goal is to guide the IT department in a long-term direction that is congruent with the long term needs of the organization.

The enterprise architect is usually more externally facing than the application architect. She will often work with standards organizations, regulators and other industry bodies to guide or understand industry-wide strategic initiatives, and define and agree industry standards and regulation.

In our experience enterprise architects can be drawn from a variety of backgrounds. The need to understand the needs of the organization and have a cross system focus tends to mean that they are former system or infrastructure architects, or sometimes, former business analysts (who are probably responsible for the functional aspects of enterprise architecture, rather than the more technical areas).

Purpose of Role

The purpose of the role of the enterprise architect is to:

- Ensure that the business processes of the organization and well understood and that there is a clear definition of how they are supported by the organization's information systems.
- Ensure that each information system (application) in the organization has a clearly defined set of responsibilities and interfaces.

- Define the structure, location and primary characteristics of the organizations data, both in motion (messaging) and at rest (stored data), including data ownership, rules for data duplication, "golden sources" (owners) of each significant part of the organization's data and so on.
- Ensure that the organization's strategy is understood and is used as an input to IT decision making, so aligning IT and organizational decision making,
- Maximize the return on investment of the IT budget by ensuring that business priorities are understood and are used to select the right areas for IT budget spending.
- Ensure that the organization's future state IT environment is defined and understood and that there is a clear roadmap that defines a credible set of steps to move from the current state to that proposed future state.
- Ensure that IT change projects align with the organization's priorities, strategy and future state architecture.

Responsibilities

The responsibilities of the enterprise architect are varied, but usually include all or some of the following:

- Functional business domain modeling of the organization and the specification of application systems required for it.
- Corporate data modeling, to create enterprise-level data models and data dictionaries, which provide standard definitions of concepts to be shared across the organization.
- Developing organization-wide models of data ownership and strategies for dealing with distributed and decentralized data.

- Creating current and future state models of the enterprise and its systems, and associated gap analysis and roadmap creation to guide the organization towards the desired future state.
- Creation and management of enterprise inventories of key IT assets such as applications, business processes or reusable software elements.
- Contributing to the organization's technology strategy.
- Defining the organization's application integration architecture (the significant information and control flows between key systems, and the data standards to be used) to allow applications to be integrated in a systematic, standardized and flexible way.
- Definition of organizational technical standards.
- Assessing, overseeing and providing governance over IT change, to ensure that it aligns with the organization's standards and strategy.

Methods and Tools

The enterprise architect typically uses methods and tools such as:

- Functional modeling tools, supporting UML or enterprise architecture specific approaches such as Archimate or TOGAF. Due to their ubiquity, desktop office products (such as Word, Visio and PowerPoint) are also often used to create less formal "box and line" diagrams.
- EA frameworks, such as TOGAF or Zachman, to guide the creation of sets of architectural models.
- Specialist EA tool sets such as Troux, ProVision or Promis Netmodeller, which provide enterprise architecture repositories and modeling tools.

- Metadata modeling tools and repositories such as ASG Rochade or Adaptive Metadata Manager.
- IT inventory products such as ARIS IT Inventory or HP Asset Manager, which allow databases of IT assets to be defined, created and managed.

Due to the high cost of some of these tools, enterprise architects often develop their own home-grown equivalents, such as building an IT inventory using a spreadsheet or relational database.

APPLICATION ARCHITECTS

Defining Characteristics

The application architect has a more even balance between problem domain and solution domain focus than her enterprise architect colleagues, as this is crucial to creating effective applications that meet the needs of the business in a cost-effective way.

The application architect tends to focus on a single system, which she is deeply involved in defining, building and often operating. Her main concern is its function and internal design, and in particular the system wide concerns and mechanisms that it embodies. She is knowledgeable about other systems in the organization at a more abstract level, typically understanding them as "black boxes" that hers interacts with.

The time horizon of an application architect is the short to medium term. She knows where her application is headed, but is more concerned with how it should be built and changed today.

The application architect is almost always grown from senior, highly capable software developers, so she has very strong technical knowledge of the process of system building.

Purpose of Role

The purpose of the application architect's role is to:

- Ensure that their application(s) have clearly defined scope and key requirements.
- Ensure that their application(s) have a well-defined, clearly implemented and suitable architecture that allows them to meet their objectives and requirements.
- Ensure that their application(s) are capable of meeting their key requirements, particularly the quality properties (non-functional requirements) required of them.
- Create a suitable architectural description for their application(s), according to the complexity of the application(s) and the needs of the environment they are working in.
- Ensure the technical integrity of the implementation their application(s), so that they are implemented in line with the architecture, follow sound software development practice, and are fit for purpose.
- Minimize implementation risk for new applications or application changes, by the use of techniques such as expert judgment, proof-of-concept implementation, technology testing and incremental, risk-driven development.
- Provide a source of expert, independent advice to provide validation and review of other applications in the organization.

Responsibilities

The responsibilities of the application architect include the following:

- Application architectural design, defining the architectural structures of the applications she is responsible for, and creating design models to support this activity.

- Creation of technical standards to be applied across her system in order to ensure commonality of approach and technical integrity.
- Creating prototype and proof-of-concept software in order to validate design ideas, investigate and assess implementation options or guide the work of software implementation teams.
- Detailed software and database design, where the design work is particularly critical to achieving important system qualities (for example perhaps being involved in the design of part of a database that is likely to have a direct effect on system performance).
- Reviewing the work of others, particularly design, software implementation and testing artifacts.
- Performing architectural assessment of her own systems and those of others.

Methods and Tools

The application architect uses the following methods and tools:

- Architecture and design approaches such as Domain Driven Design (Evans, 2003) or Attribute Driven Design (Woicik et al, 2006), the application and development of styles and patterns and the use of architectural viewpoints and perspectives (ISO, 2007).
- Software modeling techniques such as UML, Entity Relationship Modeling, informal notations such as "box and line" diagrams and again, the use of architectural viewpoints. When using formally defined notations such as UML or ERDs, the application architect quite often uses a modeling tool (such as Rational Software Modeler, MagicDraw or PowerDesigner) to help her capture her models.

- Software development and analysis tools when developing or analyzing software (such as IDEs, code analysis tools, testing tools, build and configuration management tools).
- When performing assessments, some application architects will use predefined methods like ATAM (Clements, Kazman & Klein, 2001), whereas others will define their own lightweight approaches like TARA (Woods, 2011) or use an ad hoc approach for the situation in hand.

INFRASTRUCTURE ARCHITECTS

Defining Characteristics

The infrastructure architect tends to have a broad organizational focus, but a narrow technical focus, being an expert in one or more specialist technology areas which she is responsible for right across the organization.

The focus of an infrastructure architect is strongly technical, rather than on the business domain of the organization she works in (indeed, she may well be a consultant to that organization). While she needs to have a broad understanding of the priorities of the business area she is serving, her primary skill is deep expertise in one or more technology domains.

The infrastructure architect necessarily has a cross-system focus, defining technology standards and provision at an organizational (or divisional) level, in order to meet the needs of many applications in a consistent manner. Her relationship with individual application areas is often quite formal, via management mechanisms such as service level agreements (SLAs).

The time horizon of an infrastructure architect is long term, as many of her projects will take a long time to implement, and the return on the investment is likewise only seen over the long term. She is interested in achieving simplicity, standardization, stability and cost effective technology provision, none of which is amenable to a short-term, tactical approach. This often means defining long-term roadmaps for her domain and having long-term relationships with vendors and suppliers, to maximize the value to the organization.

The infrastructure architect often influences the "quality properties" to be exhibited by applications, such as security (designing and implementing enterprise-wide mechanisms for authentication and confidentiality); availability (designing and implementing enterprise-wide mechanisms for high availability or disaster recovery); or scalability (designing and implementing enterprise-wide mechanisms for shared computational infrastructure or on-demand provision of hardware resources).

Purpose of Role

The purpose of the infrastructure architect's role is to:

- Provide a clear definition of the IT infrastructure platform for the organization, and how it is to be used to meet the needs of the organization's applications.
- Define clear standards for infrastructure technology acquisition and use in the organization.
- Select appropriate in-house or third party technology products to act as the components of the infrastructure platform, and to define how each component is used within the platform.
- Provide in-house expertise in one or more areas of infrastructure technology.
- Act as an informed point of contact with third party infrastructure product vendors and consultants, to ensure that the third parties that the organization contracts with work to meet its needs.

Responsibilities

The responsibilities of the infrastructure architect include the following:

- Infrastructure environment design, to define how shared infrastructure will work and provide a service to the organization.
- Contributing to technology strategy in her area of expertise, defining the current and future state for it and how it relates to the rest of the organization's IT strategy.
- Creating technical standards in areas relevant to her expertise, guiding the organization's adoption and use of particular technologies.
- Reviewing projects that are making use of parts of the infrastructure environment, to guide them towards appropriate and realistic use of the infrastructure and ensuring that particular applications do not cause problems for other users of infrastructure services.
- Project consultancy, to help organizations adopt and make most effective use of the infrastructure services available.
- Liaising with technology vendors who supply the organization's IT infrastructure components, and managing the relationships with important vendors.
- Keeping abreast of new technology developments, understanding how they could benefit the organization, and promoting their adoption where this is of benefit.
- Leading infrastructure implementation projects.

Methods and Tools

The infrastructure architect is not particularly well served by the rather sparse set of methods and tools available to them, particularly in comparison with enterprise architects, but typically uses the following methods and tools:

- Informal modeling tools, such as desktop office products like PowerPoint, Excel and Visio.
- Parts of enterprise architecture frameworks (such as TOGAF and Zachman) that are relevant to the definition of the areas of focus for the infrastructure architect.
- Domain or vendor specific methods or tools such as those available for network design or capacity management and modeling.
- Documentation and communication tools such as wikis, SharePoint sites and PowerPoint presentations.

RELATING ENTERPRISE, APPLICATION, AND INFRASTRUCTURE ARCHITECTS

Having defined and explained the three IT architecture roles, we now consider how they relate to each other and the influence that each role has on the other two.

The enterprise architect provides an application architect with a context for her work, and provides an infrastructure architect with strategies, priorities and requirements for enterprise wide infrastructure.

In turn, the application architect provides an enterprise architect with requirements that they have for enterprise infrastructure or standardization, based on the needs of their applications; inputs to the enterprise architecture plans and roadmaps; and validation of the enterprise architecture in practice. The infrastructure architect provides an enterprise architect with assistance in formulating enterprise wide technology plans and specific information about the cost and practicality of the enterprise architecture group's plans.

Application and infrastructure architects also interact frequently, with the application architect usually acting as the customer of the infrastructure architects, who provide standard services or infrastructure configurations, with known characteristics and qualities, which she can use as the foundation for her systems.

These interactions are illustrated by the informal diagram in Figure 2 and explained below.

To be more specific, the enterprise architect provides an application architect with the following artifacts:

- An organization-wide application architecture, to provide context and define responsibilities for her application(s).
- A corporate data model, to guide database and domain model design and application integration.
- An integration architecture and associated standards and patterns, to guide application integration.
- Standards for achieving common critical qualities, such as security, high availability and disaster recovery in a standard way within the organization (often using common organizational services).

- A technology strategy and technical standards, which also guide application design.

In return, the application architect provides an enterprise architect with the following artifacts:

- A practical, usage-based validation of the feasibility and usefulness of the enterprise architecture, based on her use of it and the requirements of the applications that she is responsible for.
- An implementation of some parts of the enterprise architecture, as embodied in her applications.
- Content for and validation of corporate standards as they are developed, based on the experience of trying to build applications in the organization.

The enterprise architect provides an infrastructure architect with the following artifacts:

- A technology strategy, into which the infrastructure architect's work will fit.
- A set of business priorities, to help the infrastructure architect focus on and prioritize the right aspects of her work.

Figure 2. Inter-architect relationships

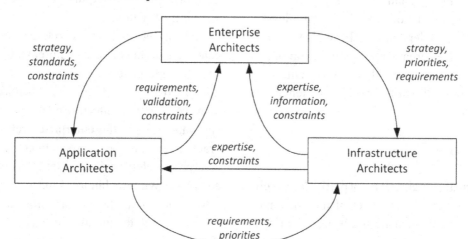

- Requirements for shared infrastructure, based on the long term needs of the organization.
- Rollout plans for major programs, to allow the necessary infrastructure services to be designed and implemented.

The infrastructure architect provides an enterprise architect with the following artifacts:

- Evaluations and certifications of products within her area of expertise, to help the enterprise architect confidently select products, knowing that they can be successfully applied within the organization.
- Technical feasibility reviews of enterprise architecture proposals, particularly those relating to shared infrastructure services.
- Cost estimates for the infrastructure aspects of proposed enterprise architecture led programs.
- Information about the vendors who supply the technology in her area of expertise, the relative positioning of different vendors and more general market information such as adoption trends.
- Briefings on emerging technologies to help the enterprise architect stay up to date.

The infrastructure architect can provide an application architect with the following artifacts:

- Application design reviews, from an infrastructure perspective.
- Consultancy or informal training on the various technologies and infrastructure services that the infrastructure architecture is responsible for.
- Design work for the infrastructure aspects of new applications.
- Assistance with selecting appropriate infrastructure products and services for particular applications and providing an un-

derstanding of the likely or known risks, problems or limitations that use of particular products or services is likely to imply.
- Cost estimates for the acquisition and use of infrastructure products and services.

An application architect is largely a consumer of the work of the infrastructure architect, but does provide input to infrastructure architecture work via the following means:

- The application architect can supply an infrastructure architect with a deployment view of her system to help the infrastructure architect understand its requirements and plan for it.
- She can supply a rollout schedule to allow the required infrastructure provision to be timed correctly.
- Her non-functional requirements are a useful input to the infrastructure architect's designs, to help identify the right infrastructure services and products to use.
- The budget for the application architect's application is a constraint on the infrastructure provision that can be specified.

DEFINING THE RELATIONSHIPS

In this section, we delve more deeply into the relationships between the three types of IT architect that we described earlier. We do this through the mechanism of a UML class diagram, shown in Figure 3, which models the key architect roles under consideration, the roles of others in the organization that they interact with, and the artifacts through which this interaction occurs.

Before describing the content of this model, it is worth briefly clarifying its utility and its limitations. Formalizing the relationships between the roles in this way is useful because it helps to add a degree of precision to what are quite loose

Figure 3. Inter-role relationships

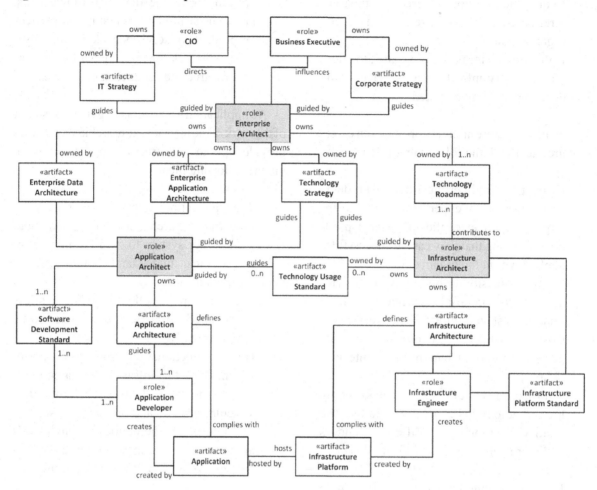

relationships, and so helps to clarify the complicated relationships between these three architectural roles. However, it is important to bear in mind that a model of this sort is inevitably a simplification of the complicated interactions between people in real organizations and shows an idealized view of the world, which is unlikely to exist in such a neat and tidy form anywhere in a real organization.

The roles that the actors in the model play are briefly described here:

- **Application Architect:** An architect concerned with the design of one or a small number of application systems.
- **Application Developer:** A software developer who is engaged with the development of one or more application systems.
- **Business Executive:** A role played by any senior non-IT manager in the organization who is interested in shaping its IT environment (typically includes the CEO, COO and CFO).
- **Chief Information Officer (CIO):** Heads the IT organization.

- **Enterprise Architect:** An architect concerned with the design of organization-wide (cross-system) IT structures.
- **Infrastructure Architect:** An architect concerned with the design of the IT infrastructure platform within an organization.
- **Infrastructure Engineer:** Someone involved in the detailed design and construction of the IT infrastructure platform.

Brief definitions of the artifacts through which the actors in the model communicate are as follows:

- **Application:** A computer system, performing one or more functions for the organization.
- **Application Architecture:** The architecture of a specific application system.
- **Corporate Strategy:** A definition of the strategy for the organization, which defines the businesses, it should be in and why, and how it plans to achieve this.
- **Enterprise Application Architecture:** An architectural definition of the organization-wide application landscape (applications, responsibilities and integration).
- **Enterprise Data Architecture:** An architectural definition of organization-wide data structure, storage and ownership.
- **Infrastructure Architecture:** An architectural definition of the organization's infrastructure platform.
- **Infrastructure Platform:** A collection of hardware and software that provides a runtime environment for the organization's application systems.
- **Infrastructure Platform Standard:** The definition of a standard approach to using one or more specific technologies within the organization's infrastructure platform.
- **IT Strategy:** The definition of the organization's objectives, principles and tactics that relate to how information technology

will support the organization's business strategy.
- **Software Development Standard:** The definition of a standard approach to some aspect of software development.
- **Technology Roadmap:** The definition of the sequence of steps and their planned timing to evolve the technology in use in the organization towards a planned future state.
- **Technology Strategy:** The definition of the organization's objectives, principles and tactics relating to the specific technologies that the organization uses
- **Technology Usage Standard:** The definition of a standard approach to using one or more specific pieces of technology within the organization.

Having defined the artifacts and roles within the model, we can now consider how they relate to each other and what this tells us about the relationships between enterprise, application and infrastructure architects.

The Chief Information Officer, who runs the IT organization, directs the work of the enterprise architects and their work is also influenced by a number of the organization's executive level business managers. The formal route for the CIO to direct the work of enterprise architects is through the IT Strategy that the enterprise architecture must support. Similarly the formal communication path between the business managers and the work of enterprise architects is through the definition of the Business Strategy that informs the enterprise architecture work.

An enterprise architect is the owner of a number of important strategic IT artifacts, namely the Technology Strategy, the enterprise's Data Architecture and Application Architecture and the Technology Roadmap that explains how the IT environment (in particular the infrastructure platform) is going to evolve in the future.

An application architect uses a number of the enterprise architect's outputs in order to inform their work, in particular the enterprise's Application Architecture and Data Architecture and the Technology Strategy that informs their choice and use of technology when designing systems.

The application architect's outputs are the Application Architecture for one or more application systems, and the Software Development Standards which define the standard approaches for software development that should be employed when developing or maintaining certain applications. These artifacts are used by the Application Developers who are responsible for the relevant application systems.

Similarly the infrastructure architects use a number of the enterprise architect's outputs when designing the organization's infrastructure platform, in particular the Technology Strategy and the Technology Roadmap (which they will also need to contribute to in their own area of specialty, to ensure that the plans that the roadmap implies are achievable).

The infrastructure architect's outputs are the Infrastructure Architecture (or their part of it) and a set of Infrastructure Platform Standards that define how particular technologies should be used within the organization's infrastructure platform. These artifacts are used by Infrastructure Engineers who are responsible for the detailed design and construction of the organization's infrastructure platform.

The infrastructure architect also influences the work of the application architect through the use of Technology Usage Standards that define how particular technologies should be used within the organization, so providing the application architect with guidance and constraints on the technologies they should use within their applications and how they should be used.

CASE STUDY

A retailer of consumer electronics goods and accessories sells its products in stores and over the Internet, and now wants to move into the mobile consumer market. However the retailer's strategy of encouraging customers to visit their shopping website from their mobile devices is not working well, since the website is poorly suited to the cell phone form factor, and offers a painfully slow user experience over a mobile connection.

The retailer has therefore decided to develop an "app" which will run on a range of Internet-enabled smartphones and portable devices, and provide similar functionality to that available on the website. The app will seamlessly align with the website from the customer's perspective – so, for example, the customer will log in to the app using the same credentials, and will be able to see their favorite items, shopping history and account details. The first version of the app will allow customers to browse part of the retailer's catalog, order goods and track their delivery status. Subsequent versions will extend the catalog and offer more features.

The app will rely on a number of supporting servers that process requests on its behalf and the overall application will be required to integrate with the retailer's existing systems for supply chain management, customer management and finance. It will also be required to integrate with the retailer's web infrastructure in a secure, scalable way.

The application architect plays a key role in defining the architecture of the new application and overseeing its implementation. However the other types of architect also make important contributions to the success of the project, as the case study illustrates.

The Enterprise Architect

As we have seen the enterprise architect focuses on the problem domain and owns the "big picture." For the shopping app, her most important contribution is to provide an enterprise functional model. This model defines the retailer's important enterprise functions, such as manufacturing, distribution and warehouse management, and the major information and control flows between them. She discusses this model with the application architect, so that they can agree where the new application "fits" into the model, and which enterprise functions it will have to interact with. The application architect uses this information to produce a first-cut definition of the scope and requirements of the app.

The enterprise architect also maintains a system landscape model which maps the enterprise functional model on to physical systems. This mapping is sometimes one-to-one (for example, the retailer has a single financial accounting system), but in many cases it is more complex – the biggest challenge being that the distribution function is implemented in a number of different systems according to region and product. The enterprise architect helps the application architect understand these systems, what functions they provide, and how the app and its servers should interact with them. The application architect uses this information to produce a more detailed specification of the app's interfaces and control flows.

Another important contribution of enterprise architecture is the definition and application of enterprise messaging standards. The enterprise architecture team has defined a standard set of messages and data items, such as order, delivery note and invoice, and all systems are expected to conform to these definitions in their interfaces. The enterprise architect works with the application architect to understand which messages should be used for which interfaces, and how these messages should be used.

Infrastructure Architect

It is always very difficult to predict the take-up of an Internet application, and for this reason the application architect is keen that the back-end infrastructure is easily scalable to deal with unexpected peaks of customer demand. The app must also comply with the retailer's technology standards for servers, storage, networking, security, and middleware.

The retailer runs several data centers each with dedicated web and application server farms which support their main website. Infrastructure components such as servers, storage, or network connectivity are usually provisioned in the form of standard services with defined characteristics (such as a server's CPU and memory configuration) and standard SLAs for deployment, management and performance.

The infrastructure architect works with the application architect to understand how this infrastructure can be used to host the app's servers and the existing enterprise services that it relies upon. He also helps the application architect define the required storage management architecture, and how interactions between the app and the data center will traverse the retailer's network and security infrastructure (firewalls, load balancers, session endpoints and so forth).

The infrastructure architect then helps the application architect define the infrastructure for the app's middle-tier components: the application servers, relational database, messaging-oriented middleware, and file transfer services. Finally, the infrastructure architect helps the application architect define the business continuity architecture which will enable the service to come back on-line quickly in the event of a severe failure.

The biggest challenge to the two architects is to understand how the app will be deployed to customers' smartphones. This is an area of which the retailer has no previous experience, so the infrastructure architect brings in an outside expert to advise on the best way forward. The solution requires some changes to the retailer's data networking and security capabilities, and the infrastructure architect oversees the implementation of these by the retailer's production engineering teams.

Application Architect

Involving the enterprise and infrastructure architect has made the application architect's life much easier. He is able to draw on their expertise and knowledge to help design aspects of the architecture – its interactions with other systems, and the infrastructure it will run on – of which he has little knowledge himself.

The communication is not just one-way, however: the enterprise architect has made a number of clarifications and improvements to the enterprise model, and has disseminated to other teams the insights she has gained. The infrastructure architect has been able to add a service for the deployment of software to customer devices to the retailer's portfolio of standard infrastructure services. This will benefit the next project that needs to write a smartphone app (there are already a couple in the pipeline).

Conversely, the application architect has been able to dedicate much more of his time to the architecture of the application itself. He is able to represent external systems and underlying infrastructure as "black boxes" in most of his models, confident that the nature and characteristics of these are correct and well understood.

CONCLUSION

In conclusion, the role of the IT architect has become well established and can be seen in action in many organizations, although we find a great diversity in job titles and descriptions. This leads to confusion about the role amongst stakeholders and the architects themselves.

By classifying architects along two axes, namely the scope and focus of their jobs, the classification problem is greatly simplified. This analysis led us to define a simple, widely-applicable taxonomy of architects, namely enterprise architects, application architects and infrastructure architects. With this insight we have been able to clearly define the roles of each and better understand the interactions between them.

The enterprise architect sets the context for system and infrastructure architects. She provides the application architect with a context for her work, and the infrastructure architect with strategies, priorities and requirements for enterprise wide infrastructure. Application architects are responsible for the architecture and design of individual systems, within an overall enterprise application architecture, using technology services designed by infrastructure architects. Infrastructure architects provide cross system infrastructure services (storage, compute, network), within a set of priorities and direction set by enterprise architects.

REFERENCES

Akenine, D. (2008). A study of architect roles by IASA Sweden. *Architecture Journal, 15*. Retrieved September 1, 2011, from http://msdn.microsoft.com/en-us/architecture/cc505968

Clements, P., Kazman, R., & Klein, M. (2001). *Evaluating software architectures: Methods and case studies*. Boston, MA: Addison-Wesley.

Ellison, R. J., & Moore, A. P. (2003). *Trustworthy refinement through intrusion-aware design (TRIAD)*. Technical Report, CMU/SEI-2003-TR-002, March 2003.

Evans, E. (2003). *Domain-driven design: Tackling complexity in the heart of software*. Boston, MA: Addison-Wesley.

Fowler, M. (2003). Who needs an architect? *IEEE Software, 20*(5), 11–13. doi:10.1109/MS.2003.1231144

IASA. (2011). *Architecture roles.* Retrieved 28 September, 2011, from http://www.iasaglobal.org/iasa/Roles.asp

IEEE. (1995). *Software, 12*(6).

ISO. (2007). *ISO/IEC 42010:2007: Systems and software engineering -- Recommended practice for architectural description of software-intensive systems.*

Kruchten, P. (2008). What do software architects really do? *Journal of Systems and Software, 81,* 2413–2416. doi:10.1016/j.jss.2008.08.025

Taylor, R., Medvidovic, N., & Dashofy, E. (2010). *Software architecture: Foundations, theory and practice.* Hoboken, NJ: John Wiley and Sons.

van't Wout, J., Waage, M., & Hartman, H. Stahlecker & M., Hofman, A. (2010). *The integrated architecture framework explained: Why, what, how.* Springer, Yi Qun, P. (2009). *IBM's ITA & ITS profession.* Retrieved September 1, 2011, from http://www.kingdee.com/news/subject/09togaf/pdf/wuzhifan.pdf

Vickers, B. (2004). Architecting a software architect. In *Proceedings Aerospace Conference 2004*, Big Sky, MT, USA, 6-13 March 2004. Piscataway, NJ: IEEE.

Weill, P. (2007). *Innovating with information systems.* Presented at 6th e-Business Conference, Barcelona, Spain, 27th March 2007. Retrieved January 5, 2012, from http://www.iese.edu/en/files/6_29338.pdf

Woicik R. et al. (2006). *Attribute driven design.* Technical Report, CMU/SEI-2006-TR-023, November 2006.

Woods, E. (2011, June). Industrial architectural assessment using TARA. In *Proceedings 9th Working IEEE Conference on Software Architecture, WICSA 2011*, Colorado, USA, 20–24 June 2011. Piscataway, NJ: IEEE Computer Society Press.

KEY TERMS AND DEFINITIONS

Application Architect: Someone who is responsible for the design, capabilities and internal structures (i.e. the architecture) of a specific set of systems, requiring a balanced blend of technology and domain knowledge, combining deep practical knowledge of the technologies needed to build and run systems, with enough detailed domain knowledge to ensure that the systems effectively meet business needs. Common synonyms for application architect include software architect, solutions architect, application architect, systems architect and technical architect.

Application Architecture: The set of key design decisions, structures and organizing principles for a software application system that define the characteristics and capabilities of the application.

Architecture: The set of design decision which define the essence and core characteristics of the system, or more formally, following ISO 4210, "the fundamental conception of a system in its environment embodied in elements, their relationships to each other and to the environment, and principles guiding system design and evolution."

Enterprise Architect: Someone who is responsible for defining the capabilities, functional components, information assets and systems required to support the activities of a business unit or of the whole organization, requiring a blend of domain and technology knowledge, and is often biased towards broad domain knowledge. Common organizational synonyms for enterprise architect include functional architect, business architect, strategic or strategy architect, domain architect, data architect, information architect and (business) stream architect.

Enterprise Architecture: The set of principles, standards and blueprints for the organization's business processes and IT infrastructure that reflect the integration and standardization requirements of the company's operating model.

Infrastructure Architect: Someone who has responsibility for the architecture of an infrastructure platform used to host many systems, probably all of those in an organization, requiring primarily specific technology knowledge, with a limited amount of domain knowledge being required. Common organizational synonyms for infrastructure architect include technical architect, technology architect, and specialist job titles such as database architect, middleware architect, network architect or storage architect.

Infrastructure Architecture: The definition of the key design characteristics of part or all of a collection of compute, storage and networking components that combine to form a unified platform on which applications can be hosted.

IT Architect: Someone who is responsible, in whole or in part, for the conception and definition of the architecture of some part of an organization's information system environment and whose work can be characterized by performing design work, a focus on stakeholders and their needs, the responsibility for system-wide concerns, the need to balance conflicting concerns, leadership and the need to manage uncertainty.

System: In the information systems domain, a system is the combination of hardware, software and human activity that supports one or more functions within an organization, such as management, operations or decision-making. This concept of a system can span an organization-wide set of applications that automate an entire-business process through a generic service that provides a facility used by other systems, to an individual small information system that automates one part of a department's work.

Chapter 2
Semantic Wiki for Tracing Process and Requirements Knowledge in Small and Medium Enterprises

Khrystyna Nordheimer
University of Mannheim, Germany

Stefan Seedorf
University of Mannheim, Germany

Christian Thum
University of Mannheim, Germany

ABSTRACT

Although the early phases in software development are important to project success, there are only a few lightweight tools for the integrated management of core software entities. Especially, small and medium-sized enterprises (SME) often lack knowledge and resources to use complex development environments. In this chapter, the authors present a wiki-based approach which allows multiple stakeholders to develop a shared understanding of business elements as well as software design elements. Business processes, requirements, and the architectural design are documented and modeled in a common wiki platform, which provides the foundation for semantic traceability. This allows users to react to changes and track down affected elements on both sides. Finally, the wiki platform supports real-time collaborative modeling of process and design models natively integrated into the Web browser.

DOI: 10.4018/978-1-4666-2199-2.ch002

INTRODUCTION

Managing the software development life cycle is a complex endeavor which requires different stakeholders to work together in a systematic, structured process. Many large organizations follow industry standard processes, such as the Rational Unified Process (RUP), or have adopted agile methods in recent years. For each life-cycle phase specialized tools are used, e.g. for project management, requirements management, software modeling, programming, testing, and configuration management. However, most developed tools and methods are hardly suitable for Small and Medium-sized Enterprises (SME), because they are too complex and require extensive training as well as high qualification of employees. SMEs often do not have the knowledge and resources at hand for systematic life-cycle management and use therefore individual solutions and tools that are usually incoherent and not linked together. This leads to inconsistency and information asymmetry between business and IT experts. Furthermore, the realization of traceability through the development process can be negatively affected.

Recently, SMEs increasingly follow the trend of outsourcing parts of their development to partnering software companies abroad (Richardson et al. 2008; Boden et al. 2007). One key problem here is the transfer of the knowledge to the partner that is needed to understand the requirements and the business domain. To this date, misunderstood requirements present a major source of development inefficiency and project failure (Maalej et al. 2009). Further, SMEs should have suitable methods and tools at hand to manage the global software lifecycle. As software development is an iterative and incremental process, the collaborating partners should be able to get a constant overview of the state of the project and to trace requirements knowledge to the software architecture and vice versa. It becomes more important through geographic distance between project management

and developers. In this context, existing software lifecycle approaches do not sufficiently address the specific needs of SME.

Within the scope of the GlobaliSE research project, we have studied the current problems of SME in software life-cycle management (SLCM). The domain in question is enterprise software. In case studies with eight SMEs we interviewed developers and customers and identified the following problems:

- Common software process models as well as underlying software tools do not meet the needs of SME. Most of them are commercial, too complex and often too expensive for SME purposes.
- Customers document their business processes either deficiently or not at all. However, the lack of business process and requirements knowledge is stated as a frequent cause for failure, especially in near- and offshoring development.
- The relationships between business processes, requirements, and software components are usually not documented and cannot be traced.

Regarding the use of tools for supporting the global software process (business process modeling, requirements engineering, change management, communication), we found that most companies use a wide range of products, partly individual developed solutions. However, we could also identify a small number of common used tools. The most widely accepted are different kinds of wikis (c.f. Louridas 2006). Majority of respondents use them mainly for documentation reasons, knowledge, customer or project management. More frequent use of wikis in SMEs is desirable, since they are inexpensive, flexible, and easy-to-use. On the downside traditional wikis are very limited when it comes to business process and requirements management. For example, the documentation is informal and non-visual. Traditional wikis are also not ideal for traceability management, as they only allow specify hyperlinks between pages. Wiki content can neither be formally stated nor automatically processed. In summary, the core problems of traditional wikis are consistency of content, accessing knowledge and reusing knowledge (Krötzsch et al. 2007).

In this chapter, we propose a wiki-based solution for the lightweight modeling, documentation and traceability management of business process, requirements, and architectural software components. The specific requirements, issues and preferences of SME are taken into account. Furthermore, we show how the proposed conceptual approach can be realized in a semantic wiki.

The remainder of this chapter is organized as follows: In the second section, wikis are introduced and categorized according to their functionality and support of the software life cycle. In the third section, the related work is discussed. In the fourth section, the lightweight software tool CLEoS based on the Semantic MediaWiki (SMW) is introduced. The platform supports the documentation of requirements, business processes, and software components as well as the management of traceability links (Dengler et al. 2009). The architecture solution for Semantic MediaWiki is further extended by SLiM, a collaborative editor for synchronous lightweight modeling. SLiM supports the synchronous distributed creation and manipulation of UML diagrams, lowering the technical entry barriers for participating in the modeling process (Thum et al. 2009).

SEMANTIC WIKIS FOR SOFTWARE DEVELOPMENT

Semantic wikis are wikis that allow imposing a knowledge model onto unstructured page content (Maalej et al. 2010). Traditional wiki pages and links between them can be annotated with types, which describe their meaning in machine-interpretable manner. This has a number of advantages in software engineering applications (Happel and Seedorf 2006). For example, a link from a *stakeholder* to a *requirement* could be annotated with *is responsible for* relationship. Such semantic annotations offer a number of benefits for the wiki users. They enable context-aware search by creation of user specific queries which can be automatically answered by the wiki engine. Using a semantic query one can easily answer the question *"who is responsible for requirement X"* or *"which requirements are managed by person Y"*. Semantic annotations can be also used for adoption of content presentation according to the needs of different stakeholders (Schaffert et al. 2007). Additional information can be shown on a wiki page as a table, an info box or a graph. Thus, the presentation of content and wiki search benefit greatly from an adaptation to the represented context (Schaffert et al. 2006). Furthermore, semantic wikis offer following features:

- **Collaborative:** Wiki platform enable collaborative editing of information in easy manner. All users can work on the same content together and get always the updated version of documents, articles, tables etc. Especially, in distributed teams effective collaboration plays an important role, reducing information inconsistency and asymmetry.
- **Semantic:** Semantic annotation of hyperlinks can be used to define relationships between the software entities which enables semantic querying and knowledge processing. It offers a basis for realization of traceability through the entire development process.
- **Extendable:** Wikis can be customized to specific needs of users. Depending on requirements of SME different additional functions or tools can be integrated as wiki

extensions. It is also possible to import data from external sources or tools and vice versa.

- **Lightweight:** Wikis are easy to use and moderately intuitive. Users do not necessary need to define and implement semantic annotations; they can use user-friendly buttons, check boxes or dropdown boxes link wiki pages. Semantic queries can be predefined and reused.

With these features semantic wikis address some of the shortcomings of traditional wikis, which were identified in section 1. To this date, they have been proposed and adapted for requirements management (Auer et al. 2006) and business process management (Dengler and Happel 2010). The support for covering other phases of the development lifecycle, however, still seems to be highly constrained. In the following section, we will describe how some of these constraints can be overcome by providing a unified wiki-based modeling and documentation platform.

CLEOS SEMANTIC WIKI APPROACH

In the first section, we analyzed from several case studies that SME still fall short of modeling business processes, requirements, and realizing traceability across the early phases of development. In the second section, wikis —which are already widely accepted— were proposed as one way of tackling these issues. However, wikis usually do not offer features for graphical modeling, and are thus of limited use when it comes to combining modeling with software documentation. Moreover, every SME that intends to use a wiki will have to create a basic structure over and over again. This impedes relating various software entities to the requirements because there is no standardized information model. Further problems

arise from the lack of forms for user-friendly input and project tracking features.

In order to solve these shortcomings and lower the setup cost, we have developed the Collaborative Lightweight Extension for Software Engineering (CLEoS). CLEoS is based on the Semantic MediaWiki (SMW), a semantic extension of the widely used MediaWiki (Krötzsch 2006). It includes a number of templates and forms for user friendly input. Users do not have to learn a wiki syntax to create business process and requirement descriptions. For the three core elements there are three following extension modules: a business process extension, a requirements extension and a software architecture extension. All three extensions have in common that they have predefined templates and forms, in addition to the structured wiki pages that define the initial information structure.

These wiki pages are based on a semantic data model consisting of concepts (*categories* in SMW) and properties for different types of software entities. For example, every business process can be broken down into activities. The concepts are mapped to a structured wiki page, and a custom template and form for editing the description is provided. There are forms for describing the traceability links between different elements, e.g. the requirements realized by a software component (see Figure 1). These forms are automatically embedded when a new page of a preconfigured type, in this example software component, is embedded.

The SMW enables asynchronous collaborative editing based on forms but it does not support graphical modeling. In order to provide such functionality we have developed an additional extension which allows synchronous graphical modeling business processes and architectural designs. The extension SLiM (Synchronous Lightweight Modeling) is tightly integrated with the other modules and is described in Thum et al.

Figure 1. Semantic data model of CLEoS

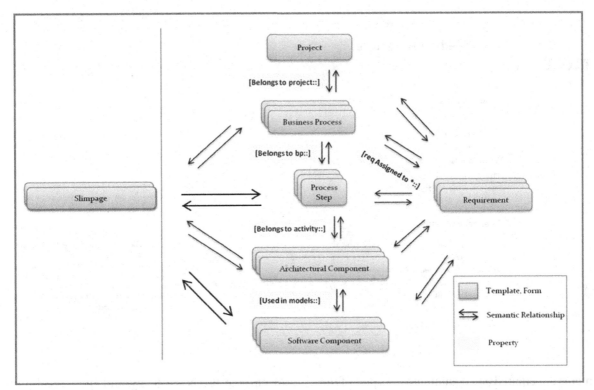

(2009). In general, CLEoS wiki provides the following features:

- Process life cycle
  - Documentation of business processes
  - Integrated collaborative modeling (SLiM Process)
- Software life cycle
  - Requirements management
  - Documentation of architectural and software components
  - Integrated collaborative modeling (SLiM UML)

The underlying semantic data model of the CLEoS wiki system is shown in Figure 1. For each concept, e.g. business process, requirement, software component etc. one wiki page will be created. Likewise, the relationships between concepts will be mapped to properties in the CLEoS wiki.

To demonstrate the added value of the CLEoS wiki and to show how it can be used in the SLCM we describe a simple scenario of the development process for an "Automated Teller Machine." In this example a user can log in to a system and choose between deposit, inquiry or withdrawal options. In the first step a new CLEoS project will be created. This wiki page contains the project description, the information about the start and the end date, responsible persons, the completeness and the current status of the project. Moreover, it gives an overview of the project structure including related business processes, process steps, requirements, architectural and software components (see Figure 2).

For simplicity and brevity of our case the development process is described top-down as follows: In the beginning of a project, analysts and business experts come up with a first version of the process model. In the next step, the require-

Figure 2. CLEoS project page

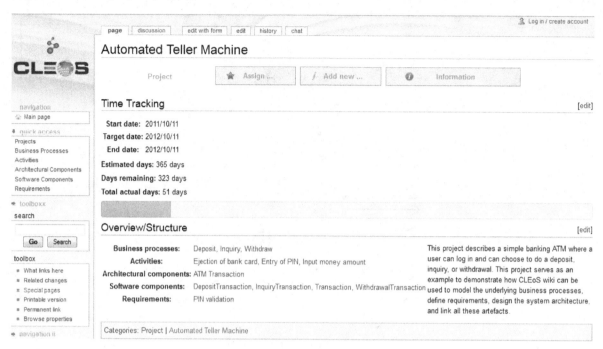

ments are elicited and documented. As part of the requirements phase, the business processes could be enhanced or redesigned. The third step is the architectural design where the system is broken down into software components. The implementation, testing, and deployment is not covered by CLEoS because these are always carried out with language-specific implementation tools. Although this simple case looks like a "waterfall process", it does not matter in which order or in how many iterations these steps are performed. If the system is developed in an agile process, CLEoS can still ensure the traceability between the elements.

Since the integrated SLiM tool allows one to edit process models synchronously on the wiki page the preliminary model can then be discussed and refined by all process stakeholders. The advantage of a wiki-based business process modeling is that it can be accessed by all users, e.g. customers who verify the process. Because the CLEoS wiki serves as a central information repository there is only a single process representation. This helps

to enforce the consistency and the traceability throughout the project.

Business Process Modeling

Communication between domain experts, business analysts, and software engineers is crucial to project success—especially in the early stages of a project. Therefore, business process modeling it is widely used in software development projects. While wikis are highly suitable for collaborative documentation, they are not equipped for visual modeling out-of-the-box. Although process modeling tools have been integrated into some wiki engines they largely remain separate entities (e.g., see the Confluence Gliffy plugin). Further, it has been shown that simple control flow patterns, e.g. multi-choice pattern and parallel-split patterns, can be mapped into a semantic wiki (Dengler & Happel 2010). In wiki-based process modeling systems, a process entity is typically mapped to a wiki page, and the sub-processes (activities or tasks) are mapped to sub-pages or separate wiki pages. It has also been shown that these structures can be read to automatically generate a graphical process model.

In the Automated Teller Machine example three following business processes can be defined: the deposit, the inquiry, and the withdrawal. For each process a wiki page of the category "Business process" will be created. Using the integrated modeling tool business experts define the process model and add further information applying the predefined template. As the business process modeling notation we provide so called *intuitive Activity Modeling language* (iAM) which consists of only six elements and is compatible to a subset of BPMN 2.0. The iAM notation can optionally be

replaced by any other business process modeling language. Figure 3 illustrates the business process model of the withdrawal.

Likewise, particular process steps are mapped to wiki pages of the category "Activity" which contain further details. In our example the process step "Entry of PIN" is mapped to a wiki page with the same name. In order to add a specific information about the process step business experts do not have to create and fill these pages manually but can use predefined templates again (see Figure 4).

Although the combination of wiki systems with graphical modeling does not match the advanced features of business process management tools it is a lightweight alternative that allows for

Figure 3. Business process "withdrawal"

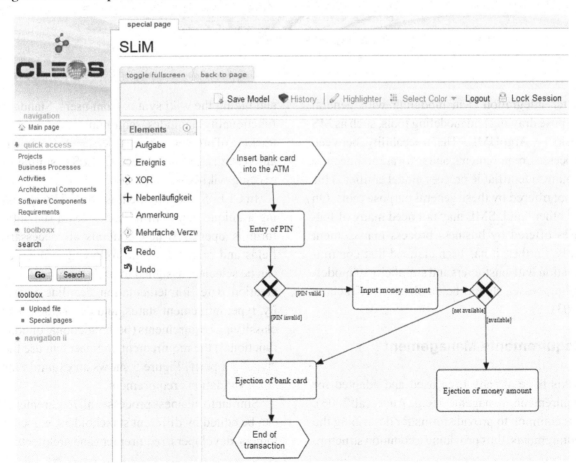

Figure 4. Process step "entry of PIN"

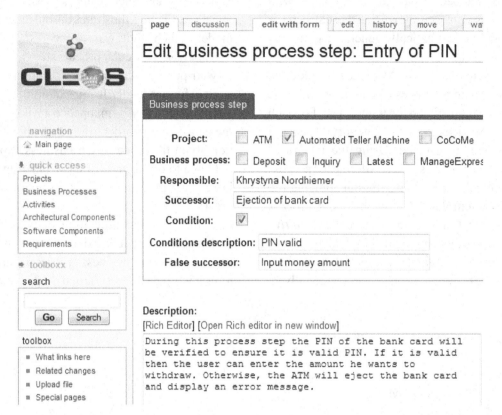

better integration than modeling with general purpose drawing and modeling tools, such as MS Visio or ArgoUML. The traceability between processes, requirements, and software architecture requires identifiable process model entities. This is not offered by these general purpose tools. On the other hand, SME may not need many of features offered by business process management tools. Further, it has been claimed that communication with customers and simplicity of modeling processes should be emphasized (Kruchten 2003).

Requirements Management

Wikis have already been used and adapted for requirements management (e.g., Auer et al. 2006). It is common to provide forms for describing the requirements, thus providing a common structure

and hiding the wiki syntax from users. Standard functionality includes requirement categories, tracking of projects, stakeholders, and implementation status. In this respect, CLEoS is similar to existing wiki-based solutions.

In CLEoS a requirement is created by choosing a unique name. In the next step a semantic form is opened which contains all necessary fields and properties. The following properties can be selected: assigned to project, responsible, creation date, implementation deadline, priority, type, implement status, and description. For classifying requirements (both functional or nonfunctional) the requirement engineer can use the "type" property. Figure 5 shows an example for "PIN validation" requirement.

Similar to business processes all requirements can be edited by different stakeholders, e.g. customers, developers, requirement and architecture

Figure 5. Requirement "PIN validation"

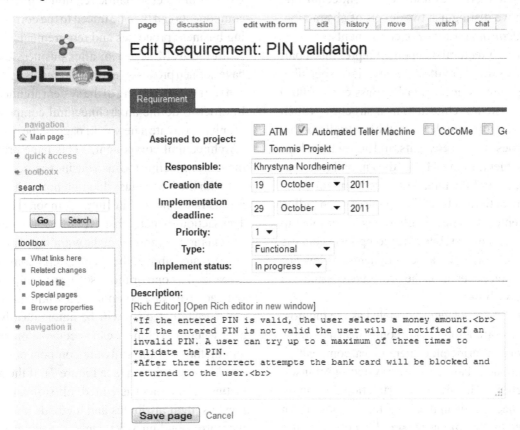

engineers etc. This helps to avoid inconsistency and information asymmetry between business and IT experts.

Architectural Design

Traditionally, the architectural design of the software is not documented using wikis. Specific development tools, e.g. UML modeling tools, are the most common way to document software architecture and design. On the other hand, the original idea for creating the first wiki engine by Ward Cunningham (1995) was to create a knowledge base for software architecture patterns. Later it has been shown that wikis provide a number of benefits for architecture documentation and architectural knowledge sharing (Bachmann

and Merson 2005; Happel and Seedorf 2007). Software development tools, however, are more likely to increase the distance between developers, analysts, and users. In our case study, it was stated that UML models are often too complex to understand and do not facilitate collaboration between different stakeholders. Using different toolsets for business processes, requirements, and software design furthermore makes it more difficult to maintain vertical traceability on heterogeneous software entities.

Therefore, CLEoS enables to describe *how* the software is designed and implemented. It provides several semantic templates and forms for describing the structural design of a software solution in a platform-independent manner. The central software entities are "components". According to literature on software architecture and design we distinguish two-levels of abstraction: *architectural* and *software* components.

An architectural component represents a part of the system architecture and is responsible for logically connected tasks. Bass et al. (2003) define system architecture as a structure, which comprises software elements, the externally visible properties of those elements, and the relationships among them. In the CLEoS data model (see Figure 1), an architectural component supports one or more activities by realizing the corresponding requirements. The "implements"-relationship describes that an architectural component consists of one or more software components. Its level of abstraction depends on the project needs and can be freely chosen.

A software system is modeled as the topmost architectural component in a component hierarchy, following the principle of hierarchical composition of component-based software systems (Atkinson et al. 2008). The levels of abstraction depend on the project needs and can be freely chosen. An architectural component should, however, not represent implementation-specific details. For example, in the given ATM scenario, the system that stores the customers' account information could be expressed as an architectural component, which supports the business processes that require transactions of bank accounts.

Software components occur at a lower level of abstraction than architectural components. They are units of composition "with contractually specified interfaces and explicit context dependencies only" (Szyperski 2001). A software component is specialized by process and entity component. Entity components represent the business concepts on which business processes operate. These include both data and repository objects and also the services that support them and their business usage (Herzum and Sims 1998)0. Process components represent business activities in the domain itself.

The CLEoS data model directly relates software components to architectural components.

By their indirect semantic relationships software components can then be traced to the corresponding business processes and requirements.

In the ATM scenario, after business experts have defined processes and requirements designers can start with modeling of the system architecture. In order to define an architectural component a user has to create a new wiki page of the category "Architectural component." This page provides the same modeling tool as a business process page but with the UML class diagram notation. Figure 6 illustrates the architectural component "ATM Transaction" which consists of four software components and supports e.g., the withdrawal process.

As stated above, the architectural component is realized as one or more software components. For each software component a wiki page of the appropriate category will be automatically created where developers can specialize properties and methods of the software component as well as add its description (see Figure 7). If the architectural component is edited, all software components, their attributes and methods mapped to the corresponding wiki pages are updated. For example, a new software component "DataVerification" is added to the architectural component in Figure 6. When the component is saved with SLiM, a new wiki page "DataVerification" is created including the already defined attributes and methods. If this software component would later be removed from the architectural component, it will be deleted only if it is not included in any other architectural component and the user confirms that the component can be deleted. This way, data integrity between the architectural models in UML and the wiki-based documentation is maintained.

The SLiM UML editor currently only supports UML class diagrams and it is therefore only possible to describe the static structure of a software system (Thum et al. 2009). One advantage compared to standalone modeling tools is that it supports ad-hoc collaboration between stakeholders at multiple sites. It is possible to discuss and

Figure 6. Architectural component "ATM transaction"

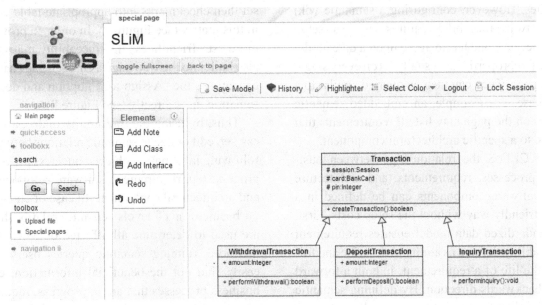

Figure 7. Software component "transaction"

modify architectural models together with other stakeholders who do not have a modeling tool installed on their computer. By enabling the web-based manipulation of UML diagrams in real-time we lower the entry barriers and enable more users to actively participate in the modeling process. The editor has been deeply integrated into CLEoS, which allows round-trip engineering of graphical models and text documentation.

Traceability Management

Semantic wikis provide the means for relating arbitrary software entities to other entities (i.e. wiki pages to other wiki pages). Although the semantic wiki paradigm has been realized in many different ways, all semantic wiki engines have in common that they allow to define typed links between pages. The wiki pages can be interpreted as entities and the typed links as properties of the entities. However, configuring a semantic wiki for software traceability requires significant setup cost because one has to agree upon a date model first. The properties are usually set on every single wiki page. They can then be queried similar to a database. For example, an embedded semantic query on the page may list all requirements that relate to a specific architectural component.

In CLEoS the relationships between business processes, requirements, and architecture and software components can be defined in a user-friendly way without the setup costs. First, a standardized data model ensures requirement traceability defined as ability to describe and follow the life of a requirement, in both a forward and backwards direction. By defining semantic relationships one can discover at all times who suggested the requirement, why the requirement exists, what requirements are related to it and how that requirement relates to other information such as systems designs, implementations and user documentation (Sommerville and Saywer 2003).

Second, it is possible to discover and manage traceability relationships with a traceability matrix integrated into the wiki. This matrix allows users to choose two page categories and the type of the semantic relationship that has to be set. After categories selection, e. g. requirement and process step, all pages that belong to the first category will appear as rows, and all pages of the second category will appear as columns. A wiki user can set then checkmarks into appropriate table cells in this matrix (see Figure 8). In order to provide more user friendliness the traceability matrix is also built into the wiki pages. On each page a user can choose the "Assign to…" option and define semantic links directly (see Figure 8).

Thus, by using the traceability matrix a user can set, edit or delete semantic relations between following information objects: business process, process step, requirement, software component, and architectural component. In case of changes on business or IT levels semantic relationships are used to determine all affected objects. Furthermore, running semantic queries users can easily find out the beneficial information, e.g. business processes that are in progress, requirements with highest priority, the responsible person for each information object etc.

RELATED WORK

First, we cover existing (semantic) wiki systems and how they relate to CLEoS. Second, the commonalities and differences to existing models for software traceability are described.

We classify existing wiki tools according to their ability to support semantic annotations and queries as well as visual modeling and editing (see Figure 9). Traditional wikis are usually limited to

Figure 8. Traceability matrix

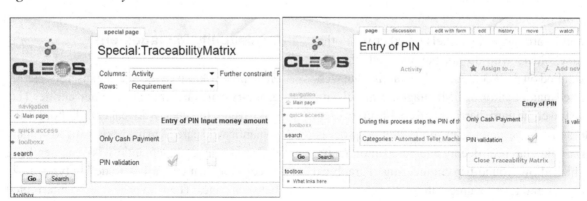

Figure 9. Wiki tools classification

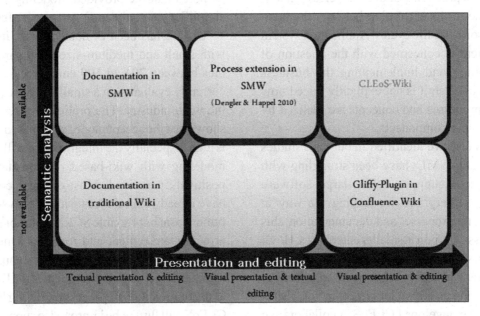

textual presentation and textual editing of information. Softwiki is a semantic wiki developed for requirements engineering (Auer et al. 2006). It supports the collaborative requirements elicitation and analysis, and focuses on developing taxonomies and ontologies from text. The prototype proposed in Hussain et al. (2009) uses semantic constructs for capturing the process definitions of a system and translates them into programming constructs. However, there is no visual modeling or editing options.

Dengler and Happel (2010) present an approach for collaborative, Wiki-based modeling of business processes and UML diagrams. A graphical presentation is generated from the semantic descriptions in the wiki. The Gliffy Confluence Plugin[1] supports graphical editing of diagrams within the Confluence Enterprise Wiki. However, diagrams are embedded as plug-in into a wiki page and are thus cannot be connected with information entities (i.e., wiki pages) in the wiki. None of tools mentioned above support real-time collaboration for distributed environments.

The approach also deals with the well-known problem of software traceability. Traceability

models have been extensively studied in software engineering. A common model for software traceability is the one suggested by Ramesh and Jarke (1999), which was later refined and extended by Hildenbrand (2008). The models however, focus on requirements traceability and do not include business processes, which may be important for understanding the requirements. Design traceability–going from requirements and processes to architectural and software components–is often neglected. CLEoS's information model is more fine-grained than the models mentioned above–it describes the actual entities instead of artifacts. Since it abstracts from the artifact level, it is independent from methods, modeling notations, or programming languages.

DISCUSSION AND CONCLUSION

Traditionally, there has been a conceptual gap between application systems and the corresponding business domain. While software systems are shaped by business processes, rules, and concepts, it is often not known how the components relate to business processes and vice versa. This is mainly due to the separation between the business and software life cycles. Application system development is concerned with the question of understanding and implementing the business domain, but often it is not explicitly traced how business processes and concepts are realized by the underlying components.

To this end, we identified in our case studies that especially SMEs have been struggling with adequate tool support. While large software developing enterprises are leading the way in standardizing processes and documentation, this is much less common in smaller enterprises. However, understanding the requirements and business processes and how they relate to the architectural design remains an important success factor. Therefore we have developed CLEoS, a collaborative lightweight platform for documenting and relating knowledge during the software life-cycle. It is not a closed solution but an extension of an open-source wiki system, the Sematic MediaWiki. It can be combined with any other software development plugins and extensions. The semantic templates, forms, and collaborative modeling editor SLiM serve as a starting point and provide a flexible way for managing business processes, requirements, and architectural designs.

CLEoS provides two distinct advantages compared to other wiki-based systems: First, the traceability matrix enables all stakeholders to view and manage traceability links in the wiki in a user-friendly way. Second, the deep integration of browser-based modeling allows for visual modeling of software components and business processes without needing any more tools. In contrast to graphical modeling tools the wiki-based text documentation is directly integrated with the diagram representation. This aims at lowering the entry barriers for other stakeholders to be involved in the elicitation and modeling processes. More importantly, it can be used as a collaborative tool in distributed development. However, it has to

be noted that the provided modeling solution is simplified and only comprises a core feature set.

CLEoS has been evaluated in six interviews with small and medium-sized software companies between 20 and 500 employees. CLEoS is currently evaluated in a small software project in the wine industry. The preliminary results have shown that the acceptance of wiki-based solutions is high–especially the integration of collaborative modeling with wiki-based documentation was positively perceived. Most of these companies have already experiences with wiki systems and prefer basic but flexible SCLM solutions, e.g. for project management and tracking. One area of improvement is the business process management, since the larger software companies see BPMN 2.0 as the future standard process modeling language. CLEoS will further be improved to support a larger subset of BPMN 2.0 and simplify the integration with external tools.

Lowering the gap between requirements and software architecture has been long known to be a key problem in software engineering. In this chapter we proposed wikis as one technical solution and presented a case example to show how the relationships can be managed with the CLEoS platform. At the heart of this problem, however, lies the communication between the different stakeholders involved in a software project. While tools can be designed in ways that lower the entry barriers, they have to be applied in a way that enhances the knowledge sharing culture in software teams.

ACKNOWLEDGMENT

This work was funded by the Ministry of Science, Research and the Arts of Baden-Württemberg, Germany, and the Landesstiftung Baden-Württemberg foundation. The authors are responsible for the content of this publication.

REFERENCES

Atkinson, C., Bostan, P., Brenner, D., Falcone, G., & Gutheil, M. (2008). Lecture Notes in Computer Science: *Vol. 5153. Modeling components and component-based systems in KobrA* (pp. 54–84). The Common Component Modelling Example. doi:10.1007/978-3-540-85289-6_4

Auer, S., Riechert, T., & Fähnrich, K.-P. (2006). SoftWiki – Agiles Requirements-Engineering für Softwareprojekte mit einer großen Anzahl verteilter Stakeholder. In Meißner, K., & Engelien, M. (Eds.), *Workshop Gemeinschaften in Neuen Medien (GeNeMe)* (pp. 97–108).

Bachmann, F., & Merson, P. (2005). *Experience using the web-based tool wiki for architecture documentation.* Technical Note CMU.

Bass, L., Clements, P., & Kazman, R. (2003). *Software architecture in practice* (2nd ed.). Addison-Wesley.

Boden, A., Nett, B., & Wulf, V. (2007). Coordination practices in distributed software development of small enterprises. *Second IEEE International Conference on Global Software Engineering*, (pp. 235–246).

Cunningham, W. (1995). *Portland pattern repository: WikiWikiWeb.* Retrieved August 11, 2011, from http://c2.com/cgi-bin/wiki

Dengler, F., & Happel, H.-J. (2010). Collaborative modeling with semantic MediaWiki. *Proceedings of the 6th International Symposium on Wikis and Open Collaboration*, Gdansk, Poland.

Dengler, F., Lamparter, S., Hefke, M., & Abecker, A. (2009). Collaborative process development using semantic MediaWiki. *Proceedings of the 5th Conf. of Professional Knowledge Management*, Solothurn, Switzerland, (pp. 97-107).

Happel, H.-J., & Seedorf, S. (2006). Applications of ontologies in software engineering. *Proceedings of Workshop on Sematic Web Enabled Software Engineering* (SWESE) at ISWC 2006, Athens, Georgia, November 5-9.

Happel, H.-J., & Seedorf, S. (2007). Ontobrowse: A semantic wiki for sharing knowledge about software architectures. *Proceedings of the 19th International Conference on Software Engineering and Knowledge Engineering (SEKE)*, Boston, USA, July 9-11, (pp. 506-512).

Herzum, P., & Sims, O. (1998). *The business component approach.* OOPSLA'98, Business Object Workshop IV.

Hildenbrand, T. (2008). *Improving traceability in distributed collaborative software development - A design science approach.* Frankfurt, Germany: Peter Lang Verlag.

Hussain, T., Balakrishnan, R., & Viswanathan, A. (2009). Semantic wiki aided business process specification. *Proceedings of the 18th International Conference on World Wide Web (WWW'09)*, (pp. 1135-1136). New York, NY: ACM.

Krötzsch, M., Vrandecic, D., & Völkel, M. (2006). Semantic Mediawiki. *Proceedings of 5th International Semantic Web Conference (ISWC06)*, (pp. 935-942).

Krötzsch, M., Vrandecic, D., Völkel, M., Haller, H., & Studer, R. (2007). Semantic Wikipedia. *Journal of Web Semantics*, *5*(4), 251–261. doi:10.1016/j.websem.2007.09.001

Kruchten, P. (2003). *The rational unified process.* Addison-Wesley Professional.

Louridas, P. (2006). Using wikis in software development. *Software*, *23*, 88–91. doi:10.1109/MS.2006.62

Maalej, W., Happel, H. J., & Seedorf, S. (2010). Applications of ontologies in collaborative software development. In I. Mistrík, J. Grundy, A.V.D. Hoek, & J. Whitehead (Eds.), *Collaborative software engineering*. Berlin, Germany: Springer.

Ramesh, B., & Jarke, M. (1999). Toward reference models for requirements traceability. *IEEE Transactions on Software Engineering, 27*(1), 58–93. doi:10.1109/32.895989

Richardson, I., Avram, G., Deshpande, S., & Casey, V. (2008). Having a foot on each shore –Bridging global software development in the case of SMEs. *IEEE International Conference on Global Software Engineering*, (pp. 13–22).

Schaffert, S., Bischof, D., Bürger, T., Gruber, A., & Hilzensauer, W. (2006). *Learning with Semantic Wikis*. First Workshop SemWiki2006 – From Wiki to Semantics, co-located with the 3rd Annual European Semantic Web Conference (ESWC), Budva, Montenegro.

Schaffert, S., Bry, F., Baumeister, J., & Kiesel, M. (2007). Semantic Wiki. *Informatik Spektrum, 30*(6), 434–439. doi:10.1007/s00287-007-0195-z

Sommerville, I., & Sawyer, P. (2003). *Requirements engineering: A good practice guide*. Wiley.

Szyperski, C. (2002). *Component software: Beyond object-oriented programming* (2nd ed.). Boston, MA: Addison-Wesley.

Thum, C., Schwind, M., & Schader, M. (2009). *SLIM—A lightweight environment for synchronous collaborative modeling*. ACM/IEEE 12th International Conference on Model Driven Engineering Languages and Systems (MoDELS'09), Denver, USA; October 04-10.

ENDNOTES

[1]   http://www.gliffy.com/confluence-plugin/

Chapter 3
Evolutionary Architecting of Embedded and Enterprise Software and Systems

Jakob Axelsson
Swedish Institute of Computer Science (SICS), Sweden & Mälardalen University, Sweden

ABSTRACT

Many industries rely heavily on embedded software and systems to maximize business value in their products. These systems are very complex, and the architecture is important to control the complexity and make development efficient. There are often also connections between the embedded system and the different lifecycle processes, and hence, to the enterprise systems supporting those processes. It is rare to start from scratch when developing new products, and instead, these companies evolve their products over time, which means that architecting needs to be evolutionary. This chapter describes what such an evolutionary architecting process can look like based on observations from industry, and how the process can be continuously improved using a maturity model. It is also presented how the embedded system relates to different elements of the enterprise architecture.

INTRODUCTION

In many companies developing technical products, such as the automotive industry, process automation, defense, or telecommunication, embedded systems and software play an increasingly important role. The embedded systems have developed from simple, stand-alone processors into a large number of computers with distribution networks and millions of lines of software. Each processor

node can have many actuators and sensors, which are sometimes very information intensive. There are also often links (wired or wireless) to other systems for information exchange. The embedded system needs to be packaged in whatever space is available in the product, and be equipped with an adequate power supply system, which often introduces both new operating modes, and electrical requirements that have implication on the software in different ways. (For an overview

DOI: 10.4018/978-1-4666-2199-2.ch003

of contemporary complex embedded systems and their challenges, see e.g. Broy *et al.*, 2007; Grimm 2003).

This increasing complexity leads to soaring development costs, and many companies strive to curb this trend by reusing software and hardware between products. At the same time, the development cost targets have to be balanced against the strict requirements of these products. They are often business-critical, or even safety-critical; they are installed in harsh environments and must be very robust against disturbances; they have a long lifetime where it is usually not acceptable to discard the overall product just because of a failure in the embedded system; and finally, they often have to be flexible to adapt to changes and upgrades after delivery to customers. This means that a substantial part of the design effort deals with supporting other lifecycle stages than just normal operation.

With these requirements, and a multiplicity of products and variants for different customers and markets, the architecture is becoming very important and is a source of increasing interest for companies developing embedded systems. An architecture can be defined as "the fundamental organization of a system embodied in its components, their relationships to each other, and to the environment, and the principles guiding its design and evolution" (IEEE, 2000). Often, a product line approach is applied, where the same platform is used as a basis, with modifications to fit individual products and customers. The decisions made by architects in the early phases influence many decisions made later on, and the architecting decisions are difficult to change further down the process (Smith and Reinertsen, 1995). With a poor architecture, downstream development activities will thus become much more expensive and time consuming.

In the embedded systems literature, there is a strong focus on systems and hardware architecture (see e.g. Sangiovanni-Vincentelli and Di Natale 2007), and this is natural since custom hardware is almost always used and there are hence many degrees of design freedom in the choice of hardware components and structure. Over the years, this focus has been complemented with increasing emphasis on software architecture as a consequence of the rising importance of software in these products. However, what is often neglected in the literature is a discussion on the links between the embedded systems in the product and the enterprise architecture, i.e. the organizing logic and IT infrastructure, of the firms that produce it or interact with it over its lifetime.

We have previously done in-depth studies of the current architecting practices at a few automotive companies (Wallin and Axelsson, 2008; Wallin *et al.* 2009). The issues found were later validated also in other industrial areas (Wallin *et al.* 2012) where embedded software and systems play an essential role. Among the issues were a lack of processes for architecture development, and that the organizations had an unclear responsibility for architectural issues. Also, there was a lack of long-term strategy to ensure that legacy does not negatively impact future decisions, and a lack of methods to evaluate the business value when choosing the architecture. In short, the organizations rely on the performance and knowledge of individuals instead of on processes and methods (a finding also supported by Hoorn *et al.*, 2011; Babar and Gorton, 2009). Several of the issues also directly relate to the fact that the embedded systems architecture is linked to enterprise architectures. This includes trade-offs when the same platform is used by several firms; relations to suppliers; and decision making which is often narrow in scope to the embedded system (or parts of it). It is indicated that the complexity of the organization and product has grown beyond what the current processes can handle.

Based on this information collected from industry, it appears plausible to assume that a mature organization would work with architecting of embedded systems and software mainly through stepwise refinement rather than large leaps. We call this an evolutionary architecting approach, in contrast with the revolutionary approach focusing on large but rare changes. Some of these companies state that they never again expect to start from fresh in their architecting, since it will be too expensive and complex. Instead, they will continue to refine their existing products. Some of the companies have tried to make major revisions of their embedded architecture, but have failed spectacularly and been forced to revert to evolution of their existing solutions. Contributing factors to this has been the overwhelming costs of changing the enterprise architectures to integrate it with the new embedded systems. It cannot be assumed that a large, mature company can upgrade all its architectures in perfect synchronization, but an asynchronous model where different parts are changed in small steps at different times is much more realistic. This is also how it is done in practice.

The purpose of this chapter is to present findings on what an evolutionary architecting process would look like and how it relates to enterprise architecting. The process is described from the point of view of the embedded system architect, and this is natural since the firm is there to produce its product and these should be in focus. The reciprocal enterprise architect view is mainly presented indirectly, since it exists to support the products, but the relations between the two views are discussed throughout. Software is what provides the functionality of that link, so the software architecture is also heavily involved in all parts of the problem.

The chapter is structured as follows. In the next section, a background to the area is given, including more information on embedded systems architecting, its relationship with enterprise architecting, and on evolutionary architecting. Since many companies have difficulties with their architecting practices, a maturity model has been developed that allows measurement of how an organization performs its architecting in order to guide improvement efforts. This model is

presented in the following section. When applying the maturity model to several organizations, it was discovered that a root cause problem was that they lack a clear process description. Therefore, the next section describes a generic process for architecting. In the last two sections, directions for future research are given, followed by the conclusion of the chapter.

BACKGROUND

In this section, some background into the area of embedded systems architecting is provided, together with its relation to enterprise architecture. It begins by looking into the process context of embedded systems architecting. This is expanded into a more complete view, presenting the different enterprise architectures that the embedded systems relate to during its lifecycle. Finally, the stepwise, evolutionary approach is discussed in relation to a revolutionary, from-scratch process.

The Context of Embedded Systems Architecting

In product development, an architecting process is closely related to other development activities. For embedded systems the overall product development is often depicted in a V-model, as shown in Figure 1. The architecting activities are mainly related to the early design, where customer functions are transformed into technical systems. In addition, the architects deal with quality attributes which are non-functional properties of the architecture, both related to performance of the products and to things like modifiability over time. They also consider the life-cycle of the product, including future development, production, service, and operation.

The interfaces of the architecting process are highlighted in Figure 2. The triggering input is a change request (CR) from product planning (a role sometimes called business analysts, or simi-

Figure 1. Development process context

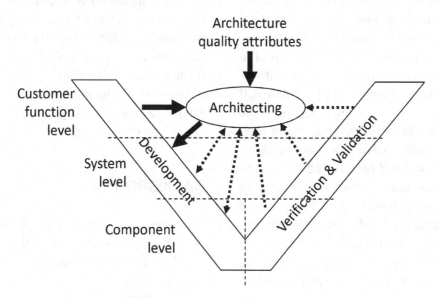

Figure 2. Interfaces of the evolutionary architecting process

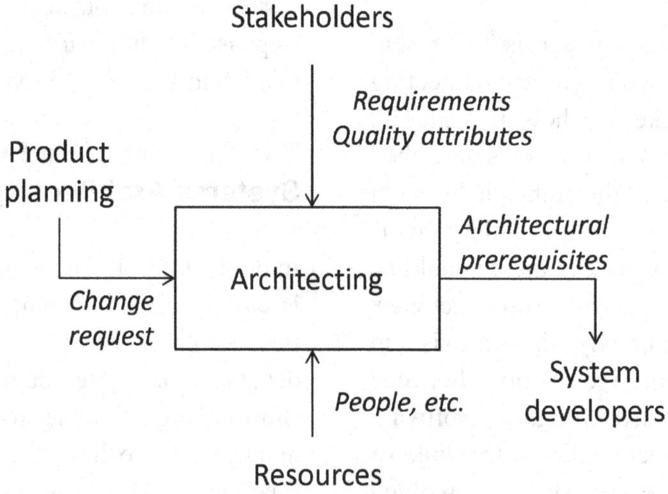

larly), usually to add a new function or enhance performance in some way. Other inputs are from various stakeholders on their needs and requirements, and the above mentioned quality attributes. Also, resources (mainly in terms of people) are required. The principle output is architectural prerequisites to system developers. These prerequisites are the architectural decisions that they need to respect in the detailed design, such as interface definitions, resource constraints, or design rules, and thus give an engineering context to their development work. In the figure, stakeholders include not only product planners but also representatives of all relevant product lifecycle stages as well as developers, in particular system developers, and testers.

Enterprise Systems Related to Embedded Systems

The architecture of the product and its embedded system can be discussed at several levels, as shown in the left part of Figure 3. At the topmost level, it is the architecture of the product, i.e., the complete car, industrial robot, or airplane, which is in focus. This is relevant to the embedded system, because it is part of that product, and many constraints are decided on that level, such as packaging, production setups, etc. Next, the overall system architecture is shown, and this includes the overall structure of both hardware and software. Finally, the software architecture is a part of the system architecture, and shows how the software in the different nodes is structured.

Analogous to the way in which the product architecture describes the structure of the product, the enterprise architecture describes the structure of a firm, as shown in the right part of the same figure. Based on the top-level enterprise architecture, which contains business processes, data models, application interfaces, and technology decisions, the IT system architecture can be derived for a system that supports different parts of the enterprise's operation, and this system contains different software systems with their own architecture.

As shown in Figure 3, the embedded systems can be related through many-to-many relations to the enterprise systems, and this is to a large degree related to the lifecycle stages of a product. As was indicated in the previous section, understanding the product lifecycle is one of the key activities of architects, and this also makes the architects who are responsible for the embedded systems intimately related to those dealing with the corresponding enterprise systems. To clarify the nature of the relations between the embedded and enterprise systems, the product lifecycle will now be described.

Figure 4 shows a generic lifecycle that most embedded systems go through. For each system, there are usually additional stages that are business specific, but this simplified model is sufficient to show the relation between embedded and enterprise systems. The following are examples of relations from the different stages:

- **Development:** Most embedded systems are not equipped with a normal computer user interface, and therefore provisions have to be made for how to communicate

Figure 3. Embedded system and enterprise system interrelations

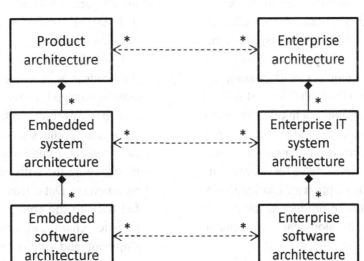

Figure 4. The embedded system and the product lifecycle stages

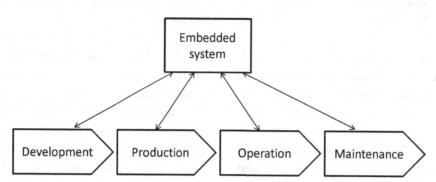

between the developer's workstation and the embedded system, for the purpose of software installation, debugging, data extraction, etc. Also, special enterprise systems must often be developed for systematic testing, including simulations of the embedded system's intended environment, which is usually not fully available during development. These installations can be very complex and costly, and should not be neglected when planning a project.

- **Production:** The embedded hardware is often produced at one or several external suppliers, and then integrated at the producer. This means that production testing is needed at the suppliers, and assembly testing at the producer. Such tests are usually automated and this requires special equipment and software. Also, software needs to be installed in the systems at some stage, either at the supplier or during assembly, and this requires an often complex enterprise system to keep track of different software versions, delivering them to the factory or supplier, and installing them correctly. This creates a connection to the enterprise logistics systems for production. (For a closer description of challenges in the relation between product development and production development, see Pernstål *et al,*. 2008.)

- **Operation:** During operation, the embedded system often provides data that is useful for its owner, and this needs to be extracted and fed into enterprise systems for analysis. This could occasionally be right into the core economy systems of the firm. Sometimes, data is also fed back to the developing company, so that they can analyze how the products are used and how effective they are, and use that information for future enhancements.

- **Maintenance:** Most physical products need some form of maintenance to keep them in shape over their lifetime, and when an embedded system is involved, this usually means that diagnostic software in the product is used to locate problems. Even though that software resides in the embedded system, its data is used by enterprise systems in a workshop for fault tracing not only of the embedded computers, but of the product as a whole. Sometimes, software is changed, either because a new version has become available since the last maintenance check, or because a mechanical problem sometimes can be corrected by changing the software, or recalibrating parameters. Data from the workshop is fed back to the enterprise systems of the logistics chain and used for determining shipment and production of spare parts, and to developers so that they can identify recurring problems in the products. It is however not always the case that the same company is organizing the maintenance, that originally shipped the product, but third-party maintenance companies exist in many industries.

To summarize, a number of existing enterprise systems are affected by the need to communicate with the embedded system, and additional enterprise systems are needed to deal with the special needs of a particular product. Also, it is important to note that it is not only the enterprise architecture of the producing company that is related to the embedded system, but also those at suppliers, customers, and maintenance organizations. As can be understood from the above discussion, having access to data throughout the lifecycle is a key to success for the producer, and should thus be a requirement when it designs its overall enterprise architecture.

Revolution vs. Evolution

As mentioned above, embedded systems are often developed using a product-line approach. When a new product-line platform is developed, there is an opportunity to do a major revision of the architecture. Changes that are typically introduced only at this time are a new communication concept, a different structure of the communication networks, or new basic software in the electronic control units (ECUs). Between these revolutionary steps, modifications such as the addition of a new ECU, a reallocation of some application software between two ECUs, or changing the connection of a sensor from one ECU to another, often occur.

The enterprise architecture is usually connected to the embedded system platform, to achieve that all embedded systems can interact with the same enterprise systems. Therefore, larger changes to the enterprise systems are difficult unless they either ensure backwards compatibility with the

previous versions with regards to the interfaces to the embedded systems, or are done when the embedded system can also be upgraded. In the other direction, changes to the embedded system must not assume unrealistic changes to the enterprise systems, in particular when these enterprise systems are outside the developing firm. As an example, it was at one firm suggested to improve the embedded system's interface used for maintenance fault tracing, but this idea had to be dropped because the third-party companies that provided maintenance for these products refused to purchase additional equipment at thousands of workshops throughout the world.

In this chapter, it is argued that an evolutionary architecting process (EAP) where changes are done in small steps is the best way to deal with the challenges in embedded and enterprise systems. This is in contrast with a revolutionary architecting process (RAP), which starts from scratch to provide the "optimal" solution. Some of the differences between these two extreme alternatives are:

- RAP is done rarely as a defined activity or project, perhaps once every 5-10 years when a new platform is introduced and each time with duration of a few years. EAP on the other hand is an ongoing process all the time. Among many other consequences, this means that few architects will experience more than very few RAP instances in their professional lives, and therefore it is very difficult to learn how to do it efficiently.
- RAP deals with the architecture as a whole, considering all the functions and systems together. EAP usually deals with changes to a singular, or a few, functions or systems within an existing framework.
- RAP tries to dimension an architecture that can support many (yet unknown) changes as smoothly as possible for a long time, whereas EAP tries to implement a specific

and concrete change in a specific architecture as efficiently as possible (while trying to assure that the resulting architecture still remains as flexible to future changes as possible, although this aspect is often less explicit in practice).

- RAP tries to predict future requirements, which is a speculative activity dealing with abstract information. One of the most important parameters is the expected rate of change which dimensions the flexibility needed. EAP deals with concrete requirements, functions and systems. This means that RAP must deal with uncertainty to a much higher extent than EAP.

- RAP requires synchronization between different related architectures, such as the embedded system architecture and the enterprise system architecture. This is however unrealistic to organize in practice and the EAP resolves this by allowing asynchronous operation of related processes.

With these differences pointed out, it should also be said that there are situations where some aspects of revolutionary nature is also conducted within EAP, simply because there is a need that was not foreseen at the time of the previous instantiation of RAP. It could appear to the reader that it is quite obvious that the RAP is preferable, but empirical studies show that many architects actually have a focus on "creating and communicating, rather than reviewing and maintaining an architecture," and thus on forward engineering (Clerc *et al.*, 2007).

Evolution of software architecture is also discussed by Erder and Pureur (2006), with a focus on IT and enterprise architecture. The authors launch the idea of evolution taking place in waves and plateaus, where the waves correspond to smaller evolutions of functionality within a stable infrastructure plateau. Chaki *et al.* (2009) and Garlan *et al.* (2009) also discuss evolutionary architecting, but for software only systems.

It is interesting to compare the EAP with Agile practices for software development. Although there are similarities, such as the emphasis on iterative completion of small steps at a time rather than long-lasting development of large chunks, or the use of a backlog, there are also differences that are related to the nature of the deliverable. Since many architects produce, in the end, information in the form of documentation and models to be used and refined by other developers, rather than executable code (Clements *et al.*, 2007), things like daily builds or test-driven development makes less sense. Also, Agile teams work intensively together, whereas architects tend to work in parallel on different change requests, making co-operation less intensive (Hoorn *et al.*, 2011). Instead, architects communicate vividly with other roles outside the architecting team (Kruchten, 2008), often serving as translators. So, although EAP is in some senses similar to Agile, it is not the same thing.

A different approach is the work of Northrop (2002) on a framework for software product lines. It consists of a large catalogue of practices and patterns that an organization should follow, according to the authors, to be successful in software product lines. The role of the architecture is emphasized, but the scope is much wider than this, addressing the entire enterprise. Also, the approach is relying on long-term planning and predefined rules to evolve the product line assets, making it fairly heavy to use and intensive in secondary documentation. The view presented in this paper is in this sense more similar to Agile, being much more lightweight and lean, and giving the architects freedom to modify the platform when needs arise. The architects in the EAP thus act reactively on pull from product development rather than being pushed by plans.

Many industries are currently heavily influenced by Japanese practices that are gathered under the label "Lean." One of the most cited aspects of Lean is *kaizen*, which stands for continuous improvement activities. The idea of evolutionary development is thus not new. However, Lean also contains the idea of *kaikaku*, meaning revolutionary change, and this has not been widely recognized in the western industry, nor has the interplay between the two been considered. Within software development, the relation appears to be the opposite, with much focus on new development, and less on continuous improvement. (The application of kaizen to software product lines is further discussed by Inoki and Fukazawa, 2007.)

MATURITY MODEL FOR ARCHITECTING

Now that the connections between the embedded system and different enterprise systems have been established, and it has been found that an evolutionary architecting process model best reflects the needs of reality, it becomes natural to ask oneself how evolutionary architecting can be performed better. As a first step, it would be beneficial to establish a way of measuring how mature an organization is in its architecting practices, and to that extent an Evolutionary Architecting Maturity Model (EAMM) (Axelsson, 2010) has been created. All the details of the model will not be described here, but it only summarizes the major principles behind it, and then turn to a discussion of findings on how real firms perform according to that model. It will also be elaborated upon how issues related to the relation between enterprise and embedded architectures are reflected in the model and empirical results. An earlier attempt to create a measurement system is reported by Bass et al.(2008), but their model does not have a process focus and is only an initial sketch with no empirical results reported. For enterprise systems, a similar framework has also been described by Kaisler et al. (2005).

The theoretical framework behind the EAMM model is the Capability Maturity Model Integration (CMMI) for Development, version 1.2 (SEI, 2006), which is based on "best practices" in software and systems engineering. It was chosen since it is the most widely used maturity model, and hence is familiar to many users. Many parts of it also make sense intuitively for architecting. However, a drawback is that it is rather heavy to use, and a lightweight, adopted version is therefore more appropriate for architecting teams.

When developing EAMM, the same structure as CMMI was used and it was axiomatically assumed that everything in CMMI is correct and relevant, unless good reasons for changing it were found. The reasons for changing are primarily based on the characteristics of the evolutionary architecting process and the organizations described above. Also, the terminology has been updated to suit the architecting activities. In a few cases, additions to, or reinterpretations of, CMMI have been made. Since architecting is an internal activity, formal appraisals are not focused. Instead, self-assessment is a more relevant tool for the architects. The result is a questionnaire of 53 questions that can be completed in about one hour.

EAMM uses the same maturity levels 1 to 5 as CMMI, but also adds a level 0 where the basic requirements are not met and the measurement becomes irrelevant. It also reuses 21 of the 22 process areas defined in CMMI. (The last, which is not used in EAMM, is Supplier Agreement Management (SAM) at Level 2. It is removed from EAMM since many architects play a minor role in supplier selection and agreement, although the suppliers should be included among the stakeholders.) Each CMMI process area relates to a number of goals that are required to be met and for each goal, a number of practices are defined, that are expected (but not required) to be implemented. Each question in the EAMM assessment questionnaire was derived by interpreting these goals and practices in the context of evolutionary architecting, and each question hence relates to a certain process area and level.

In the following subsections, the maturity levels and process areas of EAMM will be briefly described.

Level 0: Incomplete

In the EAMM, a Level 0 is included. A company at this level does not work with product lines at all, but each product has its own architecture and the ambition for reuse is low. There is no organizational responsibility for architecture across the products, and no defined process.

Level 1: Initial

A company who fulfills the requirements that it is working evolutionary based on product lines and has an organization responsible for architecting the products is at least at EAMM Level 1. At this initial level, the processes are usually ad hoc and chaotic, and success is highly dependent on the skills of the people. No process areas are defined at this level.

Level 2: Managed

At EAMM Level 2, an organizational policy is established where the roles and responsibilities of the architects are formalized with respect to other parts of the development organization. There is a need at this level to define what quality attributes should serve as guiding principles for the architects' work. These should not be connected to any specific function, and should relate primarily to the product line architecture rather than to the architecture of individual products.

A key factor in evolutionary architecting is to maintain the architecture descriptions that are used and updated when architecting each change request (CR). These cross-project assets must be defined clearly to allow efficient management, and the CMMI does not provide clear guidance on how to manage data between projects.

EAMM defines six process areas at this level, namely Requirements Management (REQM), Configuration Management (CM), Measurement and Analysis (MA), Project Planning (PP), Project Monitoring and Control (PMC), and Process & Product Quality Assurance (PPQA).

Level 3: Defined

At EAMM Level 3, processes are institutionalized in the organization, and they are improved over time and adapted for each CR through tailoring guidelines. EAMM defines 11 process areas at this level, namely Requirements Development (RD), Technical Solution (TS), Product Integration (PI), Verification (VER), Validation (VAL), Decision Analysis and Resolution (DAR), Integrated Project Management (IPM), Risk Management (RSKM), Organizational Process Definition (OPD), Organizational Process Focus (OPF), and Organizational Training (OT).

Level 4: Quantitatively Managed

At EAMM level 4, the organization uses quantitative analyses to establish a stable architecting process with predictable behavior. The two process areas Organizational Process Performance (OPP) and Quantitative Project Management (QPM) are included.

Level 5: Optimizing

At EAMM level 5, the organization continually improves its processes and architectural assets based on a quantitative understanding of the common causes of variation. It also strategically manages the architecture by identifying future bottlenecks and planning for refactoring at suitable times. The two process areas Causal Analysis and Resolution (CAR) and Organizational Innovation and Deployment (OID) are included.

Results from Applying the Maturity Model

Assessments of the evolutionary architecting practices have been carried out at five companies using EAMM. The companies are all large multinationals, whose products are highly dependent on embedded systems and software. They come from the automotive, process automation, and defense sectors. An overview of the results is given in Table 1, where the percentage indicated for each level shows how large proportion of the maximum score was achieved for the questions associated with that level, and the total score at the bottom is simply the sum of the percentages per level, and is a rough indicator of the level at which the company can be considered to be.

As can be seen in the table, the companies perform fairly consistently, and although there are differences in the exact level reached, none of these companies have come to embrace the practices at Levels 4 and 5. An interesting observation is that Company A insisted that they already do several of the practices at Level 5 and much fewer at Level 4. When digging deeper into this, we found that at this company there is a strong culture to deal seriously with all deviations and discover the root cause for them. However, it does not involve a statistical analysis of measurement data, but is done qualitatively.

An output from using the model is a more detailed table showing the scores of each process area. From that table, the architects can identify potential weaknesses and actions for improvement. This is meant as a guide for improving architecting practices, and a heuristic is to start with improvements at lower process levels to lay a foundation for the higher levels. However, in all cases the architects must value the suggestions from the EAMM, and determine if it is the right solution in their situation and if the benefit outweighs the cost.

At each level, certain areas are generally very weak in these companies. At Level 2, this is particularly the case for the Measurement and Analysis (MA) area, and the consequence of this is seen at the higher levels that are very much based on measurement of process data. But at the same level, Requirements Management (REQM) and Process and Product Quality Assurance (PPQA) stand out. The architects in these companies do not systematically define the architecturally significant requirements, nor do they provide routines for following up the quality of their work. At level 3, Verification (VER) gets low score, possibly as a consequence of the lack of requirements, and Risk Management (RSKM) is a practice very rarely employed by architects. The area Operational Process Development (OPD) is also worth mentioning. In this area, two companies scored 100% and the other three 0 or 25%. The root cause for the low scores was that the companies simply lacked even the simplest written description of the architecting process. Finally, the Decision Analysis and Resolution (DAR) is weak, and architects simply do not seem to work

Table 1. Results from applying the evolutionary architecting maturity model

Level	No. of Questions	Company A	Company B	Company C	Company D	Company E
1	3	100%	92%	92%	92%	83%
2	17	65%	37%	15%	54%	49%
3	22	66%	33%	16%	69%	38%
4	5	20%	0%	0%	20%	0%
5	6	67%	13%	17%	42%	13%
Total	53	3.17	1.74	1.39	2.77	1.82

with multiple alternative solutions and compare these systematically. Although many techniques exist for architecture analysis, such as the relatively well-known methods SAAM (Kazman *et al.,* 1994), ATAM (Kazman *et al.,* 1998), and CBAM (Kazman *et al.,* 2001), they do not appear to be used so much in practice, which is also confirmed by Babar and Gorton (2009).

When looking at the relations between the embedded and enterprise systems, the latter mainly shows up in the maturity model as stakeholder concerns. This means that it is primarily in the process areas that deal with requirements (REQM, RD) and quality assurance (VER, VAL) that these relations appear. Four of the companies scored very low in all these areas, whereas the fifth had generally good results, having a strong company culture to work seriously with requirements in all areas.

A PROCESS DESCRIPTION FOR EVOLUTIONARY ARCHITECTING

Through the EAMM, it has been possible to get a good understanding of the status of evolutionary architecting in industry. However, as was presented in the previous section, several companies are blocked from reaching higher maturity levels through the lack of a written process description. Since this seems to be such a common issue in many companies, it could be a good idea to have a basic generic process description that can be used as a starting point by a company, and then tailored to its needs. In this section, such a basic evolutionary architecting process is therefore presented, which can also be useful for companies where a process description already exist, as a means for comparison.

It should be noted that generic architecting processes are by no means a novel idea. A generic process for creating and maintaining architectures is for instance presented by Hofmeister *et al.* (2005). That process is based on a comparison

of five different software architecture design methods. However, this process and most other in literature only deal with the core architectural design work, but the framework showing how to interact with other processes and how to resolve strategic planning is lacking.

The box in Figure 2 will now be opened to look at the evolutionary architecting process from the inside. An overview of the process is given in Figure 5. The main activities are described in the following subsections.

Task Planning and Prioritization

The evolutionary architecting process is triggered by change requests originating from product planning, typically asking for a new customer feature or a performance upgrade. However, the request could also be a consequence of a change to a certain enterprise system that enforces upgrades to the embedded system.

The change requests can arrive at any time since different processes run asynchronously, so this activity is event triggered. As a first step, the architects analyze the effort needed to deal with the request, and then place the request in the architectural backlog, which is a queue of requests waiting to be dealt with. The backlog is in priority order, and whenever an architect becomes available they pick the highest priority item in the backlog.

Analyze Requirements

When an architect picks a change request from the backlog, the first step is to analyze the different stakeholders' needs, including those from architect's developing the enterprise systems, and transform these into requirements. In a mature organization, requirements are stored in a database and are version controlled, so in this activity architects update the database with new requirements related to the change request, and resolve any conflicts with existing requirements

Figure 5. The evolutionary architecting process

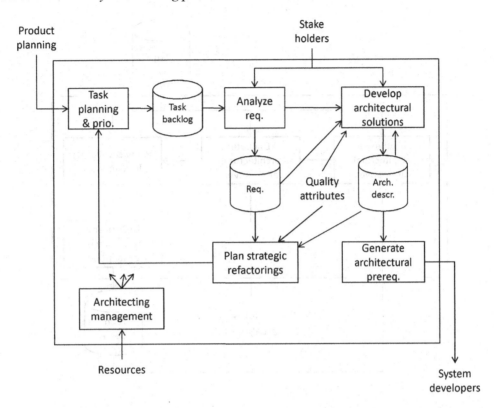

that could affect other products on the product line. Note however that architects are not concerned with the complete set of product requirements, but only those that are architecturally significant, which is a much smaller subsets.

Develop Architectural Solutions

The next activity is to develop an updated architecture that fulfils the objectives of the change request, while satisfying the new and old requirements. The main sub-activities are, as shown in Figure 6:

1. **Synthesize Architectural Alternatives:** Given the architecturally significant requirements, the architects derive alternative solutions that can be compared for merits. These do not have to be formally defined and described in all detail, but could equally be more informal sketches, as long as they

contain the necessary information. The current architectural description forms a basis for identifying the changes needed in the evolution.

2. **Evaluate Architectural Alternatives:** The alternative solutions are evaluated based on the requirements, but also on their effect on the quality attributes. Both these could be used to capture relations to the enterprise architecture.

3. **Verification and Validation:** Verification is performed to check conformance to requirements, and validation goes back to stakeholder needs.

4. **Risk Analysis:** Major uncertainties connected to the architectural decisions are analyzed, together with the consequences. If these are severe, mitigation actions are identified. These could be both technical, such as increasing tolerances in the design,

Figure 6. The activity to develop architectural solutions

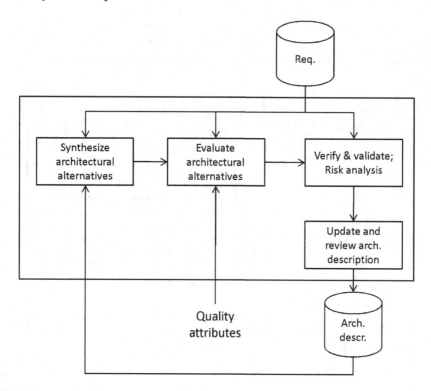

or in the form of activities, such as additional testing.

5. **Update and Review Architectural Description:** The final step is to update and review the architecture description with the new solution. A mature organization uses configuration management to keep track of different versions of the architecture description, associated with different products in the product line, and to allow parallel work by architects dealing with different change requests simultaneously.

In practice, the two activities development of the architectural solutions and analyze requirements often overlap in time, and are done iteratively. This is because which requirements are architecturally significant actually depends in part on what architectural solution is selected.

One finding from a previous study (Wallin and Axelsson, 2008) was that the lack of good analysis

methods is an area of concern for many architects. A particularly difficult analysis is the trade-off between short-term and long-term concerns. Often, the short term concerns are to implement a new functionality requested by product planning, and these give a potential for income to the company that is fairly easily quantifiable. The long term concerns, however, have to do with the quality attributes, such as maintaining flexibility for future changes, and these are more difficult to assess and put in economic terms. There are two common pitfalls in such trade-offs. The most common one is probably to optimize for current needs, making later changes expensive, and it is natural that this is more common since the short term needs are explicit and quantifiable. The other pitfall is to add excessive flexibility that is eventually not used, and this adds to complexity and cost.

One way to deal with this situation is to use real-options analysis (Bahsoon, 2003; Gustavsson and Axelsson, 2008), which is a method that allows architects to actually put a value on future flexibility. In this way, a cost-benefit analysis for flexibility can be included in the business case and traded against today's cost. However, the analysis requires architects to assess the likelihood of different future events towards which the architecture must be flexible, and to support that estimation it is very important to keep track of historic data and trends, since it would otherwise be pure guesswork.

Generate Architectural Prerequisites

Whenever there is a need of architectural prerequisites for system developers on a specific product project, architects derive those prerequisites from the current architectural description. This activity is essentially time triggered, based on the project plans of each product project.

Plan Strategic Refactoring

Refactoring is the process of changing the architecture without modifying its external behavior in any significant way. This activity is motivated by the need to make the architecture optimal over time, so that it can support evolution of the product line. As an example, after adding a number of features, parts of the architecture are bound to become bottlenecks that need to be removed by adding more capacity, simply because a resource is being overused. Or, complexity could simply have become overwhelming due to an increasing technical debt. It has previously been shown by Dersten *et al.* (2010) that a larger refactoring of the embedded system often has very large implications also on the enterprise systems, so this is an area of particular concern. In essence, refactoring is the mechanism of the EAP that makes it possible to avoid revolutionary architecting. The revolutionary steps, when all has to be redone, are thus divided in smaller pieces, each of which is of a size that can be handled in an evolutionary manner.

Refactoring is planned strategically by monitoring trends in key quality attributes over time, to predict when they will reach unacceptable levels. This, together with prognostics of change request rates, allows identification in due time of refactoring needs. This activity is hence mainly time triggered, since strategic analysis is a recurring activity. It is important to note that refactoring is here not based on vague wishes of architects or developers, but founded in facts and measurements which increases the acceptability of the consequences. Since it deals with predicting the future, sensitivity analyses are used to assess the risks associated with wrong estimates.

Once identified, the refactoring change requests end up in the same task log as all other requests, but it is particularly challenging to prioritize these changes since their value is often hard to quantify as rigorously as requests for new functionality. Only mature organizations can successfully determine when the time is right to apply a refactoring.

Architecting Management

In addition, there is a need of a management process to coordinate and support architects. This sub-process includes the following activities:

1. **Resource Management:** Each task dealing with a change request is assigned an architect who is responsible for taking it through the process.
2. **Progress Tracking:** Tasks are followed up to ensure that they follow their plans, but also to gather process performance data that can be used for further increasing the quality and performance of the process.
3. **Co-Ordination:** Usually, several change requests are being processed in parallel by different members of the architecting team, and this activity synchronizes their work to ensure that they do not create conflicting

solutions. Typically, a periodic meeting is used for this, and possibly also for the previous activity.

4. **Process Development:** The management process also is in charge of the continuous process development efforts to ensure that the overall evolutionary process remains efficient, which also entails making process measurements and planning periodic process reviews.

5. **Organizational Implications:** A final responsibility of this sub-process is to deal with identifying organizational implications of architecting decisions. In essence, it is a consequence of Conway's law (Conway, 1968), which states that an organization basically always will produce systems whose structure is a copy of the organization's communication structure. Thus, if the architects identify a need to change the technical structure, the organization will need to adapt to remain efficient, and this could also mean updates to the different enterprise systems or the overall enterprise architecture.

The process development activity can be inspired by the principles of *Lean* development, which focuses on eliminating waste, i.e. activities that are not creating customer value, and to create flow (see Gustavsson and Axelsson, 2010, for application of Lean to embedded system architecting, and Poppendieck and Poppendieck, 2003, for applications to software development in general). For this, process measurements (corresponding to maturity Levels 4 and 5) are necessary. Some wastes that often show up in architecting have to do with handoffs between people; technology debt in the form of extra work created by short-sightedness; task switching; and delays caused by people waiting for information. However, looking at architecting through the eyes of Lean also leads to an intriguing question: what is the value of architecting, and how can it be measured? Since

Lean focuses on reducing activities that do not contribute to value, having a clear idea of this is essential. One value of architecting is to provide prerequisites for system developers, and organize their work. Unfortunately, the effects of this show up downstream in the process, and can be very hard to measure. Another value is to provide a basis for future evolution, but this includes the uncertainty of what features and performance will really be needed later on, and is thus even harder to assess.

The Role of the Architect

Having defined the process for evolutionary architecting, it is worth reflecting on what this means for the role of the architect. Based on experience from industry, this role is often quite unclear, and each person tends to define his or her own deliverables and mandate. In the process presented above, the role is much clearer described and also the deliverables for which the architect is responsible. One thing to emphasize is that the architect in this process becomes a service provider that works on specific requests, rather than a "grand designer." Developers will pull information from architects, rather than architects pushing information onto developers. This provides structure to the daily work, but does not prevent the architects from also dealing with the greater picture, which is the purpose of the refactoring activities. However, today refactoring is often done based on gut feeling, but in this process it is highly data driven. This means that architects must engage much more in the collection and analysis of quantitative data, than is common today. The data is useful in many regards: to plan refactoring based on trends in quality attributes; to optimize the performance of the architecting process; and to perform flexibility vs. cost trade-offs. A very visible change will also be that architects will work in quick iterations to deal with each change request, rather than in long-enduring investigations. The fact that architects provide service to developers is also different to the way many architects work today, according to the study by Hoorn *et al.* (2011), who describe them as "lonesome decision makers working in splendid isolation" that "spend most of their time on making architectural decisions and least on documenting the results."

FUTURE RESEARCH DIRECTIONS

The framework for evolutionary architecting that is described in this paper is, based on available empirical research, in good correspondence with the practices of industry, and the process and maturity model should therefore be a useful tool for stepwise improvement of the process's efficiency and effectiveness. However, there are many questions that could be researched further.

One such question is how far one can get by evolution only. With a careful mix of gradual feature introduction and refactoring, it is probably possible to reduce the need for revolutionary steps quite a lot compared to what is common belief today. Related to this is also the question on how to plan and decide refactoring. This is a key to successfully avoiding revolutionary steps, but more research is needed on methods to decide when it is wise to actually do a certain refactoring.

However, the belief that most revolutionary steps can be avoided is based on technical and economical arguments, but there can be other reasons for revolutionary steps that are not so obvious. One is that in many companies, "heroes" are created by assuming leadership during a large change, whereas the people who make the quieter, day-by-day improvement often gets less attention. It is thus difficult to build a career from mastering an evolutionary architecting process, and much easier by being the chief architect of a revolutionary step, at least if it is reasonably successful. This could be one reason why revolutions

occur, whose objective value could be questioned. To overcome this, companies must look beyond processes and tools, and think about things like reward systems and personal attention.

Regarding the relation between embedded and enterprise architecture, more can be done. One is to find better ways to quantify the consequences that a change on one side will have on the other. Preferably, this should be a quantification in economic terms to make it a figure comparable to other factors. Also, the interplay between the two processes could be more detailed. Perhaps there is even room for finding an embedded/enterprise co-architecting scheme?

CONCLUSION

In this chapter, the architecting of embedded systems and software has been taken as a starting point. Based on previous empirical research, it has been found that this process is often in practice evolutionary, rather than revolutionary, and that there are good reasons for this. Therefore, a maturity model has been defined that can be used by a company to compare its current architecting process with a best practice process, and this model has been evaluated at a number of companies. Also, a concrete evolutionary architecting process description has been provided that can be used as a starting point for installing a new, formal process in an organization. Both from the empirical material, and in the models described in the chapter, it is clear that there is a tight interrelation between the embedded system and the enterprise systems supporting it, once the embedded system becomes a reasonably complex product. Therefore, the implications of this interrelation on the various parts of the maturity model and process description have been discussed throughout.

REFERENCES

Axelsson, J. (2010). Towards a process maturity model for evolutionary architecting of embedded system product lines. In *Proceedings 4th European Conference on Software Architecture*, Volume 2.

Babar, M. A., & Gorton, I. (2009). Software architecture review: The state of practice. *IEEE Computer*, July (pp. 26-32).

Bahsoon, R. (2003). Evaluating software architectures for stability: A real options approach. In *Proceedings of the 25th International Conference on Software Engineering (doctoral symposium)*.

Bass, L., Clements, P., Kazman, R., & Klein, M. (2008). Evaluating the software architecture competence of organizations. In *Proceedings 7th Working IEEE/IFIP Conference on Software Architecture* (pp. 249-252).

Broy, M., Krüger, I. H., Pretschner, A., & Salzmann, C. (2007). Engineering automotive software. *Proceedings of the IEEE*, *95*(2), 356–373. doi:10.1109/JPROC.2006.888386

Chaki, S., Diaz-Pace, S., Garlan, D., Gurfinkel, A., & Ozkaya, I. (2009). Towards engineered architecture evolution. In *Proceedings ICSE Workshop on Modeling of Software Engineering*.

Clements, P., Kazman, R., Klein, M., Devesh, D., Reddy, S., & Verma, P. (2007). The duties, skills, and knowledge of software architects. In *Proceedings of the 6th Working IEEE/IFIP Conference on Software Architecture* (pp. 44-47).

Conway, M. (1968). How do committees invent? *Datamation*, April.

Dersten, S., Fröberg, J., Axelsson, J., & Land, R. (2010). Analysis of the business effects of software architecture refactoring in an automotive development organization. In *Proceedings of the 36th EUROMICRO Conference on Software Engineering and Advanced Applications*.

Erder, M., & Pureur, P. (2006). Transitional architectures for enterprise evolution. *IT Professional*, (May-June): 10–17. doi:10.1109/MITP.2006.77

Garlan, D., Barnes, J. M., Schmerl, B., & Celiku, O. (2009). Evolution styles: Foundations and tools support for software architecture evolution. In *Proceeding Joint Working IEEE/IFIP Conference on Software Architecture 2009 & European Conference on Software Architecture* (pp. 131-140).

Grimm, K. (2003). Software technology in an automotive company – Major challenges. In *Proceedings of the 25th International Conference on Software Engineering* (pp. 498-503).

Gustavsson, H., & Axelsson, J. (2008). Evaluating flexibility in embedded automotive product lines using real options. In *Proceedings of the 12th International Software Product Line Conference* (pp. 235-242).

Gustavsson, H., & Axelsson, J. (2010). *Improving the system architecting process through the use of lean tools*. Paper presented at the Portland International Conference on Management of Engineering and Technology, Phuket, Thailand.

Hofmeister, C., Kruchten, P., Nord, R. L., Obbink, H., Ran, A., & America, P. (2005). Generalizing a model of software architecture design from five industrial approaches. In *Proceedings 5th IEEE/ IFIP Conference on Software Architecture* (pp. 77-88).

Hoorn, J. F., Farenhorst, R., Lago, P., & van Vliet, H. (2011). The lonesome architect. *Journal of Systems and Software*, *84*(9), 1424–1435. doi:10.1016/j.jss.2010.11.909

IEEE. (2000). *IEEE standard 1471-2000, recommended practice for architectural description of software-intensive systems*.

Inoki, M., & Fukazawa, Y. (2007). Software product line evolution method based on kaizen approach. In *Proceedings of the ACM Symposium on Applied Computing* (pp. 1207-1214).

Kaisler, S. H., Armour, F., & Valivullah, M. (2005). Enterprise architecting: Critical problems. In *Proceedings of the 38th Hawaii International Conference on Systems Sciences*.

Kazman, R., Asundi, J., & Klein, M. (2001). Quantifying the costs and benefits of architectural decisions. In *Proceedings 23rd International Conference on Software Engineering* (pp. 297-306).

Kazman, R., Bass, L., Abowd, G., & Webb, M. (1994). SAAM: A method for analyzing properties of software architecture. In *Proceedings of the 16th International Conference on Software Engineering*, (pp. 81-90).

Kazman, R., Klein, M., Barbacci, M., Longstaff, T., Lipson, H., & Carriere, J. (1998). The architecture tradeoff analysis method. In *Proceeding 4th IEEE International Conference on Engineering of Complex Computer Systems* (pp. 68-78).

Kruchten, P. (2008). What do software architects really do? *Journal of Software and Systems, 81*, 2413–2416. doi:10.1016/j.jss.2008.08.025

Northrop, L. M. (2002). SEI's software product line tenets. *IEEE Software*, (July-August): 32–40. doi:10.1109/MS.2002.1020285

Pernståhl, J., Magazinovic, A., & Öhman, P. (2008). A multiple case study investigating the interaction between manufacturing and development organizations in automotive software engineering. In *Proceedings of the Second ACM-IEEE International Symposium on Empirical Software Engineering and Measurement* (pp. 12-21).

Poppendieck, M., & Poppendieck, T. (2003). *Lean software development: An agile toolkit.* Addison-Wesley.

Sangiovanni-Vincentelli, A., & Di Natale, M. (2007). Embedded system design for automotive applications. *IEEE Computer*, October (pp. 42-51).

SEI. (2006). *CMMI for development*, Version 1.2. Software Engineering Institute, Technical Report CMU/SEI-2006-TR-008.

Smith, P. G., & Reinertsen, D. G. (1995). *Developing products in half the time: New rules, new tools*. New York, NY: John Wiley.

Wallin, P., & Axelsson, J. (2008). A case study of issues related to automotive E/E system architecture development. In *Proceedings of the 15th IEEE International Conference on Engineering of Computer Based Systems* (pp. 87-95).

Wallin, P., Johnsson, S., & Axelsson, J. (2009). Issues related to development of E/E product line architectures in heavy vehicles. In *Proceedings of the 42nd Hawaii International Conference on System Sciences*.

Wallin, P., Larsson, S., Fröberg, J., & Axelsson, J. (2012). Problems and their mitigation in system and software architecting. *Information and Software Technology, 54*(7). doi:10.1016/j.infsof.2012.01.004

Chapter 4
Software Licenses, Open Source Components, and Open Architectures

Thomas A. Alspaugh
University of California Irvine, USA

Hazeline U. Asuncion
University of Washington Bothell, USA

Walt Scacchi
University of California Irvine, USA

ABSTRACT

A substantial number of enterprises and independent software vendors are adopting a strategy in which software-intensive systems are developed with an open architecture (OA) that may contain open source software (OSS) components or components with open APIs. The emerging challenge is to realize the benefits of openness when components are subject to different copyright or property licenses. In this chapter, the authors identify key properties of OSS licenses, present a license analysis scheme to identify license conflicts arising from composed software elements, and apply it to provide guidance for software architectural design choices whose goal is to enable specific licensed component configurations. The scheme has been implemented in an operational environment and demonstrates a practical, automated solution to the problem of determining overall rights and obligations for alternative OAs as a technique for aligning such architectures with enterprise strategies supporting open systems.

INTRODUCTION

A substantial number of enterprises and independent software vendors are adopting a strategy in which software-intensive systems are developed with open source software (OSS) components or components with open APIs. It has been common for both independent or corporate-sponsored OSS projects to require that developers contribute their work under conditions that ensure the project can license its products under a specific OSS license. For example, the Apache Contributor License

DOI: 10.4018/978-1-4666-2199-2.ch004

Agreement grants enough rights to the Apache Software Foundation for the foundation to license the resulting systems under the Apache License. This sort of license configuration, in which the rights to a system's components are homogeneously granted and the system has a well-defined OSS license, was the norm and continues to this day.

However, we more and more commonly see a different enterprise software configuration, in which the components of an enterprise system do not have the same license. The resulting system may not have any recognized OSS license at all—in fact, our research indicates this is the most likely outcome—but instead, if all goes well in its design, there will be enough rights available in the system so that it can be used and distributed, and perhaps modified by others and sub-licensed, if the corresponding obligations are met [Alspaugh, Asuncion, and Scacchi 2009]. These obligations are likely to differ for components with different licenses; a BSD (Berkeley Software Distribution) licensed component must preserve its copyright notices when made part of the system, for example, while the source code for a modified component covered by MPL (the Mozilla Public License) must be made public, and a component with a reciprocal license such as the Free Software Foundation's GPL (General Public License) might carry the obligation to distribute the source code of that component but also of other components that constitute "a whole which is a work based on" the GPL'd component. The obligations may conflict, as when a GPL'd component's reciprocal obligation to publish source code of other components is combined with a proprietary license's prohibition of publishing source code, in which case there may be no rights available for the system as a whole, not even the right of use, because the obligations of the licenses that would permit use of its components cannot simultaneously be met.

The central problem we examine and explain in this chapter is to identify principles of software

architecture and software licenses that facilitate or inhibit success of the OA strategy when OSS and other software components with open APIs are employed. This is the knowledge we seek to develop and deliver. Without such knowledge, it is unlikely that an OA that is clean, robust, transparent, and extensible can be readily produced. On a broader scale, this chapter seeks to explore and answer the following kinds of research questions:

- What license applies to an OA enterprise system composed of software components that are subject to different licenses?
- How do alternative OSS licenses facilitate or inhibit the development of OA systems for an enterprise?
- How should software license constraints be specified so it is possible for an enterprise to automatically determine the overall set of rights and obligations associated with a configured enterprise software system architecture?

This chapter may help establish a foundation for how to analyze and evaluate dependencies that might arise when seeking to develop software systems that embody an OA when different types of software components or software licenses are being considered for integration into an overall enterprise system configuration.

In the remainder of this chapter, we examine software licensing constraints. This is followed by an analysis of how these constraints can interact in order to determine the overall license constraints applicable to the configured system architecture. Next, we describe an operational environment that demonstrates automatic determination of license constraints associated with a configured system architecture, and thus offers a solution to the problem we face. We close with a discussion of some issues raised by our work.

BACKGROUND

There is little explicit guidance or reliance on systematic empirical studies for how best to develop, deploy, and sustain complex software systems when different OA and OSS objectives are at hand. Instead, we find narratives that provide ample motivation and belief in the promise and potential of OA and OSS without consideration of what challenges may lie ahead in realizing OA and OSS strategies. Ven (2008) is a recent exception.

We believe that a primary challenge to be addressed is how to determine whether a system, composed of subsystems and components each with specific OSS or proprietary licenses, and integrated in the system's planned configuration, is or is not open, and what license constraints apply to the configured system as a whole. This challenge comprises not only evaluating an existing system at run-time, but also at design-time and build-time for a proposed system to ensure that the result is "open" under the desired definition, and that only the acceptable licenses apply; and also understanding which licenses are acceptable in this context. Because there are a range of types and variants of licenses (cf. OSI 2011), each of which may affect a system in different ways, and because there are a number of different kinds of OSS-related components and ways of combining them that affect the licensing issue, a first necessary step is to understand the kinds of software elements that constitute a software architecture, and what kinds of licenses may encumber these elements or their overall configuration.

OA seems to simply mean software system architectures incorporating OSS components and open application program interfaces (APIs). But not all software system architectures incorporating OSS components and open APIs will produce an OA, since the openness of an OA depends on: (a) how (and why) OSS and open APIs are located within the system architecture, (b) how

OSS and open APIs are implemented, embedded, or interconnected in the architecture, (c) whether the copyright (Intellectual Property) licenses assigned to different OSS components encumber all or part of a software system's architecture into which they are integrated, and (d) the fact that many alternative architectural configurations and APIs exist that may or may not produce an OA (cf. Antón and Alspaugh 2007, Scacchi and Alspaugh 2008). Subsequently, we believe this can lead to situations in which new software development or acquisition requirements stipulate a software system with an OA and OSS, but the resulting software system may or may not embody an OA. This can occur when the architectural design of a system constrains system requirements—raising the question of what requirements can be satisfied by a given system architecture, when requirements stipulate specific types or instances of OSS (e.g., Web browsers, content management servers) to be employed (Scacchi 2002), or what architecture style (Bass, Clements, and Kazman 2003) is implied by a given set of system requirements.

Thus, given the goal of realizing an OA and OSS strategy together with the use of OSS components and open APIs, it is unclear how to best align acquisition, system requirements, software architectures, and OSS elements across different software license regimes to achieve this goal (Alspaugh, Scacchi, Asuncion 2010, Scacchi and Alspaugh 2008).

UNDERSTANDING OPEN ARCHITECTURES

The statement that a system is intended to embody an open architecture using open software technologies like OSS and APIs, does not clearly indicate what possible mix of software elements may be configured into such a system. To help explain this, we first identify what kinds of software elements are included in common software architectures whether they are open or closed (cf. Bass, Clements, Kazman 2003):

- **Software Source Code Components:** Includes (a) standalone programs, (b) libraries, frameworks, or middleware, (c) inter-application script code (e.g., C shell scripts) and (d) intra-application script code (e.g., to create Rich Internet Applications using domain-specific languages (e.g., XUL for Firefox Web browser (Feldt 2007) or "mashups" (Nelson and Churchill 2006)).

- **Executable Components:** These are programs for which the software is in binary form, and its source code may not be open for access, review, modification, and possible redistribution. Executable binaries can be viewed as "derived works" (Rosen 2005).

- **Application Program Interfaces (APIs):** The availability of externally visible and accessible APIs to which independently developed components can be connected is the minimum condition required to form an "open system" (Meyers and Obendorf 2001).

- **Software Connectors:** In addition to APIs, these may be software either from libraries, frameworks, or application script code whose intended purpose is to provide a standard or reusable way of associating programs, data repositories, or remote services through common interfaces. The High Level Architecture (HLA) is an example of a software connector scheme (Kuhl, Weatherly, Damann 2000), as are CORBA, Microsoft's.NET, Enterprise Java Beans, and LGPL libraries.

- **Configured System or Sub-System Architectures:** These are software systems that can be built to conform to an explicit architectural design. They include software source code components, executable components, APIs, and connectors that are organized in a way that may conform to a known "architectural style" such as the Representational State Transfer (Fielding and Taylor 2002) for Web-based client-server applications, or may represent an original or ad hoc architectural pattern (Bass 2003). Each of the software elements, and the pattern in which they are arranged and interlinked, can all be specified, analyzed, and documented using an Architecture Description Language (ADL) and ADL-based support tools (Bass 2003, Medvidovic 1999).

Figure 1 provides an overall view of an archetypal software architecture for a configured system that includes and identifies each of the software elements above, as well as including free/open source software (e.g., Gnome Evolution) and closed source software (WordPerfect) components. In simple terms, the configured system consists of software components (grey boxes in the Figure) that include a Mozilla Web browser, Gnome Evolution email client, and WordPerfect word processor, all running on a Linux operating system that can access file, print, and other remote networked servers (e.g. an Apache Web server). These components are interrelated through a set of software connectors (ellipses in the Figure) that connect the interfaces of software components (small white boxes attached to a component) and link them together. Modern day enterprise systems or command and control systems will generally have more complex architectures and a more diverse mix of software components than shown in the figure here. As we examine next, even this simple architecture raises a number of OSS licensing issues that constrain the extent of openness that may be realized in a configured OA.

Figure 1. An enterprise software system architecture depicting components (grey boxes), connectors (ellipses), interfaces (small boxes on components), and data/control links

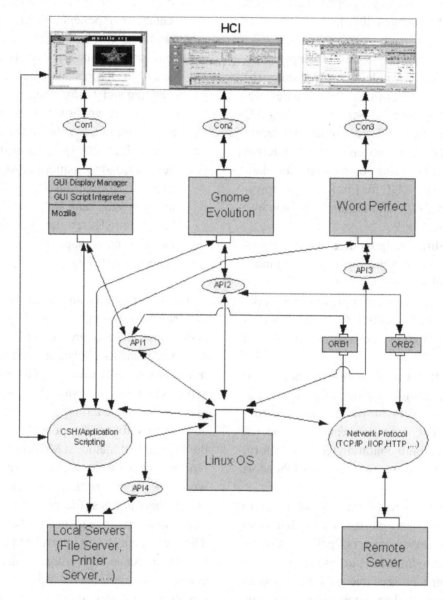

UNDERSTANDING OPEN SOFTWARE LICENSES

A particularly knotty challenge is the problem of licenses in OSS and OA. There are a number of different OSS licenses, and their number continues to grow. Each license stipulates different constraints attached to software components that bear it. External references are available which describe and explain many different licenses that are now in use with OSS [Fontana 2008, OSI 2008, Rosen 2005, St. Laurent 2004]. Software licenses may be grouped into four general categories, listed in Table 1. OSS licenses are classified as permissive, reciprocal, and propagating; all propagating licenses of which we are aware are

Table 1. Types of software licenses

License Type	Also known as	Examples	Characterized by
Permissive	Academic	Apache, BSD, MIT	Many rights; few obligations
Reciprocal	Copyleft	MPL, LGPL	Many rights; obligations on derivative works
Propagating	Strong Copyleft	GPL, AGPL	Many rights; obligations on "nearby" works
Proprietary	N/A	CTL; EULAs, TOSs	Few rights

also reciprocal, but most reciprocal licenses are not propagating. End-user license agreements (EULAs) and terms of service (TOSs) for commercial software are typically proprietary and do not grant the OSS rights of copying, source code availability, modification, and distribution.

Typical rights and obligations include:

- **A Right to Perform an Action:** "... each Contributor hereby grants to You a... copyright license to reproduce... the Work... in Source... form" (Apache License 2.0).

- **A Right to Not Perform an Action:** "In no event shall the authors or copyright holders be liable for any claim, damages or other liability" (MIT License).

- **An Obligation to Perform an Action:** "You must cause any work that you distribute or publish, that in whole or in part contains or is derived from the Program or any part thereof, to be licensed as a whole at no charge to all third parties under the terms of this License" (GPLv2).

- **An Obligation to Not Perform an Action:** "Neither the name of the <organization> nor the names of its contributors may be used to endorse or promote products derived from this software without specific prior written permission" (BSD 3-Clause License).

OSS licenses typically grant the right to copy, modify, and distribute source and binary code, while proprietary licenses typically grant only the right to possess one or a limited number of binary copies, or analogous rights to connect to a service, and often explicitly disallow modification or distribution. OSS licenses typically impose an obligation to retain copyright and license notices unmodified. Reciprocal licenses typically impose an obligation to publish source code of modified versions under the same license (the reciprocal obligation); propagating licenses are characterized by obligations to publish "nearby" software, under varying definitions of "nearby" that range over software statically linked, dynamically linked, or other means of combining. Virtually all software licenses include disclaimers of liability and warranty, and newer licenses often include various provisions for patent rights.

More and more software systems are designed, built, released, and distributed as OAs composed of components from different sources, some proprietary and others not. Systems include components that are statically bound or interconnected at build-time, while other components may only be dynamically linked for execution at run-time, and thus might not be included as part of a software release or distribution. Software components in such systems evolve not only by ongoing maintenance, but also by architectural refactoring, alternative component interconnections, and component replacement (via maintenance patches, installation of new versions, or migration to new technologies). Software components in such systems may be subject to different software licenses, and later versions of a component may be subject to different licenses (e.g., from CDDL (Sun's Common Development and Distribution License) to GPL, or from GPLv2 to GPLv3).

Software systems with open architectures are subject to different software licenses than may be common with traditional proprietary, closed source systems from a single vendor. Software architects/developers must increasingly attend to how they design, develop, and deploy software systems that may be subject to multiple, possibly conflicting software licenses. We see architects, developers, software acquisition managers, and others concerned with OAs as falling into three groups. The first group pays little or no heed to license conflicts and obligations; they simply focus on the other goals of the system. Those in the second group have assets and resources, and to protect these they may have an army of lawyers to advise them on license issues and other potential vulnerabilities; or they may constrain the design of their systems so that only a small number of software licenses (possibly just one) are involved, excluding components with other licenses independent of whether such components represent a more effective or more efficient solution. The third group falls between these two extremes; members of this group want to design, develop, and distribute the best systems possible, while respecting the constraints associated with different software component licenses. Their goal is a configured OA system that meets all its goals, and for which all the license obligations for the needed copyright rights are satisfied. It is this third group that needs the guidance the present work seeks to provide.

There has been an explosion in the number, type, and variants of software licenses, especially with open source software (cf. OSI 2008). Software components are now available subject to licenses such as the General Public License (GPL), Affero General Public License (AGPL), Mozilla Public License (MPL), Apache Public License, (APL), permissive licenses (e.g., BSD, MIT), Creative Commons, and Artistic. Furthermore, licenses such as these can evolve, resulting in new license versions over time. But no matter their diversity, software licenses represent a legally enforce- able contract that is recognized by government agencies, corporate enterprises, individuals, and judicial courts, and thus they cannot be taken trivially. As a consequence, software licenses constrain open architectures, and thus architectural design decisions.

So how might we support the diverse needs of different software developers, with respect to their need to design, develop, and deploy con- figured software systems with different, possibly conflicting licenses for the software components they employ? Is it possible to provide automated means for helping software developers deter- mine what constraints will result at design-time, build-time, or run-time when their configured system architectures employ diverse licensed components? These are the kind of questions we address in this chapter.

Software Licenses: Rights and Obligations

Copyright, the common basis for software licenses, gives the original author of a work certain exclusive rights, which for software include the right to use, copy, modify, merge, publication, distribution, sub-licensing, and sell copies. These rights may be licensed to others; the rights may be licensed individually or in groups, and either exclusively so that no one else can exercise them or (more com- monly) non-exclusively. After a period of years, the rights enter the public domain, but until then the only way for anyone other than the author to have any of the copyright rights is to license them.

Licenses may impose obligations that must be met in order for the licensee to realize the as- signed rights. Commonly cited obligations include the obligation to buy a legal copy to use and not distribute copies (proprietary licenses); the obli- gation to preserve copyright and license notices (permissive licenses); the reciprocal obligation to publish source code you modify under the same license (MPL); or the propagating obligation to publish under GPL all source code for a work "based on the Program" where the "Program" is GPL'd software (GPL).

Licenses may provide for the creation of derivative works (e.g., a transformation or adaptation of existing software) or collective works (e.g., a Linux distribution that combines software from many independent sources) from the original work, by granting those rights possibly with corresponding obligations.

In addition, the author of an original work can make it available under more than one license, enabling the work's distribution to different audiences with different needs. For example, one licensee might be happy to pay a license fee in order to be able to distribute the work as part of a proprietary product whose source code is not published, while another might need to license the work under MPL rather than GPL in order to have consistent licensing across a system. Thus we now see software distributed under any one of several licenses, with the licensee choosing from two (dual license) or three (Mozilla's tri-license) licenses.

The basic relationship between software license rights and obligations can be summarized as follows: if you meet the specified obligations, then you get the specified rights. So, informally, for the permissive licenses, if you retain the copyright notice, list of license conditions, and disclaimer, then you can use, modify, merge, sub-license, etc. For MPL, if you publish modified source code and sub-licensed derived works under MPL, then you get all the MPL rights. And so forth for other licenses. However, one thing we have learned from our efforts to carefully analyze and lay out the obligations and rights pertaining to each license is that license details are difficult to comprehend and track—it is easy to get confused or make mistakes. Some of the OSS licenses were written by developers, and often these turn out to be incomplete and legally ambiguous; others, usually more recent, were written by lawyers, and are more exact and complete but can be difficult for non-lawyers to grasp. The challenge is

multiplied when dealing with configured system architectures that compose multiple components with heterogeneous licenses, so that the need for legal advice begins to seem inevitable (cf. Fontana 2008, Rosen 2005). Therefore, one of our goals is to make it possible to architect software systems of heterogeneously-licensed components without necessarily consulting legal counsel. Similarly, such a goal is best realized with automated design-time support that can help architects understand design choices across components with different licenses, and that can provide support for testing build-time releases and run-time distributions to make sure they achieve the specified rights by satisfying the corresponding obligations.

Expressing Software Licenses

Historically, most software systems, including OSS systems, were entirely under a single software license. However, we now see more and more software systems being proposed, built, or distributed with components that are under various licenses. Such systems may no longer be covered by a single license, unless such a licensing constraint is stipulated at design-time, and enforced at build-time and run-time. But when components with different licenses are to be included at build-time, their respective licenses might either be consistent or conflict. Further, if designed systems include components with conflicting licenses, then one or more of the conflicting components must be excluded in the build-time release or must be abstracted behind an open API or middleware, with users required to download and install to enable the intended operation. (This is common in Linux distributions subject to GPL, where for example users may choose to acquire and install proprietary run-time components, like proprietary media players). So a component license conflict need not be a show-stopper if identified at design time. However, developers have to be able to determine which components' licenses conflict and to take appropriate steps at design-time, build-time, and run-time, consistent with the different concerns and requirements that apply at each phase (cf. Scacchi and Alspaugh 2008).

In order to fulfill our goals, we need a scheme for expressing software licenses that is more formal and less ambiguous than natural language, and that allows us to identify conflicts arising from the various rights and obligations pertaining to two or more component's licenses. We considered relatively complex structures (such as Hohfeld's eight fundamental jural relations (Hohfeld 1913)), but applying Occam's razor selected a simpler structure. We start with a tuple <*actor, operation, action, objects*> for expressing a right or obligation. The *actor* is the "licensee" or "licensor" for all the licenses we have examined. The *operation* is one of the following: "may", "must", "must not", or "need not", with "may" and "need not" expressing rights and "must" and "must not" expressing obligations; following Hohfeld, the lack of a right (which would be "may not") correlates with a duty to not exercise the right ("must not"), and whenever lack of a right seemed significant in a license we expressed it as a negative obligation with "must not". The *action* is a verb or verb phrase describing what may, must, or must not be done, with the *objects* completing the description. We specify objects separately from the action in order to minimize the set of actions and to simplify the formalization of relations among rights and obligations. Objects are specified by parameters ranging over specified types, represented here by

names in {}. An obligation's objects may also be specified by parameters, in [], bound to objects of the appropriate type for the corresponding right. Finally, some licenses are parameterized, represented by names in {{{}}}. See our previous work for more specifics (Alspaugh, Asuncion, and Scacchi 2009; Alspaugh, Scacchi, and Asuncion 2010; Alspaugh, Asuncion, and Scacchi 2011). A license then may be expressed as a set of rights, with each right associated (in that license) with zero or more obligations that must be fulfilled in order to enjoy that right. Figure 2 displays the tuples and associations for two of the rights and their associated obligations for the permissive BSD software license. Note that the first right is granted without corresponding obligations.

The process of expressing licenses with tuples is manual, with the majority of the effort spent identifying each action and placing it in an ontology of actions from all the licenses of interest. The ontology is needed for reasoning about the actions; from it the subsumption relationship between any two actions can be automatically determined. Some actions, such as those for the exclusive copyright rights, are widely shared among licenses; others, often those for obligations, appear only in a single license. Our approach defines actions, where possible, in terms of rights and obligations defined in U.S. law and the Berne Convention, making ontology building more scalable for large numbers of licenses. The set of tuples chosen for a license and the subsump-

Figure 2. A portion of the BSD license tuples

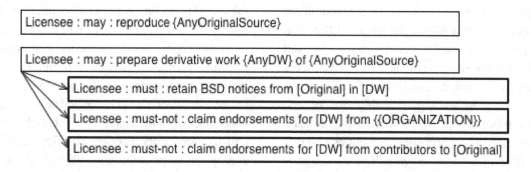

tion relationships between its actions and those of other licenses are determined by the legal interpretation of the license; the remainder of the interpretation, in our view, consists of each action's definition in the world.

The Appendix presents one interpretation of the well-known BSD license as tuples, using about a dozen distinct actions and representing about a day's work by one analyst. We find that a license can typically be expressed with a few tens of rights tuples, with each right associated with roughly one to five obligation tuples. The examples of typical rights and obligations listed above in section "Understanding open software licenses" can be interpreted as the following tuples; of course, other interpretations are also possible, and indeed the third provision (from GPLv2) has several prominent ones:

```
Licensee: may: reproduce <AnySource>
```
"... each Contributor hereby grants to You a... copyright license to reproduce... the Work... in Source... form"

```
Licensee: need not: remedy liability
with respect to <Any>
```
"In no event shall the authors or copyright holders be liable for any claim, damages or other liability"

```
Licensee: must: publish [Derivative-
Work] under GPLv2
```
"You must cause any work that you distribute or publish, that in whole or in part contains or is derived from the Program or any part thereof, to be licensed as a whole at no charge to all third parties under the terms of this License"

```
Licensee: must not: claim endorsement
of [DerivativeWork] by {{ORGANIZA-
TION}} or contributors to [Original]
```
"Neither the name of the <ORGANIZATION> nor the names of its contributors may be used to endorse or promote products derived from this software without specific prior written permission."

With this approach nearly all license provisions can be expressed: specifically, all the enactable, testable rights and obligations. Examples are shown above at the beginning of the section "Understanding Open Software Licenses" and in Figure 2. However, there are certain license provisions that are neither enactable nor testable and thus cannot be expressed in terms of an action. Some examples are:

- **Exhortation:** "The licenses for most software are designed to take away your freedom to share and change it. By contrast, the GNU General Public License is intended to guarantee your freedom to share and change free software—to make sure the software is free for all its users." (GPLv2)
- **Non-Binding Advice:** "If you wish to incorporate parts of the Library into other free programs whose distribution conditions are incompatible with these, write to the author to ask for permission." (LGPLv2.1)
- **Explanation:** "For example, a Contributor might include the Program in a commercial product offering, Product X." (Common Public License 1.0)
- **Non-Binding Request:** "It is requested, but not required, that you contact the authors of the Document well before redistributing any large number of copies, to give them a chance to provide you with an updated version of the Document." (GNU Free Documentation License 1.3)

We argue that non-enactable, non-testable provisions are not relevant to the problem we address, namely, to identify license conflicts and guide architectural design to enable specific licensing results.

We now turn to examine how OA software systems that include components with different licenses can be designed and analyzed while effectively tracking their rights and obligations.

When designing an OA software system, there are heuristics that can be employed to enable architectural design choices that might otherwise be excluded due to license conflicts. First, it is possible to employ a "license firewall" which serves to limit the scope of reciprocal obligations. Rather than simply interconnecting conflicting components through static linking of components at build time, such components can be logically connected via dynamic links, client-server protocols, license shims (e.g., via LGPL connectors), or run-time plug-ins. Second, the source code of statically linked OSS components must be made public. Third, it is necessary to include appropriate notices and publish required sources when permissive licenses are employed. However, even using design heuristics such as these (and there are many), keeping track of license rights and obligations across components that are interconnected in complex OAs quickly become too cumbersome. Thus, automated support needs to be provided to help overcome and manage the multi-component, multi-license complexity.

AUTOMATING ANALYSIS OF SOFTWARE LICENSE RIGHTS AND OBLIGATION

We find that if we start from a formal specification of a software system's architecture, then we can associate software license attributes with the system's components, connectors, and sub-system architectures and calculate the copyright rights and obligations for the system. Accordingly, we employ an architectural description language specified in xADL (Dashofy et al. 2005) to describe OAs that can be designed and analyzed with a software architecture design environment (Med-

vidovic 1999), such as ArchStudio4 (Dashofy et al. 2007). We have taken this environment and extended it with a Software Architecture License Traceability Analysis module (cf. Asuncion and Taylor 2012). This allows for the specification of licenses as a list of attributes (license tuples) using a form-based user interface, similar to those already used and known for ArchStudio4 and xADL (Dashofy et al. 2007, Medvidovic 1999).

Figure 3 shows a screenshot of an ArchStudio4 session in which we have modeled the OA seen in Figure 1. OA software components, each of which has an associated license, are indicated by darker shaded boxes. Light shaded boxes indicate connectors. Architectural connectors may or may not have associated license information; those with licenses (such as architectural connectors that represent functional code) are treated as components during license traceability analysis. A directed line segment indicates a link. Links connect interfaces between the components and connectors. Furthermore, the Mozilla component as shown here contains a hypothetical subarchitecture for modeling the role of intra-application scripting, as might be useful in specifying license constraints for Rich Internet Applications. This subarchitecture is specified in the same manner as the overall system architecture, and is visible in Figure 5. The automated environment allows for tracing and analysis of license attributes and conflicts.

Figure 4 shows a view of the internal XML representation of a software license. Analysis and calculations of rights, obligations, and conflicts for the OA are done in this form. This schematic representation is similar in spirit to that used for specifying and analyzing privacy and security regulations associated with certain software systems (Breaux and Anton 2008).

With this basis to build on, it is now possible to analyze the alignment of rights and obligations for the overall system:

- **Propagation of Reciprocal Obligations:** Reciprocal obligations are imposed by the license of a GPL'd component on any other component that is part of the same "work based on the Program" (i.e. on the first component), as defined in GPL. We follow one widely-accepted interpretation, namely that build-time static linkage propagate the reciprocal obligations, but that "license firewalls" such as dynamic links or client-server connections do not. Analysis begins, therefore, by propagating these obligations along all connectors that are not license firewalls.

- **Licensing Conflicts and Incompatibilities:** An obligation can conflict with another obligation contrary to it, or with the set of available rights, by requiring a copyright right that has not been granted. For instance, the Corel proprietary license for the WordPerfect component, CTL (Corel Transactional License), may be taken to entail that a licensee must not redistribute source code, as a specific obligation. However, an OSS license, GPL, may state that a licensee must redistribute source code. Thus, the conflict appears in the modality of the two otherwise identical obligations, "must not" in CTL and "must" in GPL. A conflict on the same point could occur also between GPL and a component whose license fails to grant the right to distribute its source code. Similar conflicts may arise between obligations and desired rights. We discuss this further below.

This phase of the analysis is affected by the overall set of rights that are required. If conflicts arise involving the union of all obligations in all components' licenses, it may be possible to eliminate some conflicts

Figure 3. An ArchStudio 4 model of the open software architecture of Figure 1

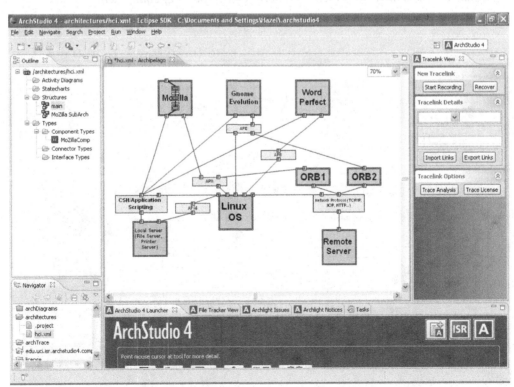

Figure 4. A view of the internal schematic representation of the Mozilla Public License

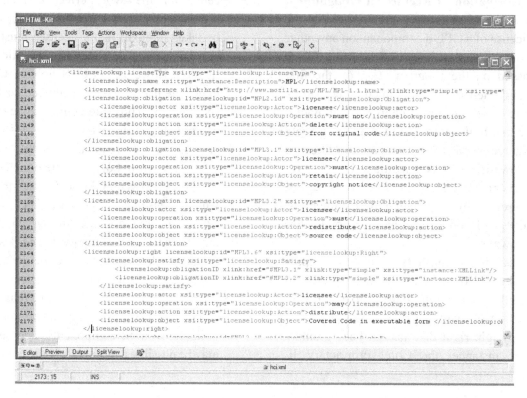

Figure 5. License conflicts have been identified between two pairs of components

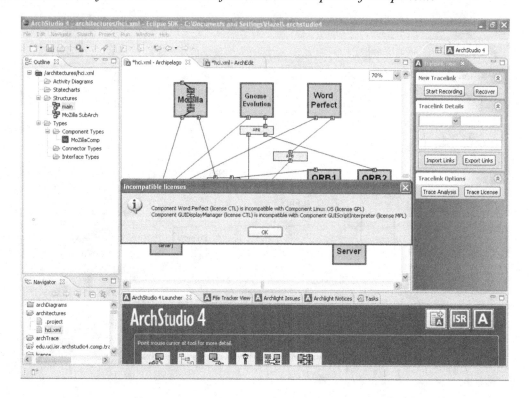

by selecting a smaller set of rights, in which case only the obligations for those rights need be considered.

Figure 5 shows a screenshot in which the License Traceability Analysis module has identified obligation conflicts between the licenses of two pairs of components ("WordPerfect" and "Linux OS," and "GUIDisplayManager" and "GUIScriptInterpreter").

- **Rights and Obligations Calculations:** The calculation begins from each right desired for the system as a whole. The right is examined for each component of the system: the right is either freely available (i.e. not an exclusive right defined in copyright or other law), subsumed by some right granted by the component's license, or unavailable. The license tuples for the component are examined for one that subsumes the desired right. If there is no such tuple, then the desired right is unavailable for the component and thus for the system containing it. But if there is such a tuple, it is instantiated for the component, and the associated obligations are instantiated in parallel. Each instantiated obligation is added to the set of obligations for the system. In addition, the correlative right (Hohfeld 1913) to perform each obligation must be obtained; the calculation recurses with each correlative right as the desired right. The calculation terminates when all chains of rights and obligations have terminated in either a freely-available right or an unobtainable right. The result is a set of available instantiated rights, each associated with zero or more instantiated obligations and their correlative rights, and a set (hopefully empty) of unobtainable rights (Alspaugh, Asuncion, and Scacchi 2011).

Several kinds of problems may be identified: (1) desired or correlative rights may be unobtain-

able; (2) the desired rights may entail obligations that conflict and cannot both be satisfied; (3) desired or correlative rights may be obtainable, but cannot be exercised because they conflict with an obligation; and (4) all desired rights may be available, but the entailed obligations may be more than the system's developers or eventual users are willing to undertake. Examples of specific obligations are:

- **OSS:** "Licensee must retain copyright notices in the binary form of module.c"
- **Reciprocal OSS:** "Licensee must publish the source code of component.java version 1.2.3"
- **Proprietary EULA:** "Licensee must obtain a proprietary license for a copy of component.exe"
- **Proprietary ToS:** "Licensee must obtain a proprietary license for use of service http://service.com".

Figure 6 shows a report of the calculations for the hypothetical subarchitecture of the Mozilla component in our archetypal architecture, exhibiting an obligation conflict and the single copyright right (to run the system) that the prototype tool shows would be available for the subarchitecture as a whole if the conflict is resolved; a production tool would also list the rights (none) currently available.

If a conflict is found involving the obligations and rights of linked components, it is possible for the system architect to consider an alternative linking scheme, employing one or more connectors along the paths between the components that act as a license firewall, thereby mitigating or neutralizing the component-component license conflict. This means that the architecture and the environment together can determine what OA design best meets the problem at hand with available software components. Components with conflicting licenses do not need to be arbitrarily excluded, but instead may expand the range of

Figure 6. A report identifying the obligations, conflicts, and rights for the architectural model

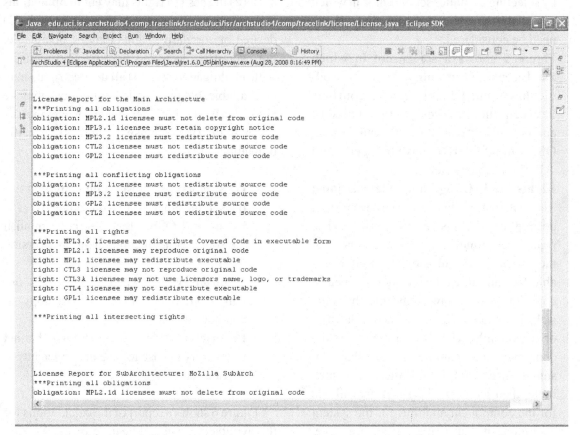

possible architectural alternatives if the architect seeks such flexibility and choice.

At build-time (and later at run-time), many of the obligations can be tested and verified, for example that the binaries contain the appropriate notices for their licenses, and that the source files are present in the correct version on the Web. These tests can be generated from the internal list of obligations and run automatically. If the system's interface were extended to add a control for it, the tests could be run by a deployed system.

The prototype License Traceability Analysis module provides a proof-of-concept for this approach. We encoded the core provisions of four licenses in XML for the tool—GPL, MPL, CTL, and AFL (Academic Free License)—to examine the effectiveness of the license tuple encoding and the calculations based upon it. While it is clear

that we could use a more complex and expressive structure for encoding licenses, in encoding the license provisions to date we found that the tuple representation was more expressive than needed; for example, the actor was always "licensee" or "licensor" and seems likely to remain so, and we found use for only four operations or modalities. At this writing, the module shows proof of concept for calculating with reciprocal obligations by propagating them to adjacent statically-linked modules; the extension to all paths not blocked by license firewalls is straightforward and is independent of the scheme and calculations described here. Reciprocal obligations are identified in the tool by lookup in a table, and the meaning and scope of reciprocality is hard-coded; this is not ideal, but we considered it acceptable since the legal definition in terms of the reciprocal licenses will not change frequently. We also focused on the design-time analysis and calculation rather than build- or run-time as it involves the widest range of issues, including representations, rights and obligations calculations, and design guidance derived from them.

We do not claim our approach is a substitute for advice from legal counsel; it is not (and if we claimed it were such a claim would be illegal in many jurisdictions). The encoding of the BSD license in the Appendix is merely an example; we have not developed "the" interpretation, but rather an approach with which many alternative interpretations can be expressed and then worked from. Our key contribution is an approach through which inferences can be drawn about licensing issues for a particular design architecture or build- or run-time configuration, based on a particular set of license interpretations. During our research we have discussed our approach with a number of people in the legal field, including a law professor, a law student working in intellectual property law, an international law researcher, and several lawyers. Our approach implements an inference system on Hohfeld's jural relations (Hohfeld 1913), which are viewed as foundational in U.S. legal scholarship; follows an inference process accepted by persons with legal training; and uncovers the same kinds of concerns a knowledgeable and thorough analyst would. It provides a way for organizations to express their own interpretations of software licenses, and use those interpretations to rapidly and consistently identify license conflicts, unavailable rights, and unacceptable obligations resulting from a particular architectural configuration. We believe this empowers organizations to steer clear of known problems and highlight issues for analysis by legal counsel.

Based on our analysis approach, it appears that the questions of what license (if any) covers a specific configured system, and what rights are available for the overall system (and what obligations are needed for them) are difficult to answer without automated license-architecture analysis. This is especially true if the system or sub-system is already in operational run-time form (cf. Kazman and Carrière 1999). It might make distribution of a composite OA system somewhat problematic if people cannot understand what rights or obligations are associated with it. We offer the following considerations to help make this clear. For example, a Mozilla/Firefox Web browser covered by the MPL (or GPL or LGPL, in accordance with the Mozilla Tri-License) may download and run intra-application script code that is covered by a different license. If this script code is only invoked via dynamic run-time linkage, or via a client-server transaction protocol, then there is no propagation of license rights or obligations. However, if the script code is integrated into the source code of the Web browser as persistent part of an application (e.g., as a plug-in), then it could be viewed as a configured sub-system that may need to be accessed for license transfer or conflict implications. A different kind of example can be anticipated with application programs (like Web browsers, email clients, and word processors) that employ Rich Internet Applications or mashups entailing the use of content (e.g., textual character fonts or geographic maps) that is subject to copyright protection, if the content is embedded in and bundled with the scripted application sub-system. In such a case, the licenses involved may not be limited to OSS or proprietary software licenses.

In the end, it becomes clear that it is possible to automatically determine what rights or obligations are associated with a given system architecture at design-time, and whether it contains any license conflicts that might prevent proper access or use at build-time or run-time, given an approach such as ours.

SOLUTIONS AND RECOMMENDATIONS

Software system configurations in OAs are intended to be adapted to incorporate new innovative software technologies that are not yet available. These system configurations will evolve and be refactored over time at ever increasing rates (Scacchi 2007), components will be patched and upgraded (perhaps with new license constraints), and inter-component connections will be rewired or remediated with new connector types. An approach for addressing licensing issues at design time such as the one we present here will be increasingly important. As such, sustaining the openness of a configured software system will become part of ongoing system support, analysis, and validation. This in turn may require ADLs to include OSS licensing properties on components, connectors, and overall system configuration, as well as in appropriate analysis tools (cf. Bass, Clements, and Kazman 2003, Medvidovic 1999).

Constructing licensing descriptions is an incremental addition to the development of the architectural design, or alternative architectural designs. But it is still time-consuming, and may present a somewhat daunting challenge for large pre-existing systems that were not originally modeled in our environment.

We note that expressing a software license in our tuples necessarily implies selecting an interpretation of the provisions of the license. Individuals and small organizations may simply choose a representative or commonly-accepted interpretation, but enterprises will of necessity seek legal counsel and construct their own interpretations aligned with their advice. An enterprise must also consider the scope of our approach, which focuses on exclusive rights to "do" that are constant over a defined time span, as the copyright rights are. Patent rights, for example, are fundamentally different, being exclusive rights to "prevent from doing" rather than to "do." For example, the owner of a copyright has the right to copy the work, and may license that right to others who may then make copies. In contrast the owner of a patent has the right to prevent others from using the algorithm, process, or invention, and may only grant a license by which the owner will forbear from preventing the licensee from using the patented matter rather than a straightforward right to use it; this license has no effect if some other overlapping patent exists or is granted in the future, and the other patent owner can still prevent the licensee of the first patent from using it. A number of the prominent OSS licenses such as GPLv3 have provisions for indemnifying licensees against patent infringement involving the licensed material, and our approach supports considering these provisions at system design time.

Advances in the identification and extraction of configured software elements at build time, and their restructuring into architectural descriptions is becoming an endeavor that can be automated (cf. Choi 1990, Kazman 1999, Jansen 2008). Further advances in such efforts have the potential to automatically produce architectural descriptions that can either be manually or semi-automatically annotated with their license constraints, and thus enable automated construction and assessment of build-time software system architectures.

The list of recognized OSS licenses is long and ever-growing, and as existing licenses are tested in the courts we can expect their interpretations to be clarified and perhaps altered; the GPL definition of "work based on the Program," for example, may eventually be clarified in this way, possibly refining the scope of reciprocal obligations. Our expressions of license rights and obligations are for the most part compared for identical actors, actions, and objects, then by looking for "must" or "must not" in one and "may" or "need not" in the other, so that new licenses may be added by keeping equivalent rights or obligations expressed equivalently. Reciprocal obligations, however, are handled specially by hard-coded algorithms to traverse the scope of that obligation, so that addition of obligations with different scope, or the revision of the understanding of the scope of an existing obligation, requires development work. Possibly these issues will be clarified as we add more licenses to the tool and experiment with their application in OA contexts.

Lastly, our scheme for specifying software licenses offers the potential for the creation of shared repositories where these licenses can be accessed, studied, compared, modified, and redistributed.

CONCLUSION

The relationship between enterprise software systems that employ an open architecture, open source software, and multiple software licenses has been and continues to be poorly understood. OSS is often viewed as primarily a source for low-cost/free software systems or software components. Thus, given the goal of realizing an enterprise strategy for OA systems, together with the use of OSS components and open APIs, it has been unclear how to best align software architecture, OSS, and software license regimes to achieve this goal.

The central problem we examined in this chapter was to identify principles of software architecture and software copyright licenses that facilitate or inhibit how best to insure the success of an OA strategy when OSS and open APIs are required or otherwise employed. In turn, we presented an analysis scheme and operational environment that demonstrates that an automated solution to this problem exists. Furthermore, in related work, we have gone on to formally model and analyze the alignment, matching, subsuming, and conflicting relationships among interconnected enterprise software components that are subject to different licenses (Alspaugh, Asuncion, and Scacchi 2009, Alspaugh, Scacchi, and Asuncion 2010).

We have developed and demonstrated an operational environment that can automatically determine the overall license rights, obligations, and constraints associated with a configured system architecture whose components may have different software licenses. Such an environment requires the annotation of the participating software elements with their corresponding licenses, which in our approach is done using an architectural description language. These annotated software architectural descriptions can be prescriptively analyzed at design-time as we have shown, or descriptively analyzed at build-time or run-time. Such a solution offers the potential for practical support in design-time, build-time, and run-time license conformance checking and the ever-more complex problem of developing large software systems from configurations of software elements that can evolve over time.

NOTES

The BSD license is a template license parameterized by the name of the organization that is the licensor; <ORGANIZATION> in the license text, represented by parameter {{ORGANIZATION}} in the tuple syntax.

BSD grants its own distinct set of rights: redistribution (not distribution, though it is implied) and use, with the right of modification implied but not explicitly granted. This interpretation expresses them in terms of the standard U.S. copyright rights of reproduction, preparation of derivative works, and distribution of copies, similar to the Berne Convention rights.

BSD grants some rights and imposes some obligations that seem superfluous or problematic, and this interpretation provides one rationalization of them. For example, for R1 BSD imposes the obligation to retain the BSD notice, but this right is for the unmodified source, so the obligation has no effect (of course the notice is retained, because the source is unmodified). Another example is the right to use, which is freely available unless the program in question infringes a patent; but BSD contains no provisions for granting a license to infringe any of the licensor's patents and the licensor cannot grant one for other patents, so the grants of the right to use seem superfluous and were ignored in this interpretation.

ACKNOWLEDGMENT

The research described in this report has been supported by grant #0808783 from the U.S. National Science Foundation, and grant N00244-10-0077 from the Acquisition Research Program at the Naval Postgraduate School. No endorsement implied.

REFERENCES

Alspaugh, T. A., & Antón, A. I. (2007). Scenario support for effective requirement. *Information and Software Technology*, *50*(3), 198–220. doi:10.1016/j.infsof.2006.12.003

Alspaugh, T. A., Asuncion, H. A., & Scacchi, W. (2009). Intellectual property rights for heterogeneously licensed systems. In *Proceedings 17th International Requirements Engineering Conference (RE09)*, Atlanta, GA, 24-33, September 2009.

Alspaugh, T. A., Asuncion, H. A., & Scacchi, W. (2011). Presenting software license conflicts through argumentation. In *Proceedings 23rd International Conference on Software Engineering and Knowledge Engineering (SEKE'11)*.

Alspaugh, T. A., Scacchi, W., & Asuncion, H. A. (2010). Software licenses in context: The challenge of heterogeneously licenses systems. *Journal of the Association for Information Systems*, *11*(11), 730–755.

Asuncion, H. (2008). Towards practical software traceability. In *Companion of the 30th International Conference on Software Engineering*, (pp. 1023-1026). Leipzig, Germany.

Asuncion, H. U., & Taylor, R. N. (2012). Automated techniques for capturing custom traceability links across heterogeneous artifacts. In *Software and Systems Traceability* (pp. 129–146). Springer-Verlag. doi:10.1007/978-1-4471-2239-5_6

Bass, L., Clements, P., & Kazman, R. (2003). *Software architecture in practice* (2nd ed.). New York, NY: Addison-Wesley Professional.

Breaux, T. D., & Anton, A. I. (2008). Analyzing regulatory rules for privacy and security requirements. *IEEE Transactions on Software Engineering*, *34*(1), 5–20. doi:10.1109/TSE.2007.70746

Choi, S., & Scacchi, W. (1990). Extracting and restructuring the design of large systems. *IEEE Software*, *7*(1), 66–71. doi:10.1109/52.43051

Dashofy, E., Asuncion, H., Hendrickson, S. A., Suryanarayana, G., Georgas, J. C., & Taylor, R. N. ArchStudio 4: An architecture-based meta-modeling environment. In *28th International Conference on Software Engineering (ICSE '07), Companion Volume*, (pp. 67–68). 20–26 May 2007.

Dashofy, E. M., Hoek, A. d., & Taylor, R. N. (2005). A comprehensive approach for the development of modular software architecture description languages. *ACM Transactions on Software Engineering and Methodology*, *14*(2), 199–245. doi:10.1145/1061254.1061258

Feldt, K. (2007). *Programming Firefox: Building rich internet applications with XUL*. Sebastopol, CA: O'Reilly Press.

Fielding, R., & Taylor, R. N. (2002). Principled design of the modern web architecture. *ACM Transactions on Internet Technology*, *2*(2), 115–150. doi:10.1145/514183.514185

Fontana, R., Kuhn, B. M., Molgen, E., et al. (2008). *A legal issues primer for open source and free software projects*. Software Freedom Law Center, Version 1.5.1. Retrieved from http://www.softwarefreedom.org/resources/2008/foss-primer.pdf

Hohfeld, W. N. (1913). Some fundamental legal conceptions as applied in judicial reasoning. *The Yale Law Journal, 23*(1), 16–59. doi:10.2307/785533

Jansen, A., Bosch, J., & Avgeriou, P. (2008). Documenting after the fact: Recovering architectural design decisions. *Journal of Systems and Software, 81*(4), 536–557. doi:10.1016/j.jss.2007.08.025

Kazman, R., & Carrière, J. (1999). Playing detective: Reconstructing software architecture from available evidence. *Journal of Automated Software Engineering, 6*(2), 107–138. doi:10.1023/A:1008781513258

Kuhl, F., Weatherly, R., & Dahmann, J. (2000). *Creating computer simulation systems: An introduction to the high level architecture.* Upper Saddle River, NJ: Prentice-Hall PTR.

Medvidovic, N., Rosenblum, D. S., & Taylor, R. N. (1999). A language and environment for architecture-based software development and evolution. In *Proceedings 21st International Conference Software Engineering (ICSE '99)* (pp. 44-53). Los Angeles, CA: IEEE Computer Society.

Meyers, B. C., & Obendorf, P. (2001). *Managing software acquisition: Open systems and COTS products.* New York, NY: Addison-Wesley.

Nelson, L., & Churchill, E. F. (2006). Repurposing: Techniques for reuse and integration of interactive services. *Proceedings 2006 IEEE International Conference Information Reuse and Integration.*

OSI. (2011). *The open source initiative.* Retrieved from http://www.opensource.org/

Rosen, L. (2005). *Open source licensing: Software freedom and intellectual property law.* Upper Saddle River, NJ: Prentice-Hall PTR. Retrieved from http://www.rosenlaw.com/oslbook.htm

Scacchi, W. (2002). Understanding the requirements for developing open source software systems. *IEE Proceedings. Software, 149*(1), 24–39, February. doi:10.1049/ip-sen:20020202

Scacchi, W. (2007). Free/open source software development: Recent research results and emerging opportunities. *Proceedings of European Software Engineering Conference and ACM SIGSOFT Symposium on the Foundations of Software Engineering,* Dubrovnik, Croatia, (pp. 459-468).

Scacchi, W., & Alspaugh, T. A. (2008). Emerging issues in the acquisition of open source software within the U.S. Department of Defense. *Proceedings 5th Annual Acquisition Research Symposium,* Vol. 1, (pp. 230-244). NPS-AM-08-036, Naval Postgraduate School, Monterey, CA

St. Laurent, A. M. (2004). *Understanding open source and free software licensing.* Sebastopol, CA: O'Reilly Press.

Ven, K., & Mannaert, H. (2008). Challenges and strategies in the use of open source software by independent software vendors. *Information and Software Technology, 50,* 991–1002. doi:10.1016/j.infsof.2007.09.001

KEY TERMS AND DEFINITIONS

Architectural Description Language (ADL): A formal language or notational scheme for explicitly specifying the elements of a software system architecture including the system's components, component interfaces, and connectors that collectively denote the overall architectural configuration of the system. ADLs are a convenient way to specify an OA software system.

Architecture Development Environment: An integrated ensemble of software tools whose collective purpose is to facilitate the interactive development of software system architecture models using an ADL, ideally in a form that can be also used to subsequently develop or consistently derive the build-time and run-time versions of the specified software system architecture.

Automated Software License Analysis: A technique for automatically analyzing the propagation of software copy rights and obligations across interconnected software components that are part of an explicit, open architecture software system.

Open Architecture (OA): A software system architecture that is explicitly specify, model, or visually render the software components of a system, the connectors that interconnect data or control flow between components via each component's interfaces, that collectively denote the overall architectural configuration of a system in a form that can be accessed, studies, modified or redistributed.

Open Source Software: Software whose source code is available for external access, study, modification, and redistribution by end-users, accompanied by a software copyright agreement (software license) that insures these rights are available to anyone who satisfies the explicitly declared obligations included in the licenses. See the Open Source Initiative (OSI 2011) for other definitions of open source software. In contract, closed source software generally denotes proprietary whose source code is not available for external access, study, modification or redistribution by end-users, and therefore may also be available as restricted use, executable components.

Software Licenses: A contractual agreement conveyed from software developers, owners, or producers to external users of the software most typically through explicit copyright declarations or an end-user license agreement (EULA).

Software Traceability: A technique for navigating or tracing relationships between elements of a software system, and/or documentation of its software engineering.

APPENDIX: AN INTERPRETATION OF THE BSD 3-CLAUSE LICENSE

General Obligations for the License as a Whole

O1. Licensee: must-not: seek remedy based on warranty or liability with respect to [Any].

Rights and Corresponding Obligations

R1. Licensee: may: reproduce {AnyOriginalSource}
R2. Licensee: may: reproduce {AnyOriginalBinary}
o2.1. Licensee: must: distribute the BSD notice with [Any]
R3. Licensee: may: prepare derivative work {AnyDerivativeWork} of {AnyOriginalSource}
o3.1. Licensee: must: retain BSD notices from [Original] in [DerivativeWork]
o3.2. Licensee: must-not: claim endorsement for [DerivativeWork] by {{ORGANIZATION}}
o3.3. Licensee: must-not: claim endorsement for [DerivativeWork] by contributors to [Original]
R4. Licensee: may: prepare derivative work {AnyDerivativeWork} of {AnyOriginalBinary}
o4.1. Licensee: must: distribute the BSD notice with [Any]
o4.2. Licensee: must-not: claim endorsements for [DerivativeWork] from {{ORGANIZATION}}
o4.3. Licensee: must-not: claim endorsements for [DerivativeWork] from contributors to [Original]
R5. Licensee: may: distribute copies of {AnyOriginalSource}
o5.1. Licensee: must: retain the BSD notice in [Any]
R6. Licensee: may: distribute copies of {AnyOriginalBinary}
o6.1. Licensee: must: distribute the BSD notice with [Any]

Section 2
Crossing Enterprise, System, and Software Architecture Boundaries

Chapter 5
Mitigating Mobile Diversity with RESTful Services

Tristan Wehrmaker
Leibniz Universität Hannover, Germany

Kurt Schneider
Leibniz Universität Hannover, Germany

ABSTRACT

Mobile devices create new opportunities for companies. However, innovative applications can cause challenges for software and system architecture. In this chapter, the authors describe a trap to fall into when starting a promising mobile application in a shortsighted way. When the application gets popular and successful, diversity of mobile platforms increases. Many users have an almost emotional relationship to their own smartphone or platform and may not be willing to change it. In order to make the mobile application available to more users, a company may be tempted to add a "simple" extension to accommodate other platforms. Thus, the diversity in devices leads to diversity in distributed object technologies and with it to problems in complexity and compatibility. The authors describe an approach that counters this problem with RESTful services. They use the ConTexter system for illustrating experiences with the problem and for evaluating a proposed solution. The chapter shows the key issues the authors had to solve while migrating ConTexter to a RESTful platform.

1. INTRODUCTION

Many people carry smartphones, tablets or other mobile devices with them all the time. More and more companies seize the chance of mobile distributed applications to improve their access to people and the flow of information. In this chapter, we describe an unfavorable trap of shortsighted propagation. It is closely related to the Distributed Disaster anti-pattern described by Brown et al. (2000).

Risky new ideas are typically explored with a small and homogeneous user community to start with. The new application is explored using a single technological platform (e.g., hardware and operating system). Paradoxically, problems arise exactly if those attempts are successful: If the initially small user group likes the application,

DOI: 10.4018/978-1-4666-2199-2.ch005

it is often spread to other people, without careful redesign. When the system spreads beyond its initial target group and throughout the enterprise, diversity of mobile platforms increases. This is the root of the here-described problem. The application that was previously intended as proof of concept turns into an application that is in productive use. There are too many users that have the application installed in their devices and the development team has no access to them anymore. In addition the resources are often too limited to discard the existing application and to start from the beginning. There are good reasons to fall into this trap again and again.

Many users have an almost emotional relationship to their own smartphone or platform. They are not willing to change. In order to make the mobile application available to more users, a company may add a "simple" extension to their server side system to accommodate other platforms – and opt for architectural diversity. At this point add-ons and bypasses start to mess up the initially simple architecture.

Performance and maintainability suffer due to compromised architectural clarity when smartphones, computers and other handhelds introduce diversity. Many diverse implementations of clients and servers have to be maintained, which leads to problems in complexity and compatibility.

The concepts in this chapter were developed upon our experiences with this problem and are reported using the case study of our ConTexter system as presented in Schneider et al. (2010). It is also used to evaluate a proposed solution approach. The development of ConTexter accidentally got lured into the above-mentioned trap. ConTexter is an advanced feedback system. ConTexter is considered as yet another mobile application example with all its strengths and weaknesses. A case study section below describes it in more detail. We discuss the REST architectural style and how it can help to mitigate the above-mentioned problems. We suggest using REST from the start of the development. However, we also present mitigation steps for a situation in which the development already got caught in the trap of shortsighted propagation.

The chapter is structured as follows. Section 2 describes the background of this chapter with explanations of the central terms *mobile application* and *client-server communication* in conjunction with an introduction into REST and RESTful services. Section 3 discusses the diversity in mobile applications. It highlights the trap of shortsighted propagation and shows our ConTexter system, which serves as case study and example of how to get caught in the trap. Section 4 will describe how to bypass the trap with RESTful services. This includes recommendations on how RESTful services can be implemented and how to proceed when migrating to technologies for RESTful services. Future research directions will be shown in section 5. It evaluates the proposed solution approach, discusses recommendations on when to use it and describes how it might be improved in the future. Section 6 finally gives a conclusion about this chapter.

2. BACKGROUND

2.1 Mobile Applications

The diversity of mobile devices is in the focus of this chapter. Christensen (2009) describes the term "'smart mobile device'" as follows:

"Smart" Mobile Devices typically describes devices that are continuously connected to a TCP capable network, with a hand-held form factor and a large, high quality graphics display. These devices generally have significant computing power, and support mainstream programming technologies for their development (Christensen, 2009).

For example smartphones and tablets fall into this category. Mobile devices are based on specific platforms. We characterize a mobile platform as an environment consisting of an operating system, offering an SDK utilizing a specific programming language and supporting technologies for accessing the hardware of a mobile device. Currently popular mobile platforms are for instance iOS by Apple Inc., Android by the Open Handset Alliance, Windows Phone 7 by Microsoft Corp., or webOS by Hewlett-Packard Company.

Finally a mobile application is an application developed for a mobile device based upon a mobile platform. Besides the differentiation according to the type of the device (smartphone or tablet) and according to the platform the application runs on (iOS, Android, etc.) mobile applications can be distinguished because of their residence. A mobile application can either be native to the device or browser-based. Native applications reside directly on the device. They can take full advantage of the hardware access offered by the platform and are mostly written in the programming languages that are intended by the platforms (Objective-C at iOS, Java at Android, etc.). Browser-based applications do not get installed on the device itself, but reside on the web and get accessed through the browser of the device. They are typically written with web technologies like HTML5 and JavaScript. Browser-based applications offer only a limited access to the hardware of the device. Merely few standardized APIs are offered to access the sensors and system functions. Like the Geolocation API[1] that gives access to the actual geo coordinates using for example the GPS sensor of the device.

Native applications only run on devices that are based on the platform they are developed for, while browser-based applications should run on every platform similarly in theory. Depending on the use cases of the developed application, it can make sense to implement it as native or browser-based application. Alternatives for creating applications that run on various mobile platforms are so called cross-platform frameworks like PhoneGap[2] or Rhodes[3]. Those enable the development of native applications using web technologies. Applications that are using those frameworks are able to utilize most of the devices sensors and other device capabilities. These kinds of applications are beyond the scope of this chapter, because we will focus on the client-server-communication, which is introduced in the next section.

2.2 Client-Server Communication

When working with mobile devices it is often usual to let a server run complex calculations. In many cases there is data that must be stored on a server because it is needed in a larger context. An opportunity to realize a decoupled and standardized communication between the mobile devices as client and a server are so called web services. The World Wide Web Consortium (W3C) defines web services as follows:

A Web service is a software system designed to support interoperable machine-to-machine interaction over a network. It has an interface described in a machine-processable format (specifically WSDL). Other systems interact with the Web service in a manner prescribed by its description using SOAP messages, typically conveyed using HTTP with an XML serialization in conjunction with other Web-related standards (Booth et al., 2004).

This definition associates web services to solutions that are realized based on the Web Service Description Language (WSDL) and SOAP. With the increasing relevance of the Web 2.0 and of mobile devices, these traditional web services have turned out to be too heavyweight. Hence services based on REST got popular. Roy T. Fielding analyzed the architecture of the web and inferred from it the Representational State Transfer (REST) architectural style (Fielding, 2000). REST embraces the web and the underlying technologies (HTTP, URI and so on). Instead of using the Hypertext Transfer Protocol (HTTP) as transport-level protocol for other application-level protocols like SOAP, REST is designed to use HTTP as the application-level protocol it was specified for. Thus REST is the most natural way to develop systems that act in the ecosystem of the web.

Richardson and Ruby recommend a resource-oriented architecture (Richardson & Ruby, 2007) based on the principles of REST. Core concepts are in short:

- Everything that is of some kind of interest is capsuled in a resource.
- Every resource on the web is addressable by a Uniform Resource Identifier (URI).
- All resources have a Uniform Interface defined by the HTTP verbs (GET, PUT, POST, DELETE, etc.).
- As resources themselves cannot be transferred over the Internet, there are representations of these resources.
- The representations are connected through hyperlinks.
- All requests to a RESTful service are stateless.

How these concepts can get implemented will be described later in this chapter, when it comes to our proposed solution approach. An application is called RESTful if it sticks to the principles of REST. Webber et al. (2010) use a maturity model developed by Richardson to distinguish the levels of an application on their way of getting RESTful. Yan Liu et al. (2008) describe a method for reengineering legacy systems with RESTful services. Thereby they do not especially go into mobile applications and legacy systems with existing service capabilities. But they discuss how to identify the resources that have to be present in the system. Moreover, Tilkov (2011) describes different types of resources. He distinguishes between primary resources, corresponding to the concepts of the system, list resources, containing references to the primary resources, and others. Schreiner (2011) shows an approach on how to derive a meta model from these resource types.

3. DIVERSITY IN MOBILE APPLICATIONS

3.1 Shortsighted Propagation

When developing an application – in our case for a mobile platform – the development will often be carried out for one single platform in the beginning for economic reasons or for prototyping. This happens especially if the decision makers do not know about the existence of the here-described problems. The decision for one mobile platform (e.g. Android, iOS or Windows Phone) may for example depend on the familiarity of the development team with the particular development environment. In this chapter we want to call attention for the problems that might occur when making such decision.

Thereby every platform has its own traits. Besides different possibilities for accessing the hardware of the device, the most platforms define their own standards for communicating with and for accessing a server. Every platform favors a particular distributed object technology. On the Android platform there are for example Remote Method Invocation (RMI) and serialized Java object streams. iOS offers Distributed Objects (DO). Windows Phone 7 supports its own proprietary solution called .Net Remoting.

Thus, we assume that the application is developed for only one platform in the beginning. Therefore, it uses the communication techniques of this platform. That leads us to a trap that we call shortsighted propagation. This behavior of the development team is shortsighted because other platforms were not considered. However, chances are there will be potential users of the application in the future who prefer those other platforms.

It is assumed that the application will be developed for the Android platform. It is obvious that the developers would use the technology that is featured by this platform or that they are already familiar with. Although an easier start in development is advantageous, it leads to a solution that is closely coupled to one platform. In case of the Android platform it might be obvious to use RMI for calling methods on the server. However, a device based on the iOS platform for example cannot deal with RMI interfaces.

There are still too much diverse hardware, operating systems, and software platforms in mobile application development. When the application gets popular the user base starts to grow. Some potential users will favor different mobile platforms. Hence, other platforms need to be supported. Since they use different mechanisms, workarounds must be introduced. The application gets messed up with extensions and plug-ins for each additional platform.

The result of such approach is an unmaintainable environment. Every time something has to be extended or adjusted, every interface has to be changed. This is an error-prone process.

The trap of shortsighted propagation is closely related to the Distributed Disaster anti-pattern proposed by Brown et al. (2000). The authors state that the main exceptions of the anti-pattern are when the software development is done for prototyping purposes. In contrast to the Distributed Disaster anti-pattern, the here-described approach assumes that a prototypical mobile application can leave the prototype stadium because it got spread to many users that are not necessarily accessible anymore like described above. Then the mobile application is in productive use and may already have got caught in the trap of shortsighted propagation.

3.2 Case Study

In this section we present our case study. Therefore, our ConTexter system is presented in short, followed by an explanation of how we got caught in the trap of shortsighted propagation.

The ConTexter System for Spontaneous Feedback

IT ecosystems (Lentz & Bleizeffer, 2007) consist of dynamically interacting subsystems, components, and services containing software. Companies provide parts of IT ecosystems, e.g. for airports, train stations, and shopping malls. Due to the complex interaction of subsystems, overall behavior cannot be completely anticipated or engineered. IT ecosystems constantly evolve by adapting to new user requirements and to changes in their environment. On-going improvement requires feedback from users. However, feedback is not easy to get. We have developed an approach facilitating feedback in context. It is gathered by mobile devices like smartphones.

A number of trends in modern technology and society have created a new situation. So far, the only way for unsatisfied customers of software and systems to complain was by calling or writing to providers. However, spending extra time and effort for identifying and contacting the responsible provider prevented most people from giving feedback. Why would someone spend time and money to provide feedback?

Effective support for evolution needs to cover (1) identifying the component or subsystem a user wants to address, (2) the ability to send feedback at very low effort and cost, and (3) support for interpreting incoming feedback. In Schneider et al. (2010), we present an architecture, a framework, and an application example to put stakeholder feedback into context. Contextualized feedback supports providers in driving the IT ecosystem evolution. In Schneider (2011) we address the added value of focusing spontaneous feedback using a tool like ConTexter.

Tools to support this approach need to facilitate and guide the identification of appropriate addressee subsystems in the IT ecosystem. We suggest using heuristics on geographical and logical proximity to identify addressees for feedback:

Context can be captured implicitly and at minimal effort by locating users automatically. In addition, tailor-made mechanisms for pre-sorting feedback are proposed to facilitate analysis of feedback and fast improvement reaction (Schneider, 2011). The essential use cases associated with our ConTexter tool are:

1. Providers of services, software or elements of an IT ecosystem that are interested in feedback define a number of entities and maybe further feedback options that help users to focus their feedback.

2. Whenever a stakeholder invokes ConTexter:
    a. The mode of feedback is selected (positive, neutral, negative or proposal).
    b. A heuristic context matching algorithm selects and presents a short list of potential addressees.
    c. The user makes the final selection of the most appropriate entity.
    d. Some entities may have frequently-selected options assigned. By checking one or more of those options, stakeholders save typing effort. In addition, providers can sort and count selected options automatically.
    e. Finally, videos, pictures, or audio messages can be recorded and attached. This is easier than writing long texts,

and it might be easier to analyze due to the higher level of detail and concrete information included with the feedback.

3. ConTexter routes all incoming feedback directly to the provider who has defined the selected entity. Based on the entities and options selected during the above steps, feedback is presorted and statistically analyzed. Only those messages containing rich attachments or texts require intense manual attention.

The flow of giving feedback in ConTexter is shown in Figure 1. In this example the user wants to complain about the ticket machine at a train station. Due to a malfunction the user missed the desired train. For this reason he wants to give feedback over his situation. Thus, he starts his mobile ConTexter application and chooses to complain by tapping the "negative" button. Meanwhile, the system searches for entities whose context he is in. Besides the train station, the system finds the ticket machine as well by heuristics. After the user chooses the ticket machine he can select from predefined options of this entity and give a free text input. Before sending the feedback to the service the user shoots a photo of the ticket machine to emphasize his statement.

Figure 1. The flow of giving feedback in a ticket-buying scenario

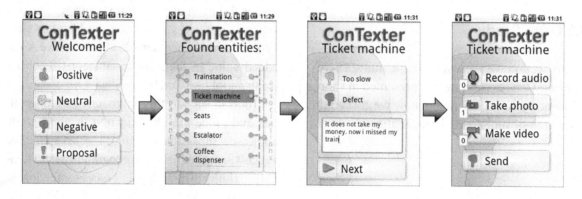

All other features are omitted here for the sake of brevity. They are not essential to convey the mission and operation of the ConTexter system with respect to the architectural aspects discussed here.

Shortsighted Propagation

During the development of ConTexter, the above-mentioned symptoms of falling into the trap of shortsighted propagation started to occur. In the beginning of the development it was considered a proof of concept. ConTexter was not intended to be used by a wider user base in the first run. So supporting other platforms was not on the agenda.

The development of ConTexter started with Android 1.6 on the client side. The reason for this choice was the openness of the Android system. Our developers had an easy start. The server side was implemented offering communication interfaces with a mix of RMI, HTTP-POST wrapped JSON and a proprietary session mechanism for identifying the clients and the feedback they are actually giving. The client and the server where tightly coupled through the proprietary protocols they used. Therefore, every change on the server side unavoidably led to changes on the client side.

Because the system was used by a small group of users' new versions of the client application could be distributed to the users at acceptable effort. After a while the previously small user group started to grow and the need of supporting devices using the iOS platform arose due to the popularity of iPhones. Figure 2 shows the environment of the ConTexter at that time. ConTexter already had two different interfaces to communicate with two different devices. On the one hand the server was connected to a desktop administration tool via Java Remote Method Invocation (RMI). On the other hand the android clients were connected via an HTTP POST – RPC style service transferring documents in the JavaScript Object Notation (JSON) and serialized Java objects for identifying the user session. RPC stands for Remote Procedure Call, which is a way to communicate with a server by calling methods over HTTP. The description which method has to be called is defined within the message that is thereby send to the server. Standardized protocols that are based upon RPC are e.g. XML-RPC and SOAP.

Opening a branch to a second operating system affected protocol details and the entire system and software architecture. The original architecture was essentially built upon serialized Java objects. It was not possible to continue using it with the iOS platform since iOS cannot deal with that data format.

The architecture was not laid out for other platforms, so we had two alternative options to proceed:

1. Adding plug-ins to the server side system, which enable the communication with iOS-clients.
2. Implementing a more generic interface compatible with almost every platform.

The first solution leads to two interfaces that both need to be maintained. With every additional platform, such as Windows Phone or webOS, dedicated solutions would become necessary. In addition, these extensions immensely increase the complexity of the architecture.

Figure 2. The components of the ConTexter system with the used transfer technologies

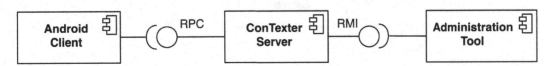

The second solution would mean to provide an additional interface to be maintained as well. But the legacy interface has not to be maintained in the long run. We decided to follow this approach because we wanted to avoid falling into the trap of shortsighted propagation again if other platforms would be added to the architecture. Our goal is to have only one interface that needs to be maintained, instead of two or more.

Since we assume that such situations will occur again, we describe key issues when migrating an application to an open and extendable architecture. It can be used with almost any kind of client platform. Furthermore we provide solutions to these key issues.

4. MITIGATING DIVERSITY WITH RESTFUL SERVICES

Our proposed solution approach is based on the paradigms of RESTful HTTP. Figure 3 shows the desired solution. The server has only one unique interface. All clients refer to this interface. That makes it extendable and connectable to different client application.

The decision for the implementation as RESTful service came from the comparison of different approaches like SOAP services. It emerged that SOAP services introduce too many constraints and a huge tool chain. In contrast REST services are working on a bunch of well-tested and widely used standards like HTTP, URI and MIME. The web shows the ability of these services to be scalable and lightweight. So it fits best for distributed applications with diverse types of client applications and devices. We propose the usage of REST in a mobile scenario because the devices are often connected through a cellular network, which currently offers a very limited bandwidth, where the overhead introduced by SOAP messages can heavily affect the user experience.

REST can be the common ground of different and diverse mobile platforms. All devices that are programmable and accommodate a web browser will be able to deal with RESTful services. This includes smartphones of various kinds, and even IP-TV sets. This means that diversity in client devices does not lead to diversity in server implementations.

We recommend the following approach for migrating proprietary systems to RESTful applications. When migrating ConTexter we observed some things that need a closer inspection. First we will depict how to design the RESTful web service. Afterwards we will describe the migration of the legacy interfaces to the architecture of the RESTful web service.

Figure 3. Desired solution for the interface over which clients can communicate with the server

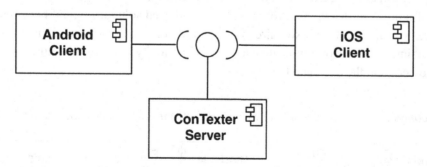

4.1 Defining the RESTful Service

According to the principles of REST the following steps need to be done to implement a RESTful service:

1. *Find the resources.* The main concepts of the system have to be defined as resources. In the ConTexter example the concepts are e.g. entities, the user can give feedback to, media artifacts belonging to the feedback or the feedback itself. Often resources can be derived from the classes in the domain model. But other concepts such as the relation between an entity and a feedback can be resources too, even if they are for example not persisted into a database.

2. *Define the URIs for accessing the resources.* Every resource is identified by a unique Uniform Resource Identifier (URI). That way there is not only one endpoint that the client has access to, but also it can access every resource independently.

3. *Define the Uniform Interface.* HTTP defines the verbs/methods GET, PUT, POST, DELETE amongst others. They formulate a contract between a server and a client on how the client can interact with each resource. Thereby not all of these methods have to be implemented by every resource. For example, it may not be a good idea to modify a feedback using an HTTP-PUT request after it is created. However, it is very important not to define methods that are outside the HTTP specification. That would break the Uniform Interface, because not all clients know about the newly created methods. This would lead again to a closed proprietary solution.

4. *Determine the formats for the representations.* Because a resource itself cannot be retrieved or transmitted over the net, we must define representations of these resources. The most common formats for structured data are the Extensible Markup Language (XML) and the JavaScript Object Notation (JSON). Both formats have their own advantages and disadvantages. XML has a better tool support than JSON. However, JSON has a much smaller syntax than XML. That means less data to transmit between client and server. For this reason we decided to offer a JSON formatted output for the mobile clients of ConTexter. But we also offer XML representations for other clients that would prefer this format.

5. *Define the connections between the representations.* A main concept of REST is the connectedness. That means that the resources are connected with each other through links inside their representations. The connections are due to the relations between the resources or different states a resource can reach. A main advantage of this approach is, that a client application only needs to know one entry point into the server application. The server can control the path of the client through the application by offering only links that fit to the current application state. This behavior is often called Hypermedia As The Engine Of Application State (HATEOAS). It can be compared to HTML pages inside a browser that offer only links to other pages that make sense from the users location within the web application.

In web applications it is often necessary to identify associated activities of a user. An often-used technique to achieve this is sessions. A session contains all information that belongs to a user. Thus, the state of the client application is held on the server side. In contrast, one of the main concepts of REST is statelessness. This means that the client state only belongs to the client, and the server state only to the server. Thus the server remembers nothing about the client. Every request from the client to the server must contain all information to handle the request and to re-

Box 1. A resource defined using the Jersey framework

```
@Path("/helloworld")
public class HelloWorldResource {

    @GET
    public Response get() {
        return Response.ok().entity("Hello World").build();
    }
}
```

turn a response. This approach makes RESTful services extremely scalable, because a request can be routed to another server, or can be handled by an intermediary proxy. While migrating the ConTexter we noticed that most information about the client that needs to be persisted on the server side can be encapsulated inside of resources. In our ConTexter example the data belonging to a user and the process of giving feedback can be encapsulated within the feedback resource. The feedback can have different states like "initialized", "media added", "completed" and so forth.

When the RESTful service got implemented, the mobile development team can start to implement the new clients and to migrate their legacy mobile application to work with the new RESTful service. For the technical implementation we used the Jersey framework, which is the reference implementation of the Java API for RESTful Web Services (JAX-RS). Thus, our application is written in Java. It is running in a Glassfish Application Server, which is in turn the reference implementation of the Java EE 6 specification. The JAX-RS standard allows an annotation-based implementation of RESTful services. Thereby it

is possible to develop a RESTful service with just a few annotations.

Box 1 depicts a sample resource. The @Path annotation marks a class as resource class. It accepts a parameter that defines the URI path over which the resource can be accessed. The Jersey servlet will automatically dispatch all incoming requests to the appropriate resource. The annotation @GET labels a Java method that will react on HTTP-GET requests to this resource. Other annotations for POST, PUT and DELETE exist analog.

The Response class is a builder for HTTP responses. It provides convenient methods for returning the corresponding HTTP response codes and response headers. Thus it is possible to implement full-fledged resources through very simple means. For every concept in ConTexter we implemented a resource as well as resources that represent lists of these resources. The implementation of representations is in Jersey supported by message body readers and message body writers. It includes predefined readers and writers for JAXB and Jackson for an annotation-based definition of XML and JSON representations. But also own reader and writer can be provided. This will be helpful when it comes to the migration of the proprietary protocols.

4.2 Migration to a RESTful Service

One problem with distributed mobile applications is that the distributor has no access to the distributed versions. Because the old mobile clients would break when offering the new server implementation, it comes in handy to offer a legacy interface

Figure 4. Initial situation

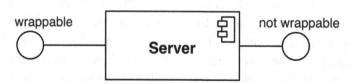

Figure 5. Legacy server interface

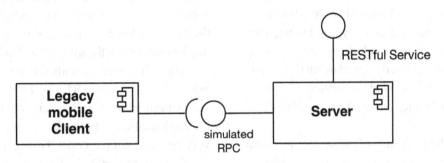

Figure 6. Interfaces after finishing the migration

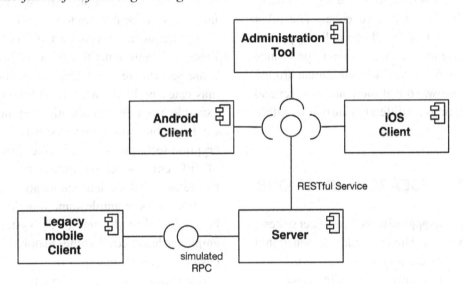

that acts on the same infrastructure as the new implementations but does provide functionality needed by old clients. While analyzing ConTexter we found interface technologies that can be realized with techniques for RESTful services and some that cannot. Figure 4 shows this discrepancy. Hence, we have to distinguish between these two types of interfaces.

As above mentioned there are two kinds of interfaces in the ConTexter example. The RPC style service on the one hand is implemented using the HTTP-POST method on remote procedures defined by different URI paths with the message in the request body. The request body consists of JSON data and serialized Java objects. The migration here is simple to be achieved. The client does

not need to be changed. It can simply send his messages as usual. The server has to offer the URI paths identifying the methods and a message body reader and writer for the proprietary data format sent by the client. Figure 5 shows the application with the legacy interface simulating the communication paths needed by the legacy applications.

On the other hand there are distributed object technologies, like RMI, that cannot be side effect free wrapped by HTTP. RMI for instance can be tunneled over HTTP, but this cannot be done without modifications to the server infrastructure and the client application. So there is no direct replacement for this. When designing applications that run on and embrace the web, it seems odd to implement the administration user interface as a desktop application. So the preferred way is to offer a browser based administration interface. This is recommended anyway for testing purposes. If there has to be a desktop application in any case this should be designed using the RESTful interface as any kind of device with web browsing capabilities can make use of RESTful services.

The complete structure of our system is shown in Figure 6. The server now offers two interfaces, whereby one is only for legacy purposes and does not need to be maintained as the legacy clients are not maintained anymore either. The other interface serves now for all other client applications and those implemented in the future. Since we migrated ConTexter the environment around it started to grow, so that there are now several client applications for different kind of jobs within the system.

5. FUTURE RESEARCH DIRECTIONS

Our approach was applied to the ConTexter system, as described above. This case study demonstrated the feasibility of the migration. The ConTexter system has an open and extendable interface now. Thus, an ecosystem of special purpose client applications for different platforms has been established to manage various behaviors of the system. This shows that it is now simpler to communicate with the server. Because no proprietary interfaces are used, a variety of possible platforms are able to access the services offered by the server, even those that are not mobile.

Our solution approach can now be applied to other situations, offering a migration path to circumvent the trap of shortsighted propagation. The migration is recommended for scenarios where mainly interfaces are involved that can be wrapped by HTTP as shown in section 4.2. In contrast, it may not be recommended to migrate when the most involved interfaces are not wrappable because it would break the client application.

tions, which have to be reimplemented to interact with the server. It is in any case advantageous, if the business logic is cleanly separated from the implementation of the interfaces. Thus, it is easier to replace the interface with a RESTful one. During the development of RESTful services with the Jersey Framework a multiplicity of classes has to be implemented. These classes contain mostly very few and simple code. This recurring effort can be encountered in the future with methods of model-driven software development. Thus, it can be explored, if the migration for specific original interfaces can be done automatically.

Furthermore, it has to be analyzed, if all non-functional requirements can be satisfied. Thus, some security relevant features of the systems may cause problems with RESTful services. For example proprietary authentication mechanisms can be problematic if they depend on special encryption techniques. Besides the differentiation of different devices we further can distinguish by the intended use and the location. In a banking system for example some functions may not be available for all users of the system. A bank employee has access to other features than a bank customer. Rights management or authorization and authentication can achieve this but in some domains it may be too insecure. Then additional particular interfaces have to be introduced.

6. CONCLUSION

This chapter showed how legacy systems with proprietary service interfaces could be migrated to systems with a RESTful service interface. It covered and characterized the trap of shortsighted propagation, which causes applications that run into a situation where they are unmaintainable concerning the addition of other mobile platforms. A presentation of our case study ConTexter was followed by a discussion about the use of the REST architectural style as an adequate basis for innovative mobile applications. It outlined the key migration steps from a messed-up architecture to a RESTful architecture and described problems we got into and showed proposed solutions.

We evaluated the migration process by applying it to our ConTexter system. In the ConTexter system we ran into problems with extending it for other mobile platforms. We analyzed our system and found the trap of shortsighted propagation. So we searched for methods that could help us with implementing an interface for our system that is as open and extendable as possible. Hence, we derived a migration process that consists of two main steps.

On the one hand is the design and implementation of the RESTful service. There were five tasks to be done:

1. Finding the resources.
2. Defining the URIs for accessing the resources.
3. Defining the Uniform Interface.
4. Determining the formats for the representations.
5. Defining the connections between the representations.

It turned out that (1) is the most comprehensive activity, because it is often not clear which resources are needed and how they exactly have to be structured. A good starting point for defining the resources are the classes in the domain model. For the definition of URIs (2) it turned out that there are different opportunities on how these URIs can get structured. While it can be important to build human-readable URIs, REST makes no constraints how a URI should look like, as long as it is unique. While defining the uniform interface (3), it is possible to give very fine-grained access to the resources by only allowing specific operations on them. Since the annotations like @GET infer functionality the code is better documented as in conventional interfaces. With the HTTP methods a developer that is familiar with the concepts of REST can immediately understand the Uniform

Interface. Determining the formats for the representations (4) is a simple task if keeping with standard and wide used formats like XML and JSON. Especially for mobile applications it is important to choose a lightweight format that has less transmission overhead. The task of defining the connections between the representations (5) turned out in our case to be simple because we only had to add links to subordinated resources and not to more advanced state transitions. Another issue was the transfer of the session mechanisms that have to be represented in form of resources.

On the other hand is the migration of the legacy interface to a RESTful service. It turned out that a distinction between interfaces that can be wrapped with HTTP and those that cannot is necessary. The wrappable interfaces can be implemented with technologies for RESTful services, whereas other interfaces have to be replaced in conjunction with the corresponding interface in the client applications that use these server interfaces.

In summary, the trap of shortsighted propagation leads to an immense effort in migrating. We believe that this effort is worth it if additional platforms have to be supported by the system. We suggest using REST from the beginning to avoid the troubles caused by the trap of shortsighted propagation. Diversity is a fact of life, and a driver for architectural decisions. Some of that diversity may be given a rest, however, by migrating to RESTful architecture.

REFERENCES

Booth, D., Haas, H., McCabe, F., Newcomer, E., Champion, M., Ferris, C., & Orchard, D. (2004). *Web services architecture*. Retrieved September 15, 2011, from http://www.w3.org/TR/ws-arch/

Brown, W. J., Malveau, R. C., McCormick, H. W., & Thomas, S. W. Theresa Hudson (Ed.) (2000). *Anti-patterns in project management*. New York, NY: John Wiley & Sons.

Christensen, J. H. (2009). Using RESTful web-services and cloud computing to create next generation mobile applications. In *Proceedings of the 24th ACM SIGPLAN Conference Companion on Object Oriented Programming Systems Languages and Applications (OOPSLA '09)* (pp. 627-633). New York, NY: ACM.

Fielding, R. T. (2000). *Architectural styles and the design of network-based software architectures.* Ph.D. dissertation, University of California, Irvine. Retrieved September 15, 2011, from http://www.ics.uci.edu/fielding/pubs/dissertation/top.htm

Lentz, J. L., & Bleizeffer, T. M. (2007). *IT ecosystems: Evolved complexity and unintelligent design.* In CHIMIT 2007, Cambridge, MA, USA

Liu, Y., Wang, Q., Zhuang, M., & Zhu, Y. (2008). Reengineering legacy systems with RESTful web service. *Proceedings of COMPSAC, 08,* 785–790.

Richardson, L., & Ruby, S. (2007). *RESTful web services.* O'Reilly Media.

Schneider, K. (2011). Focusing spontaneous feedback to support system evolution. In *Proceedings of the IEEE 19th International Requirements Engineering Conference (RE '11)* (pp. 165-174).

Schneider, K., Meyer, S., Peters, M., & Schliephacke, F. Mörschbach & J., Aguirre, L. (2010). Feedback in context: Supporting the evolution of IT-ecosystems. In M. Ali Babar, M. Vierimaa, & M. Oivo (Eds.), *Proceedings of the 11th International Conference on Product-Focused Software Process Improvement (PROFES 2010)* (pp. 191-205). Berlin, Germany: Springer-Verlag.

Schreiner, S. (2011). Modeling RESTful applications. In C. Pautasso & E. Wilde (Eds.), *Proceedings of the Second International Workshop on RESTful Design (WS-REST '11)* (pp. 15-21). New York, NY: ACM.

Tilkov, S. (2011). *REST und HTTP: Einsatz der Architektur des Web für Integrationsszenarien* (2nd ed.). Dpunkt Verlag.

Webber, J., Parastatidis, S., & Robinson, I. (2010). *REST in practice: Hypermedia and systems architecture.* O'Reilly Media.

ADDITIONAL READING

Allamaraju, S. (2010). *RESTful Web services cookbook.* O'Reilly.

Apple Inc. (2011). *Introduction to CFNetwork programming guide.* Retrieved September 28, 2011, from http://developer.apple.com/library/ios/#documentation/Networking/Conceptual/CFNetwork/Introduction/Introduction.html

Berner-Lee, T., Fielding, R., & Masinter, L. (2005). *Uniform resource identifier (URI): Generic syntax.* Retrieved September 23, 2011, from http://www.ietf.org/rfc/rfc3986.txt

Bray, T., Paoli, J., Sperberg-McQueen, C. M., & Maler, E. (2008). *Extensible markup language (XML) 1.0 (Fifth Edition): W3C recommendation 26 November 2008.* Retrieved September 23, 2011, from http://www.w3.org/TR/2008/REC-xml-20081126/

Crockford, D. (2006). *The application/JSON media type for JavaScript object notation (JSON).* Retrieved September 23, 2011, from http://www.ietf.org/rfc/rfc4627.txt

Engelke, C., & Fitzgerald, C. (2010). Replacing legacy web services with RESTful services. In C. Pautasso, E. Wilde, & A. Marinos (Eds.), *Proceedings of the First International Workshop on RESTful Design (WS-REST '10)* (pp. 27-30). New York, NY: ACM.

Fielding, R., Gettys, J., Mogul, J., Frystyk, H., Masinter, L., Leach, P., & Berners-Lee, T. (1999). *Hypertext transfer protocol -- HTTP/1.1.* Retrieved September 23, 2011, from http://www.w3.org/Protocols/rfc2616/rfc2616.html

Fowler, M. (2010). *Richardson maturity model: Steps toward the glory of REST.* Retrieved September 4, 2011, from http://martinfowler.com/articles/richardsonMaturityModel.html

Goncalves, A. (2010). *Beginning Java EE 6 with GlassFish 3.* Apress. doi:10.1007/978-1-4302-2890-5

Gregorio, J., & de Hora, B. (2007). *The atom publishing protocol.* Retrieved September 23, 2011, from http://www.ietf.org/rfc/rfc5023.txt

Hadley, M., Pericas-Geertsen, S., & Sandoz, P. (2010). Exploring hypermedia support in Jersey. *Proceedings of the First International Workshop on RESTful Design (WS-REST '10)* (pp. 10-14). New York, NY: ACM.

Liskin, O., Singer, L., & Schneider, K. (2011). Teaching old services new tricks: Adding HATEOAS support as an afterthought. In C. Pautasso & E. Wilde (Eds.), *Proceedings of the Second International Workshop on RESTful Design (WS-REST '11)* (pp. 3-10). New York, NY: ACM.

Mitra, N., & Lafon, Y. (2007). *SOAP version 1.2 part 0: Primer (2nd ed.): W3C recommendation 27 April 2007.* Retrieved September 28, 2011, from http://www.w3.org/TR/2007/REC-soap12-part0-20070427/

Nottingham, M., & Sayre, R. (2005). *The atom syndication format.* Retrieved September 23, 2011, from http://tools.ietf.org/rfc/rfc4287.txt

Oracle Corporation. (2011a). *GlassFish server open source edition 3.1 quick start guide.* Retrieved September 15, 2011 from http://glassfish.java.net/docs/3.1.1/quick-start-guide.pdf

Oracle Corporation. (2011b). *Jersey 1.9.1 user guide.* Retrieved September 15, 2011, from http://jersey.java.net/nonav/documentation/latest/user-guide.html

Pautasso, C., Zimmermann, O., & Leymann, F. (2008). RESTful web services vs. "big" web services: Making the right architectural decision. In *Proceedings of the 17th International Conference on World Wide Web (WWW'08)* (pp. 805-814). New York, NY: ACM.

Peng, Y.-Y., Ma, S.-P., & Lee, J. (2009). REST-2SOAP: A framework to integrate SOAP services and RESTful services. In *Proceedings of the 2009 IEEE International Conference on Service-Oriented Computing and Applications (SOCA).*

Popescu, A. (2010). *Geolocation API specification: W3C candidate recommendation 07 September 2010.* Retrieved September 28, 2011, from http://www.w3.org/TR/2010/CR-geolocation-API-20100907/

Wehrmaker, T., Gärtner, S., & Schneider, K. (2011). *ConTexter: End-user feedback-driven requirements engineering.* Retrieved January 26, 2012, from http://vimeo.com/twehrmaker/contexter-demonstration

Winer, D. (2003). *XML-RPC specification.* Retrieved September 28, 2011, from http://www.xmlrpc.com/spec

ENDNOTES

1. See http://www.w3.org/TR/geolocation-API/
2. See http://phonegap.com/
3. See http://rhomobile.com/products/rhodes/

Chapter 6
Enterprise Applications:
From Requirements to Design

Christine Choppy
LIPN, University Paris 13, France

Denis Hatebur
University Duisburg-Essen, Germany

Maritta Heisel
University Duisburg-Essen, Germany

Gianna Reggio
Universita di Genova, Italy

ABSTRACT

The authors provide a method to systematically develop enterprise application architectures from problem descriptions. From these descriptions, they derive two kinds of specifications: a behavioral specification describes how the automated business process is carried out. It can be expressed using activity or sequence diagrams. A structural specification describes the classes to be implemented and the operations they provide. The structural specification is created in three steps. All the diagrams are expressed in UML.

1. INTRODUCTION

We provide a method to systematically develop enterprise application architectures from problem descriptions. The problem descriptions are based on Jackson's problem frame approach (Jackson, 2001). For enterprise applications, we have developed a specialized problem frame that takes the specifics of such applications into account

(Choppy & Reggio, 2006). In particular, new domain types – such as *business worker* and *business object* – are introduced. We describe the requirements through problem diagrams that are instances of the enterprise application frame and of other problem frames.

In addition to Jackson's problem frame approach, we represent the business model underlying the business application by a domain

DOI: 10.4018/978-1-4666-2199-2.ch006

knowledge diagram. Such a diagram identifies the domains relevant for the business process to be automated and states how they are related. It serves to analyze the business process to be automated and helps to construct the appropriate instances of the enterprise application frame, thus obtaining the problem diagrams.

From the problem diagrams, we derive two kinds of specifications: a behavioral specification describes how the automated business process is carried out. It can be expressed using activity or sequence diagrams. A structural specification describes the classes to be implemented and the operations they provide. This specification is expressed as a class diagram, where all operations are specified in OCL.

With these different models, we have described the software development problem in a detailed way, taking into account the specifics of business applications. This makes it possible to develop a suitable software architecture in a systematic way. We proceed similarly as described in earlier work (Choppy, Hatebur, & Heisel, 2011), where we derive software architectures from problem descriptions for arbitrary software. In this work, we make use of the fact that the software development problem is decomposed in subproblems that fit to the enterprise application frame. Taking into account the identified business objects, we focus on how these objects can best be stored and accessed. In this context, questions of distributing the software to be developed and the information to be stored are addressed, too.

In a first step, we create an initial architecture. To obtain that architecture, we first have to decide on the responsibilities of the software to be developed (which is called *machine* in the problem frames approach). We have to inspect all domains occurring in the problem diagrams and decide if they will be part of the machine or not. Some domains may reside in the environment but still need to have an internal representation in the machine. The rules given in (Choppy & Reggio, 2006) support this task. Moreover, the initial

architecture reflects the problem decomposition that was obtained by applying the problem frame approach. Each subproblem machine becomes a component in the initial architecture.

The initial architecture need not be implementable, because the interaction between the different components has not yet been taken into account. Therefore, we transform the initial architecture into an implementable architecture. To create the implementable architecture we have to consider technical requirements, for example that some functionality should be implemented on another computer. In business applications, there is usually a database, which may be located on a different computer than the machine we are building. In that case, we have to split the problem diagrams and create corresponding subproblem diagrams that separate the different machines accordingly. Conversely, in many cases, only one database is used to store different kinds of information, such that the components representing the different domains have to be merged into the database component. Moreover, we introduce coordinator components, considering the formal descriptions of the business model, and facade components. Finally, we allocate all machines that solve the different problems or subproblems and the considered domains to physical components of the machine to be built.

The implementable architecture that is obtained in this way does not follow a particular architectural style. If, for example, a layered architecture is wished for, the implementable architecture can further be transformed into a layered one, as is described in (Choppy et al.., 2011).

All the diagrams that we present in this chapter are expressed in UML instead of the original notation used by Jackson (Jackson, 2001). This makes it possible to exploit the additional expressive power provided by UML class diagrams and also to represent software architectures and problem descriptions in the same notational framework. Carrying over the problem-frame approach to UML is achieved by defining a UML profile for problem frames (Hatebur & Heisel, 2010). That profile forms the basis for a tool called UML4PF, which is currently under development at the University of Duisburg-Essen. UML4PF[1] supports requirements analysis using problem frames and deriving software architectures from problem descriptions. It is based on the Eclipse development environment, extended by an EMF-based UML tool. Using UML4PF, users can set up diagrams in UML notation that are translations of the original problem frame notation. Most notably, UML4PF can be used to check semantic validation conditions expressed in OCL. Such conditions concern on the one hand the semantic integrity of single models. One the other hand, also the coherence between different models can be checked.

The work presented here builds on and enhances previous work. The method for deriving architectures from problem descriptions (Choppy et al.., 2011) is now tailored and elaborated, taking the specifics of developing enterprise architectures into account and integrating the business frame presented in (Choppy & Reggio, 2006).

The rest of the chapter is organized as follows. In Section 2, we introduce the basic concepts and notations we use in our work. Section 3 is devoted to the requirements analysis phase that we carry out using the enterprise application frame. As an example, we consider an online shop. Section 4 describes how we derive the architecture of the business application from the problem descriptions set up in the requirements analysis phase. Related work is discussed in Section 5, and we conclude in Section 6.

2. BACKGROUND, CONCEPTS, AND NOTATIONS

In this section, we introduce the basic concepts we use in this work, problem frames that we represent using UML tools, and various diagrams (context diagrams, problem diagrams, domain knowledge diagrams, and composite diagrams), and we express properties using OCL constraints.

2.1 Context Diagrams

The different diagram types make use of the same basic notational elements. As a result, it is necessary to explicitly state the type of diagram by appropriate stereotypes. In our case, the stereotypes are *<<ContextDiagram>>*, *<<ProblemDiagram>>*, *<<ProblemFrame>>*, and *<<TechnicalContextDiagram>>*. These stereotypes extend (some of them indirectly) the meta-class *Package* in the UML meta-model. According to the UML superstructure specification ("UML Revision Task Force", 2009), it is not possible that one UML element is part of several packages. For example a class *Client* should be in the context diagram package and also in some problem diagrams packages.[2] Nevertheless, several UML tools allow one to put the same UML element into several packages within graphical representations. We want to make use of this information from graphical representations and add it to the model (using stereotypes of the profile). Thus, we have to relate the elements inside a package explicitly to the package. This can be achieved with a dependency stereotype *<<isPart>>* from the package to all included elements (e.g., classes, interfaces, comments, dependencies, associations).

The context diagram in the fourth figure contains the machine domain(s), the relevant domains in the environment, and the interfaces between them. Domains are represented by classes with the stereotype *<<Domain>>*, and the machine is marked by the stereotype *<<Machine>>*. Instead of *<<Domain>>*, more specific stereotypes such as *<<BiddableDomain>>*, *<<LexicalDomain>>* or *<<CausalDomain>>* can be used. Since some of the domain types are not disjoint, more than one stereotype can be applied on one class.

2.2 Problem Frames

Problem frames are a means to describe software development problems. They were proposed by Michael Jackson (Jackson, 2001), who describes them as follows:

A problem frame is a kind of pattern. It defines an intuitively identifiable problem class in terms of its context and the characteristics of its domains, interfaces and requirement.

Problem frames are described by frame diagrams, which basically consist of rectangles, a dashed oval, and different links between them, see Figure 1). The task is to construct a *machine* that establishes the desired behavior of the environment (in which it is integrated) in accordance with the requirements.

Rectangles with a domain stereotype denote domains that already exist in the application environment. Jackson (Jackson, 2001, p. 83f) considers three main domain types:

- "A **biddable domain** usually consists of people. The most important characteristic of a biddable domain is that it is physical but lacks positive predictable internal causality. That is, in most situations it is im-

possible to compel a person to initiate an event: the most that can be done is to issue instructions to be followed." Biddable domains are indicated by *B* (e.g., *User* in Figure 1).

- "A **causal domain** is one whose properties include predictable causal relationships among its causal phenomena." Often, causal domains are mechanical or electrical equipment. They are indicated with a *C* in frame diagrams. Their actions and reactions are predictable. Thus, they can be controlled by other domains.

- "A **lexical domain** is a physical representation of data – that is, of symbolic phenomena. It combines causal and symbolic phenomena in a special way. The causal properties allow the data to be written and read." Lexical domains are indicated by *X* (e.g., *Workpieces* in Figure 1).

A rectangle with a double vertical stripe denotes the machine to be developed, and requirements are denoted with a dashed oval. The connecting lines between domains represent interfaces that consist of shared phenomena. Shared phenomena may be events, operation calls, messages, and the like. They are observable by at least two domains, but controlled by only one domain, as indicated

Figure 1. Simple Workpieces problem frame

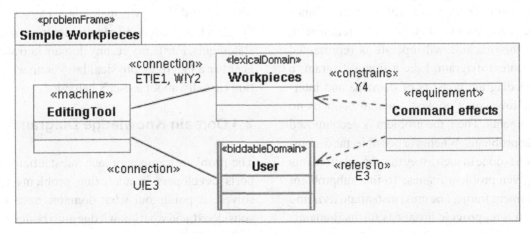

by an exclamation mark. For example, in Figure 1 the notation *U! E3* means that the phenomena in the set *U! E3* are controlled by the domain *User* and observed by the *EditingTool*. To describe the problem context, a connection domain between two other domains may be necessary. Connection domains establish a connection between other domains by means of technical devices. Connection domains are, e.g., video cameras, sensors, or networks.

A dashed line represents a requirement reference, and an arrow indicates that the requirement constrains a domain.[3] If a domain is constrained by the requirement, we must develop a machine, which controls this domain accordingly. In Figure 1, the *Workpieces* domain is constrained, because the *EditingTool* changes it on behalf of user commands to satisfy the required *Command effects*.

Jackson (Jackson, 2001) introduces five basic problem frames (*Transformation, Simple Workpieces, Information Display, Commanded Behaviour* and *Required Behaviour*) that can be combined and/or adapted to fit the problem studied. Research on problem frames led to define more complex problem frames corresponding to large classes of applications (e.g. geographic problem frames (Nelson, Cowan, & Alencar, 2001) for geographic information systems). In previous work, we presented a problem frame for enterprise/business applications (Choppy & Reggio, 2006), and here, we will show how we can use it to develop the system architecture.

Software development with problem frames proceeds as follows: first, the environment in which the machine will operate is represented by a context diagram. Like a frame diagram, a context diagram consists of domains and interfaces. However, a context diagram contains no requirements. Then, the problem is decomposed into subproblems. Whenever possible, the decomposition is done in such a way that the subproblems fit to given problem frames. To fit a subproblem to a problem frame, one must instantiate its frame diagram, i.e., provide instances for its domains,

interfaces, and requirement. The instantiated frame diagram is called a problem diagram.

Besides problem frames, there are other elaborate methods to perform requirements engineering, such as i* (Yu, 1997), Tropos (Bresciani, Perini, Giorgini, Giunchiglia, & Mylopoulos, 2004), and KAOS (Bertrand, Darimont, Delor, Massonet, & Lamsweerde, 1998). These methods are goal-oriented. Each requirement is elaborated by setting up a goal structure. Such a goal structure refines the goal into subgoals and assigns responsibilities to actors for achieving the goal. We have chosen problem frames and not one of the goal-oriented requirements engineering methods to derive architectures, because the elements of problem frames, namely domains, may be mapped to components of an architecture in a fairly straightforward way.

2.3 Problem Diagrams

In a problem diagram (see e.g., the seventh figure the knowledge about a sub-problem described by a set of requirements is represented. A problem diagram consists of sub-machines of the machines given in the context diagram, the relevant domains, the connections between these domains and a requirement (possibly composed of several related requirements), as well as of the relation between the requirement and the involved domains. A requirement refers to some domains and constrains at least one domain. This is expressed using the stereotypes <<*refersTo*>> and <<*constrains*>>. They extend the UML meta-class *Dependency*. Domain knowledge and requirements are special statements. Furthermore, any domain knowledge is either a fact (e.g., physical law) or an assumption (usually about a user's behavior).

2.4 Domain Knowledge Diagrams

The problem frame approach substantially supports developers in analyzing problems to be solved. It points out what domains have to be considered, and what knowledge must be described and reasoned about when analyzing a problem in depth. Developers must elicit, examine, and describe the relevant properties of each domain. These descriptions form the domain knowledge, which is represented by domain knowledge diagrams. Domain knowledge consists of assumptions and facts. Assumptions usually describe required user behavior, whereas facts describe properties of the problem environment, regardless of how the machine is built. To express mandatory behavior of domains in the environment we have introduced domain knowledge diagrams (see e.g., the third figure).

2.5 Composite Diagrams

Composite structure diagrams ("UML Revision Task Force", 2009) are a means to describe architectures (see e.g., the fourteenth figure). They contain named rectangles, called parts. These parts are components of the software. In an object-oriented implementation components are instantiated classes. Each component may contain other (sub-) components. Atomic components can be described by state machines and operations for accessing internal data. In our architectures, components for data storage are only included if the data is stored persistently. Otherwise they are assumed to be part of some other component. Parts may have ports, denoted by small rectangles. Ports may have interfaces associated to them. Provided interfaces are denoted using the "lollipop" nota-

tion, and required interfaces using the "socket" notation. Figure 2 shows how interfaces in problem diagrams are transformed into interfaces in composite structure diagrams.

The partial problem diagram shown on the left-hand side of Figure 2 states that the phenomena *phen1* and *phen2* shared between the machine and a domain are controlled by the machine. In the composite structure diagram (with associated interface class) shown in the middle of Figure 2, this is expressed by a required interface *P1_if* of the part component of the machine, which is the same as for the whole machine. Shared phenomena controlled by a domain correspond to provided instead of required interfaces of the part and the machine, respectively. Because of this direct correspondence, we do not use the socket and lollipop notation in the following, but use connectors between ports as shown on the right-hand side of Figure 2. These connectors can be implemented e.g. as data streams, function calls, asynchronous messages or hardware access.

The architecture of software is multi-faceted: there exists a structural view, a process-oriented view, a function-oriented view, an object-oriented view with classes and relations, and a data flow view on a given software architecture. We use the structural view from UML 2.0 that describes the structure of the software at runtime. After that structure is fixed the interfaces need to be refined using sockets, lollipops and interface classes to describe the possible data flow. Then the cor-

Figure 2. Notation for architectures

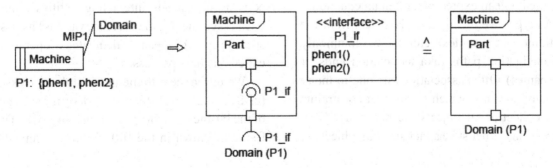

responding active or passive class with its data and operations can be added for each component. Thereby the process-oriented and object-oriented views can be integrated seamlessly into the structural view. That approach and the corresponding process are described in (Heisel & Hatebur, 2005).

2.6 OCL

The Object Constraint Language (OCL) (UML Revision Task Force, 2010, Warmer & Kleppe, 2003) is part of UML ("UML Revision Task Force", 2009). It is a notation to describe constraints on object-oriented modeling artifacts such as class diagrams and sequence diagrams. A constraint is a restriction on one or more elements of an object-oriented model.

OCL constraints are denoted in the UML model they belong to or in a separate document. We only use the constraint type class invariant, which is a constraint that must hold before and after execution of a method, but can be violated during method execution. The basic format of an OCL class invariant is as follows:

context *identifier* **inv**: *boolean expression*

where **context** is a keyword to mark the relative model element indicated by *identifier* from which other model elements can be referenced. The keyword **self** can be used within *boolean expression* to access the **context**. The *identifier* is a class, attribute name, association name, operation name, or the like. The keyword **inv** describes that this constraint is an invariant and *boolean expression* is some boolean expression, often an equation.

As types we mostly use classifiers from the UML model the context refers to. We commonly use navigation paths (aka association ends or role names). Often associations are one-to-many or many-to-many, which means that constraints on a collection of objects are necessary. OCL expressions either state a fact about all objects in the collection using quantification or facts about the collection itself.

3. ENTERPRISE BUSINESS MODELLING: AN APPROACH À LA PROBLEM FRAME

In this section we introduce the Business Frame for enterprises and the associated (UML) Business Model, illustrating both with an application to the *Electronic Commerce* case study.

All in all, we perform the following steps in the requirements analysis phase of business application systems:

1. Set up an enterprise business diagram (domain knowledge diagram).
2. Set up a context diagram.
3. Instantiate Enterprise Application Frame.
4. Derive behavioral specifications.
5. Derive structural specifications.
6. Set up software lifecycle.

We discuss these steps in the following sections.

3.1 Enterprise Business Diagram (Domain Knowledge Diagram)

Before starting the development of an enterprise application it is important to accurately understand and model the business in which the application will operate. This activity is called business modeling and will result in a so-called business model.

We assume that the business to be modeled consists of various interacting entities (called business entities) that achieve the various business-specific goals by means of dedicated cooperations called business processes.

We introduce a frame in the style of Jackson (cf. Sect. 2.2) to help to get abstractly the structure of the business, before modeling it in UML. That frame is shown in the fifth figure. Technically, the business frame is a frame with a domain for each business entity, where the business processes are described in terms of composite phenomena.

The business frame domains (examples can be found in Figure 3), that are the business entities, can be classified as:

- **Business Objects:** The entities which are subject to the business (e.g., a catalogue, an insurance contract document), and are lexical domains. Business objects are passive and cannot cause any events.
- **Business Workers:** The human entities acting in the business (e.g., a manager, a clerk), and are biddable domains.
- **Systems:** Software systems or mechanical apparatus with a role in the business (e.g., Payment System handling the payments or a scanner for paper documents). The systems are causal domains.

The business entities may be further classified in internal and external w.r.t. the business; the internal ones are those under the responsibility of the enterprise managing the business. The rule for deciding whether an entity is internal or external is the following: in case of a reorganization of the business by the managing enterprise, an internal entity may be modified, whereas an external one may not; thus Payment System is external, whereas a stock or a clerk are internal (indeed the enterprise may change the stock organization or the way the clerk works, but not the way the *Payment System* performs). This is displayed using the corresponding stereotypes (e.g. *<<businessObject>>*, *<<businessWorker>>*, *<<externalSystem>>*, etc. in Figure 3). The external entities are marked with the corresponding stereotypes, and their box is left uncolored (e.g., in Figure 3 Payment System is an external system), while for simplicity the stereotypes for the internal ones do not include "internal' but their box is colored.

The classification in internal and external entities is completely orthogonal to the classification in business objects, workers and systems. All these domains are considered as given, and this marking is implicitly assumed.

Figure 3. Electronic commerce domain knowledge diagram

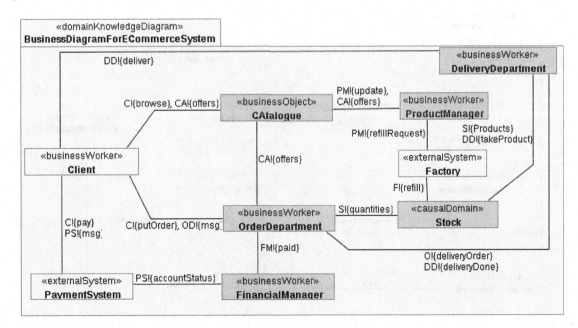

In a Business Frame the domains are connected by composite phenomena that correspond to the business processes. The domains connected in a business process are called the participants of the process. We consider a business process as a cooperation between business workers, business objects and systems (both internal and external).

We illustrate our approach on the *Electronic Commerce* from Choppy & Reggio (2006, 2005), that is a system for selling products via the internet. We consider the following requirements for this system:

R1: A *Client* can browse the offers in the *Catalogue* and check the availability.

R2: When a *Client* puts an order, if the product is available in the stock and the debit request is granted, then the product is taken from the *Stock* (reducing the quantity) and delivered to the *Client*; otherwise, an error message is returned.

R3: The *Product Manager* can update the *Catalogue* (add, remove, change entries).

Figure 3 shows the Domain Knowledge Diagram for our *Electronic Commerce*. This frame exhibits internal business workers (e.g., *Manager*), internal business objects (e.g., *CAtalogue*[4]), and external systems (e.g., *Factory Payment System*).

The activity diagram in the ninth figure shows the behavior of the business workers for the selling process. For the description of the activity before any machine is developed, we have no *StockRepresentation* but the *Stock* itself and the activity *UpdateStockRepresentation* is not necessary.

3.2 Context Diagram

Given the understanding provided in the domain knowledge diagram, the context diagram is then established by introducing the enterprise application to be developed represented by a machine (in Figure 4, machine EC) and its corresponding interfaces to handle the requirements. Note that now the machine *EC* is responsible to handle the client order, which was previously under the responsibility of the *OrderDepartment*.

Figure 4. Electronic commerce context diagram

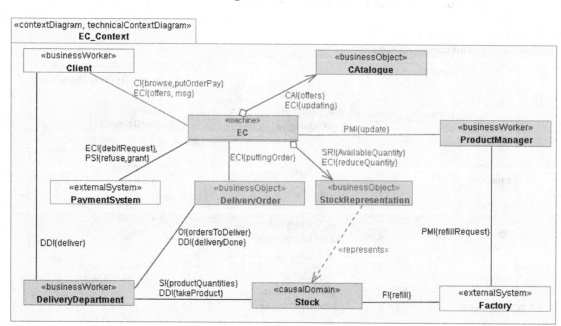

3.3 Enterprise Application Problem Frame

The Enterprise Application problem frame in Figure 5 displays the various kinds of domains to be taken into account (<<*businessObject*>>, <<*businessWorker*>>, <<*externalSystem*>>) in an enterprise application. These domains are interfaced with the requirements through a constraining reference and the relevant phenomena. They are also interfaced with the *EnterpriseApplication* (that is the <<*machine*>> to be developed), and the relevant multiplicity applies. Notice that internal business objects are part of the enterprise application.

In the following, the Enterprise Application problem frame will be instantiated into problem diagrams describing the various subproblems.

Electronic Commerce: Initial Subproblem Description and Problem Diagrams

At this stage, the initial subproblems are identified and described using problem diagrams (instances of the Enterprise Application problem frame).

In our *Electronic Commerce* case study, the initial subproblems are *EC_browse* (Figure 6), *EC_sell* (Figure 7), and *EC_upCat* (update Catalogue) (Figure 8).

Problem *EC_browse* (cf. Figure 6) refers to a causal *Stock* domain with which the machine has no interface. Our approach is to introduce a lexical domain that is a representation of the causal domain with an interface to the machine. We add an assumption (or requirement) stating that the state of the lexical domain corresponds to the state of the causal domain. The rationale is that our business software is not embedded – therefore we do not introduce an interface between the machine and a causal domain being not a computer. We also add new representation domains to the con-

Figure 5. Enterprise application problem frame (EA frame)

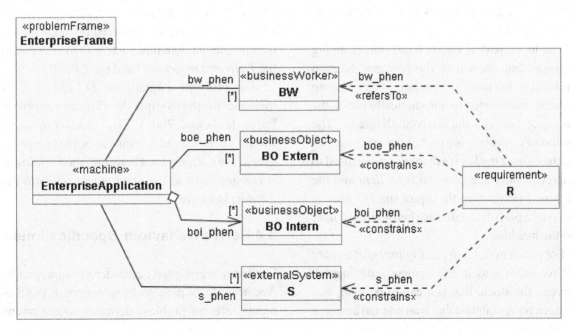

Figure 6. Problem diagram for EC_browse

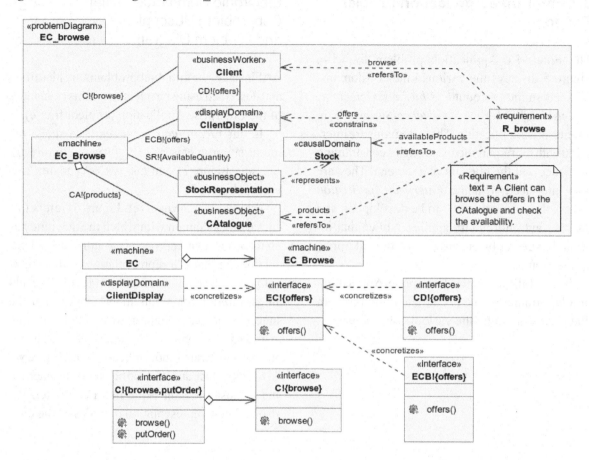

text diagram, and a stereotype for dependency: <<*represents*>>.

The lower part of Figure 6 contains mapping diagrams that show how the problem diagram is related to the context diagram. Such mapping diagrams are needed to automatically check the coherence between the different diagrams. The machine *EC_browse* is a part of the machine *EC*, and the *ClientDisplay* is a display domain used to concretize interface between the *Client* and the machine. Furthermore, the suproblem *EC_browse* uses only a part of the interface between the *Client* and the machine.

For problem *EC_sell* (cf. Figure 7), let us note that we again – as in *EC_browse* – distinguish between the stock, that is a causal domain, and the stock representation that is an internal business

object (with the dependency relation <<*represents*>>). We also show shared phenomena between problem domains, such as *deliver* between the *DeliveryDepartment* and the *Client*.

The problem diagram for *EC_upCat* is an instance of the Simple Workpieces problem frame (Jackson, 2001). The *ProductManager* should be able to add, remove, or change products in the *CAtalogue*. Therefore, the *CAtalogue* is constrained and the requirement refers to the *ProductManager*.

3.4 Derive Behaviour Specifications

Until now, we only have considered requirements. According to the problem frame approach, requirements refer to problem domains. Descriptions

Figure 7. Problem diagram for EC_sell

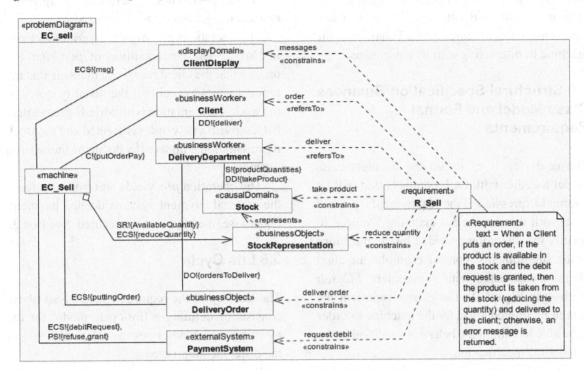

Figure 8. Problem diagram for EC_upCat

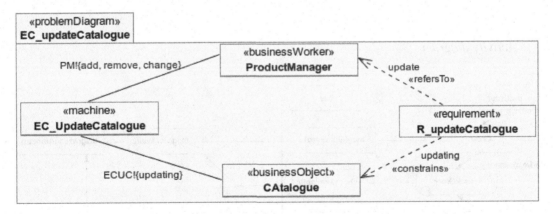

describing the behavior of the machine are called specifications. Specifications are implementable requirements. They are derived from requirements by using domain knowledge. Specifications treat the machine as a black box and describe how the machine reacts to external stimuli and how it behaves in order to achieve the requirements. For more details, see (Jackson & Zave, 1995).

The behavior of the machine can be specified using either activity diagrams or sequence diagrams. Here we present an activity diagram for problem *EC_sell* in Figure 9. Swimlanes are used to structure the diagram with respect to the various actors. As already stated in Section 3.2, the machine *EC_Sell* takes the roles of the *OrderDepartment* and *FinancialManager*. Therefore, the swimlanes of the activity diagram given in Figure 9 annotated with *OrderDepartment* and *FinancialManager* represent the behavior of the machine in interacting with its environment.

3.5 Structural Specification/Business Class Model and Formal Requirements

The next step is to set up the business class model together with OCL contracts that will be a formal expression of the requirements (pre and post) with the initial class diagram. We need to specify the operation provided by the machines in the subproblems. For our example, the class diagram associated with subproblem *EC_sell* is given in Figure 10. The classes represent the data to be implemented by the machine in order to be able to exhibit the behavior specified in the behavioral specification.

The OCL contract for the operation *putOrder-Pay* of the machine *EC_Sell* is given in Box 1. The precondition states that all input data are valid. The postcondition says that the (private) operations *putOrder* and *pay* are called.

The operations *putOrder* and *pay* are defined in Box 2. The postcondition of *putOrder* expresses that the client receives a message that the product is not available if the quantity stored in the stock representation is not strictly greater than 0. Otherwise a new order is created and the stock representation is updated by deducing the ordered quantity.

The operation *pay* yields an error message if the external payment systems decline payment. Otherwise, the payment is executed. See Box 3.

3.6 Life Cycle

The last step of the requirements analysis phase consists of defining a life-cycle model for the machine, which describes the relations between the different subproblems.

We specify the possible activities from the viewpoints of the main actors in terms of the identified subproblems. In our case study, the

Figure 9. Activity diagram

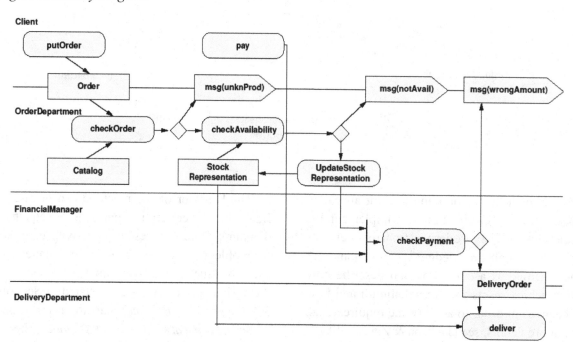

Figure 10. Business class model of EC sell

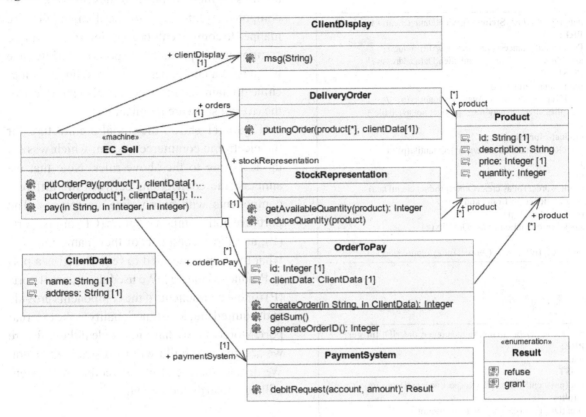

Box 1. OCL contract for putOrderPay of EC_Sell

```
putOrderPay(product: String [*], clientData: ClientData, accountData:
String)
PRE:
Product.allInstances().id->includesAll(product) and
clientData.name<>" and clientData.address<>"
POST:
let otpid: Integer =
putOrder(product,clientData)
in
self.pay(accountData, orderToPay->select(o| o.id = pid)
->asSequence()->first().getSum() otpid)
```

client can browse the catalogue several times before buying some product, which we express by *C=Browse*;Sell*. The managers update the catalogue, as expressed by *M=upCat*. Clients and managers can act in parallel: *System=C∥M*.

We need the life-cycle model later, when we have to decide if a coordinator component should be introduced in the software architecture.

4. ARCHITECTURE

We develop the software architecture for enterprise application systems in two steps. First, we set up an initial architecture that is then transformed into an implementable architecture.

Box 2. Operations putOrder and pay

```
putOrder(product: String [*], clientData: ClientData): Integer
PRE:
Product.allInstances().id->includesAll(product)
and clientData.name<>" and clientData.address<>"
POST:
not product->forAll(p |
stockRepresentation.getAvailableQuantity(p)>0
) implies clientDisplay^msg('product not available')
and
product->forAll(p |
stockRepresentation.getAvailableQuantity(p)>0
)
and
result = orderToPay.createOrder(product,clientData)
->asSequence()->first() and
product->forAll(p |
stockRepresentation^reduceQuantity(p)
)
and orderToPay->size()=orderToPay@pre->size()+1
```

Box 3. Payment

```
pay(accountData: String, sum: Integer, orderID: Integer)
PRE:
true
POST:
not (paymentSystem.debitRequest(accountData,sum)='grant')
implies
clientDisplay.msg('Cannot debit amount')
POST:
paymentSystem.debitRequest(accountData,sum)='grant'
implies
self^paid(orderID)
```

4.1 Initial Architecture

In the initial architecture we collect information from the requirements analysis phase. On the one hand, we decide which domains of the problem diagrams are transformed into components of the software architecture. On the other hand, we transform interfaces of the problem diagrams into ports and interfaces of the software architecture.

First, each machine domain of a problem diagram becomes a component in the initial architecture, which has the same name as the machine domain in the context diagram. Second, business objects become components, because they are lexical and thus can exist only inside the machine. Business workers and external systems

are outside the machine and thus do not become components. Interfaces of the domains that are mapped to components become interfaces to these components (represented by ports). If an interface belongs to a component corresponding to a machine domain, its interfaces are also interfaces of the overall software architecture.

Figure 11 shows the initial architecture for the electronic commerce system, which was set up according to the above rules. Note that we annotate the connections between the different components with appropriate stereotypes. The ports are both component ports (CP) or just ports (P), and the second part of their name refers to what they are connected to (e.g. P_PM is a port to Product Manager). We used the external ports (P) for the components if the components provide and required the same functionality as the external port. Moreover, we have to decide if the software we are going to build will be distributed or not. We decide that the electronic commerce system will be a distributed system.

4.2 Implementable Architecture

In the second step of the architectural design, we transform the initial architecture into an implementable architecture. If the initial architecture is annotated as distributed, it must be decided how the distribution will be achieved. Moreover, if a component is connected to several external ports, a facade component will be introduced. If from the life-cycle model it follows that some interactions have to take place before other interactions can be performed, a coordinator component is necessary.

In our example, we do not need a coordinator component, because placing an order (*Sell*) is possible without prior browsing. However, we decide that for security reasons the processing of orders and the processing of payments should be performed on different computers. As a consequence, we split the problem diagram *EC_sell* into two new problem diagrams as shown in Figures 12 and 13.

Figure 11. Initial architecture of electronic commerce

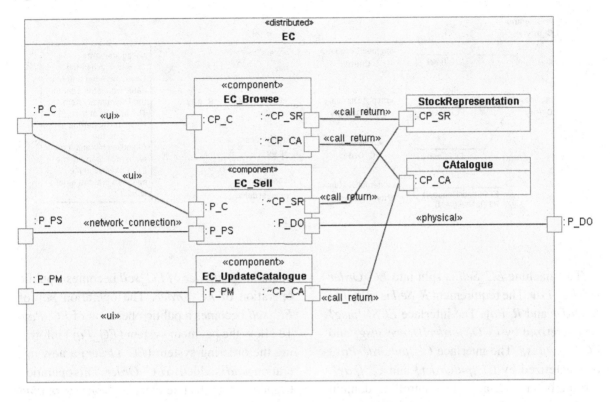

Figure 12. Problem diagram for EC_order

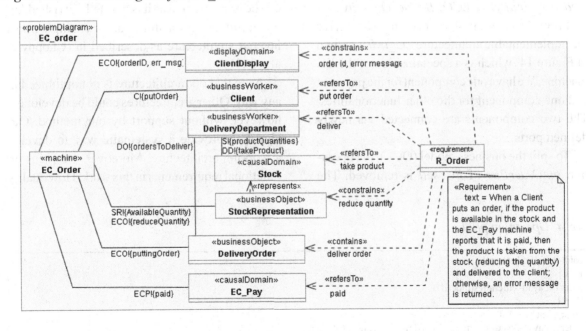

Figure 13. Problem diagram for EC_pay

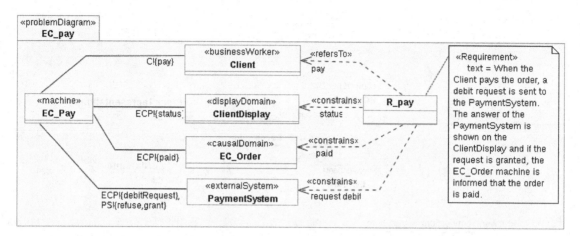

The machine *EC_Sell* is split into *EC_Order* and *EC_Pay*. The requirement *R_Sell* is split into *R_Order* and *R_Pay*. The interface *ECS! {msg}* is concretized by *ECO! {orderID, err_msg}* and *ECP! {status}*. The interface *C! {putOrderPay}* is concretized by *C! {putOrder}* and *C! {pay}*. For the other interfaces the controlling domain needs to be *EC_Order* instead of *EC_Sell*. Therefore the interface names change, e.g., from *ECS! {reduceQuantity}* to *ECO! {reduceQuantity}*.

From the new problem diagrams, we derive the implementable architecture *EC_IMPL* shown in Figure 14, which is a specialization of the EC machine. We have one component for the payment and one component for the other functionalities. The two components are connected via newly defined ports.

To split the business model (OCL), the operation *putOrderPay* of *EC_sell* is removed. The operation *putOrder* of *EC_sell* becomes a public operation of *EC_Order*. The operation *pay* of *EC_sell* becomes a public operation of *EC_Pay*. To allow the payment system (*EC_Pay*) informing the ordering system (*EC_Order*) a new operation *paid* is added to *EC_Order*. This operation triggers the product delivery with *orders^puttingOrder*. See Box 4.

The software architecture given in Figure 14 can be implemented as it is defined. If wished for, it can further be transformed, for example into a layered architecture as described in (Choppy et al.., 2011).

Note that our architecture is not optimized in any way. Other architectures could be developed, however, without support by our method. Our aim is to provide a systematic way to develop a working architecture. Moreover, we focus on functional requirements in this work. How quality

Box 4. Operation paid

```
paid(orderID: Integer)
PRE:
orderToPay.id->includes(orderID)
POST:
let otpay: OrderToPay =
orderToPay->select(otp| otp.id=orderID)->asSequence()->first()
in
orders^puttingOrder(otpay.product.id->asSet(),otpay.clientData)
```

Figure 14. Implementable architecture of electronic commerce

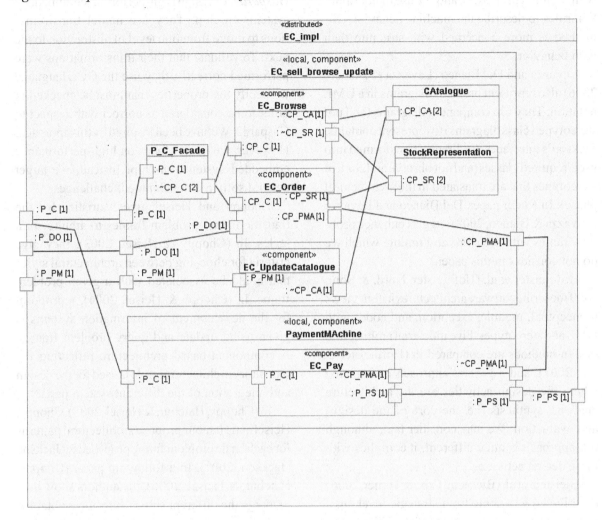

requirements can be taken into account, too, is discussed in (Alebrahim, Hatebur, & Heisel, 2011).

5. RELATED WORK

Hall, Rapanotti et al. (Hall, Jackson, Laney, Nuseibeh, & Rapanotti, 2002, Rapanotti, Hall, Jackson, & Nuseibeh, 2004) introduce architectural concepts into problem frames (introducing "AFrames") so as to benefit from existing architectures. In (Hall et al.., 2002), the applicability of problem frames is extended to include domains with existing architectural support, and to allow

both for an annotated machine domain, and for annotations to discharge the frame concern. In (Rapanotti et al.., 2004), "AFrames" are presented corresponding to the architectural styles Pipe-and-Filter and Model-View-Controller (MVC), and applied to transformation and control problems. In contrast, we keep requirements and architectural documents separate.

Barroca et al. (Barroca, Fiadeiro, Jackson, Laney, & Nuseibeh, 2004) extend the problem frame approach with coordination concepts. This leads to a description of coordination interfaces in terms of services and events (referred to respectively here as actuators and sensors) together with required properties, and the use of coordination rules to describe the machine behavior. Our method is more concerned with structure than with behavior.

Lavazza and Del Bianco (Lavazza & Bianco, 2006) also represent problem diagrams in a UML notation. They use component diagrams (and not stereotyped class diagrams) to represent domains. Jackson's interfaces are directly transformed into used/required classes (and not observe and control stereotypes that are translated in the architectural phase). In a later paper, Del Bianco and Lavazza (Lavazza & Bianco, 2008) suggest enhance problem frames with scenarios and timing, which we do not consider in this paper.

Hofmeister et al. (Hofmeister, Nord, & Soni, 1999) describe software architectures in four views (conceptual, module, execution, and code) with UML and stereotypes. Five industrial architecture design methods are compared in (Hofmeister et al.., 2007), and a general approach is extracted where the design activities are the architecture analysis, synthesis (i.e. the core of the design) and evaluation. We may consider that, although our approach is quite different, it complies with these design activities.

Bleistein et al. (Bleistein, Cox, & Verner, 2006) describe how to come from strategic level business requirements to machine level requirements. They also use problem diagrams, but combine them with VMOST (Sondhi, 1999). VMOST is a technique for deconstructing business strategies into core components. The presented approach complements our procedure for deriving the specifications of the components in the implementable architecture.

Attribute Driven Design (ADD) (Wojcik et al., 2006) is a method to design a conceptual architecture. It focuses on the high-level design of an architecture, and hence does not support detailed design.

Charfi et al. (Charfi, Gamatié, Honoré, Dekeyser, & Abid, 2008) use a modelling framework,

Gaspard2, to design high-performance embedded systems-on-chip. They use model transformations to move from one level of abstraction to the next. To validate that their transformations were performed correctly, they use the OCL language to specify the properties that must be checked in order to be considered as correct with respect to Gaspard2. We have been inspired by this approach. However, we do not focus on high-performance embedded systems-on-chip. Instead, we target general software development challenges.

Choppy and Heisel give heuristics for the transition from problem frames to architectural styles. In (Choppy & Heisel, 2003), they give criteria for choosing between architectural styles that could be associated with a given problem frame. In (Choppy & Heisel, 2004), a proposal for the development of information systems is given using update and query problem frames. A component-based architecture reflecting the repository architectural style is used for the design and integration of the different system parts.

In (Choppy, Hatebur, & Heisel, 2005), Choppy, Heisel and Hatebur propose architectural patterns for each basic problem frame proposed by Jackson (Jackson, 2001). In a follow-up paper (Choppy, Hatebur, & Heisel, 2006), the authors show how to merge the different sub-architectures obtained according to the patterns presented in (Choppy et al., 2005), based on the relationship between the subproblems. Hatebur and Heisel (Hatebur & Heisel, 2009) show how interface descriptions for layered architectures can be derived from problem descriptions.

In a more recent paper (Choppy et al.., 2011), Choppy, Heisel and Hatebur describe how to derive software architectures from problem diagrams in a general setting. This paper emphasizes the integrity conditions that have to hold for the different models that are set up in the process.

6. CONCLUSION AND PERSPECTIVES

In this chapter, we have presented a method that supports the development of enterprise application systems. It covers the phases requirements analysis and architectural design. Requirements analysis is based on a specialization of the problem frame approach to enterprise applications, in particular, a specific enterprise application frame. The business processes to be automated are explicitly represented using domain knowledge diagrams. The result of the requirements analysis phase is a set of problem diagrams, each covering a relevant aspect of the software development problem. These diagrams form the basis of the architectural design phase, which makes use of the information collected in the analysis phase. The architectural design takes into account the specifics of enterprise application systems, in particular the business objects that have to be stored appropriately, often using databases.

Different diagrams expressed in UML are set up during requirements analysis as well as architectural design.

In summary, the contributions of our work are the following:

- We provide a systematic development method for enterprise systems, based on well-structured requirements documents.
- The specifics of enterprise systems are taken into account by specific domain types and a specialized enterprise problem frame.
- From the problem description, most interfaces and the data specification can be derived in a systematic way.
- The different artifacts developed with our method are linked; thus, traceability and change propagation are supported.
- The method is tool-supported, which relieves developers of tedious modeling and validation tasks.

Future work on this trend includes to adapt and extend the validation conditions to take into account the enterprise problem frame and our approach that includes domain knowledge diagrams and diagrams to describe the behavior (here activity diagram). We also intend to semi-automatically generate the architectures for enterprise systems.

REFERENCES

Alebrahim, A., Hatebur, D., & Heisel, M. (2011). A method to derive software architectures from quality requirements. In T. D. Thu & K. Leung (Eds.), *Proceedings of the 18th Asia-Pacific Software Engineering Conference (APSEC)* (pp. 322–330). IEEE Computer Society.

Barroca, L., Fiadeiro, J. L., Jackson, M., Laney, R. C., & Nuseibeh, B. (2004). Problem frames: A case for coordination. In *Coordination Models and Languages, Proceedings 6th International Conference Coordination* (pp. 5-19).

Bertrand, P., Darimont, R., Delor, E., Massonet, P., & van Lamsweerde, A. (1998). GRAIL/KAOS: An environment for goal driven requirements engineering. In *ICSE'98 - 20th International Conference on Software Engineering.*

Bleistein, S. J., Cox, K., & Verner, J. (2006, Mar). Validating strategic alignment of organizational IT requirements using goal modeling and problem diagrams. *Journal of Systems and Software, 79*(3), 362–378. doi:10.1016/j.jss.2005.04.033

Bresciani, P., Perini, A., Giorgini, P., Giunchiglia, F., & Mylopoulos, J. (2004). Tropos: An agent-oriented software development methodology. *Autonomous Agents and Multi-Agent Systems, 8*(3), 203–236. doi:10.1023/B:AGNT.0000018806.20944.ef

Charfi, A., Gamatié, A., Honoré, A., Dekeyser, J. L., & Abid, M. (2008). Validation de modèles dans un cadre d'IDM dédié à la conception de systèmes sur puce. In *4èmes Jounées sur L'ingénierie Dirigée par les Modèles (IDM 08).*

Choppy, C., Hatebur, D., & Heisel, M. (2005). Architectural patterns for problem frames. *IEE Proceedings – Software, Special Issue on Relating Software Requirements and Architectures, 152*(4), 198–208.

Choppy, C., Hatebur, D., & Heisel, M. (2006). Component composition through architectural patterns for problem frames. In *Proc. XIII Asia Pacific Software Engineering Conference (APSEC)* (pp. 27–34). IEEE.

Choppy, C., Hatebur, D., & Heisel, M. (2011). Systematic architectural design based on problem patterns. In Avgeriou, P., Grundy, J., Hall, J., Lago, P., & Mistrik, I. (Eds.), *Relating software requirements and architectures* (pp. 133–159). Springer. doi:10.1007/978-3-642-21001-3_9

Choppy, C., & Heisel, M. (2003). Use of patterns in formal development: Systematic transition from problems to architectural designs. In *Recent Trends in Algebraic Development Techniques, 16th WADT, Selected Papers* (pp. 205–220). Springer Verlag.

Choppy, C., & Heisel, M. (2004). Une approche à base de "patrons" pour la spécification et le développement de systèmes d'information. In *Proceedings Approches Formelles dans L'assistance au Développement de Logiciels* (pp. 61–76). AFADL.

Choppy, C., & Reggio, G. (2005). A UML-based approach for problem frame oriented software development. *Journal of Information and Software Technology, 47*, 929–954. doi:10.1016/j.infsof.2005.08.006

Choppy, C., & Reggio, G. (2006). Requirements capture and specification for enterprise applications: A UML based attempt. In J. Han & M. Staples (Eds.), *Proc of the Australian Software Engineering Conference (ASWEC 2006), IEEE* (p. 19-28).

Hall, J. G., Jackson, M., Laney, R. C., Nuseibeh, B., & Rapanotti, L. (2002, 9-13 September). Relating software requirements and architectures using problem frames. In *Proceedings of IEEE International Requirements Engineering Conference (RE'02).* Essen, Germany.

Hatebur, D., & Heisel, M. (2009). Deriving software architectures from problem descriptions. In *Software Engineering 2009 – Workshop Band* (pp. 383–302). GI.

Hatebur, D., & Heisel, M. (2010). Making pattern- and model-based software development more rigorous. In J. S. Dong & H. Zhu (Eds.), *Proceedings of International Conference on Formal Engineering Methods (ICFEM)* (LNCS Vol. 6447, pp. 253–269). Springer.

Heisel, M., & Hatebur, D. (2005). A model-based development process for embedded systems. In T. Klein, B. Rumpe, & B. Schätz (Eds.), *Proceedings of the Workshop on Model-Based Development of Embedded Systems.* Technical University of Braunschweig. Retrieved from http://www.sse.cs.tu-bs.de/publications/MBEES-Tagungsband.pdf

Hofmeister, C., Kruchten, P., Nord, R. L., Obbink, H., Ran, A., & America, P. (2007). A general model of software architecture design derived from five industrial approaches. *Journal of Systems and Software, 80*(1), 106–126. doi:10.1016/j.jss.2006.05.024

Hofmeister, C., Nord, R. L., & Soni, D. (1999). Describing software architecture with UML. In *Proceedings of the First Working IFIP Conference on Software Architecture* (pp. 145–160). Kluwer Academic Publishers.

Jackson, M. (2001). *Problem frames: Analyzing and Structuring Software Development Problems*. Addison-Wesley.

Jackson, M., & Zave, P. (1995). Deriving specifications from requirements: an example. In *Proceedings of 17th International Conference on Software Engineering* (pp. 15–24). ACM Press.

Lavazza, L., & Bianco, V. D. (2006). Combining problem frames and UML in the description of software requirements. *Fundamental Approaches to Software Engineering, LNCS 3922*.

Lavazza, L., & Bianco, V. D. (2008, February). Enhancing problem frames with scenarios and histories in UML-based software development. *Expert Systems - The Journal of Knowledge Engineering, 25*(1).

Nelson, M., Cowan, D., & Alencar, P. (2001). Geographic problem frames. In *Fifth IEEE International Symposium on Requirements Engineering* (pp. 306–307).

Rapanotti, L., Hall, J. G., Jackson, M., & Nuseibeh, B. (2004, 6-10 September). Architecture driven problem decomposition. In *Proceedings of 12th IEEE International Requirements Engineering Conference (RE'04)*. Kyoto, Japan.

Sondhi, R. (1999). *Total strategy*. Airworthy Publications International Ltd.

UML Revision Task Force. (2009, February). *OMG unified modeling language: Superstructure*. Retrieved from http://www.omg.org/docs/formal/09-02-02.pdf

UML Revision Task Force. (2010, February). *Object constraint language specification*.

Warmer, J., & Kleppe, A. (2003). *The object constraint language 2.0: Getting your models ready for MDA* (2nd ed.). Pearson Education.

Wojcik, R., Bachmann, F., Bass, L., Clements, P., Merson, P., & Nord, R. (2006). *Attribute-driven design (ADD) (Version 2.0)*. Software Engineering Institute.

Yu, E. (1997). Towards modelling and reasoning support for early-phase requirements engineering. In *Proceedings of the 3rd IEEE International Symposium on Requirements Engineering* (pp. 226 – 235).

ENDNOTES

[1] Available at http://uml4pf.org

[2] Alternatively, we could create several Client classes, but these would have to have different names.

[3] In the following, since we use UML tools to draw problem frame diagrams, all requirement references will be represented by dashed lines with arrows and stereotypes *<<refersTo>>*, or *<<constrains>>* when it is constraining reference.

[4] *CAtalogue* controls phenomena CA! {offers}, hence its name with a capital A.

Chapter 7
Using Genetic Algorithms to Search for Key Stakeholders in Large–Scale Software Projects

Soo Ling Lim
University College London, UK

Mark Harman
University College London, UK

Angelo Susi
Fondazione Bruno Kessler, Italy

ABSTRACT

Large software projects have many stakeholders. In order for the resulting software system and architecture to be aligned with the enterprise and stakeholder needs, key stakeholders must be adequately consulted and involved in the project. This work proposes the use of genetic algorithms to identify key stakeholders and their actual influence in requirements elicitation, given the stakeholders' requirements and the actual set of requirements implemented in the project. The proposed method is applied to a large real-world software project. Results show that search is able to identify key stakeholders accurately. Results also indicate that many different good solutions exist. This implies that a stakeholder has the potential to play a key role in requirements elicitation, depending on which other stakeholders are already involved. This work demonstrates the true complexity of requirements elicitation – all stakeholders should be consulted, but not all of them should be treated as key stakeholders, even if they appear to be significant based on their role in the domain.

DOI: 10.4018/978-1-4666-2199-2.ch007

INTRODUCTION

Large software projects are complex. They involve thousands, or even hundreds of thousands of stakeholders (Cleland-Huang & Mobasher, 2008). These stakeholders range from customers who pay for the software system, to users who interact with the system, developers who build and maintain the system, and legislators who impose rules on the development and operation of the system. They have different and sometimes conflicting requirements. They also have different degrees of influence on the project (Glinz & Wieringa, 2007).

In order for the resulting software system and architecture to be aligned with the enterprise and stakeholder needs, the stakeholders' voices must be heard (Lim & Finkelstein, 2011). In addition, key stakeholders – stakeholders who contribute significant and valuable information to the requirements elicitation process – must be identified and engaged throughout the project (Gause & Weinberg, 1989; Glinz & Wieringa, 2007). Nevertheless, stakeholders can lack knowledge, interest or time to be adequately involved in the project (Alexander & Robertson, 2004). Previous studies have found that most developers experience difficulty identifying and engaging with key stakeholders (Alexander & Robertson, 2004; Gause & Weinberg, 1989). As a result, software projects often fail due to the omission of these stakeholders and lack of input from them (Lim, 2010).

This paper focuses on discovering key stakeholders who influence the outcome of requirements elicitation. In large projects, this is a known challenge (Cheng & Atlee, 2007). To consider all stakeholders would be impractical and often infeasible. However, considering only a subset of stakeholders is risky. As requirements are elicited from stakeholders, involving the wrong set of people gives rise to incomplete requirements, which leads to the development of the wrong product.

Previous work proposes the use of social network analysis – a technique increasingly being used in software engineering – to identify and prioritise stakeholders (Lim, Quercia, & Finkelstein, 2010). However, such approaches make the assumption that the stakeholders' influence in the project is determined solely by their position in the network, which does not always hold (Lim et al., 2010). Exactly how to determine if an individual is a key stakeholder is not well understood.

This work proposes the use of genetic algorithms to identify key stakeholders and their *actual* influence in a project, given the stakeholders' requirements priorities and the actual priorities of the requirements that are implemented in the project. The aim of the work is to increase the understanding of key stakeholders using search-based techniques. In addition, the proposed method can be used in an incremental development process in which the analyst applies the method to the data collected from the previous increment, and use the results to inform elicitation in the current increment. This is one of the first applications of search-based techniques to analyse software project stakeholders. Stakeholder analysis is an ideal candidate for genetic algorithms, because the direct calculation of influence is not feasible as the search space is vast, noisy and multimodal, yet the evaluation of candidate solutions is fast (Goldberg, 1989). The proposed method is applied to data collected from a large real-world software project. The results are analysed using quantitative data collected from project documentation and stakeholder interviews.

The rest of the paper is organised as follows. The next section describes the background and related work, and the section after that introduces the proposed search-based technique for stakeholder analysis. The evaluation section describes the research questions, the large-scale software project used in the study, and the experiments. It also reports the results of the study. The final sections discuss future work and conclude.

BACKGROUND

Social Networks for Stakeholder Analysis

In requirements elicitation, recent work proposed the use of social network analysis to identify and prioritise stakeholders in large software projects (Lim et al., 2010). A web-based tool has been developed to support the method and has been used in more than ten software projects (Lim, Damian, & Finkelstein, 2011). In this method, stakeholders are asked to recommend other stakeholders who should be involved in the project. A recommendation is a triple:

<stakeholder name, stakeholder role, salience>

where stakeholder role is the stakeholder's position or customary function in the project (Sharp, Galal, & Finkelstein, 1999), salience is a number on an ordinal scale (e.g., 1–5) indicating the stake-holder's influence in the project (e.g., 1 is low influence and 5 is high influence), as perceived by the stakeholder who made the recommendation. An example recommendation from Bob is <Alice, data protection officer, 4>.

The recommendations are used to build a social network in which the nodes are the stakeholders and the links are their recommendations. Then, various social network measures (Table 1) are used to prioritise the stakeholders. Each social network measure produces a score for each stakeholder. Stakeholders with the same roles are grouped together. Roles are ranked based on the highest scores of their constituent stakeholders, and within roles, stakeholders are ranked based on their scores (Lim et al., 2010). The output is a prioritised list of stakeholder roles, and for each role, a prioritised list of stakeholders, ordered by decreasing score. The previous work has found that the betweenness centrality measure produced the most accurate result (Lim et al., 2010), and subsequent previous work has used the measure to

Table 1. Social network measures

Measure	Prioritisation of Stakeholder S in a Network (Lim et al., 2010)	Assumptions
Betweenness Centrality (Brandes, 2001)	Sums the number of shortest paths between pairs of stakeholders that pass through S.	Stakeholders who are widely recommended by disparate groups of stakeholders are more influential.
Load Centrality (Brandes, 2008)	Sums the amount of information passing through S.	The links between stakeholders represent information flow, and stakeholders with more information flowing through them are more influential.
Closeness Centrality (Scott, 2000)	Sums the inverse average shortest-path distance from S to all reachable stakeholders.	The faster it is for stakeholders' recommendation to reach S the more influential S is.
PageRank (Page, Brin, Motwani, & Winograd, 1999)	A stakeholder strongly recommended by many highly ranked stakeholders is ranked higher, and the recommendations of a highly ranked stakeholder have more weight, which, in turn, raises the ranking of their recommended stakeholders.	Stakeholders who receive more recommendations are more influential and their recommendations are more accurate.
Degree Centrality (Scott, 2000)	Ranks S using the number of recommendations that S makes and receives.	Stakeholders who make and receive a lot of recommendations are more influential.
In-Degree Centrality (Scott, 2000)	Ranks S using the number of recommendations that S receives.	Stakeholders who receive a lot of recommendations are more influential.
Out-Degree Centrality (Scott, 2000)	Ranks S using the number of recommendations that S makes.	Stakeholders who make a lot of recommendations are more influential.

weight stakeholders for requirements prioritisation (Lim & Finkelstein, 2011). This existing method is used as the baseline approach in this work for comparison purposes.

Social network analysis has been widely used in software engineering. For example, Lopez-Fernandez, Robles, and Gonzalez-Barahona (2004) used social networks to analyse the information in software revision control repositories; Damian, Marczak, and Kwan (2007) used social network analysis to study collaboration, communication, and awareness among project team members. Previous work has also used social network analysis to predict software failure. For example, Zimmermann and Nagappan (2008) used social networks to predict programs that are more likely to have defects. Wolf, Schroter, Damian, and Nguyen (2009) used social network analysis to predict whether a software integration will fail based on the communication structures of software project teams. Meneely, Williams, Snipes, and Osborne (2008) modelled developer collaboration relationships using social networks and showed that it can help to predict software failures at the file level.

Search-Based Software Engineering

Search-based software engineering is a field that applies search-based optimisation techniques to address software engineering problems. A wide range of optimisation techniques has been used, such as local search, simulated annealing, genetic algorithms, and genetic programming, as reviewed in (Harman, 2007). These techniques have been applied to various software engineering activities such as requirements analysis, project management, software refactoring, test data generation, and bug fixing, as reviewed in (Harman, 2007). A common characteristic in these works is that perfect solutions are impractical or impossible in many software engineering problems (Harman, 2007). As such, metaheuristic search-based optimisation techniques are used to search for

good solutions. The search is guided by a fitness function, which serves to differentiate good solutions from poor ones. This shifts the emphasis from solution construction to solution description, and the researcher defines what is required rather than how the solution should be constructed. The search-based methods are then left to generate creative solutions for the defined fitness function.

This work uses a genetic algorithm (GA) as the search-based technique. A GA is an algorithm that mimics biological evolution as a problem-solving strategy (Goldberg, 1989). Given a specific problem, the input to the GA is a set of potential solutions to that problem, and a metric called a fitness function that allows each candidate to be quantitatively evaluated. Candidate solutions are often randomly generated, but they can also be known solutions, and the aim of the GA is to improve them. The algorithm is as follows:

1. Randomly generate an initial population.
2. Compute and save the fitness for each individual in the current population.
3. Define selection probabilities for each individual in the current population so that the selection probabilities is proportional to the fitness for each individual.
4. Generate a new population by probabilistically selecting individuals from the current population to produce offspring via genetic operators.
5. Repeat Step 2 until the maximum number of generations is reached or until an acceptable fitness score is obtained.

In requirements engineering, the application of search-based techniques focuses on requirements optimisation and prioritisation. For example, in software release planning, Greer and Ruhe (2004) used genetic algorithm-based approaches to optimise requirements allocation, and assess and optimise the extent to which the ordering conflicts with stakeholder priorities. Tonella, Susi, and Palma (2010) proposed prioritising requirements using interactive genetic algorithms and constraint handling. Zhang (2010) used multi-objective search-based techniques to optimise requirements in different contexts, such as balancing requirements and resources, and balancing the extent of requirements satisfaction for each stakeholder. Finkelstein, Harman, Mansouri, Ren, and Zhang (2009) proposed using search to analyse the tradeoffs between different stakeholders' notions of fairness in requirements allocation, where there are multiple stakeholders with potentially conflicting requirement priorities and different views of what constitutes a fair solution.

Despite the recent interest in search-based requirements optimisation, little work has been conducted on using search-based techniques to analyse stakeholders. The only previous work related to this topic is the recent work which explored the use of evolutionary computation to analyse the relationship between stakeholders' social networks and their involvement in the project (Lim & Bentley, 2011). The work builds different model social networks to represent various types of stakeholder activity in a project. Then, it uses Cartesian Genetic Programming to correlate the social network of a real software project against each model.

SEARCHING FOR KEY STAKEHOLDERS

This work proposes the use of search as a method to identify key software project stakeholders:

1. A list of requirements and corresponding requirement priorities for each stakeholder.
2. The actual priorities of the list of requirements implemented in the project (based on post project knowledge).
3. The assumption that more influential stakeholders are more likely to make the priorities of the project requirements resemble their personal priorities.

Given these, this work proposes to use a genetic algorithm (GA) to search for the real influence of each stakeholder in the project.

The work assumes that the project team has used existing requirements elicitation methods (e.g., use cases or goal modelling (van Lamsweerde, 2009)) to produce a set of requirements for the project. Requirements are defined at different levels of abstraction, and a high-level requirement can be refined into several more specific requirements (van Lamsweerde, 2009). As such, the requirements are organised in a hierarchy (Figure 1). Achieving all the lower-level require-

Figure 1. Hierarchy of requirements

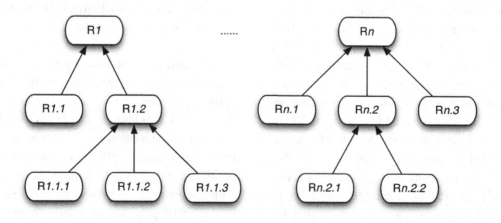

ments belonging to the same parent requirement means that the parent requirement is achieved. An example hierarchy of requirements for an access control system can be seen in Figure 2.

Each stakeholder assigns ratings to the set of requirements identified by the project team. A rating is a number on an ordinal scale (e.g., 1–5) reflecting the importance of the requirement to the stakeholder (e.g., 1 means that the requirement is not very important to the stakeholder; 5 means that the requirement is very important). Different stakeholders can have different ratings on the same requirements (Greer & Ruhe, 2004; Lim & Finkelstein, 2011). The set of requirements identified by the project team may be incomplete. As such, stakeholders can also provide other requirements not already in the set and rate the requirements. Stakeholders are asked to rate requirements rather than rank them, because previous work has shown that large projects can have hundreds of requirements, and stakeholders experienced difficulty providing a rank order of requirements when there are many requirements (Lim & Finkelstein, 2011).

Each requirement is assigned an *Importance* value, calculated using Equation 1:

$$Importance_R = \sum_{i=1}^{n} ProjectInfluence_i \times r_i$$

(1)

where *ProjectInfluence*$_i$ is a value denoting stakeholder *i*'s influence in the project, r_i is the rating

provided by stakeholder *i* on requirement *R*, and *n* is the total number of stakeholders who rated on requirement *R* (Lim & Finkelstein, 2011). (In the existing method, the *ProjectInfluence* value is calculated using social networking measures of stakeholder recommendation networks sorted by the stakeholders' role in the project, as described in the background section, with details of the calculation available in Lim and Finkelstein (2011).)

The requirements are ranked based on their *Importance* value, whereby requirements with higher *Importance* values are ranked higher. In assigning the ranks, fractional ranking (also known as "1 2.5 2.5 4" ranking) is used such that if a tie in ranks occurs, the mean of the ranks involved is assigned to each of the tied items. The requirements are prioritised within their hierarchy, so that the output is a ranked list of high-level requirements, for each high-level requirement, a ranked list of requirements, and for each requirement, a ranked list of specific requirements.

Using this method, the project team arrives with a prioritised list of requirements. Nevertheless, the *ProjectInfluence* values are an approximation of the stakeholders' real influence in the project, especially in large projects where no individuals have the global perspective (Cleland-Huang & Mobasher, 2008). Errors in these values produce incorrect prioritisation of the requirements. Throughout the project, incorrectly prioritised requirements will surface, and be rectified as the project continues. For example, stakeholders who are overlooked will voice their requirements

Figure 2. Example hierarchy of requirements

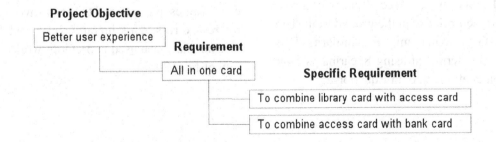

during the project, and in the worst case, after the system has been deployed (Lim & Finkelstein, 2011). Hence, after the system has been deployed, post project knowledge reveals the actual priority of the requirements in the project. This actual prioritisation of requirements project is known as the ground truth and can be collated from project documentation (in a well-documented project) (Lim, 2010).

With the ground truth and the stakeholders' ratings on the requirements, the stakeholders' actual *ProjectInfluence* can be derived. In this work, key stakeholders are determined by the actual *ProjectInfluence* values – the higher the value, the more influential the stakeholders. The GA is used to evolve the *ProjectInfluence* values in order to search for good solutions, i.e., a set of *ProjectInfluence* values such that the resulting prioritised list of requirements (using Equation 1) is close to the ground truth. A simple binary-coded elitist GA with tournament selection, single point crossover and bitwise mutation is used (Bentley & Wakefield, 1997; Goldberg, 1989). The phenotype is defined as an array of weights, one for each stakeholder in the project who has provided ratings. Weights are coded in the genotype as 8 bit binary numbers, each corresponding to a positive integer with the range from 0 to 255. Using this method, key stakeholders – those who positively influence the end result of the prioritisation – will be identified, with their project influence values determined by the weights. Stakeholders whose requirements are not needed can be removed entirely by setting their weight to zero.

The fitness of the solution corresponds to the similarity between the priority of the requirements produced from the evolved *ProjectInfluence* values and their priority in the ground truth. The aim of the GA is to maximise the similarity. This similarity is determined using Spearman's rank correlation coefficient, ρ, in Equation 2:

$$\rho = \frac{\sum_{i=1}^{n}(x_i - \overline{x})(y_i - \overline{y})}{\sqrt{\sum_{i=1}^{n}(x_i - \overline{x})^2 \sum_{i=1}^{n}(y_i - \overline{y})^2}} \tag{2}$$

where n is the total number of requirements, x_i is the rank for requirement i in the prioritised list of requirements produced using the evolved *ProjectInfluence* values and y_i is the rank for requirement i in the ground truth. Values of ρ range from +1 (perfect correlation), through 0 (no correlation), to −1 (perfect negative correlation). A positive ρ means that high priorities in the ground truth list are associated with high priorities in the list of identified requirements. As the requirements are organised in a hierarchy (Figure 1), the fitness is calculated differently depending on the level of hierarchy being evaluated. For the top-level requirements (R_1 to R_n in Figure 1), the fitness is simply the rank correlation for requirements R_1 to R_n (using Equation 2). For the second-level requirements ($R_{1.1}$ to $R_{n.3}$ in Figure 1), rank correlation is measured for each list of second-level requirements with the same parent (ρ_1 for $R_{1.1}$ and $R_{1.2} \ldots \rho_n$ for $R_{n.1}$ to $R_{n.3}$). Then, the fitness is the average correlation for all the lists calculated using Equation 3:

$$\rho_{average} = \frac{\rho_1 + \rho_2 \ldots + \rho_n}{n} \tag{3}$$

The fitness for the third-level requirements is calculated the same way as the second-level requirements. Finally, if the ground truth has a rank order, but the rank returned by the GA has equal values, ρ is mapped to zero to avoid divide by zero errors. This hierarchical based fitness measure has been used in previous work (Lim & Finkelstein, 2011).

EVALUATION

The experiments investigate the ability of the GA to search for the stakeholder weights in a real-world software project, given their ratings on the requirements and the ground truth. The evaluation asks the following research questions and aims to increase our understanding about key stakeholders.

RQ1. GA vs. Existing Method: As mentioned in the previous section, the existing method calculates project influence using the output from betweenness centrality sorted by the stakeholders' roles in the project (Lim & Finkelstein, 2011). This measure was used in the existing method because previous work (Lim & Finkelstein, 2011; Lim et al., 2010) found it to be most accurate in prioritising stakeholder roles among the measures described in the background section. Using this method, a stakeholder with a low score may be ranked high, if he shares the same role with a stakeholder with a high score. RQ1 asks: How does the solution from the existing method compare to the solutions identified by the GA?

RQ2. Social Network Measures: The use of social network measures sorted by stakeholder roles assumes that stakeholders' influence is determined by their role in the project (Lim & Finkelstein, 2011). RQ2 investigates the assumption by asking: How optimal are the raw outputs from social network measures (not sorted by roles) compared to the output from the existing method (sorted by roles)? Can the GA optimise the raw outputs from the social network measures further?

RQ3. All or Nothing: Traditional requirements engineering methods involve a small subset of stakeholders, but recent work has proposed inclusive methods that involve all stakeholders (Cleland-Huang & Mobasher, 2008). RQ3 asks: Can the GA find better results if it begins with the assumption that all stakeholders should be involved, or if it begins with no stakeholders involved?

RQ4. Rating Effect: Besides the project influence value, the importance value for each requirement also depends on the stakeholders' ratings. Previous work has shown that it is not always possible to elicit complete rating values from the stakeholders, and the data cleaning used to populate missing data fields may distort the stakeholders' actual intentions, causing a bias in the results (Lim & Finkelstein, 2011). RQ4 asks: How does data cleaning of rating values affect the results?

RALIC Datasets

RALIC is the acronym for Replacement Access, Library and ID Card. RALIC was a large-scale software project to replace the existing access control system at University College London and consolidate the new system with library access and borrowing. RALIC has a large and complex stakeholder base with more than 60 stakeholder groups and approximately 30,000 users. Besides students, staff and visitors who use the system, the project stakeholders include faculty and academic departments, as well as administrative divisions such as the estates and facilities division, human resource division that manages staff information, library systems, security systems, and so on. These stakeholders have different and sometimes conflicting requirements. The project duration was 2.5 years, and the system has already been deployed at UCL.

In this work, the following datasets from the RALIC project were used (Lim, 2010). The RALIC datasets are available at: http://www.cs.ucl.ac.uk/staff/S.Lim/phd/dataset.html. For reasons of privacy, the names of stakeholders were annonymised in this paper.

- **Recommendations:** The RALIC stakeholders were surveyed to collect their recommendations on other stakeholders. A total of 68 stakeholders provided recommendations and 127 stakeholders were identified. Recommendation data is used to build the social network of stakeholders.

- **Raw Ratings:** The stakeholders rated a predefined list of requirements, from 0 (not important) to 5 (very important), and −1 for requirements they actively do not want. Stakeholders also added requirements not in the predefined list and rated those requirements. The requirements were organised into a hierarchy of three levels: project objectives, requirements, and specific requirements. A total of 76 stakeholders provided their ratings. All unrated requirements at any level of the hierarchy are given a rating of zero.

- **Propagated Ratings:** The previous work (Lim & Finkelstein, 2011) cleaned the raw ratings data to eliminate missing data as follows. If a stakeholder rates a high-level requirement but does not rate the lower-level requirements, then his rating propagates down to the lower-level requirements. If a stakeholder rates a lower-level requirement but does not rate the high-level requirement, then his rating propagates up to the high-level requirement, and if more than one lower-level requirement is rated, then the maximum rating is propagated. To answer RQ4, the raw ratings data and propagated ratings data were compared.

- **Ground Truth:** This ground truth was built using post project knowledge, reflecting the list of requirements implemented in the project, prioritised based on their actual importance (Lim & Finkelstein, 2011).

Experiments

The following experiments were conducted to answer the research questions described previously, with variations made to the initial population

and datasets. Variations were made in order to investigate how the initial population affects the trajectory of subsequent evolution in the search space. Experiments 1 to 3 used the propagated ratings dataset, and Experiment 4 used the raw ratings dataset.

Experiment 1. GA vs. Existing Method: To answer RQ1, Experiment E1.1 initialised the GA with a random population; Experiment E1.2 initialised the GA with the output from the existing method (i.e., betweenness centrality sorted by stakeholder role) to investigate if the existing *ProjectInfluence* values are already optimal or whether they can be further optimised.

Experiment 2. Social Network Measures: To answer RQ2, this experiment initialised the population with the output from the social network measures in Table 1 (not sorted by stakeholder roles): betweenness centrality (E2.1), load centrality (E2.2), closeness centrality (E2.3), PageRank (E2.4), degree centrality (E2.5), in-degree centrality (E2.6) and out-degree centrality (E2.7).

Experiment 3. All or Nothing: To answer RQ3, Experiment E3.1 initialised the population with zero weights and E3.2 initialised it with maximum weights.

Experiment 4. Rating Effect: Previous experiments used propagated ratings data. To answer RQ4, this experiment repeated Experiments 1 to 3 using the raw ratings data. The experiments were labelled E4.1, E4.2, and E4.3 respectively.

All experiments were run 20 times. The GA used a tournament size of 5 and elitism of 2 individuals. To discourage premature convergence, crossover was used with a probability of 1.0 and mutation was used with a probability of 0.1 per individual. The population size was 200 and the maximum number of generations was 1000. (The source code for the GA is written by Bentley and

Wakefield (1997) and is available at: http://www. cs.ucl.ac.uk/staff/p.bentley/sourcecode.html. We added tournament and elitism to the code. The code was written in C, with typical execution times of about 10 seconds per run, on a 2.4GHz dual core MacBook.)

The termination criteria were either when the maximum number of generations was reached or when evolution obtained a perfect fitness value. The weights produced by the social network measures were normalised values between 0 and 1, while the GA produced integer values from 0 to 255. As such, the weights from the social network measures used to initialise the population in Experiments 1, 2 and 4 were scaled such that the maximum weight was equal to 100, in order to allow the GA to increase the weights if needed. In Experiment E3.2 (maximum weights), the initial weight for each stakeholder was 255.

RESULTS AND DISCUSSION

Table 2 summarises the results for the existing method and social network measures calculated in this work to provide a baseline comparison for the experiment results. For the existing method and each measure in Table 1, this table reports the correlation for the three hierarchy levels (project objectives, requirements, and specific requirements) and their average. The existing method produced the best average correlation for all three hierarchy levels ($\rho = 0.6186$) as shown in the first row of Propagated Ratings Data in Table 2. Overall, propagated data produced higher average correlation, demonstrating that propagation was able to clean the data to fit the current social network measures. Data propagation increased the correlation of objectives and requirements, with $\rho = 0.8088$ and 0.5825 respectively, but decreased the correlation for specific requirements, with $\rho = 0.4645$. For specific requirements, raw data produced higher correlation with the ground truth

Table 2. Original correlation on propagated ratings data (P) and raw ratings data (R)

Data	Measure	Objectives	Requirements	Specific Requirements	Average
P	Existing method	0.8088	0.5825	0.4645	0.6186
	Betweenness	0.8829	0.2568	0.4267	0.5221
	Load	0.8829	0.2449	0.4267	0.5182
	Closeness	0.6791	0.3571	0.4518	0.4960
	PageRank	0.7717	0.3492	0.4891	0.5367
	Degree	0.6977	0.3460	0.5027	0.5155
	In-degree	0.7162	0.3492	0.4916	0.5190
	Out-degree	0.6791	0.3421	0.4518	0.4910
R	Existing method	0.6497	-0.1043	0.8105	0.4520
	Betweenness	0.6497	-0.0741	0.7358	0.4371
	Load	0.6497	-0.0741	0.7358	0.4371
	Closeness	0.6497	-0.1537	0.6852	0.3937
	PageRank	0.6688	0.1108	0.7541	0.5112
	Degree	0.6497	0.1155	0.7412	0.5021
	In-degree	0.6688	0.1308	0.7301	0.5099
	Out-degree	0.6497	-0.1577	0.7296	0.4072

with the best correlation of $\rho = 0.8105$ from the existing method (see first row of Raw Ratings Data in Table 2).

Table 3 summarises the results for all four experiments, reporting, for each experiment, the dataset, the initial population, and the correlation for the three hierarchy levels. The GA was always able to find better weights than those produced by the existing method and social network measures (Table 2). This indicates that the assumptions made by the social network measures to produce weights were not always valid for identifying key stakeholders, because their weights were evidently sub-optimum. The rest of this section discusses the results for each experiment.

Result 1: GA vs. Existing Method

The GA found comparative, and in some cases better solutions than the solution from the existing method (RQ1).

When the GA was initialised with a random population (E1.1), it was able to find comparatively good solutions, with correlation values up to 0.8947 (Table 3 E1.1). For specific requirements, it managed to find better solutions than when initialised with values from the existing method (E1.2). In the existing method, the allocation of project influence based on roles added the assumption that stakeholders' knowledge in the project is

Table 3. Results for experiments 1 to 4 (standard deviation in brackets)

E	Data	Initial Population	Objectives	Requirements	Specific Requirements
1.1		Random	0.8947 (0.0187)	0.7028 (0.0224)	0.7648 (0.0543)
1.2		Existing method	0.9451 (0.0238)	0.7463 (0.0179)	0.7160 (0.0246)
2.1		Betweenness	0.9864 (0.0015)	0.8348 (0.0295)	0.8155 (0.0125)
2.2		Load	0.9847 (0.0068)	0.8470 (0.0300)	0.8255 (0.0052)
2.3		Closeness	0.8835 (0.0230)	0.7483 (0.0134)	0.7965 (0.0160)
2.4	P	PageRank	0.9581 (0.0102)	0.7844 (0.0305)	0.8055 (0.0251)
2.5		Degree	0.8934 (0.0143)	0.7403 (0.0178)	0.7964 (0.0141)
2.6		In-degree	0.9130 (0.0313)	0.7505 (0.0122)	0.8113 (0.0121)
2.7		Out-degree	0.9070 (0.0246)	0.7486 (0.0164)	0.8057 (0.0198)
3.1		Minimum (0)	0.9890 (0.0035)	0.9228 (0.0223)	0.8345 (0.0036)
3.2		Maximum (255)	0.7717 (0.0000)	0.6240 (0.0043)	0.6207 (0.0000)
4.1		Random	0.6914 (0.0011)	0.3056 (0.0237)	0.8764 (0.0079)
		Existing method	0.6902 (0.0000)	0.3231 (0.0099)	0.8717 (0.0212)
		Betweenness	0.6918 (0.0011)	0.3681 (0.0113)	0.8842 (0.0173)
		Load	0.6934 (0.0048)	0.3710 (0.0120)	0.8830 (0.0192)
		Closeness	0.6902 (0.0007)	0.3279 (0.0132)	0.8621 (0.0155)
4.2	R	PageRank	0.6903 (0.0005)	0.3256 (0.0144)	0.8779 (0.0187)
		Degree	0.6902 (0.0000)	0.3081 (0.0194)	0.8719 (0.0133)
		In-degree	0.6905 (0.0008)	0.3220 (0.0119)	0.8710 (0.0195)
		Out-degree	0.6902 (0.0000)	0.3232 (0.0107)	0.8663 (0.0145)
4.3		Minimum (0)	0.8242 (0.0000)	0.4820 (0.0530)	0.9135 (0.0078)
		Maximum (255)	0.6880 (0.0000)	0.1962 (0.0227)	0.8633 (0.0260)

determined by their role in the project. Interviews with the stakeholders revealed that this was not always the case. Some stakeholders (such as Song the gym manager, Hicks the developer, Faulk the head of Research Department of Speech, Hearing and Phonetic Sciences, and Holmes the system maintainer) had marginal roles in the project, but had significant knowledge and interest about the project. The GA significantly increased their project influence weights (by a value of 100 or more out of a total of 255) to produce better overall requirements prioritisation.

Stakeholders with high project influence in objectives were not always influential in requirements and specific requirements. In E1.1, good solutions for different hierarchy levels have low correlation with one another. In E1.2, all three hierarchy levels were initialised with the same set of weights from the existing method. The GA made different corrections to the weights in the initial population depending on the hierarchy of requirements that was being measured. The correlation between the magnitude of corrections made to the stakeholders' weights for objectives, requirements and specific requirements was less than 0.1.

The GA showed that it was possible to find good sets of requirements from a large number of different combinations of stakeholders, sometimes not including those with significant roles as identified by the project team. Different runs of the same experiment produced best solutions that consisted of different combinations of stakeholders and weights. The best solutions between runs had low correlation with one another, and in the experiment initialised with a random initial population, the correlation between two best solutions are often around 0, indicating no correlation. This result suggests that in a practical application of the proposed solution, the analyst can select one of these equivalent solutions, based on the availability of the stakeholders.

Result 2: Social Network Measures

The raw outputs from the social network measures were sub-optimal but better than the output from the existing method, and the GA was able to optimise the raw outputs significantly (e.g., an improvement in correlation from 0.24 to 0.85 for load centrality requirements) (RQ2).

As mentioned in RQ1, the existing method used the output from betweenness centrality sorted by the stakeholders' roles to produce their *ProjectInfluence* values. When the GA was initialised with betweenness centrality weights that are not sorted by roles (E2.1), it produced a better correlation than when initialised with output from the existing method (E1.2), for all levels of requirements (e.g., for requirements, correlation of 0.8348 as compared to 0.7463 in Table 3). Again, this demonstrates that prioritising stakeholders by their roles in the project adds assumptions that do not always hold, hence producing a sub-optimal solution.

Among all the social network measures, the GA initialised with output from betweenness centrality (E2.1) and load centrality (E2.2) produced prioritised lists of requirements that had the highest correlation with the ground truth, with load centrality having a better correlation for requirements and specific requirements (Table 3). These two measures also had the highest original correlation before the GA was applied (Table 2). This showed that among the social network measures evaluated in this work, the assumptions made by these two measures produced stakeholder weights that were most valid for identifying key stakeholders.

Evolution corrected the assumptions made by the social network measures that did not hold for a particular stakeholder. For betweenness centrality, initial stakeholders who made recommendations but were not recommended, and stakeholders who did not make recommendations (even if they are highly recommended) received a project influence of 0. Interviews revealed that in RALIC, some stakeholders were not widely known (e.g., Rick the senior supplier of the project), but their formal roles in the project meant they had influence in the project. Other stakeholders, such as Lam the disability officer, did not make recommendations as they were unavailable during the recommendation period, and as a result, received betweenness of 0. In the search for better solutions, the GA corrected the weights for these stakeholders. For out-degree centrality (E2.7), stakeholders who did not recommend other stakeholders received an influence value of 0. The GA corrected the weights for stakeholders who did not recommend other stakeholders but voiced important requirements in the project. As such, although out-degree performed the worst before the GA was applied (Table 2), the GA was able to improve the correlation to be better than that of degree and closeness centrality (Table 3 E2.7).

Result 3: All or Nothing

The GA found the best results when it was initialised with all stakeholders having zero weights, and the worst results when it was initialised with all stakeholders having maximum weights (RQ3).

Evolving from an initial population of zero weights produced the highest correlation with the ground truth for all three hierarchy levels (Table 3 E3.1). Starting with no stakeholders meant that the GA was free to choose any set of stakeholders, and the GA was more selective. For example, in objectives, many stakeholders continued to have zero weights, and two stakeholders, librarian Reed and gym manager Song, appeared as key stakeholders in 15 out of 20 runs. During the interviews, these stakeholders revealed knowledge about the project that was not possessed by other stakeholders. For example, Reed correctly pointed out that external library users were significant stakeholders in the project.

Similar to the previous experiments, the GA selected a wide range of different stakeholders. In some runs, these stakeholders (Reed and Song) had zero weights, and other stakeholders were combined to get a good solution. This illustrated that a good set of requirements can be constructed from many different subsets of stakeholders, so the concept of who is a "key stakeholder" depends on which other stakeholders have already been identified. This finding is useful for elicitation, because some key stakeholders can be unavailable at times. Similar to previous experiments, the key set of stakeholders was different for each hierarchy level. For example, although Reed appeared in most runs as a key stakeholder for project objectives, in the 20 runs for specific requirements, he was never a key stakeholder (weight = 0 for all runs).

However, there were some stakeholders whose knowledge was very specific, and few other stakeholders had the knowledge. Hence for the requirements to be complete, those stakeholders must be involved. For example, in specific requirements, Lam appeared 20 times, but with an average weight of 0.17. This was because she was the only stakeholder who gave complete requirements regarding access control for disabled staff and students. As such, to get a good set of requirements, Lam must be considered, even though she did not have a formal or significant role in the project.

Initialising the population with all stakeholders having maximum weight (E3.2) produced the worst results for all three hierarchy levels (Table 3). This illustrated that it was not helpful to assume the requirements of all stakeholders were equally important. With all stakeholders considered as highly important, the GA found it difficult to get good solutions. For example, in specific requirements, only 3 stakeholders' weights were not reduced, but these stakeholders were marginally involved, and one reported having no interest in the project.

Result 4: Rating Effect

Data cleaning improved the correlation for project objectives and requirements, but decreased the correlation for specific requirements. Evolution was able to improve the correlation for all three hierarchy levels for the raw ratings dataset (RQ4).

The GA was able to produce higher correlations in specific requirements when using raw ratings (Table 3 E4.1 to E4.3) as compared to when using propagated ratings (Table 3 E1 to E3). Nevertheless, for objectives and requirements, propagated data was able to produce higher correlation (Table 3 E1 to E3). The assumptions behind upward propagation were more valid than downward propagation. Upward propagation assumes that if a stakeholder cares about a specific requirement, they would care equally about the parent requirement (Lim & Finkelstein, 2011). Indeed, when a stakeholder in RALIC rated a specific requirement but not its parent requirement, the parent requirement tended to be equally important to the stakeholder. Downward propagation assumes that specific requirements when unrated by the stakeholder have the same rating as their parent requirement (Lim & Finkelstein, 2011). In RALIC, when a stakeholder rated a requirement but not the specific requirement, it was less likely for the specific requirements to be equally important. For example, a stakeholder who wanted to combine all access control features into one card (requirement) did not agree with combining a bankcard with his access card (specific requirement).

Propagated ratings data enabled existing social networking measures to work more effectively, producing more accurate requirements prioritisation as compared to raw ratings data (Table 2). But the GA was able to provide more meaningful results with raw data – the key stakeholders identified by the GA were more sensible and consistent compared to those who were involved in the project.

FUTURE WORK

This study is based on data from a single project. As such there must be some caution generalising the results to other projects. Future work should conduct similar analysis on different software projects in different organisations. A tool has been developed to collect stakeholders' ratings (Lim et al., 2011), and as more projects use the tool, more data will be collected and can be analysed using the method proposed in this work. Future work should also investigate the robustness of the proposed method when many stakeholders do not provide ratings and when stakeholders provide dishonest or politically motivated ratings.

This work focuses on key stakeholders as stakeholders who contribute significant and useful knowledge to the requirements elicitation process. In a software project, there are various types of key stakeholders, such as those who influence the funding of the project and those who make decisions in the project. Future work should extend the analysis to other types of key stakeholders as well as provide a conceptual understanding of the characteristics of a key stakeholder. In addition, different methods to elicit requirements priorities from stakeholders can also affect the rating data (e.g., 100-point allocation or ranking), and should be investigated in future work.

Although the GA was always able to improve on the weights produced by the existing method and social network measures, in some runs, the improvement was minor and the GA converged prematurely (e.g., within 10,000 fitness evaluations). This was caused by the extensive epistasis in the representation (where two or more genes are linked, and the effect of each one partly depends on the values of the others) (Goldberg, 1989). Changing one gene may have different effects on the solution depending on the values of the other genes. Future work should address this issue by creating a more evolvable genotype representation, so that the GA can find better solutions quicker.

In addition, interactive optimisation approaches could be investigated so that multiple factors that influence a stakeholder's involvement in the project can be considered and the analyst can select among the solutions with equivalent fitness. Finally, future work should also address the dependencies among the requirements. These dependencies influence the ground truth, and in turn, influence the identification of key stakeholders.

CONCLUSION

Large software projects have many stakeholders. The identification and engagement of key stakeholders is important in order to align the software system and architecture with stakeholder needs. This paper investigates the validity of the assumption behind using social network measures to identify key stakeholders. It proposes the use of search-based techniques to identify the key stakeholders and their actual influence in the requirements elicitation process, given the stakeholders' requirements and the actual set of requirements that is implemented in the project.

Results show that a good set of requirements can be constructed from many different subsets of stakeholders, so the concept of who is a "key stakeholder" depends on which other stakeholders have already been identified. Results also show the assumptions embodied in existing social network measures do not always hold, as such, they sometimes miss out key stakeholders. The work demonstrates a clear need for the development of more appropriate measures tailored to software stakeholders.

Consequently, this work demonstrates the true complexity of requirements elicitation – it is vital that all stakeholders are consulted, but it may be equally important that not all of them are treated as key stakeholders, even if they appear to be significant considering their role in the domain.

REFERENCES

Alexander, I., & Robertson, S. (2004). Understanding project sociology by modeling stakeholders. *IEEE Software*, *21*(1), 23–27. doi:10.1109/MS.2004.1259199

Bentley, P. J., & Wakefield, J. P. (1997). Finding acceptable solutions in the pareto-optimal range using multiobjective genetic algorithms. In Chawdhry, P. K., Roy, R., & Pant, R. K. (Eds.), *Soft computing in engineering design and manufacturing* (pp. 231–240). Springer Verlag London Limited. doi:10.1007/978-1-4471-0427-8_25

Brandes, U. (2001). A faster algorithm for betweenness centrality. *The Journal of Mathematical Sociology*, *25*(2), 163–177. doi:10.1080/0022250X.2001.9990249

Brandes, U. (2008). On variants of shortest-path betweenness centrality and their generic computation. *Social Networks*, *30*(2), 136–145. doi:10.1016/j.socnet.2007.11.001

Cheng, B. H. C., & Atlee, J. M. (2007). Research directions in requirements engineering. *Proceedings of the Conference on the Future of Software Engineering*, (pp. 285-303).

Cleland-Huang, J., & Mobasher, B. (2008). Using data mining and recommender systems to scale up the requirements process. *Proceedings of the 2nd International Workshop on Ultra-Large-Scale Software-Intensive Systems*, (pp. 3-6).

Damian, D., Marczak, S., & Kwan, I. (2007). Collaboration patterns and the impact of distance on awareness in requirements-centred social networks. *Proceedings of the 15th IEEE International Conference on Requirements Engineering (RE)*, (pp. 59-68).

Finkelstein, A., Harman, M., Mansouri, S. A., Ren, J., & Zhang, Y. (2009). A search based approach to fairness analysis in requirement assignments to aid negotiation, mediation and decision making. *Requirements Engineering Journal, 14*(4), 231–245. doi:10.1007/s00766-009-0075-y

Gause, D. C., & Weinberg, G. M. (1989). *Exploring requirements: Quality before design*. Dorset House Publishing Company, Inc.

Glinz, M., & Wieringa, R. J. (2007). Guest editors' introduction: Stakeholders in requirements engineering. *IEEE Software, 24*(2), 18–20. doi:10.1109/MS.2007.42

Goldberg, D. E. (1989). *Genetic algorithms in search, optimization, and machine learning*. Addison-wesley.

Greer, D., & Ruhe, G. (2004). Software release planning: An evolutionary and iterative approach. *Information and Software Technology, 46*(4), 243–253. doi:10.1016/j.infsof.2003.07.002

Harman, M. (2007). *The current state and future of search based software engineering*. Paper presented at the Future of Software Engineering Conference (FoSE), Minneapolis, USA.

Lim, S. L. (2010). *Social networks and collaborative filtering for large-scale requirements elicitation*. PhD Thesis, University of New South Wales, Australia.

Lim, S. L., & Bentley, P. J. (2011). Evolving relationships between social networks and stakeholder involvement in software projects. *Proceedings of the Genetic and Evolutionary Computation Conference (GECCO)*, (pp. 1899-1906).

Lim, S. L., Damian, D., & Finkelstein, A. (2011). StakeSource2.0: using social networks of stakeholders to identify and prioritise requirements. *Proceedings of the 33rd International Conference on Software Engineering (ICSE)*, (pp. 1022-1024).

Lim, S. L., & Finkelstein, A. (2011). StakeRare: Using social networks and collaborative filtering for large-scale requirements elicitation. *IEEE Transactions on Software Engineering, 38*(3), 707–735. doi:10.1109/TSE.2011.36

Lim, S. L., Quercia, D., & Finkelstein, A. (2010). StakeNet: Using social networks to analyse the stakeholders of large-scale software projects. *Proceedings of the 32nd International Conference on Software Engineering (ICSE) -Vol. 1*, (pp. 295-304).

Lopez-Fernandez, L., Robles, G., & Gonzalez-Barahona, J. M. (2004). Applying social network analysis to the information in CVS repositories. *Proceedings of the International Workshop on Mining Software Repositories (MSR)*, (pp. 101-105).

Meneely, A., Williams, L., Snipes, W., & Osborne, J. (2008). Predicting failures with developer networks and social network analysis. *Proceedings of the 16th International Symposium on the Foundations of Software Engineering (FSE)*, (pp. 13-23).

Page, L., Brin, S., Motwani, R., & Winograd, T. (1999). *The pagerank citation ranking: Bringing order to the Web*. Stanford InfoLab.

Scott, J. (2000). Social network analysis: A handbook. *Sage (Atlanta, Ga.)*.

Sharp, H., Galal, G. H., & Finkelstein, A. (1999). Stakeholder identification in the requirements engineering process. *Proceedings of the Database & Expert System Applications Workshop (DEXA)*, (pp. 387–391).

Tonella, P., Susi, A., & Palma, F. (2010). Using interactive GA for requirements prioritization. *Proceedings of the 2nd Symposium on Search Based Software Engineering (SSBSE)*, (pp. 57-66).

van Lamsweerde, A. (2009). *Requirements engineering: From system goals to UML models to software specifications*. John Wiley & Sons, Inc. doi:10.1109/ICSE.2003.1201266

Wolf, T., Schroter, A., Damian, D., & Nguyen, T. (2009). Predicting build failures using social network analysis on developer communication. *Proceedings of the 31st International Conference on Software Engineering (ICSE)*, (pp. 1-11).

Zhang, Y. (2010). *Multi-objective search-based requirements selection and optimisation*. PhD Thesis, King's College London.

Zimmermann, T., & Nagappan, N. (2008). Predicting defects using network analysis on dependency graphs. *Proceedings of the 30th International Conference on Software Engineering (ICSE)*, (pp. 531-540).

Section 3
Architecture Processes, Tools, and Techniques

Chapter 8

An Approach for Integrated Lifecycle Management for Business Processes and Business Software

Stefanie Betz
Karlsruhe Institute of Technology, Germany

Erik Burger
Karlsruhe Institute of Technology, Germany

Andreas Oberweis
Karlsruhe Institute of Technology, Germany

Ralf Reussner
Karlsruhe Institute of Technology, Germany

Alexander Eckert
FZI Research Center for Information Technologies, Germany

Ralf Trunko
FZI Research Center for Information Technologies, Germany

ABSTRACT

The lifecycles of business processes and business software interact with each other since business software is used to support business processes, and requirements on business software are derived from business processes. By integrating these lifecycles, it is possible to test if the business software meets the process-based requirements as well as to identify which impacts changes of the software product have on the business process. In this chapter, the authors give an introduction into these interdependencies. Foundations of lifecycle management, business process modeling, and performance engineering are presented, followed by the description of a framework for an integrated lifecycle management for business processes and business software. This framework is based on business process simulation and software performance prediction. The evaluation of the framework is described by applying it to an example of use and the results are discussed. The chapter closes with a conclusion and an outlook on future work.

DOI: 10.4018/978-1-4666-2199-2.ch008

INTRODUCTION

Business processes and business software both possess specific lifecycles. These lifecycles interact with each other, since business software is used to support the execution of business processes. Thus, requirements on business software are derived from the business processes to be supported. These requirements are, however, variable. During its "life," a business process is subject to various changes (e.g. new legal basic conditions, restructuring of an organization, technological progress, new business strategy, changed target values for key performance indicators), which lead to changed or new requirements for the corresponding business software. Requirements are the central interface between the business process and the software product. The requirements specification is the basic input for the design of the software architecture. Thus, changes in a business process cause changes in the business software architecture via requirements changes. The other direction of influence is, however, also possible: business software may be improved by the software vendor (independently of the customers' business processes), creating new releases, updates or versions (which mean a change of the underlying software architecture). The modified business software may impact the execution of the business process. The impact may be of positive (e.g. reduction of media disruptions) or negative (e.g. longer execution time) nature. In this context, the software vendor can show the benefits that the modified business software has on the customer's business processes in order to convince the customer of buying the modified software. Furthermore, companies developing individual software often offer after sales services for their customers or maintain the software based on a contract with the customer. These software developing companies should be enabled to react more efficiently and effectively on changes of process-based requirements by an integrated lifecycle management for business processes and business software. An integration of both lifecycles creates benefits for both the software vendor (provision of better sales arguments) and the customer (quick and adequate adaptation of the business software according to changes in business processes). For these reasons, the lifecycle of business software should be closely associated to the planning and execution of the business processes in a company. The better both are synchronized, the more efficient is the company. To the same degree, if the framework requirements of a company are changing, the company has to adapt its business processes and the related business software. Thus, it is reasonable to argue for both the business process and the business software with the term "lifecycle" and for its methodic handling with an engineer-like approach. Hence, an integrated consideration of the lifecycles of business processes and their supporting business software is evident.

Requirements Management represents the interface between the lifecycles of business processes and business software. Besides the functional requirements, which can be (more or less) directly derived from the business processes to be supported, also non-functional requirements play an important role concerning the development and maintenance of customer-specific business software. One of the major non-functional requirements on business software is performance, due to the often critical nature of business processes. The performance of business processes is measured using specific key performance indicators (KPIs), e.g. duration, costs. Target values of KPIs represent requirements to the business software. These requirements are mapped on one or more software metrics. In this way, it is possible to test if the business software meets the process-based requirements. Based on the determination of process performance by simulating business process models and the performance prediction of a software product using architecture simulation, a framework for an integrated lifecycle management for business processes and business software has been developed.

Currently, there is no solution available to support business process management within the application lifecycle management in terms of an integrated lifecycle management. In Figure 1, a schematic picture of the business process lifecycle is shown (upper half). Below, the business software lifecycle is presented. The software development phases focus on agile and iterative development methods. Especially small and medium-sized enterprises (SMEs) often use agile development methods, because of the quick reaction times and flexible approach. The arrows in Figure 1 exemplarily symbolize interactions between the two lifecycles. The modeling phase of the business process lifecycle influences for example the requirements phase of the business software lifecycle: During modeling and analysis of a business process (in the process lifecycle), requirements can be identified at the same time (in the business software lifecycle). The deployment of the business processes could influence the launch, service and support phase of the business software lifecycle. The approach to bridge the gap between the two lifecycles is realized by a continuous requirements

management representing the interface between the two lifecycles and by appropriate software tool support. With this approach, the functionality of business software can be adapted to process-based changes more efficient and effective. On the other side, software producers are able to test and analyze the impact of updates, new versions or new products on the business processes of their customers without implementing or changing the software on customer's side.

The integration of both lifecycles (as mentioned above) is one goal of the research project *GlobaliSE: Globalized Software Engineering – Development of Flexible Business Software Using Global Resources* (04/2009-03/2012). GlobaliSE is a German research project funded within the research association "business software" by the Ministry for Science, Research and Arts of the federal state of Baden-Wuerttemberg. The core topic of the project is the lightweight support for the complete lifecycle of top-quality, company-specific software systems practicable for SMEs considering offshoring aspects. This contribution is based on results of the project.

In order to offer a tool-support for the framework developed in GlobaliSE, three already existing tools have been adapted:

Figure 1. Integrated lifecycle management of business process and business software

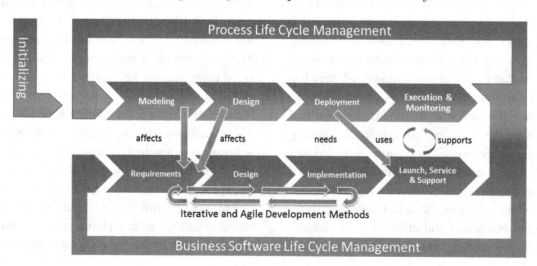

1. The framework uses Semantic MediaWiki (Dengler & Happel, 2010) as the central access point for both the customer and the software developer. In summary, SMW is used for the textual description of business processes, the description of requirements, the definition of key performance indicators, the solution of target conflicts, the descriptions of software components, the linkage of business processes, requirements, and software components. Semantic MediaWiki[1] is a free, open-source extension to MediaWiki, which allows for searching, organizing, tagging, browsing, evaluating, and sharing the content of a wiki. In contrast to traditional wikis which contain only text computers cannot understand or evaluate, Semantic MediaWiki allows for using a wiki as a collaborative database by adding semantic annotations. Furthermore, many extensions have been developed in order to extend In addition, a large number of related extensions have been created that extend the editing, displaying, and browsing abilities of the Semantic MediaWiki, e.g. the process format used in our approach.

2. For graphical modeling of business processes and their simulation, an interface to the process modeling tool Horus Business Modeler (Schuster & Rathfelder, 2010) has been developed. The tool is Java-based and builds on the Eclipse Rich Client Platform. Horus Business Modeler is an intuitive to use tool for the graphical modeling and simulation of business processes. Documentation and analysis functions as well as a database-supported repository complete the functionality spectrum. Business processes, which can be refined into hierarchical structures in order to keep the clarity of the business process schemas, take center stage in the Horus Business Modeler. Business processes can be linked with roles, resources, and organizational structures, supplemented by goals, risks, and critical success factors (i.e. key performance indicators). Horus Business Modeler uses variants of high-level Petri nets for the graphical modeling of business processes. Using the token game of Petri nets, simulation experiments and manual simulation of business processes are possible. The graphical modeling constructs (places, transitions, arcs, tokens, etc) are described using the Petri Net Markup Language (PNML).

3. For the design of software architectures and the prediction of their performance, the Palladio Workbench (Becker, Koziolek, & Reussner, 2009) is used. The Palladio approach is based on the Palladio Component Model (PCM), a domain-specific language for the description of component-based software architectures. It is designed with a special focus on the prediction of Quality-of-Service attributes like performance and maintainability. The Palladio Workbench serves as an "architecture simulator" for the prediction of these properties during early stages of the development lifecycle. The approach can, however, also be applied to existing architectures through the use of specific reverse engineering methods (Krogmann, Kuperberg, & Reussner, 2010).

In this contribution, the need for an integrated lifecycle management is motivated. The fundamentals of the approach in terms of lifecycle management, business process management, performance measurement as well as quality prediction and awareness are described in detail. A framework for an integrated lifecycle management is introduced, which supports the modeling and analysis of business processes, the requirements engineering, and the design of software architectures as well as the performance prediction for both business processes and software architectures. A use case (development of a *WebMediaStore*) is described which serves for the evaluation of the approach and the framework. The results and the limitations of the approach are discussed. Finally, conclusions on the results reached so far are drawn and an outlook on future work is given.

FOUNDATIONS AND RELATED WORK

The central foundations of this contribution lie in the areas business process modeling, requirements management, software architectures and software performance prediction as well as application lifecycle management.

Requirements management is an essential part of the software development process and a crucial success factor for software companies. During the development process and the usage of business software, changes in business processes can occur, which cause new or changed software requirements and may affect the designed software architecture. Requirements determine the properties that a software system has to possess. In the continuous requirements management, requirements are also subjected during the use of business software. Partly changes happen in operational processes (process instances), which do not have an effect on the related business software. Only if the process schema has to be changed, the change has an effect on the related business software. For this relationship, business process management and software architectures must be set in relation with requirements management.

Courses of action, interrelations, tasks, and dependencies but also bottlenecks in business processes can be illustrated using business process modeling. A process designer usually uses a top down approach, i.e. he or she starts with modeling a business process on a high abstraction level, followed by a stepwise refinement to more detailed processes down to the level of single process steps. The resulting business process models are the basis for the derivation of functional requirements for customer-specific business software supporting the execution of the business

processes. Popular methods for the modeling of business processes are e.g. Event-Driven Process Chains (EPC) (Scheer, Thomas, & Adam, 2005), Business Process Modeling Notation (BPMN) (BPMN, 2011), or Petri Nets (Reisig, 1985). In the area of business process management exists only a small number of lifecycle management publications that follow, however, very heterogeneous interests. In (Matthes, Neubert & Steinhoff, 2009) for example, a lifecycle model for business processes is presented, with focus on the reuse of individual process fragments to improve the quality of modeling and productivity. (Ploesser, Recker & Rosemann, 2008) describe a business process lifecycle focusing on change management, but this is inevitably associated with the entire application lifecycle, which is not mentioned. Depending on the performed process change, a distinction between the different classes "substitution", "adaption" and "evolution" is made as a strategy of change management. Thus, the authors especially want to improve the response times generally, means increasing productivity in (software) companies. (Papazoglou & van den Heuvel, 2007) specify a lifecycle by means of a service-oriented architecture based on a business process language. Based on WS-BPEL (OASIS, 2011), web services nets (WS-BPEL-Code) can be used for modeling and execution of business processes (Koschmider & Mevius, 2005). The published concept in (Papazoglou & van den Heuvel, 2007) can be used for a lifecycle management system (based on BPEL). A similar approach with a different focus is presented in (Chatha, Ajaefobi & Weston, 2007). This decision support system should support managers in business process reengineering projects, but it is not intended as a general solution, because of the detailed domain advises.

Application lifecycle management addresses all software engineering phases correlated with roles carrying out and digital artifacts used in the different phases. Usually, tools that facilitate and integrate requirements management, architecture design, coding, testing, tracking, and release management are used in this context and manage the artifacts. As a new task, business process management (from the customer side) should be combined with the software development process (from the software developer side) in order to bridge the gap between business software development and its usage within business processes. An integrated application lifecycle model for the development, periodic maintenance and further development of business software does not yet exist, although scientific approaches like JIL (Sutton 1997) have tried to tackle the problem of software lifecycle management. A standard of the International Organization for Standardization (ISO) for software in general is established. Based on the "Standard for Information Technology - Software Process Assessment" (ISO 15504) a "Standard for Software Lifecycle Processes" (ISO 12207) has been achieved and is compatible with existing maturity models like CMMI (Kneuper, 2008) or SPICE (Marshall & Mitchell, 2004). A good summary of lifecycle models generally for the software product area gives (Kneuper, 2008). In addition, there is the IEEE Guide for Software Engineering (ISO/IEC 9003:2004 Software engineering -- Guidelines for the application of ISO 9001:2000 to computer software), which maps aspects of quality management to software engineering, including instructions for lifecycle management. Quality management is, as already in business process management, driver for a lifecycle management in business software engineering.

However, none of the mentioned approaches integrates the lifecycle management of business processes with the lifecycle management of business software. In (Wetzstein, Ma, Filipowska, Kaczmarek, Bhiri, Losada, Lopez-Cobo, & Cicurel, 2007), a mapping approach for linking business processes with software components is presented. The technique, which is based on semantic technology and web services, combines various development phases, so that, as in all parts of an IT system, a reuse is possible. However, the

implementation has not been precisely specified and is in contrast to our approach less general.

The Palladio Component Model (Becker et al., 2009) is a meta-model for the description of component-based software architecture, with a special focus on performance prediction. The Palladio approach can be used in forward engineering scenarios as well as for the analysis of existing software. In forward engineering, developers may use the performance modeling and prediction techniques as a basis for design decisions; for existing systems, reverse engineering methods are available to extract component-based architectures. The feature that distinguishes Palladio from other performance prediction approaches like UML Marte (OMG, 2006) or KLAPER (Grassi, 2007) is its parametric design: Performance properties like execution time or resource demands are not expressed as fixed values, but as parametric dependencies of external influence factors like usage profile, execution environment, and calls to external services. Analysis and simulation result in probabilistic distributions which describe key performance indicators like execution time, memory consumption and network (see Figure 2).

Thus, it is possible to model the externally visible behavior of a system without having to know the details of implementation (grey box view), which often contain specific knowledge that should not be exposed in order to keep company secrets. Palladio offers an abstraction layer that enables analysis of performance without exposing this information.

A FRAMEWORK FOR INTEGRATED LIFECYCLE MANAGEMENT

For the realization of an integrated lifecycle approach, a framework has been developed in the GlobaliSE project. Focus of the approach is on changes on schema-level of a business process and the monitoring of non-functional requirements.

Figure 2. Performance prediction with Palladio (Reussner et al., 2011)

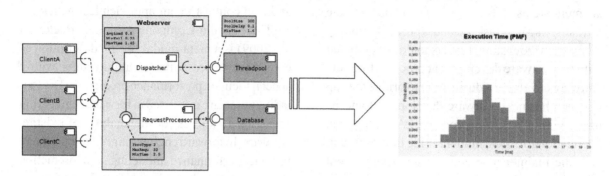

Based on the results of workshops with associated project partners from industry, specific challenges for an integrated lifecycle management have been identified:

- On customers' side, business processes are often undocumented or inadequately documented (especially if the customer is an SME).
- Interdependencies between business processes and software architectures are barely known.
- On customers' side, there is often no comprehensive overview on the own business processes.
- A linkage of software artifacts and process activities is rarely be done.
- There are often areas of conflict between software product quality and short-term changed customer requirements.

One main problem in business environments in general is that most of the companies use their own tools assortment. Some companies model their business processes, others not. Even worse, some companies buy individual software solutions, which determine a particular usage and are not interoperable to other software solutions. Thus, we had to find a common basis. It is a promising approach to use wikis as a central work place, the common basis in the internal IT environment of a company. Wiki-systems are of special interest for the target group of the project, since SMEs are particularly interested in low-cost, but at the same time flexible tools, which are usable without high installation or training effort. Traditional wikis only contain text, which is difficult to parse with a program. The Semantic MediaWiki (SMW) is a better solution for a later content reuse. By using SMW, it is possible to add semantic annotations to turn a wiki into a service like a relational database with groupware extension. In this way, it is possible to query every bit of information inside the wiki. Semantic MediaWiki is an extension of the popular Wiki-engine MediaWiki with knowledge models. One main advantage of Semantic MediaWiki compared with traditional Wiki-systems is the linkage of a lightweight documentation and modeling with a semantic knowledge model. The semantic data format allows for the integration of heterogeneous information from the whole lifecycle. The central usage of Semantic MediaWiki offers diverse advantages:

- Semantic MediaWiki is available for free.
- The tool is advanced by a community.
- It is a scalable, stable, and lightweight application.

- Semantic MediaWiki constitutes a knowledge basis with possibility for import and export.
- It offers a user-friendly input (e.g. via forms).
- There are diverse extensions to be used.
- Integration of the tools via a data interface.

The Semantic MediaWiki is used as central entry point and supports the cooperation between software developer and customer, since the usage of a Wiki is generally uncomplicated also on customers' side. Using Semantic MediaWiki, customer and software developer can capture together the business processes (e.g. in form of user stories or use cases) and derive textual process descriptions. These process descriptions in turn serve as the basis for a graphical process modeling. The textual description of business processes in SMW takes place via predefined forms and afterwards a transformation of theses textual descriptions into a graphical business process model happens.

There are several relationships in the Semantic Media Wiki displayed by semantic annotations. Semantic queries are formulated that provide information about individual links. So it is possible, for example, to quickly determine which requirements are derived from which business process and by which architectural and software components they are realized. To capture the semantic relationships between the elements to use, we designed a Semantic Media Wiki extension that implements a Traceability Matrix. Within this matrix, relationships between various elements of two categories (such as between business processes and requirements) are set by using check boxes. In this way, it is possible to determine which software components and documents are directly affected of the changes.

A central concept of the framework is quantitative factors in terms of key performance indicators. The innovative idea of the lifecycle approach of GlobaliSE is the linkage of concepts of key performance indicators for business processes and for

software architectures. In this way, business processes and business software can target-oriented be adapted to changing conditions.

By analyzing business process models, it is possible (besides qualitative properties, e.g. structural properties, reachability analysis) to determine also quantitative properties, from which indicators can be derived, which can be used as a basis for the assessment of software architectures. The performance of business processes is measured using specific key performance indicators (duration, costs, consumption of resources etc.). If such a key performance indicator (KPI) has to achieve a specific target value, it represents a (non-functional) requirement to the business software. This requirement is mapped on one or more software metrics. In this way, it is possible to test if the business software meets these process-based, non-functional requirements.

In the area of software architectures, it is possible to predict the performance of a software product using the Palladio Component Model (PCM) and the PCM-based Palladio Workbench, which is available for free. On business process side, the process performance can be determined by simulating the Petri net based business process models and measuring the relevant KPIs using Horus, which is available as a freeware tool. Horus enables for a formal graphical modeling; additionally, roles and resources can be modeled; the resulting process models can be simulated. Horus is a Petri net-based tool for the modeling and analysis of business processes. Advantages of Horus are the usage of a mathematical funded, formal modeling language, the additional possibility of modeling roles, resources, and organizational structures and in particular the possibility to simulate the resulting business process models.

A change in a business process can be described either textually in the Semantic MediaWiki or graphically by modifying the Petri nets in Horus. The derived requirements concerned by this change are highlighted automatically. In this way, the components of the corresponding software architecture can easily be identified and analyzed. If the software architecture is changed, the linked requirements are also highlighted, which facilitates the identification of the concerned KPIs.

In order to identify the relevant and available KPIs, it is necessary to regard their sources:

- Target values of KPIs are extracted from the requirements.
- KPIs of business software or its architecture are provided by an analysis using PCM.
- These KPIs in turn can be used for the simulation of business processes in Horus in order to generate process KPIs.
- However, if no simulation happens, it is conceivable to use KPIs like the (estimated) duration of an activity, which result from the analysis using PCM or manual user input (e.g. at the modeling).

If the textual process descriptions in the SMW are changed, it has an effect on the corresponding business process models. Using key performance indicators during simulation or execution of business processes, it is possible to give a feedback if changes in the business processes or the used business software are necessary. Requirements for the business software are derived from the process descriptions in SMW. These requirements are linked with both the underlying process activities and the implementing software architecture components. This happens in particular against the background of a traceability of requirements, which interrelations with the business process and the business software side as well as the quick allocation of affected architecture components in case of business process changes have to be visible. Architecture components derived from the requirements in SMW can be transferred to the tool Palladio in form of a specification model. Using Palladio, non-functional properties of software architectures (e.g. performance) can be tested. These non-functional properties can be described in form of key performance indicators and be returned to SMW.

A software architecture change is represented by the specification models of the concerned architecture components. These changed specification models can be tested using Palladio and serve as a basis for key performance indicators of non-functional properties of a software architecture. For an impact analysis of software architecture changes on business processes, a linkage between KPIs of non-functional properties of a software architecture and the KPIs of the business process is necessary. The decision for a software architecture can influence a software system in such a way, that e.g. duration, mode or time of usage of a software in a business process is changed or sub processes have to be re-aligned or rearranged for efficiency reasons. Furthermore, it is possible that new activities within a business process are necessary or older activities become redundant. Thus, KPIs of a software architecture should be determined for activities within a business process, which are related to the software system.

In order to establish a linkage between software architecture and business process, it is obvious to relate KPIs for non-functional properties of a software architecture to typical KPIs for business processes. It is conceivable to determine the throughput time of a process activity by means of the response time. In the run-up to this, data transformations from the Palladio Component Model have possibly to be done and it has to be more detailed analyzed, if the operationalization of a process KPI using PCM-data is possible by implication.

In (Korherr, 2008), BPMN, UML and EPCs have been extended by measures and goals. The underlying model of these extensions is shown in Figure 3. A measure measures type-dependently the performance of a business process and serves in this way as a quantification of process goals concerning a business process. The allocation of measures and process goals provides a basis for the extension of a process description, which

Figure 3. Generic metamodel of goals and performance measures based on (Korherr, 2008)

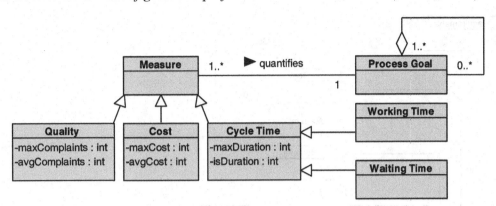

is flexible by the definition of further measure types. Regarding the limitations of the number of measures for business processes by the used modeling and simulation software, it is possible to think about the integration of KPIs.

It is obvious to link process goals with (non-functional) requirements. In this way, it is possible to assess if a requirement could be met by achieving of one or more process goals. Whilst process goals are linked with business processes, the level of granularity for the related KPIs has to be determined. Regarding business processes, the information model of GlobaliSE provides the elements *Business Process*, *Atomic Process*, *Composite Process*, and *Process Step*. In the SMW Process Format, the smallest atomic unit is called *Process Step*, which belong to a *Process*. It is conceivable to represent both KPIs for single activities (Process Steps) and (aggregated) KPIs on process level using the process format of SMW. For example, if an activity within a process is executed by a software, a change of this software could lead to a changed activity duration and therefore to a different process duration.

A common extension of the process format in this regard is shown in Figure 4. The linkage of requirement and process, enabled by the traceability matrix, includes additionally process goals, which are derived from the requirements. If the goals and therewith the requirements can

be achieved, is due to the measures. For these KPIs, further types can be introduced, which cover e.g. time, cost and quality factors. Aggregated measures are combined KPIs, which can be extracted from single measures (of Process Steps). Whilst Process Steps are solely linked with single measures, a process in the Process Format can include, besides aggregated measures, also single measures, e.g. if the process contains only one activity or process step.

In order to link KPIs of business processes with KPIs of software architectures, the granularity level has to be decided, on which KPIs of both sides can be mapped or exchanged. For business processes, it is conceivable that both an activity and a complete business process consist of a use case of an application. In order to use the capabilities of PCM, a use case should possess a certain size (e.g. with splits and cycles). Accordingly, the linkage of uses cases and business processes is more obvious (compared with use cases and activities), since within a use case single activities can be executed by the process stakeholders.

Besides the linkage with use cases, resources can be identified within a business process model, which are demanded by the activity.

Measures which can be determined via simulation using PCM are always linked with a use case. Accordingly, KPIs for use cases can be determined

Figure 4. Extension of the process format

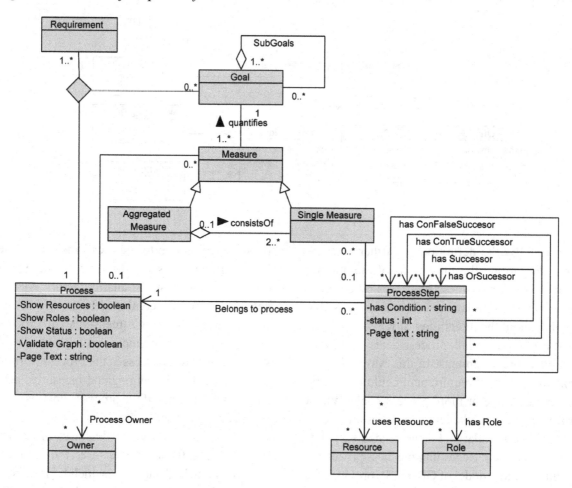

like, e.g. a complete processing duration for a use case. Single KPIs for a component in turn depend on a concrete use case and therefore have to be determined for a specific use case or (regarding process view) for a specific business process or activity. In SMW, business processes can be linked with components. Since a use case possesses at least one component, an activity has to be linked with at least one component. KPIs which have to be saved for components in SMW also have to be linked with a specific use case. This can be achieved e.g. by associating a use case with a business process or an activity and components with the activity, whereupon KPIs have to be part of the relation between activity and components. In our approach, business processes and activities

are linked with one use case of PCM and KPIs are determined at the granularity level of the use case.

Typical business process KPIs for use at simulation are:

- **Cycle Time:** Total time an entity needs for one process cycle.
- **Entity Count:** Number of entities which have been processed by a business process or which are currently in process.
- **Resource Utilization:** Percentage of time, in which a resource is in a specific status.
- **Activity Cost:** Cost for one activity, dependent of the associated entities and resources and the time span, for which they are associated with the activity.

The mapping of PCM KPIs and business process KPIs arises as follows:

- **Time Dimension:** PCM can determine a response time for a use case. The response time of a request for a certain task is defined as the time span between the request and the end of the response to that request (LL73). If a use case is associated with a business process, the response time of the use case complies with the cycle time of the business process. If the use case is associated with an activity, the response time of the use case complies with the processing time of the activity. According to this, minimal and maximal values of the response time can be used to define corresponding minimal and maximal cycle times or processing times.

- **Cost Dimension:** On the basis of PCM, it is conceivable to link costs with the degree of utilization of specific resources. In this way, e.g. costs for computing times, utilization of external (web) services or maintenance can be calculated relative to the utilization of the resource and aggregated on the level of a use case. Corresponding process or activity costs can be assigned to a business process or an activity.

- **Business Process KPIs to PCM KPIs:** According to the entity count of a business process or an activity, workloads for use cases can be derived. In this way, minimum, maximum and average values of the entity count can be used to test different workload scenarios for a use case. The workload influences, amongst others, the response time or the resource utilization of a use case.

By using this framework, a company is able to directly integrate the business process models (via requirements management) into the software development process. The software development can be aligned with changing business processes in a time- and cost-saving way without media breaks and manual import effort.

EXAMPLE OF USE

To exemplify the interactions between the Semantic Mediawiki (SMW), Palladio Component Model and Horus Business Modeler we assume that we aim to improve a business process of the *WebAudioStore* described in (Becker, 2009) and (Koziolek et al., 2006). The exemplary case consists of a component-based on-line music store. Besides offering downloadable music to customers, the web store should enable musicians to upload and sell their creations for a small fee. The performance properties of the system have been modeled using the Palladio Component Model. In our example, we depicted the business process of submitting audio files to the web store. By providing different software architecture alternatives of the deployed business software, we want to improve the execution times and thus fulfill the requirements of the process by extending the example case with a usage model which is derived from the business process.

One requirement of the business process is to reduce the cycle time of the submission process. In our example the cycle time of the submission process should be less than 1000 seconds for the majority of the process instances. We specify this requirement in the SMW and associate it with its measure "cycle time" to the submission process. In the next step a business process model of the submission process must be defined. The Semantic Result Formats extension for the SMW is used to represent a business process. The process itself is pictured in the sixth figure as a Petri net model which will be simulated later with Horus Business Modeler.

At first, a user has to create an account and verify his email address to use an account. Then, he has to provide information about the album he wants to sell through the web store and upload the corresponding audio files. Afterwards, the user can preview his submission. He also can decide to make changes to his initial submission by revising his submission. We assume that there is a 20% chance that a user revises his submission. Finally, after having paid the submission fees by using a payment interface, the user has to confirm his submission to end the submission process.

We want to focus on the "upload audio files" activity which is critical for the submission process and its duration heavily relies on the response time of the underlying business software. For this purpose we specify a PCM usage model for the "upload audio files" activity which is then executed with the existing component-based architecture of the WebAudioStore.

The WebAudioStore as depicted in Figure 5 is used to sell music files over a web interface. If a user wants to sell a file he can upload it to the application server from where it can be purchased. The files are stored in a MySQL database on a separate server. The dashed line indicates optional components which are affected by the change in the business process described in the next section. In the original case study (Becker, 2009) and (Koziolek et al., 2006) an additional compression algorithm (OGG) was introduced to save space in the database, at the cost of additional computation costs.

The architecture of the WebAudioStore has been implemented as a PCM model with perfor-

mance properties and use case models which contain stochastic information on arrival rates of users and file sizes of uploaded files. The results of this performance analysis contain execution times and resource demands (i.e., CPU, network) for standard use cases. With a cost model for CPU time and network (which depends on the deployment of the system), these results can be used to estimate the hardware costs for the use cases.

The WebAudioStore example contains a use case for uploading files, which is performance critical. Since we want to improve the response time of the "upload audio files" process step, we will analyze the variation point of the encoding adapter depicted in Figure 5: as a design alternative, it is introduced to improve the upload time by using a more effective compression algorithm. This algorithm however is computationally more intensive and costs an amount of time. The effects of the introduction of the optional algorithm have been investigated thoroughly in (Koziolek et al., 2006), so we will not describe them in detail here. The speedup in response time is sufficient to fulfill the requirements mentioned above, as we will show in the following paragraphs.

The resulting frequency distribution of the usage model's response time is stored in the SMW. In the next step the submission business process schema is being exported as a PNML file to Horus and converted to an equivalent petri net. Besides of the business process schema, the determined response time frequency distributions are imported

Figure 5. The WebAudioStore architecture (from Koziolek et al., 2006)

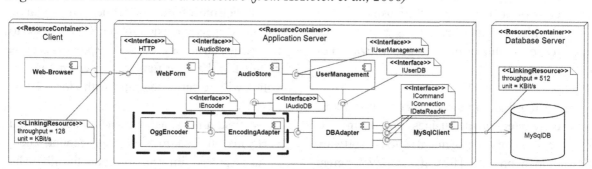

into Horus, too. In Horus we use one of those frequency distributions to describe the processing time of the "upload album file" activity. For the remaining activities, which received no data input from PCM simulations, we specify the processing time by assigning a constant value to it. The petri net of the submission process as well as its corresponding activity process times are pictured in Figure 6. Please note that no processing time for the activity "upload audio files" is provided, because its processing time is described by the response time frequency distribution received from a PCM simulation run.

To perform the business process simulation in Horus we specify that thousand business process instances are being generated and one instance is being created every 10 minutes. For our first

simulation run we use the PCM results of the web store architecture which does not use an additional compression algorithm. The simulation provides cycle times for every instance of the submission process. Figure 7 shows a histogram of the submission process' cycle times.

While most process instances have a cycle time between 800-1200 seconds there are some instances with much higher cycle times (with a maximum of 4145 seconds). Those high cycle times are caused when a user decides to revise his submission, because the time intensive activity of uploading audio files must be repeated. A redesign of the submission process could be a way to minimize the occurrences of cycle times higher than 1200 seconds. However, to fulfill the requirement of cycle time reduction even for us-

Figure 6. Petri net model of the web store submission process

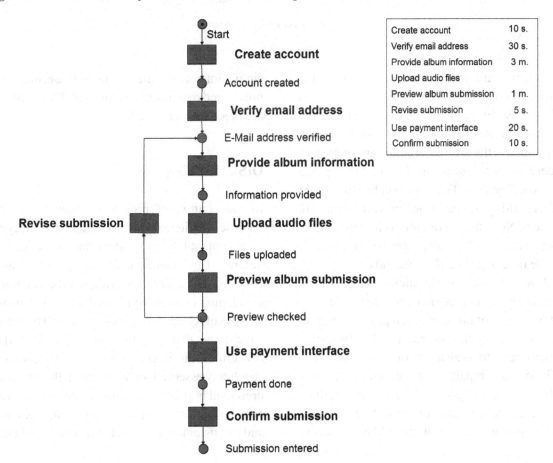

Figure 7. Histogram – Submission process

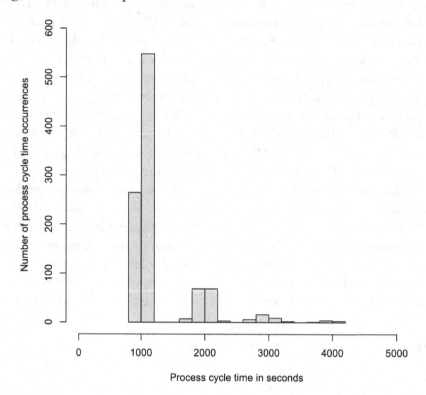

ers which don't revise their submissions, the aforementioned design alternative for the used web store software should be evaluated.

This time we use the response time frequency distribution of the software architecture alternative to describe the processing time of the "upload audio files" activity. The corresponding histogram of the resulting process cycle times are pictured in Figure 8. Now, the maximum cycle time is 3325 seconds and 81.3% of all process instances have a cycle time less than 1000 seconds.

If we assume for simplicity that we have specified a process requirement which demands that over 50% of all submission process instances must have a cycle time less than 1000 seconds, we still have to evaluate if that requirement is fulfilled. To compare the measured cycle times with the specified goals of the initially defined requirements, the simulation results determined with Horus are stored in the SMW for every

simulation run. For the considered case, the aforementioned requirement is fulfilled if the software architecture is changed.

DISCUSSION

In the context of project GlobaliSE, several specific challenges for an integrated lifecycle management have been identified (as mentioned before). The identification of these challenges is based on interviews with twelve software-developing German SMEs and a comprehensive analysis of relevant specialist literature. The results have shown that a lightweight support for SMEs concerning the integration of both lifecycles is absolutely essential. In this context, the approach presented in this contribution offers several benefits for both the software developing company and its customers and meets the mentioned chal-

Figure 8. Histogram – Submission process (alternative)

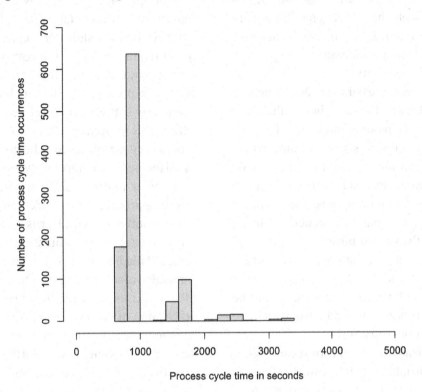

lenges. For software developers, the following advantages are evident:

- Fulfillment/compliance with process-based requirements
- Support for common requirements analysis with customer
- Traceability of impacts of changes on business process- or software-side
- Architecture-based software test via integrated business process simulation
- Prediction of performance properties at design time
- Evaluation of design decisions
- Discussion of different architecture suggestions

Benefits for the customers are as follows:

- Faster reaction of software developers on process-based changes
- Usage test of new product or update before procurement
- Compliance of performance requirements

The target of the presented approach is the development of business information systems as individualized software, which supports business processes. Thus, the approach is not intended for the development of any kind of software. A barrier for the usage of our approach could be to convince companies to implement and use three new tools, since companies often already use their own tool assortment. On the other hand, many companies do not use software tooling for the descriptions of lifecycles at all. The lightweight nature of the GlobaliSE toolset lowers the entry barriers to lifecycle tools for SMEs. In this context, it is essential to validate the realization of the advantages mentioned above, i.e. an evaluation of the presented approach in cooperation with partners from industry is necessary.

Two main hypotheses of the approach should be validated: Firstly, the lowering of the entry barriers and faster process modeling. This can be achieved by an analysis of the time which is needed for learning how to use the Semantic Media Wiki-based approach in comparison to industry-standard heavyweight business process modeling tools. Secondly, the benefit of using a combined software and business lifecycle approach in a software evolution scenario, where external influences such as legal changes require adaptation of the business processes, should be measured in terms of time and costs which are needed to adapt the software.

These facts leads to a conclusion regarding our approach and an outlook on future work to be done as described in the final section of this chapter.

CONCLUSION AND FUTURE WORK

In this contribution, we presented our approach for an integrated lifecycle of business processes and business software, which was developed within the German research project GlobaliSE. The approach supports the modeling and analysis of business processes, the requirements engineering, and the design of software architectures as well as the quality prediction for both business processes and software architectures. The integrated lifecycle management is based on the definition and linkage of key performance indicators for business processes and the used business software. The application of the approach we demonstrated by an example of use, which comprises the improvement of a business process of an audio web store by providing different software architecture alternatives of the deployed business software.

Our approach is driven by key performance indicators. Targets or target corridors for process key performance indicators represent non-functional requirements for the corresponding business software. For traceability purposes, business processes/ process activities are linked with their supporting software architecture components by defining the respective requirements (derived from process key performance indicators) as use cases (used for the simulation of software architectures).

In order to offer an IT-supported realization of our approach, we extended and linked three existing software tools: Horus Business Modeler for the modeling and simulation of business processes, Palladio Workbench for the modeling and simulation of software architectures, and Semantic MediaWiki as the central access point for the description of business processes, the definition and analysis of key performance indicators, the derivation of requirements, and the description of specification models for software architectures. By linking these three tools, an integrated consideration of changes on both business process side and business software side is possible. Since the usage of Wiki technology is easy understandable and very popular, an integration of the customer into the requirements engineering phase is possible, i.e. the customer is able to describe his business processes in natural language using the Semantic MediaWiki and can derive requirements from these processes together with the software developer. Business processes described by using Semantic MediaWiki can be transformed into Petri net models and exported to the Horus Business Modeler. Using this tool allows for the execution of several different analysis techniques, including simulation, in order to analyze both the structural correctness of the business process and the achievement of goals for process key performance indicators (which represent non-functional requirements for the used business software). The usage of Palladio Workbench allows for the simulation of different software architecture constellations. The results of these simulations can be used within the business process simulation using Horus Business Modeler. Simulation results of both business processes and software architectures are visualized in the Semantic MediaWiki. In this way, a software developer is able to check if the (changed) requirements (derived from the business processes) can be met with specific software architecture before implementing the software.

At the publication date of this contribution, GlobaliSE is still an ongoing project. The IT-supported realization of the approach has only a prototypical status. In order to provide evidence for its practical use and the realization of its advantages as mentioned before, it is necessary to validate the toolset in real life. For this purpose, several associated project partners from industry have agreed to implement and test the toolset by reconstructing already completed development/maintenance projects. After project completion, the final results will be published and the toolset will be available for free to interested companies.

REFERENCES

Becker, S., Koziolek, H., & Reussner, R. (2009). The Palladio component model for model driven performance prediction. *Journal of Systems and Software, 82*, 3-22. Retrieved from http://dx.doi.org/10.1016/j.jss.2008.03.066

Business Process Model and Notation (BPMN). (2011). Retrieved January 29, 2012, from http://www.omg.org/spec/BPMN/2.0/

Chatha, K. A., Ajaefobi, J. O., & Weston, R. H. (2007). Enriched multi-process modelling in support of lifecycle engineering of business processes. *International Journal of Production Research, 45*(1), 103–141. doi:10.1080/00207540600607150

Dengler, F., & Happel, H. J. (2010). Collaborative modeling with semantic mediawiki. In *Proceedings of the 6th International Symposium on Wikis and Open Collaboration*. Gdansk, Poland: ACM.

Grassi, V., Mirandola, R., & Sabetta, A. (2007). Filling the gap between design and performance/reliability models of component-based systems: A model-driven approach. *Journal of Systems and Software, 80*(4), 528–558. doi:10.1016/j.jss.2006.07.023

Kneuper, R. (2008). *CMMI: Improving software and systems development processes using capability maturity model integration (CMMI-Dev)*. Rocky Nook.

Korherr, B. (2008). *Business process modeling – Languages, goals, and variabilities*. PhD thesis, Vienna University of Technology.

Koschmider, A., & Mevius, M. (2005). *A Petri Net based Approach for process model driven deduction of BPEL code*. OTM Confederated International Conferences, Agia Napa, Cyprus.

Koziolek, H., Happe, J., & Becker, S. (2006). Parameter dependent performance specification of software components. In *Proceedings of the Second International Conference on Quality of Software Architectures (QoSA2006), Lecture Notes in Computer Science, vol. 4214*. Berlin, Germany: Springer-Verlag.

Krogmann, K., Kuperberg, M., & Reussner, R. (2010). Using genetic search for reverse engineering of parametric behaviour models for performance prediction. *IEEE Transactions on Software Engineering, 36*(6), 865–877. doi:10.1109/TSE.2010.69

Marshall, S., & Mitchell, G. (2004). Applying SPICE to e-learning: An e-learning maturity model? In *ACE '04: Proceedings of the Sixth Conference on Australasian Computing Education*, (pp. 185-191). Dunedin, New Zealand.

Matthes, F., Neubert, C., & Steinhoff, A. (2009). *A. federated application lifecycle management based on an open web architecture.* Karlsruhe, Germany: Workshop Design for Future – Langlebige Softwaresysteme, GI-Arbeitskreis Langlebige Softwaresysteme (L2S2).

Oasis WS-BPEL TC. (2011). *Web services business process execution language, version 2.0.* Retrieved May 23, 2011, from http://docs.oasis-open.org/wsbpel/2.0/OS/wsbpel-v2.0-OS.html

Object Management Group (OMG). (2006). *UML profile for modeling and analysis of real-time and embedded systems (MARTE)* RFP (real-time/05-02-06). Retrieved from http://www.omg.org/cgi-bin/doc?realtime/2005-2-6

Papazoglou, M., & van den Heuvel, W.-J. (2007, October). Business process development lifecycle methodology. *Communications of the ACM, 50*(10). doi:10.1145/1290958.1290966

Ploesser, K., Recker, J., & Rosemann, M. (2008). Towards a classification and lifecycle of business process change. In *Proceedings of 9th Workshop on Business Process Modeling, Development and Support (BPMDS '08): Business Process Life-Cycle: Design, Deployment, Operation & Evaluation*, Montpellier, France.

Reisig, W. (1985). *Petri Nets: An introduction. EATCS: Monographs on Theoretical Computer Science (Vol. 4).* Springer-Verlag.

Reussner, R., Becker, S., Burger, E., Happe, J., Hauck, M., Koziolek, A., et al. (2011). *The Palladio component model.* Technical report, Karlsruhe, Germany.

Scheer, A., Thomas, O., & Adam, O. (2005). Process modeling using event-driven process chains. In Dumas, M., van der Aalst, W. M., & ter Hofstede, A. H. (Eds.), *Process-aware information systems: Bridging people and software through process technology.* Hoboken, NJ: John Wiley & Sons. doi:10.1002/0471741442.ch6

Schönthaler, F., Vossen, G., Oberweis, A., & Karle, T. (2012). *Business processes for business communities: Modeling languages, methods, tools.* Springer-Verlag.

Sutton, T., & Osterweil, L. J. (1997). The design of a next-generation process language. In *Software Engineering – ESEC/FSE '97 (Vol. 1301).* Lecture Notes in Computer Science Berlin, Germany: Springer. doi:10.1007/3-540-63531-9_12

Wetzstein, B., Ma, Z., Filipowska, A., Kaczmarek, M., Bhiri, S., & Losada, S. … Cicurel, L. (2007). Semantic business process management: A lifecycle based requirements analysis. In *Proceedings of Workshops on Semantic Business Process and Product Lifecycle Management (SBPM 2007) at the 4th European Semantic Web Conference (ESWC 2007)*, Innsbruck, Austria.

ENDNOTES

[1] http://semantic-mediawiki.org/wiki/Introduction_to_SMW

Chapter 9
High-Level Modeling to Support Software Design Choices

Gerrit Muller
Buskerud University College, Norway

ABSTRACT

The IT industry is suffering from severe budget overruns and ill-performing IT services. Some of the problems that have caused IT project disasters could have been anticipated in the early project phases and mitigated in the project follow-up by modeling the system context and the software design. This chapter shows how to make models of varied views and at varied levels of abstraction to guide software design choices. Models of the enterprise provide understanding of the objectives. Models of the specification provide understanding of system performance and behavior. Models of the design provide understanding of design choices, such as the allocation of functions, resource usage, selection of mechanisms for communication, instantiation, synchronization, security, exception handling, and many more aspects. High-level models are simple models with the primary goal to support understanding, analysis, communication, and decision making. The models have various complementary representations and formats, e.g. visual diagrams, mathematical formulas, and quantitative information and graphs. Model-driven and model-based engineering approaches focus mostly on artifacts to analyze and synthesize software and hardware. High-level models complement model driven approaches by linking the system context to more detailed design decisions. High-level modeling as discussed in this chapter is based on research performed in industrial settings; the so-called industry-as-laboratory approach.

INTRODUCTION

The success rate of large scale IT projects is disastrously low. Regularly, failures of IT projects of tens of millions of Euros are reported. McManus and Wood-Harper (McManus 2008) analyzed a set of IT projects and possible causes for failure. They note that these projects are inherently large and complex, that often stakeholders' communication and management is insufficient, that projects often fail to meet customer expectations, and they observe an overreliance on project and development methodologies.

Concrete examples of failed projects are large web-based health care or travel booking systems that are improperly dimensioned and hence can-

DOI: 10.4018/978-1-4666-2199-2.ch009

not cope with the actual load. In both cases, the development focus has been on functionality and software mechanisms, ignoring operational performance needs. Estimation of operational needs and performance of the selected solution could have signaled performance problems in the early project stages.

In this chapter, we show a high-level modeling technique that, in a short amount of time, creates insight in the problem space and the consequences of options in the solution space. It is called high-level modeling because we strive for understanding and identification of issues. High-level modeling is on purpose simplifying problems and solutions at the cost of accuracy. However, even with limited accuracy a lot of understanding can be created. Critical qualities may have to be modeled later in much more detail to provide a proper confidence level.

The term "high level" refers to the amount of abstraction, and hence simplification, that is used in the high-level models. Figure 1 shows a number of high-level models mapped on a pyramid representing the number of details in the models. The pyramid figures are elaborated in Sections 2.4 and 4.1 of (Muller 2011). These high-level models are simplified so far that "manual" analysis and reasoning by humans can be done.

One example of a failed IT project is the travel management system at a large multinational company. The development of this system was outsourced to a renowned IT house. The system was tested in one of the departments before it was rolled out in the entire company. Once it was introduced throughout the company the response time degraded to hours, rather than seconds as expected. It is our experience that a few low level software design choices, such as the granularity of transactions or locking, or the granularity of instantiations and notifications, can make or break the performance of the overall design. We claim that the consequences of these choices can be predicted early in the design by a combination of simple models and measurements.

Typical for the IT domain is that architecture itself is partitioned into three layers: enterprise architecture, information architecture, and systems architecture. Enterprise architecture focuses on people, processes, and enterprise business, functionality, and performance. Information architecture describes the underlying information flow and structure. Systems architecture addresses among others partitioning, function allocation, interfaces, dimensioning, and communication protocols of hardware and software components. These layers are well separated in the IT domain.

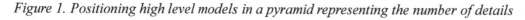

Figure 1. Positioning high level models in a pyramid representing the number of details

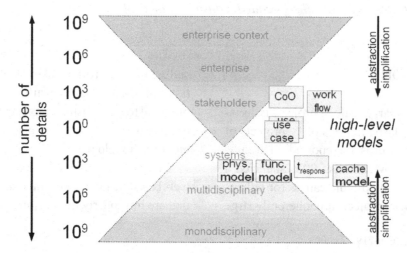

This separation facilitates independence of work packages, and reflects ideals such as separation of concerns. At the same time, it causes many of the mentioned problems because most stakeholders are not aware of the many interdependencies between these layers; for example an enterprise work flow might conflict with a chosen server decomposition and allocation causing severe performance bottlenecks.

This chapter describes how simple, low-effort models can be created and used together to obtain a better understanding of the problem and solution space. This improved understanding facilitates better decisions and helps to avoid nasty surprises late in the project.

BACKGROUND

Modeling is widely promoted in the software and systems engineering communities, with names as Model-Driven Engineering (MDE) (Schmidt 2006) or Model-Based Systems Engineering (MBSE) (Estefan 2007). However, most effort in MDE is spent on more detailed modeling for design analysis and for automated synthesis of hardware and software. MBSE is more focused on artifacts: how to replace document artifacts by model artifacts? High-level modeling as discussed in this chapter is focused on exploration of problem and solution space to increase understanding and hence to support decision making.

This chapter is based on the research at the Embedded Systems Institute in Eindhoven, in amongst others the Boderc (Heemels 2007), Darwin (vd Laar 2011), and Falcon projects (Hamberg 2011). One of the partners is the University of Twente, as shown by the dissertations by Bonnema (Bonnema 2008) and Borches (Borches 2010).

The research model that is used to research this field is Industry as Laboratory (Potts 1993). The research takes place in an industrial setting on an actual industrial problem. The researchers participate in the industrial project and at the same time observe and measure the impact of the methods and techniques that are used.

High-level modeling is not the sole remedy for large IT project failures. Proper project management, requirements engineering, processes, methods, techniques, and tools are all prerequisites for success. Many processes, methods, techniques, and tools emphasize notations, formalisms, and artifacts that are needed to apply them repeatable and predictable. The high-level modeling is a complementary competence or set of skills. Although the high-level models look simple, a significant intellectual skill set is required to make them. The methods, tools, and techniques used for high-level modeling are fundamental mathematics and physics, and general purpose tools ranging from pen and paper to Visio, Excel, or scripting languages. The way of working is closely related to Systems Thinking, see (Boardman 2008), (Hitchins 2003), and (Lawson 2010).

The high level modeling approach has been used in workshops and courses in various domains: defense, food processing, semiconductor equipment, semiconductors, health care, maritime, manufacturing, and energy. All participants in these courses and workshops are able to collect data and make some models. However, making relevant high-level models proves to be a significant challenge. Typical incubation time for the application of the main modeling ideas is more than one year.

High-level modeling is not highly formalized since the concerns to be addressed are quire heterogeneous. One of the main challenges is to keep the focus on the most relevant issues. This requires a certain amount of pragmatism that is advocated in several other communities, such as the agile movement (see <www.agilemodeling.com>) and Lean Product Development, (see (Mascitelli 2006)).

HIGH-LEVEL MODELING

The general idea of high-level modeling is to model the system in its context. Figure 2 elaborates the context one step further. It distinguishes the black box view on the system ("what") from the internal design choices ("how"). It also partitions the context in a usage context (who is using the system when and how) and life cycle context (what do suppliers and service providers need and do during the life cycle of the system).

Stakeholders in the usage and life cycle context have needs that transform into a requirements specification at black box level. This specification is often a compromise between needs in both contexts and opportunities and constraints in design and technology.

The models are made to support exploration of specifications and solutions, and hence to support decision making. We need to make related models at these levels to facilitate exploration. In general, models can be positioned in a goals-means hierarchical graph: the enterprise objectives (goals) are served by system functionality and performance (means); system functionality and performance (goals) are achieved by design concepts and technology choices (means). High-level models are models that zoom in on a few, most critical, branches in this graph.

Figure 2. The system in usage context and life cycle context with examples of models

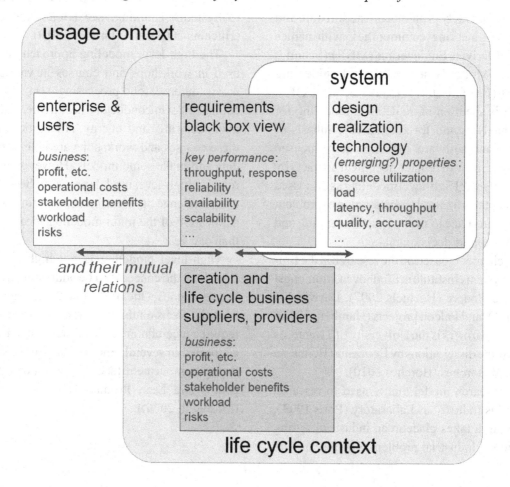

Modeling Method

The method can be summarized as an iterative repetition of the following time-boxed steps:

1. Identify issues.
2. Identify parameters and functions both as goals and means.
3. Create simple models relating goal parameters and means parameters.
4. Explore multiple solution concepts (means) and their quantitative behavior.
5. Select one or more concepts that fit best.

Typical time-boxes will start with very short time-boxes of 15 minutes, and will increase after a few iterations to time-boxes of half or a full day. The combination of iteration and time-boxes forces architects to see problem and solutions from multiple perspectives. In that way, architects more quickly synthesize a "big picture". The rapid iteration forces architects to zoom-in and –out, and to change viewpoints; they are sampling the problem and solution space. The rapid iteration should help architects to see where they have to zoom-in. Frequently architects and designers disappear in depth in one topic, discovering later that this topic was not relevant; they wasted their time, caused by a lack of understanding.

In a later section, we will show an example where the goal is good consumer experience by fast response and where several cache strategies are explored as (part of) a solution. Another example is the objective to make the effort of updating product descriptions affordable where solution concepts are (semi-) automated inputs.

Modeling Perspectives

Figure 2 shows some examples of parameters per view. The usage context typically will be an enterprise using a variety of systems to run its business. The enterprise operates in normal economic conditions, imposing profit and other financial expectations. There will be focus on operational costs, but also stakeholder benefits such as customer value. Figure 2 shows only a few aspects that play a role at enterprise level. Many more aspects relating to time, cost, risk, and staff will be visible at the managerial balanced scorecard. Balanced scorecard is a technique introduced by Kaplan (Kaplan 1976) to capture multiple views and parameters in a compact overview to support managers in decision making. The use of multiple views based on stakeholders and their concerns follows (ISO/IEC/IEEE 2011).

The requirements specification describes the system as black box: what must the system do (functions), how well must it do it (quantifications of qualities, e.g. performance, reliability), what interfaces must the system have, how must the system behave under various circumstances (use cases, exceptions, boundary conditions).

The design of the system includes partitioning, interface definition and management, function allocation, concept selection, technology selection. Design finally results in a system realization. The actual properties of the realization have to fulfill the requirements specification.

The life cycle starts with needs and ideas. These ideas are transformed into a realization through system development. System development creates a system design, and all processes and tools needed to purchase parts, manufacture, install, maintain, and dispose the system. The life cycle context is a complex interplay of suppliers and service providers. In the life cycle, normal economic conditions apply as in the usage context.

INTRODUCTION TO EXAMPLE CASE: WEB BOOKSHOP

We will use a hypothetical web-based bookshop as example for this chapter, like <www.amazon.com>. Such bookshop is a global enterprise that interfaces to the consumers mostly through Internet. Most of the operational organization behind the website stays invisible for consumers. We will introduce this case briefly by discussing two of the four views described above: usage context, and design, realization, and technology. We will elaborate the case further after providing more insight in the high-level modeling approach.

In such project we would at least meet a variety of architects: enterprise, information, software, and systems architect. The language and the concerns of these architects are quite different. The enterprise architect is concerned about business, operational and organizational issues. The information architect has abstracted from most of these concerns by working on the information model and data dictionaries. The software architect is often involved in the implementation framework with its related technology choices for communication, data base, and programming language. Finally, the systems architect is defining the hardware infrastructure. The risk of this typical task decomposition is loss of context understanding between these architects.

Usage Context

Consumers browse the catalog, order books, and trace orders via the bookshop's website. A variety of fields with information are provided on a single page: structured access to products and services through a catalogue or search engine, "hot" information such as bestsellers, special offers, or interests of other consumers, personalized information, standard information with legal conditions, contact data, etc, and advertisements. The styling of such a site is frequently updated; the look and feel is part of the company image and is subject to the need to be fashionable. An example of such page is www.amazon.com.

Bookshop employees take care of among others the logistics of the goods flow, management of the portfolio, and customer relation management. The bookshop has relations with many publishers, suppliers, and distributors. Hence, interoperability of internal systems and external systems of relat-

ing parties is crucial for an effective operation. Bookshop employees typically will have access to relevant data through work and goods flow applications.

Design, Realization, and Technology

The current "standard" IT-solution for this kind of system is a 3-tier Service-Oriented Architecture (SOA). Figure 3 shows a typical physical architecture for a SOA. The three tiers are:

- **Database Servers:** Here all data are maintained about product, relations, suppliers, etc.
- **Web Servers:** Where the client information is composed from data in the various databases.
- **Clients:** Applications running on consumer devices such as laptops and smart phones. Here the information is presented to the consumer and consumer interaction takes place.

Primary idea behind the 3-tier SOA is separation of concerns. The database tier can be distributed over the owners of the information, the web server tier contains the actual business logic and the actual interaction and presentation is distributed over a wide variety of (fashion sensitive) consumer devices.

Figure 3 classifies the physical building blocks in main functional resources: storage, communication, processing, and presentation. In fact these same resources are present when any physical block is opened. For example, one of the web servers is shown with its internals, showing internal communication channels, internal caches (storage) and multiple cores (processing). The topology of resources, the allocation of functions to resources, and properties of individual resources determines to a large degree cost, performance, reliability, and scalability.

Figure 3. Service-oriented physical architecture

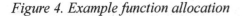

Figure 4 shows an example of how functions can be allocated to the tiers. At client side two types of interactions are shown: consumer and enterprise. Bookshop employees in the enterprise access the other tiers via clients, for example to enter logistics or financial data, or to update product or consumer data. The database is partitioned according to the types of data: product descriptions, logistics, financial, and customer relation data.

MULTIPLE MODELS

The essence of a system can be captured in about 10 models/views (Hole 2006). This multitude of models is needed to get an all-round understanding of the problem and solutions. We follow Bonnema (Bonnema 2008) and recommend using functional models, construction (or physical) decomposition, and quantification as basic set of models. We elaborate these three types of models

Figure 4. Example function allocation

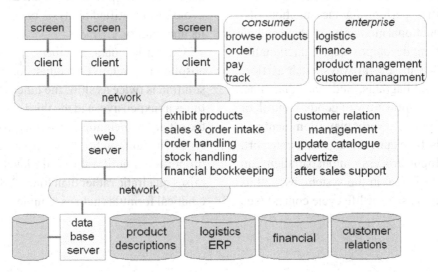

in the context of high-level modeling in the next subsections. For a more elaborate description of possible models and visualizations see (Muller 2004, Muller 2007).

Construction Decomposition

The first step taken by project organizations is to partition the project, and hence the system, in smaller entities such as subsystems, packages, modules, or components. The partitioning plays multiple roles: it supports a partitioning of the organization in teams and subteams, and it supports logistics and life cycle support. In hardware systems this partitioning is called the physical decomposition or physical architecture. In software systems we use the term construction decomposition. The construction decomposition is often explicitly visible in the repository. These decompositions are normally the same as the work breakdown structure, the organizational counterpart of the technical decomposition. The logistics counterpart is often called the Bill of Materials (BoM). Many stakeholders think in terms of parts in this decomposition.

Simple Functional Models

Functional models show how the system works. Functional models focus on functionality rather than the entities performing the functionality. That makes functional models more abstract than the construction decomposition. Functionality can be modeled in several ways, such as flow models, activity diagrams, and state diagrams. Flow models can show flow of goods, control, or information. Typically, verbs play a dominant role in flow models, for example load, store, transport, or order. The Input-Process-Output paradigm can be used both technical in the system, as well as organizational in usage or life cycle context (see Fricke 2000).

We have observed that software developers tend to have a strong functional focus, abstracting away from physical decomposition. However, sometimes their way of expressing themselves is a mix of construction decomposition (how do we define the software in building blocks and components) and functions. Single building blocks often correspond to one or more functions. However, it is the dynamic instantiation that determines the functional behavior of the system. A "pure" functional model explains what the system does dynamically without the more static allocation or partitioning considerations.

Quantification, Data, and Formulas

Quantification helps to make discussions more tangible. Characteristics of parts and functions can be quantified: how fast, how much, how big, what cost, etc. Gilb (Gilb 2005) explains that multiple numbers can be specified for a single requirement, such as the record value, the desired value, the acceptable value, and the current realized value. These numbers can come from many sources, e.g. provided as input by sales, harvested from literature or Internet, estimated by the developers, or measured. Whatever the source of data is, modelers need to know the credibility and accuracy of data. The use of (known) uncertain data can help to provide more understanding than avoiding quantified analysis because of fear for its uncertainty.

Quantified data, numbers, provide us with absolute and relative insights; for example, this solution is twice as slow, the other solution is ten times as expensive, and the third solution will fail too often. Mathematical formulas provide another type of insight, such as "performance and cost are proportional until a threshold level where costs raises quadratic rather than linear." Simple mathematical formulas help us to understand relationships between characteristics, especially between goal characteristics and means characteristics.

More Views

There are many more views that can be relevant for the subject of interest. For example: concurrency and synchronization, resource usage, exception handling, start-up (initialization) and shut-down, configuration and installation, persistency, and information models. As discussed in (Hole 2006) enough views or models are needed to understand the topic. However, if too many view or models are used then stakeholders get confused and the overview is lost.

APPLYING HIGH-LEVEL MODELING ON WEB BOOKSHOP

In this section we apply the modeling method step by step on the web bookshop case.

1. **Identify issues.** We recommend doing a customer key driver analysis as means to identify issues; see Chapter 3 in (Muller 2011). For the bookshop owner customer experience and operational costs will be part of the customer key drivers. These key drivers can be further decomposed, see the left-hand side of Figure 5. For example, customer experience will depend on product portfolio (up-to-date, complete), look and feel (fashionable, intuitive), quality of product descriptions, and site responsiveness. Similarly, operational costs can be decomposed into among others cost of computing infrastructure, staffing costs, distribution and storage costs of goods, and exception handling costs. Some of these drivers have tensions. For example, the quality of product descriptions, and the completeness of the product portfolio will take a lot of effort, which increases staffing costs. Site responsiveness can be achieved by

over dimensioning computing infrastructure, which again increases operational costs.

2. **Identify parameters and functions both as goals and means.** The next step is to make the discussion more tangible by being specific in functions and parameters. For example, site responsiveness can be expressed in end-to-end response times for specific customer actions, such as browsing and ordering products, or paying and tracking orders. These system level specifications are the result of the internal design of query, retrieve, and rendering of the information and the design of the resource utilization, e.g. networks, processors, and stores. Figure 5 shows the resulting graph of the first two steps.

3. **Create simple models relating goal parameters and means parameters.** For example, we might express customer satisfaction as function of the contributing drivers, site responsiveness as function of the main functions of the site, and browse performance as function of internal design and resource utilization. The simplest form might be that customer experience is the weighted sum of responsiveness, description quality, look and feel, actuality, and completeness. Similarly, responsiveness can be the weighted sum of end-to-end response times of browsing, ordering, paying, and tracking. The end-to-end response time might need a slightly more elaborated model based on an internal functional model, a resource model, an allocation of functions to resources, and the concurrency design.

4. **Explore multiple solution concepts (means) and their quantitative behavior.** At the end of Step 3 we can assess the actual state by comparing the status quo to the desired objectives. If there are shortcomings, then we can start looking into alternative solutions. If browsing speed is limiting user experience too much, then we can look into

Figure 5. Graph showing partial goals-means hierarchy of the web-based bookshop

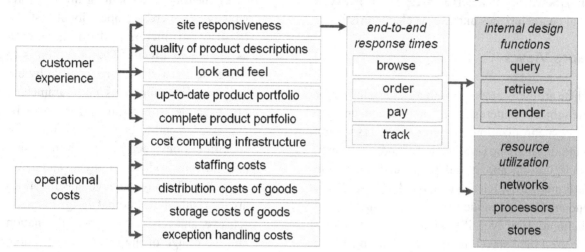

alternative function allocations, concurrency designs, or dimensioning of resources. The exploration of multiple solutions helps to understand the sensitivity of results for various improvements.

We need to model the impact of improvements on other drivers too. For instance, if we increase resource dimensions, then the cost of the computing infrastructure will increase. We recommend using a Pugh matrix (Pugh 1981) to compare concepts. A Pugh matrix uses a list of criteria to assess concepts. Some of these criteria might require a simple model to get a quantitative understanding of such criterion.

5.   **Select one or more concepts that fit best.** Architecting is a continuous struggle between striving for convergence (focus), and the need to be open-minded (divergence). Step 4 is diverging, Step 5 is converging. We do not need to reduce our design options to a single concept. LEAN product development advocates keeping a set of concepts alive under the name set-based design (Ward 1995), often in combination with late decision making. The purpose of this step is to reduce the set of alternatives

to a manageable size that will be elaborated in next iterations.

Example Customer Experience, End-to-End Response Time

We have identified customer experience as one of the key drivers in the usage context. Figure 5 shows how this customer key driver in the usage context relates to design and realization choices. In this subsection we make a few models to elaborate this relation. Figure 6 shows a simplified and enriched activity diagram for the end-to-end response time for browsing products. In this example, we assume that some user action, like pressing a button, starts the activity and we define the end moment when the product is fully shown.

The use case itself is trivial: the customer presses the next button and waits to see the picture of the next product. As consequence, the client requests the picture from the web server and waits for it. Once the picture is received it will be processed to scale it to the proper size and display it on the monitor. The web server either has the picture in cache, in which case it is returned immediately, or it propagates the request to the database containing the product pictures and information. At the bottom a time-scale is shown

Figure 6. Response time model to show a picture of a book

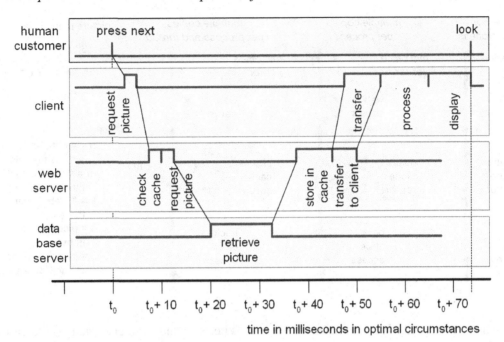

for the execution of this use case, assuming optimal circumstances.

This simple response time model can be used to explore and analyze the response time further. Crucial questions are:

- What is the desired response time to guarantee a positive customer experience?
- What variation of response time is acceptable for a positive customer experience?
- What functions and parts contribute to the response time?
- What functions and parts contribute to the variation of the response time?

Note that for customer experience the end-to-end response time is most relevant. This end-to-end time and its variation are determined by own systems such as web servers, but also external factors such as networks and client configurations.

When the answers give rise to worries, then alternate solutions can be explored to achieve desired performance. For example, assume that

both network layers add significant to the variation of the response time, then greedy caches might be considered in the web servers (to minimize network contribution of the network to the databases) and in the clients (to minimize network contribution between clients and web servers). The validity of such a caching approach depends on typical usage and load conditions, which in turn will have to be modeled (or measured).

Figure 7 shows an example of three design alternatives for handling pictures of the products in the web server. The solution using the least memory is a solution where the three processes (interfacing to the database back office, the caching process, and the web service to the client) each have only a single copy of the picture in memory. Most realizations have multiple copies of a single picture in memory in each process, like the second design option. For performance and concurrency reasons processes or threads can be instantiated several times, shown as the third option. The total amount of memory used for pictures can now be

Figure 7. Example model of memory use for three design options

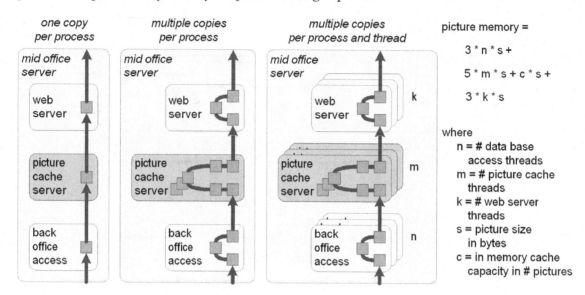

expressed as formula with five parameters *n, m, k, s, and c;* see Figure 7 for the legend.

Figure 8 uses this formula to substitute numbers for six use cases. The *small shop* use case needs so little memory that the all pictures might fit in the L3 cache of the processor. The *highly concurrent* use case still fits entirely in main memory.

When size and number of pictures increases, then we need more virtual memory, potentially slowing down the picture delivery. When high concurrency is combined with many large images, then the server will operate mostly from disk; disk speed will start to dominate the performance.

Figure 8. Substituting number into the formula for the picture memory use

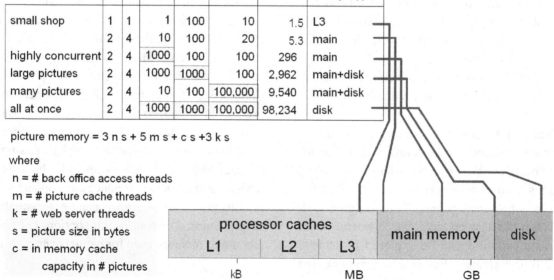

The example in Figure 8 only takes picture storage into account for browsing. Other product-related information is ignored. These models only provide the memory use for pictures when browsing. In real situations other concurrent services might be running that will interfere with this picture retrieval.

All models that we have made are quite simple; not much effort is required to make these models. However, even these very simple models provide insight in potential bottlenecks that may threaten customer key drivers (in this example end-to-end response time as part of customer satisfaction). Similar simple models can be used to explore potential solutions. The benefit is that we do not have to commit or spend lots of resources before we know if solutions make sense.

Example Cost of Change during Life Cycle

We look at the cost of change during the system life cycle as second example. The product portfolio of a bookshop will continuously change, reflecting supply and demand. Figure 9 shows an example of issues that play in keeping a portfolio up-to-date. Portfolio updates are triggered by changes in current products or by publication of new content. The changes have to be made in the databases and the new content has to be added to the databases. When the changes and additions have been made properly, then these will propagate through the tiers and become visible at client level.

The update and addition workflow sounds simple. However, since staff is a significant cost factor, we need to know how much this actually costs and if cost reductions are possible to increase efficiency. We can make a simple model based on number of changes and new publications, and cost per update or addition. At the realization side mundane problems may have large impact on the update effort. For example, the incoming content definitions might be in legacy data formats while the web shop is designed to use XML based data. The software might be designed to make perfect conversions, such that no human verification is required. Unfortunately, a stack of compatibility problems often makes it impossible to do such

Figure 9. How new content definitions impact the system

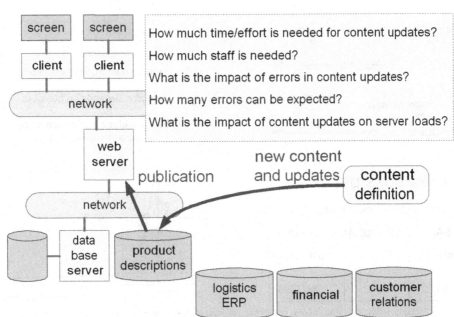

conversion completely automatic. The high-level modeling can guide the specification and design to achieve a proper amount of automation and quality of data conversion.

A complicating factor for this model is that we need to understand the workflow one step deeper in order to understand quality control and measures for quality control. Small errors (e.g. wrong price, wrong identification) might have large business impacts. In this case we recommend making simple models of quality (where, when, what, and how can errors be introduced; what is their impact; what are countermeasures; what is the expected workflow including quality control). The results of this model can impact the choice of external interface and formats, and the degree of automation of updates and additions.

Any model needs calibrated data to produce meaningful results. In this example, we can measure the amount of time needed to make or verify updates or additions. Similarly we can look for historic data for the expected number of additions. Figure 10 shows some very simple Internet research to get some calibration for the amount of new books that are published per year. We can see that large western countries publish

hundreds of thousands new books per year. It can be expected that upcoming economies with an order of magnitude more inhabitants (and hence potential authors) might increase the number of new books per years into millions.

The number of global new books per year is not yet very meaningful for our bookshop. We need to know how many new publications are selected for inclusion in the portfolio. The business and sales strategy of the bookshop will determine how many new titles are selected. Figure 10 shows that traditional bookshops such as WH Smith tend to focus on a limited amount of titles with high sales volume. At the other hand, web-based bookshops, take advantage of their virtual presence to offer a wide variation of books with lower selling volumes. This so-called "long tail" produces a large business volume; a large amount of titles times a small volume might beat the large volume of popular books.

The number of new books published in 2005 in UK and USA only exceeds 1000 new titles per day. This number can be used to make initial estimates for the effort involved in introducing new books in the portfolio.

Figure 10. Amount of new books published in one year

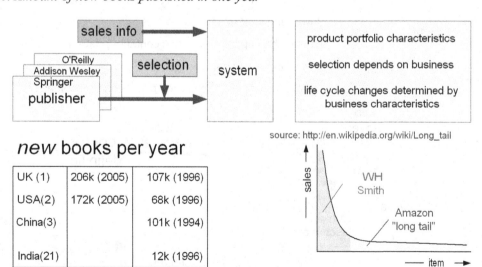

new books per year

UK (1)	206k (2005)	107k (1996)
USA(2)	172k (2005)	68k (1996)
China(3)		101k (1994)
India(21)		12k (1996)

source: http://en.wikipedia.org/wiki/Books_published_per_country_per_year

Figure 11. Model of updating effort

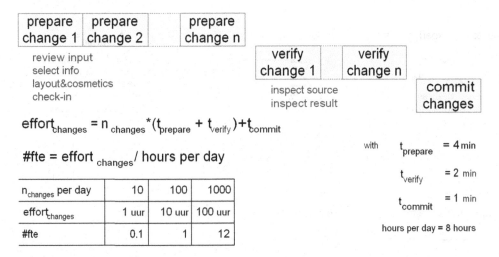

We need to elaborate the workflow one step more to be able to estimate the cost of making changes to existing products and adding new books. Figure 11 shows a simple workflow for making changes. Three stages are used: preparation, verification, and commitment. During preparation, the input data is reviewed, information is selected that needs to be included, layout and cosmetics are defined, and the resulting product description is checked in. During verification, both input data and the result are inspected. The commitment releases the descriptions into the databases and makes access through the client and web servers possible.

Figure 11 shows below the workflow formulas for the effort involved in making changes, some assumed cost per elementary action, and the quantitative results when these assumed costs are substituted in the formulas. This simple analysis shows that a specialized bookshop with 10 changes per day needs 0.1 full time equivalent (fte) to keep data descriptions up-to-date. A bookshop with a much broader offering, e.g. offering most books in the tail, needs a small office with staff to keep the product descriptions up-to-date. These very rough numbers can be used to think about options such as fully automated product

updates in relation to the potential staff cost reduction.

In this example we have shown that simple models can help to make qualities such as maintainability, expandability, scalability, and flexibility more tangible. This helps to manage expectations, and to improve the design. For example, we can avoid overdesigning flexibility (a common problem in software, over-generic designs). However, we can consciously decide what balance we need in these qualities and effort.

THE BIG PICTURE

Systems engineers have the difficult task to create "the big picture." Unfortunately, the big picture is a paradox: it requires all data to be useful; however, the overview that the big picture should bring is lost by the multitude of data. High-level modeling is a first step in creating parts of the big picture. The idea is that combining several high-level models helps individuals to get closer to the big picture. In this section we discuss how several high-level models have to be used together to get closer to the big picture. Later we will discuss the flip-side of all simplifications: the credibility of the high-level models.

Figure 12. Relating multiple models

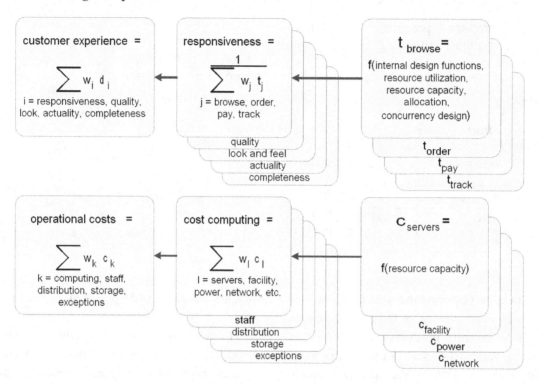

Relating High-Level Models

In the two examples we have shown and discussed several models supported by several diagrams or views. The increased understanding and the decision making support is achieved by relating several models. Figure 12 shows the models related to the customer experience and responsiveness in relation to each other. We take customer experience as starting point, decomposing it in multiple contributing drivers. Every driver can be modeled; we show the model for responsiveness, modeled as one divided by a weighted sum of response times. The browsing time is shown as function of many design choices. One of the design choices is the capacity of resources. The resource capacity has an immediate cost impact; the cost of computing is the sum of many cost factors, the cost of the servers is one of them.

We have modeled the customer experience extremely simple as a weighted sum of the con-

tributions. This simplification might not be valid, as every simplification we applied. The field of user experience, covered by disciplines as human factors and industrial design, is much less tangible than conventional engineering. The lack of tangibility is no excuse to ignore the experience; it is a challenge to simplify the available knowledge sufficiently, such that a meaningful discussion is facilitated. In the example of responsiveness, it might be that we can better replace the response time in the formula by a metric as function of the response time. For example, quite often the response time appreciation is rather non-linear: responses below 0.1 s are perceived as instantaneous, while response between 0.1 and 1 second are perceived as "fast." Improving a system from 0.6 to 0.4 second does not improve the user experience significant, since the response is still not instantaneous.

A similar diagram can be constructed for the change effort example. The starting point for that diagram is the customer experience with main focus on quality of descriptions, and actuality and completeness of the product portfolio. The second starting point is the operational cost model with focus on staff costs and exception handling costs. The change workflow model feeds into both models.

In practice, these different concerns have tensions and are potentially conflicting. For example, cost reduction is often achieved by reducing server capacity, which might reduce responsiveness. Part of trying to get closer to the big picture is to identify and understand these tensions. To keep the examples simple enough we have ignored these mutual dependencies. (Muller 2004) provides a technique called "Threads-of-Reasoning" that targets tensions from mutual dependencies.

Credibility of High-Level Models

Models are simplified representations of part of the real world used for communication, documentation, analysis, simulation, decision making, and verification. Simplification in models is the key to achieve all these goals. Simplification helps to reduce a complex and chaotic reality in a more simple and structured representation that can be explained and discussed in a limited amount of time.

Simplification means that results of models always need to be used with care. Some simplifications may cause unreliable results. Users of models must ensure that a model is applicable for the purpose, and be aware of the accuracy of the results.

High-level models, as discussed in this chapter, are highly simplified. The purpose of high-level models is to increase understanding, and facilitate exploration and decision making in a broader context. However, we need to be aware that stacking simplifications of the models and uncertainties in the data results in uncertain and inaccurate results. One of the main values of high-level modeling is the discussion about the models

and the numbers. By making high-level models we are forced to make our assumptions explicit. For example, what size of product portfolio do we have in mind, what operational margins do we assume, what automation we expect, etc. Often the relative relation of parameters is meaningful, while the absolute value might be quite uncertain. For example, the cost of change that we estimated might be an order of magnitude off. However, the ratio between preparation and verification might be reasonably accurate. The simple workflow model will trigger lots of discussions: do we use a three-stage approach, do we use a single commitment model, do we do all steps "manually," etc.

An example of an oversimplification is that we assumed that customer experience is reversely proportional to the response time. However, in reality this relationship has a kind of staircase form. For example, user experience is ranked as poor above 1 second response time, while response times between 0.1 and 1 second are ranked as good and response times below 0.1 second are ranked as extremely good. This staircase shape of the ranking relates to customer perceptions and expectations. Response times above one second are perceived a sluggish, response times below 0.1 second are perceived as immediate or continuous. Complicating factor is that perceptions and expectations are a function of the context and time; when the competition shows continuous browsing, then that might become the de facto expectation.

Figure 13. Enterprise context, enterprise, IT-system as hierarchy

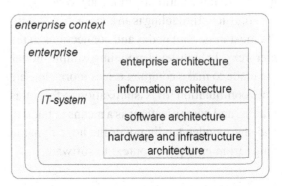

ALIGNING ENTERPRISE AND IT-SYSTEM, AND THEIR ARCHITECTURES

We can view enterprise context, enterprise, and IT-system as a hierarchy; see Figure 13; in this hierarchy of systems we have a typical hierarchy of architectures. The IT-system is the context of the software; the software architecture is a means to realize the IT-system. Similarly, an enterprise is the context of an IT-system; the information, software, hardware, and infrastructure architectures are means to realize the It system that serves the enterprise. Finally, satisfied customers in the enterprise context are the ultimate goal of the enterprise supported by the enterprise architecture. By viewing these entities as hierarchy, we can see that the rationale for entities "lower" in the hierarchy can be partitioned in objectives given by the "higher" entities in this hierarchy, and the capabilities and constraints of the "lower" entities.

Aligning enterprise and IT-system, and their architectures can be done by connecting higher level goals to lower level goals so that the lower levels will provide proper means. The graph in Figure 5 is showing such graph that relates customer experience in the enterprise context in several steps with software architecture choices.

In the case that we discussed, we did relate the enterprise concern of customer experience to response time to fundamental software design choices and we related the rate of change in the product portfolio (an enterprise concern) to the workflow of making updates, to the design of importing information from legacy systems.

High-level modeling is an approach to identify the most important nodes and connections in this hierarchy. In high-level modeling, simple models are made to make complex issues more tangible. The combination of visualizations, formulas, graphs, and quantifications is a means to build up and share understanding over the huge dynamic range from enterprise context to software.

In general, we strive for generic solutions and architectures, using abstraction as means to capture architectures compact and concise. The risk of creating and documenting architectures (enterprise, system or software) is that the architectures become so abstract and generic that understanding is lost. High-level modeling complements the architecting approach by quantifying and visualizing a limited set of use cases. These high-level models not only help to create and share understanding but also help to validate the architectures. These high-level models force architects to substantiate claims like "Pattern X makes the software architecture better maintainable."

HIGH-LEVEL MODELING IN PRACTICE

In workshops and courses the development teams are guided through a process to create an initial set of high-level models to identify major issues. In general, development teams tend to be solution focused with insufficient context understanding. In other words, many solution-oriented decisions have been taken, without the means to discuss the impact in the customer context. Some developers even have the tendency to abstract from this context knowledge and strive for a generic solution. The high-level modeling effort forces them to think about the customer context and the life cycle context. The steps in the process help developers to become concrete such that the problems and solution can be discussed and understood.

This way of working and thinking is not easy for most developers. It is not a straight forward recipe that results in the best answer. Rather it requires a continuous evaluation of the models that are made in terms of relevance, level of detail, accuracy, and effort. It also requires an open mind to find the proper type of model and an effective visualization. Most developers are used to more well-defined problems with predefined techniques that systematically bring them from problem to solution. When confronted with a heterogeneous environment with a broad set of stakeholders, they discover that their conventional approaches no longer work. This field of tension is well known in the systems engineering community, where debates rage whether good processes and tools suffice ("traditional systems engineering"), or that the way of thinking is crucial ("systems thinking").

At the end of the workshop or course, participants comment that they understand the necessity to understand customer and life cycle context in relation to the system of interest. However, at that moment most of them are not yet capable to make sensible high-level models themselves. They need to acquire more domain knowledge (knowledge of customer and life cycle context), and they need a richer set of modeling means (notations, representations, mathematical approaches). It is gratifying to meet past course participants several years later and to see that they actually apply the high-level modeling approach and recognize its added value to all other necessary project, engineering and design means. It is not realistic to expect that all developers can learn and apply high-level modeling. A significant part of the developer's population will never embrace high-level modeling and is happy to contribute in building the solution rather than answering questions like, "Do we address the right problem?" or "Will this solution solve the problem properly?"

FUTURE RESEARCH DIRECTIONS

Most disciplinary research emphasizes accuracy and completeness, resulting in extensive models, supported by formalisms and tools. However, challenges at system level are to cope with heterogeneity of information and uncertainties in inputs. More research is needed to find methods that help architects and designers to cope with heterogeneity and uncertainties.

Heterogeneity can be shown by comparing keywords of the various levels of models. Enterprises operate in a competitive economic world,

guided and constrained by legal regulations, controlled by financial institutions, embedded in an ecological, political, and social environment, populated with a wide variety of humans from paying customers to criminals. All these factors somehow relate to factors at system level, such as performance, reliability, operational cost, and security approach. Finally, we get to the technical world, where designers discuss patterns, concurrency, layering, etc. High-level modeling is an approach to relate across semantic boundaries.

Uncertainties increase when the scope increases. Performance of a single-server single-application system might be deterministic. However, multi-server multi-application systems might show chaotic behavior with its inherent uncertainties. These complicating factors are present from micro to macro scale. At micro scale we see a proliferation of caches, clock domains, smart optimizations (e.g. out-of-order scheduling) that all increase uncertainty of aggregated numbers. At macro scale we have to cope with uncertainties of the human world with fashion, hypes, crises, and other political, social, and economic complexities.

Both heterogeneity and uncertainties keep increasing, due to an increased level of integration in and of enterprises and systems in enterprises. The increased integration requires more and more interoperability. Demographic and economic trends, the quick rise of the upcoming economies as China, India, Brazil, and Turkey, increase the enterprise scope and bring additional cultural and political complexity. At the same time enterprises are forced into working faster and developing solutions faster. The global heart beat is increasing, resulting in more time pressure on system development.

We need practical and understandable means for architects and designers to cope with heterogeneity and uncertainties in a world that demands faster and faster results. Research is needed to understand the target group of architects and designers better so that methods and techniques can be developed and validated to support them.

CONCLUSION

We have discussed an approach of using simple high-level models to help architects and designers to get a quick understanding of the problem in a broader context and of potential solutions. Simple models are related in a goals-means hierarchy. Starting point are the goals of an enterprise in its societal context and with its life cycle needs. Models at enterprise level typically are heterogeneous and have to cope with uncertainties in inputs. When moving down in the hierarchy models grow gradually more technical, and at the same time more homogeneous.

We recommend modeling multiple views in time-boxed iterations. Typically, physical or construction decompositions are used (because many stakeholders think in these terms), functional models are needed, and quantified understanding is needed by using formulas and actual numbers. Other views may be added, customized toward the problem; architects normally use 10-12 views. The iterations need to be quick to help the modelers to get an overview of the whole problem and solutions space that can guide them in further elaborations. Iterations may start with one hour and increase their duration to a week; this corresponds to time-boxes per view of 15 minutes to one day.

The high-level nature, and the short time-boxes, can only be achieved by significant simplifications. Such simplifications help in understanding, discussion and communication. At the same time, simplifications limit the credibility of the results of the model. Results have to be used with great care, being aware of the simplifications that went into the high-level models.

REFERENCES

Boardman, J., & Sauser, B. (2008). *Systems thinking: Coping with 21st century problems*. CRC Press. doi:10.1201/9781420054927

Bonnema, M. (2008). *FunKey architecting - An integrated approach to system architecting using functions, key drivers and system budgets*. Doctoral dissertation, University of Twente, the Netherlands.

Borches, D. (2010). *A3 architecture overviews; A tool for effective communication in product evolution*. Doctoral dissertation, University of Twente, the Netherlands.

Estefan, J. A. (2007). *Survey of candidate model-based engineering (MBSE): Methodologies Rev A*. INCOSE MBSE Focus Group. Retrieved July 11, 2011, from www.omgsysml.org/MBSE_Methodology_Survey_RevA.pdf

Fricke, E., Schulz, A., Wehlitz, A., & Negele, H. (2000). A generic approach to implement information-based system development. *Proceedings INCOSE 2000,* Minneapolis. Retrieved from www.gfse.de/se/pubs/downloads/Info_based_SD_INC2000.pdf

Gilb, T. (2005). *Competitive engineering: A handbook for systems engineering, requirements engineering, and software engineering using pLanguage*. London, UK: Elsevier Butterworth-Heinemann.

Hamberg, R., & Verriet, J. (Eds.). (2011). *Automation in warehouse development*. Dordrecht, The Netherlands: Springer.

Heemels, M., & Muller, G. (Eds.). (2007). *Boderc: Model-based design of high-tech systems*. Eindhoven, The Netherlands: Embedded Systems Institute.

Hitchins, D. K. (2003). *Advanced systems thinking, engineering and management*. Artech House.

Hole, E., & Muller, G. (2006). *Architectural descriptions and models*. White Paper Resulting from Architecture Forum Meeting. Retrieved July 12, 2011, from http://www.architectingforum.org/whitepapers/SAF_WhitePaper_2006_2.pdf

ISO/IEC/IEEE. 42010. (2011). *Systems and software engineering—Architecture description.* Retrieved from http://www.iso-architecture.org/ieee-1471/

Kaplan, R. S., & Norton, D. P. (1996). Using the Balanced Scorecard as a strategic management system. *Harvard Business Review,* (January-February): 76.

Lawson, H. (2010). *A journey through the systems landscape.*

Mascitelli, R. (2006). *The lean product development guidebook: Everything your design team needs to improve efficiency and slash time to market.*

McManus, J., & Wood-Harper, D. (2008). *A study in project failure.* Retrieved February 5, 2012, from http://www.bcs.org/content/ConWebDoc/19584

Muller, G. (2004). *CAFCR: A multi-view method for embedded systems architecting; Balancing genericity and specificity.* PhD thesis, University of Delft. Retrieved from http://www.gaudisite.nl/ThesisBook.pdf

Muller, G. (2007). *System modeling and analysis: A practical approach.* Retrieved February 7, 2012, from http://www.gaudisite.nl/SystemModelingAndAnalysisBook.pdf

Muller, G. (2011). *Systems architecting: A business perspective.* CRC Press.

Potts, C. (1993). Software-engineering research revisited. *IEEE Software, 10*(5), 19–28. doi:10.1109/52.232392

Pugh, S. (1981). Concept selection: A method that works. In V. Hubka (Ed.), *Review of Design Methodology: Proceedings International Conference on Engineering Design,* Rome, (pp. 497–506). Zürich, Switzerland: Heurista.

Schmidt, D. C. (2006). Model-driven engineering. *IEEE Computer, 39*(2). Retrieved July 11, 2011, from http://www.cs.wustl.edu/~schmidt/PDF/GEI.pdf

Ward, A. C., Liker, J. K., Cristiano, J. J., & Sobek, D. K. II. (1995). The second Toyota paradox: How delaying decisions can make better cars faster. *Sloan Management Review, 36*(3), 43–61.

ADDITIONAL READING

Gorbea, C., Fricke, E., & Lindemann, U. (2008). The design of future cars in a new age of architectural competition. *Proceedings of the ASME 2008 International Design Engineering Technical Conferences & Computers and Information in Engineering Conference IDETC/CIE 2008* August 3-6, 2008, Brooklyn, New York, USA.

KEY TERMS AND DEFINITIONS

Big Picture: An expression used for the holistic perspective: look at problem and solution as a whole. Unfortunately, the paradox is that we are never able to grasp the big picture entirely.

Credibility: A characteristic of a model that indicates how trustworthy the outcome of the model is.

Functional Models: Models that explain how the parts of the system operate; typical functional models contain verbs, where the verbs express the action.

High-Level Modeling: Modeling whereby abstraction simplified models a recreated and analyzed to facilitate decision making and communication.

Life Cycle Context: The context of the system from initial conception to final commissioning of the system.

Usage Context: The context of the system where the system is used with customers and users as primary stakeholders.

View: A way of looking and describing problem and solutions; typical views take a specific concern of a stakeholder as starting point.

Chapter 10

Decisions Required vs. Decisions Made:
Connecting Enterprise Architects and Solution Architects via Guidance Models

Olaf Zimmermann
IBM Research GmbH, Switzerland & ABB Corporate Research, Switzerland

Christoph Miksovic
IBM Research GmbH, Switzerland

ABSTRACT

Contemporary enterprise architecture frameworks excel at inventorying as-is and at specifying to-be architecture landscapes; they also help enterprise architects to establish governance processes and architectural principles. Solution architects, however, expect mature frameworks not only to express such fundamental design constraints, but also to provide concrete and tangible guidance how to comply with framework building blocks, processes, and principles – a route planner is needed in addition to maps of destinations. In this chapter, the authors show how to extend an existing enterprise architecture framework with decision guidance models that capture architectural decisions recurring in a particular domain. Such guidance models codify architectural knowledge by recommending proven patterns, technologies, and products; architectural principles are represented as decision drivers. Owned by enterprise architects but populated and consumed by solution architects, guidance models are living artifacts (reusable assets) that realize a lightweight knowledge exchange between the two communities – and provide the desired route planners for architectural analysis, synthesis, and evaluation.

DOI: 10.4018/978-1-4666-2199-2.ch010

INTRODUCTION

A key objective of enterprise architects is to align the existing and the future IT systems with the business model and the strategic direction of an enterprise. Architecture frameworks support enterprise architects when they inventory the existing (as-is) and when they specify the future (to-be) architecture landscapes; they also help them to establish governance processes and architectural principles. However, solution architects that work on specific implementation projects expect mature frameworks not only to express such fundamental design constraints, but also to provide concrete and tangible guidance how to comply with framework building blocks, processes, and principles. In other words, a route planner is needed in addition to maps of destinations.

In practice, we have come across the following collaboration issues between enterprise architects and solution architects that call for such a route planner:

1. **Availability Issues:** Experienced, knowledgeable enterprise architects have been appointed, who managed to define to-be architectures and to release enterprise-wide architectural principles. However, they did not find the time yet to author additional documentation *how* to adhere to these principles and they are slow to respond to requests for reviews and/or project participation. Consequently, the enterprise architecture artifacts are ignored by projects teams or, even worse, "pseudo-compliance" is declared at an early stage, but never really strived for and, consequently, never actually reached.
2. **Consumability Issues:** To-be architectures and/or architectural principles are documented, but difficult to understand and to relate to design concerns on projects. Such issues are often caused by inadequate levels of abstraction and detail: if specified on rather high levels, enterprise architecture artifacts run the risk of being perceived to be full of obvious truisms and/or trivial; on the contrary, rather detailed specifications take a long time to create, comprehend, and maintain; they might also be impossible to implement under economic constraints.
3. **Enforcement and Acceptance Issues:** Workable enterprise architecture guidelines are in place, as well as a governance process. However, the guidelines established by the enterprise architects (for the benefit of the whole enterprise) are not followed properly because project teams do not fully appreciate their value; due to their narrower design scope, they view these guidelines as unwelcome additional design constraints. In practice, we also observed that solution architectures often pass formal quality reviews with certain obligations; e.g., architectural smells are reported and refactorings are suggested to reduce technical debt (Brown, Nord, & Ozkaya, 2011). However, such obligations are not always followed up upon. In such settings, solution architects can expect to "get away" with violations of architectural principles, which typically are justified by short term business priorities and stakeholder pressure.

These issues are further complicated when third parties such as external consulting firms and outsourcing providers with different goals and concerns get involved; this is often the case in practice today.

Examples of architecture design issues that often require the attention of enterprise architects are:

- The architectural principle that all sensitive data has to be secured: security is not a single requirement, but a set of responses to certain threats requiring a risk analysis and risk management (mitigation) strategy, as well as a security requirements engineering effort. For instance, a data sensitivity classification scheme might be missing entirely. In other cases, such schemes only exist in rudimentary forms; specifically, examples or concrete advice how to classify application data such as customer profiles, orders, and invoices are rarely given. This example illustrates issues 1 and 2 from above (no availability and poor consumability).

- A data classification scheme exists and distinguishes uncritical from critical Personal Information (PI) and from highly critical Sensitive Personal Information (SPI); an infrastructure-level security zone model including network transport-level firewalls has been defined as well. However, the enterprise-wide security architecture does not specify whether HTTPS connections using server-side certificates (128 bit) are good enough to protect zone-to-zone traffic that goes through firewalls if this traffic carries SPI. Such assessment requires links from business-level compliance rules to logical (functional) application architectures and then to physical infrastructure architectures; such links often are not modeled explicitly so that traceability cannot be provided. This scenario also exemplifies issues 1 and 2 (lack of availability and limited consumability).

- The security architecture on the enterprise level clearly states that if SPI is transferred across firewalls, HTTPS has to be used; however, this decision is overruled and an unsecured HTTP channel is established by opening a particular port for a tactical application supposed to go live soon due to urgent business needs (e.g., to respond to a product announcement recently made by a competitor); this tactical solution remains operational for several years although violating an architectural principle from the enterprise level. This example illustrates/instantiates issue 3 from above (lack of enforcement and acceptance).

Other examples of architectural decisions that call for guidance from the enterprise level are: technology platform choices, vendor preferences, how to deal with regulatory and legal constraints, including audit requirements such as completeness, accuracy, validity and restricted access (Julisch, Sutter, Woitalla, & Zimmermann, 2011), usage of open source software (often a separate principle or decision is required per open source license scheme such as Apache or GNU Public License) (Haischt & Georg, 2010), and so forth. Additional examples, also pertaining to the design of logical (functional) application architectures and to application integration, are presented in our previous publications (Zimmermann, 2009).

These examples illustrate the gap between enterprise architecture and solution architecture that exists in the industry. The gap has multiple facets—objectives, terminology, methods, techniques, and tools of the two communities differ substantially. In our opinion, enterprise architecture only has a chance to have a sustainable impact on the business and IT projects if this gap is overcome; to do so, extensions to existing methods are required.

Objective: To close the gap between enterprise architects and solution architects, this chapter introduces a novel way for these communities to improve their communication and knowledge exchange:

How can enterprise architects support project-level solution architects with concrete managerial and technical advice regarding the architectural decision identification, making, and enforcement activities required to ensure that the system under construction meets the expectations of its primary stakeholders (i.e., users, sponsors), but also respects the constraints imposed by implementation governance authorities (e.g., enterprise architects, auditors)?*

In response to this question, we propose to let enterprise and solution architects share architectural decision models that collect key issues and proven solutions to them. In this effort, we leverage, combine, and extend concepts from The Open Group Architecture Framework (TOGAF) (The Open Group, 2009) and from SOA Decision Modeling (SOAD) (Zimmermann, 2011). Specifically, we show how to extend TOGAF with SOAD guidance models that capture architectural decisions recurring in a particular domain such as Service-Oriented Architecture (SOA) design (Krafzig, Banke, & Slama, 2005). Such guidance models codify architectural knowledge by recommending proven patterns, technologies, and products; architectural principles are represented as decision drivers. Owned by an enterprise architect but populated and consumed by solution architects, guidance models are living artifacts and reusable assets that realize a lightweight knowledge exchange between the two communities.

Being integrated into TOGAF, guidance models can provide the desired route planners for architectural synthesis on implementation projects. Enterprise-level decision making is out of our scope for the time being; the presented concepts are designed to also work on that level. One can view TOGAF as an "über-guidance model" for enterprise architecture construction: TOGAF does not formally model decisions in an explicit guidance model, but still comprises a knowledge repository. Note that a solution constructed in an implementation project may be a marketed product such as an Enterprise Resource Planning (ERP) package or a client-specific solution (resulting from one-of-a-kind application development or integration).

INTRODUCTION TO THE CASE STUDY: PREMIER QUOTES GROUP (PQG)

To be able to exemplify our approach, we now introduce a basic scenario from the insurance industry. The scenario concerns a fictitious company and is simplified due to space constraints; however, business scenario, existing enterprise application architectures, and technical design considerations in the case originate directly from our rich project experience in several industry sectors (e.g., financial services, telecommunications, and automotive).

Let us assume that PremierQuotes Inc., an insurance company, acquired DirtCheap Insurance, another insurance company, and formed the PremierQuotes Group (PQG) to fulfill the growth expectations of its stakeholders (Zimmermann, Tomlinson, and Peuser, 2003). The two merged companies have just consolidated their customer care, contract, and risk management applications. Let us assume that the unified contract application communicates with a customer database and a policy backend to serve end users via three customer self service, agent, and back office channels. Risk management application and policy backend are COBOL applications running on the IBM System z platform. The contract application is a Java Enterprise Edition (JEE) application. Customer care is a software package; its Web application part consists of PHP scripts. An external data source, currently provided by a government information server on the Internet, is integrated, providing crime statistics (fraud history) by geographical area in a proprietary file format.

The three physical tiers are the client tier, the mid tier hosting presentation, domain, and resource (data) access logic, and the backend tier. World-Wide Web (WWW) infrastructure connects the client tier with the mid tier (over the Internet for the customer self service channel and the agent channel, over an intranet for the back office channel). Traditional Enterprise Application Integration (EAI) middleware (e.g., message-oriented middleware) is used to connect the mid tier with the backend tier.

Figure 1 illustrates a representative subset of this Enterprise Application (EA) landscape at PQG.

The client tier contains all application components directly serving the users. Examples are Web browsers and rich client applications running on Personal Computers (PCs) used by customers, agents, and back office staff. The mid tier comprises the three applications. These applications are logically layered into presentation, domain, and resource (data) access logic layers. Typical responsibilities of the mid tier are input validation, processing control, session state management, calculations, and manipulations of enterprise resources. The backend tier stores enterprise resources persistently and coordinates concurrent

access to the enterprise resources (i.e., customer profiles, offers, and policies). This tier hosts database servers, but also other systems which in themselves may be physically tiered, but are located external to the company or in another organizational domain. The policy backend and the government information server are examples. Various communication channels exist within and between tiers (Figure 1).

BACKGROUND: APPLYING THE OPEN GROUP ARCHITECTURE FRAMEWORK (TOGAF)

There is a wide range of methods, artifact classification taxonomies, and entire frameworks that can be adapted by enterprise architects to manage enterprise architecture landscapes such as the one at PQG. Prominent examples include The

Figure 1. PQG enterprise applications: System contexts, architecture overview (as-is situation)

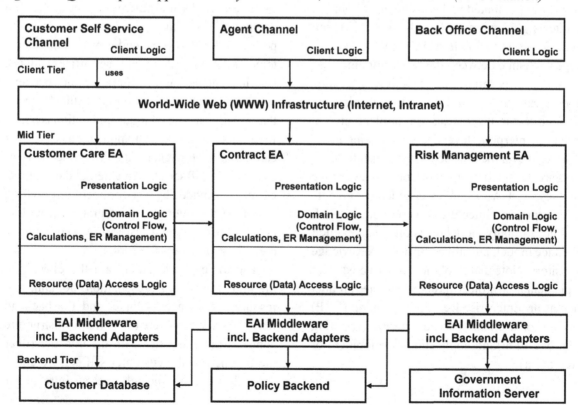

Open Group Architecture Framework (TOGAF) (Open Group, 2009), the Department of Defense Architecture Framework (DoDAF) (Department of Defense, 2010), the Enterprise Unified Process (EUP) (Ambler, Nalbone, & Vizdos, 2005), which is an extension of the Rational Unified Process (RUP) (Kruchten, 2003), and the Zachman Framework (Sowa & Zachman, 1992). The Zachman Framework was one of the first of its kind to provide a comprehensive approach for the classification of enterprise architectural artifacts. Numerous proprietary architecture frameworks from commercial (professional) service providers such as consulting firms exist as well.

Among these frameworks, TOGAF can be viewed as representative – or even as a de facto standard – due to its general availability, maturity, comprehensiveness, and wide acceptance in many countries around the world. We applied TOGAF ourselves in a number of enterprise architecture engagements for clients in several industries. Hence, we will focus on the structure and content of the TOGAF 9 framework in this chapter. Our integration concepts are designed to also work with other enterprise architecture frameworks.

TOGAF Overview

TOGAF originally has its roots in the Technical Architecture Framework for Information Management (TAFIM) (Department of Defense, 1996), which focused more on the infrastructure and technical aspects of enterprise architecture. TOGAF 8.1 eventually widened the scope of TOGAF to feature business, data, and application architectures more prominently. At the time of writing, TOGAF 9 was the latest (current) edition (The Open Group, 2009). It includes major enhancements over previous versions to better address state-of-the-art concepts such as iterative architecture development, SOA, specific security architecture considerations, and capability-based planning.

The main components and key concepts in TOGAF 9 are (The Open Group, 2009):

- The Architecture Development Method (ADM) is the core of TOGAF. It describes a step-by-step approach to developing and maintaining an enterprise architecture.
- The ADM guidelines and techniques component contains a collection of blueprints, recommendations, and best practices for applying the ADM. Examples include architectural principles, architectural patterns, governance of SOA initiatives, and migration planning techniques.
- The TOGAF architecture content framework provides a meta-model for architectural content that allows the major architectural artifacts to be consistently defined, structured, and presented. An example of such an artifact is a reusable architecture building block (component) for audit tracking that must be utilized for the development of new business applications.
- Enterprise continuum and tools discusses appropriate taxonomies and tools to categorize and store the outputs of architecture activities within an enterprise and elaborates the concept of an architecture repository. The enterprise continuum supports a very broad architectural scope, covering generic IT system services such as transaction processing, information integration architecture topics, industry-specific architectures like insurance or telecommunications architectures, and enterprise-specific architectures. Thus, the enterprise continuum can be seen as an "umbrella framework" for the TOGAF architecture content framework (which typically focuses on enterprise-specific architectures).
- The TOGAF reference models component introduces two fundamental architectural reference models, namely the TOGAF

Technical Reference Model (TRM), which provides a high-level taxonomy for the description of application software, application platforms, and communications infrastructures, and the Integrated Information Infrastructure Reference Model (III-RM). The III-RM is a reference model for application components to support information integration across domains (e.g. between the sales and invoicing business units of an enterprise).

• An architecture capability framework discusses the organization, processes, skills, roles, and responsibilities required to establish and operate an architecture practice within an enterprise.

As stated in Chapter 2.10 of TOGAF 9, many TOGAF concepts, artifacts and deliverables are generic in order to address a wide variety of enterprises in different industries. TOGAF 9 therefore defines a specific process step for tailoring (Chapter 6.4.5, Select and Tailor Architecture Framework) (The Open Group, 2009). According to our practical experience, TOGAF can be adapted for many functional and technical domains, providing a great deal of flexibility. However, these adaptation and tailoring capabilities require considerable effort (to enhance and refine the TOGAF framework for a specific enterprise).

Architecture Development Method

In contrast to many other enterprise architecture frameworks, TOGAF provides the Architecture Development Method (ADM) as its core component. ADM provides a sound repeatable process for developing architectures. According to Chapter 2.4 of TOGAF 9, this process includes activities such as establishing an architecture framework, developing architecture content, identifying and prioritizing implementation projects, and governing the realization of architectures (The Open Group, 2009). An iterative and incremental development style is explicitly promoted and elaborated in Chapter 19 of TOGAF 9 (The Open Group, 2009).

Figure 2 presents the eight ADM phases (as well as a subset of the artifacts produced in these phases):

A. Architecture Vision
B. Business Architecture
C. Information Systems Architecture
D. Technology Architecture
E. Opportunities and Solutions
F. Migration Planning
G. Implementation Governance
H. Architecture Change Management
J. Requirements Management

There is an additional preliminary phase which describes the initial preparation and startup activities required to set up a new enterprise architecture process; this phase is not shown in Figure 2. The phases form a cycle (with requirements management as a recurring phase across the entire cycle), which typically is traversed in a highly iterative manner. This cyclic organization of the phases allows enterprise architects to frequently validate (intermediate) results against the original expectations and to introduce new requirements, both on the level of the whole ADM cycle and on the level of a particular phase.

Phase A focuses on scoping decisions regarding the planned ADM cycle, on stakeholder identification, on validation of enterprise principles, standards and guidelines, as well as on the development of an architecture vision. In other words, the business case for the ADM development cycle is defined during this phase.

The phases B, C and D support the development of the business, data, application and technology architecture models. Ideally, traceability between these architecture models and the general enterprise principles and strategies is pursued.

Figure 2. TOGAF ADM with key artifacts and phases (adapted from The Open Group, 2009)

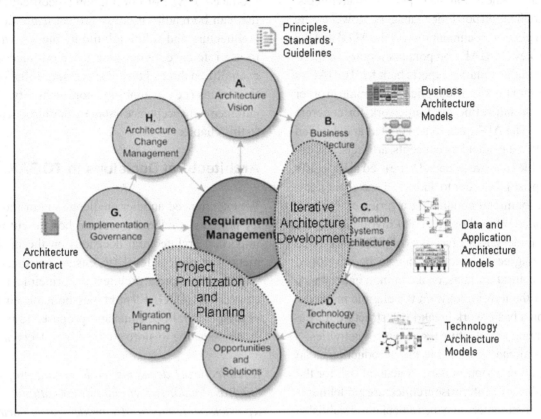

The phases E and F deal with the identification and the planning of projects that support the strategic requirements of the enterprise.

Once important projects from the perspective of the enterprise requirements are defined, the phase G specifies the governance activities for these implementation projects. In this context, the architecture contract is a key deliverable that defines the responsibilities and obligations of both a particular implementation project and the enterprise architecture group. It is discussed in more detail the subsection of this chapter that discusses architectural decisions in TOGAF (see below).

Phase H defines the architecture change management processes required to keep the architecture models current. For example, changes to the business or technology environment or lessons learned from implementation projects are consolidated and requirements for architecture model updates are defined.

TOGAF in Practice

Based on our personal experience with the adoption of TOGAF in various enterprises, we identified a number of recurring challenges. Fundamentally, the ADM is a very useful instrument for establishing the basis for an enterprise architecture management process. It provides a process-oriented view on the typical enterprise architecture activities and defines essential artifacts (work products). This process-oriented view makes the ADM as well as the overall TOGAF framework tangible and therefore eases their deployment. Moreover, the process-oriented view increases the chances of TOGAF for getting accepted by stakeholders such as business domain experts, data architects, and application portfolio managers. However, the rather generic documentation of the ADM and the other key TOGAF components requires experienced subject matter experts both for TOGAF as well as for the specific application domain in order to tailor and refine the framework for concrete usage. The ADM has to be adapted and detailed (just like the other key concepts, artifacts, and deliverables that are intended to be used in a specific enterprise). In order to address these challenges, we recommend conducting a series of TOGAF Adoption Workshops (TAWs) involving all key stakeholders. Key objectives of these workshops are to agree on available and to be developed architectural artifacts, on a common understanding of the terminology, on the eligible methods, and on a basic work breakdown structure for the upcoming architecture development activities.

As already outlined in the introduction as an integration/adoption issue, a general risk for the acceptance of enterprise architecture guidelines is that implementers may be reluctant to establish a trust relationship with the enterprise architecture staff. This is a fundamental conflict: enterprise architects set guidelines and constrain projects for the benefit of the whole enterprise; however, projects often do not see the need for such guidelines and constraints because by definition they have a much narrower scope. The classic function of enterprise architecture as a strategic planning tool works quite well in practice (a.k.a. upstream enterprise architecture, with relatively coarse models and focus on migration and transition planning). These functions correspond to TOGAF ADM phases E (opportunities and solutions) and F (migration planning). However, the connection to implementation programs (a.k.a. downstream enterprise architecture) often does not work well according to our experience: solution architects and enterprise architects have difficulties to collaborate effectively, e.g., during ADM phase G. As a consequence, enterprise architecture does not

produce the type of information (specifications) that can be readily used by project teams (e.g., architecture and solution building blocks, easy-to-use reference models, etc.). We outlined and exemplified three of the most pressing collaboration issues (i.e., availability, consumability, and enforcement/acceptance issues) in the introduction to this chapter.

Architectural Decisions in TOGAF

We experienced another challenge in our industry projects: guidance is needed how to enforce important architectural decisions on the implementation project level (to ensure consistency with the enterprise architecture principles). In chapter 41.5, TOGAF 9 promotes the management of architectural decisions and proposes to use a governance log to store architectural decisions:

[architectural] decisions made during projects (such as standards deviations or the rationale for a particular architectural approach) are important to retain and access on an ongoing basis. [...] Having sight of the key architectural decisions that shaped the initial implementation is highly valuable, as it will highlight constraints that may otherwise be obscured (The Open Group, 2009).

The governance log calls for capturing decisions with rationale, but without any details when and how to do this. This is where solution delivery processes like RUP are supposed to step in on the implementation project level. However, we are not aware of any detailed advice in existing enterprise architecture frameworks and software engineering methods on the types of decisions that typically must be made at a certain step in implementation governance, let alone any guidance for the actual implementation-level decision making.

Let us now have a look at the interfaces between the two roles from a TOGAF ADM perspective. The main interaction activities between enterprise and solution architects occur during TOGAF ADM Phase G (implementation governance). Chapter 15.4 of TOGAF defines phase G as the phase that

guides the implementation from an enterprise architecture perspective. The enterprise architects have to provide architectural oversight for the implementation and ensure that the implementation projects conform to the enterprise architecture. Specifically, the implementation governance phase defines activities and steps to guide development of solutions deployment and perform enterprise architecture compliance reviews (The Open Group, 2009).

We believe that the enterprise architect should not only follow this advice, but also coach and support the solution architects throughout the implementation project – if enterprise architects only conduct reactive compliance reviews rather late in the project, they might struggle to get their review findings accepted as changes already have become costly to implement. An early and continuous involvement helps to ensure that the architectural decisions in an implementation project adhere to the enterprise-level directions throughout the project; it may also serve as a reliable architectural frame that allows agile practices to be applied during construction.

Architectural decisions on the implementation project level that potentially impact the overall enterprise architecture must be made in awareness of enterprise-wide managerial and technical directions. If such decisions are not carefully made, business applications may become difficult to integrate with each other, or even worse, regulatory standards may be violated (as illustrated by the three exemplary design issues from the introduction). As mentioned previously, TOGAF therefore defines the architecture contract deliverable to be developed at the beginning of the implementation governance phase. The architecture contract comprises an agreement between the implementation project partners and the enterprise architects that

states the suitability of the developed solution architectures and the project implementation deliverables. According to chapter 49.1 in TOGAF 9, this includes the adherence to the enterprise principles, standards, and requirements of the existing or developing solution architectures, risk management procedures, and a set of processes and practices that ensure proper usage and development of all architectural artifacts (The Open Group, 2009). For instance, the guiding principles and constraints regarding the design options chosen by the solution architect to solve the three exemplary security design issues given in the introduction to this chapter (dealing with data classification and transport channel protection) could be summarized in such architecture contract, providing rationale for option selections.

Enterprise Architecture in the PQG Case Study

Let us assume that an enterprise architect was appointed shortly after the takeover of Dirt Cheap insurance. Having evaluated candidate assets (mostly by screening by studying online resources such as white papers from vendors, consulting firms, and analysts, but also by issuing a Request For Information (RFI) to several architecture consulting firms and evaluating their responses), he/she selects TOGAF as the architecture framework to steer the future evolution of the application landscape at PQG. As a first step towards TOGAF adoption, the ADM is tailored in a TOGAF Adoption Workshop (TAW); this TAW is organized with the help of services provided by of one of the consulting firms that responded to the RFI. Next, in ADM phase A (architecture vision) the goals of the current ADM cycle are defined; in the PQG case, this includes the development of suitable architecture models to identify synergies with the acquired IT systems from DirtCheap Insurance and to assess information integration opportunities. Infrastructure rationalization and consolidation targets (in terms of required cost saving figures per year) are also stated in the architecture vision deliverables.

ADM phases B (business architecture), C (information systems architecture) and D (technology architecture) are conducted next. In these phases, the as-is and to-be architectures are elaborated to the levels of detail that were agreed upon during phase A. Figure 1 from the previous section (system context and architecture overview diagram for as-is enterprise application landscape) is an output of phase C.

During the ADM phase E (opportunities and solutions), gap analyses between the as-is and to-be architectures are conducted and evaluated, resulting in the identification of major shortcomings in the customer enquiry processing of PQG. As a consequence, a recommendation to the PQG Chief Executive Officer (CEO) is made to launch a strategic initiative that improves the customer enquiry processing. The objectives of the initiative are to improve customer service, measured by the conversion rate (i.e., ratio between accepted offers and enquiries processed), and to increase profit by not making an offer if there is a high risk of fraudulent claims. The CEO decides to launch this initiative as it directly supports his business strategy for PQG.

In the following ADM phase F (migration planning) the enterprise architect proposes to the Chief Information Officer (CIO) to launch an application development and integration project, with the goal to develop a new process-centric Customer Enquiry System (CES) which reuses logic from the existing systems to support the strategic business initiative launched in phase E. A lead solution architect for the CES project is appointed, as well as business analysts, a project manager, and a development team.

Let us assume that architectural principles also have been established in the form that is recommended by TOGAF: name-statement-rationale-implications (The Open Group, 2009). For instance, client data such as addresses and accounting information is stored in the customer database and processed by the customer care and the contract management applications (see Figure 1); due to an architectural principle from phase A that all sensitive data has to be secured, this data is classified as Sensitive Personal Information (SPI) that is valued as a strategic corporate asset to be protected against tampering and loss during transport.

RECURRING ARCHITECTURAL DECISIONS AS DESIGN GUIDES

In the previous chapter we motivated the importance of architectural decisions from a TOGAF perspective. Now we approach this topic from an implementation project-centric point of view.

Background and Motivation

Architects make many decisions when creating designs. Both classical and recent books on software architecture (Bass, Clements, & Kazman, 2003; Rozanski & Woods, 2005; Eeles & Cripps, 2010) emphasize how important it is to get the key decisions right. However, it is rather difficult to generalize what the key decisions are, let alone when and how to make them. Therefore, these decisions are often made ad hoc. Architectural knowledge management has become an important research and development topic since 2004 (Kruchten, Lago, & van Vliet, 2006). For instance, decision capturing templates have been published (Tyree & Ackerman, 2005) and modeling tools been prototyped (Ali Babar, Dingsøyr, Lago, & van Vliet, 2009).

Architectural decisions have been characterized as a subset of design decisions that is architecturally significant (Eeles & Cripps, 2010), hard to make (Fowler, 2003a], and costly to change (Booch, 2009). The following definition adopts these themes and adds several qualification heuristics (Zimmermann, 2011):

Architectural decisions capture key design issues and the rationale behind chosen solutions. They are conscious design decisions concerning a software-intensive system as a whole, or one or more of the core components and connectors of such system (in any given view). The outcome of architectural decisions influences the non-functional characteristics of the system such as its software quality attributes.

According to this definition, architectural decisions are made when selecting a programming language, an architectural pattern, an application container technology, or a middleware asset. For instance, integration patterns such as BROKER discuss the many forces distributed systems are confronted with, e.g., location independence and networking issues (Buschmann, Henney, & Schmidt, 2007); these forces qualify as decision drivers. Hence, adding an EAI middleware that implements the BROKER pattern to an architecture is an architectural decision that should be justified and documented in the governance log for the project (see previous section).

Capturing decisions after-the-fact (i.e., retrospectively) has been recognized to be important both by the enterprise architecture community (The Open Group, 2009) and by the software architecture community (Kruchten, 2003); however, many inhibitors such as lack of immediate benefits also have been identified (Ali Babar, Dingsøyr, Lago, & van Vliet, 2009). Relaxing one assumption – documentation rigor – and making a new one – multiple projects in an application genre follow the same architectural style (i.e., they share principles and patterns) – allows graduating architectural decisions from documentation artifacts to design guides:

As an architect specializing on a particular application genre and employing a certain architectural style, I would like to know about the design issues that I have to resolve and the solution options that have been successfully applied by my peers when

they were confronted with these design issues – what do they know that I don't know?

After this repositioning from documentation to design, recurring architectural decisions become reusable assets just like methods and patterns. Novel usage scenarios arise. For instance, recurring issues may help to prioritize design and development work items and may serve as checklists during reviews. In this chapter, we investigate how recurring architectural decisions can improve communication between enterprise architects and solution architects. As a first step, let us now identify the architectural decisions required in the case study.

Architectural Decisions in CES Project at PQG (Case Study)

In the beginning of their architecture design work, solution architects should select an appropriate architectural style. Service-Oriented Architecture (SOA) (Zimmermann, 2009) is a state-of-the-art option; a more conservative alternative is to develop three separate three-tier applications (Fowler, 2003) (assuming that both styles have been approved by the PQG enterprise architect).

Many follow-up design issues arise before any of the two top-level design options can be implemented:

Strategic Design Issues

Assuming that SOA is the preferred option, a particular SOA reference model should be selected, which includes agreeing on terminology and identifying relevant pattern languages, and setting technology and product procurement direction. The business strategy (e.g., planned mergers and acquisitions, or divestitures and outsourcing) and strategic IT principles (e.g., to prefer or ban open source assets and to prefer certain software vendors and server infrastructures) must be considered. The architectural principles around security and data privacy from the introduction to this chapter belong to this category of requirements and design constraints. Hence, design guidance from the enterprise architecture level is particularly appreciated in this context.

Conceptual Design Issues

Next, conceptual patterns must be selected and adopted, decomposing the ones that define SOA as an architectural style. All pattern components have to be refined, e.g., the router capability that is a core element of the Enterprise Service Bus (ESB) pattern (Zimmermann, 2009). Functional and non-functional requirements, business rules, and legacy constraints influence the conceptual design work.

In the CES case, the business analyst identified customer care, contract, and risk management services. It is now required to design service providers for these services. The granularity of the service contracts in terms of number of service operations and structure of request and response messages must be decided. Once such service contracts are in place, it becomes possible to design service consumers.

The detailed design and configuration of the ESB triggers another set of concerns: According to the ESB definition in (Zimmermann, 2009), message exchange patterns and formats, as well as mediation, routing, and adapter patterns have to be selected (or banned). In this pattern selection and adoption process, format transformations, security settings, service management (e.g., monitoring), and communications transactionality must be defined precisely.

The service composition design also must be refined if this SOA pattern is selected. The choice of a central process manager implementing workflow concepts as opposed to distributed state management in individual applications is an important architectural concern (Zimmermann, 2009). Other key architecture design issues regarding service composition are where to draw the line

between composed and atomic services, how to interface with the presentation layer (in terms of request correlation and coordination), and how to integrate legacy workflows, e.g., those residing in software packages. System transaction boundaries and higher level error handling strategies such as compensation handlers have to be defined as well.

Platform-Related Design Issues

Implementation technologies for the conceptual patterns must be selected and profiled, for instance WS-* technologies (Weerawarana, Curbera, Leymann, Storey, & Ferguson, 2005) or other integration technologies. Once technologies have been chosen, implementation platforms must be selected and configured. Many of the SOA patterns are implemented in commercial or open source middleware assets. It must be decided whether middleware assets should be procured and how the chosen ones should be installed and configured. Performance, scalability, interoperability, and portability are important types of quality attributes when selecting and configuring implementation platforms; enterprise-level guidance regarding strategic vendor preferences and software licensing policies helps to ensure that the decisions made on different projects are consistent with each other, that opportunities for synergies are not missed (e.g., discounts), and that unnecessary costs are avoided (e.g., hidden integration effort introduced by incompatible middleware products).

In summary, PQG has several architecture alternatives to realize CES, including a) SOA or b) three-tiered client-server applications integrated via traditional EAI middleware. Making this decision is only the start of the architecture design; detailed design work follows. Numerous design issues are encountered, which qualify as architectural decisions. The design issues differ substantially depending on the architectural style and patterns chosen. Numerous forces influence the decision making: Quality attributes in categories such as reliability, usability, efficiency (performance, scalability), maintainability, and portability drive the selection of architectural style, the adoption of conceptual patterns, and the design of their platform-specific refinements. Many dependencies exist between the design issues encountered on the CES project, but also from and to those on other projects. Guidance from the enterprise architect is desired.

SOA Decision (SOAD) Modeling

To give recurring architectural decisions a guiding role during architecture design and implementation governance, related project experience has to be captured and generalized in an effective and efficient manner. This is a knowledge engineering activity. SOA Decision Modeling (SOAD) (Zimmermann, Koehler, Leymann, Polley, & Schuster, 2009) is a knowledge management framework that supports such an approach: SOAD provides a technique to systematically identify the decisions that recur when applying a certain architectural style (such as SOA) in a particular application genre (such as enterprise applications). SOAD enhances existing metamodels and templates (Tyree & Ackerman, 2005; IBM Unified Method Framework, 1998) to distinguish *decisions required* from *decisions made*. Platform-independent decisions are separated from platform-specific ones; the alternatives in a conceptual model level reference architectural patterns such as those presented in (Buschmann, Henney, & Schmidt, 2007; Fowler, 2003, Hohpe & Woolf, 2004, Zdun, Hentrich, & Dustdar, 2007). Decision dependency management allows architects to check model consistency and prune irrelevant decisions. A managed issue list guides through the decision making process. To update design artifacts according to decisions made, decision outcome information can be injected into design model transformations (Zimmermann, 2011).

In support of reuse, the SOAD metamodel defines two forms of models:

- Guidance models identifying *decisions required* (formerly known as Reusable Architectural Decision Models (RADMs) (Zimmermann, 2009) and
- Decision models logging *decisions made* (formerly known as architectural decision models).

Figure 3 shows the relations and the internal structure of these two types of models (Zimmermann, 2009).

A guidance model is a reusable asset containing knowledge about architectural decisions required when applying an architectural style in a particular application genre. An *issue* informs the architect that a particular design problem exists and that an architectural decision is required. It presents types of decision drivers (e.g., quality attributes and architectural principles) and references potential design alternatives which solve the issue along with their pros (advantages), cons (disadvantages) and known uses (previous applications). It may also make a recommendation about the alternative to be selected in a certain requirements context. Issues and alternatives, authored by a knowledge engineer, use the future tense and a tone that a technical mentor would choose in a personal conversation.

A guidance model captures architectural knowledge from already completed projects that employed the architectural style for which the guidance model is created. Project-specific decision models are created from such guidance models in a tailoring step. Such a tailoring step is conceptually similar to and inspired by method tailoring and adoption activities (e.g., TOGAF adoption as outlined in the previous section); it might involve deleting irrelevant issues, enhancing relevant ones, and adding issues not included

Figure 3. Guidance model and decision model elements

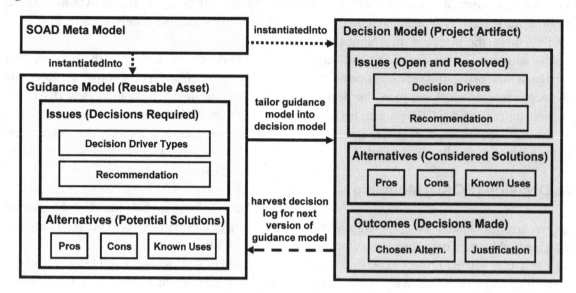

in a guidance model. The guidance model does not have a direct counterpart in TOGAF; it can be seen as an additional artifact in the enterprise continuum.

As shown in Figure 3, a decision model is an architecture documentation artifact that contains knowledge about architectural decisions required, but also captures information about architectural decisions made. A decision outcome is the record (log) of a decision actually made on a project and its justification. Outcomes can be viewed as a form of design workshop minutes and are therefore documented in present or past tense. In a TOGAF context, such decision log forms an important part of the governance log.

A decision model may reuse one or more guidance models. Information about decisions made can be fed back to the guidance model after project closure via informal or formal lessons learned reviews and/or asset harvesting activities. The required updates to the guidance models can be defined during ADM Phase H, architecture change management. Such guidance model updates have the objective to further improve the breadth, depth, and quality of the architectural knowledge in the enterprise continuum.

Decision Identification and Knowledge Harvesting Activities in SOAD

Guidance model creation activities are described in detail in our previous work, e.g., in Chapter 5 and Appendix A of (Zimmermann, 2009) and Chapter 12 of (Ali Babar, Dingsøyr, Lago, & van Vliet, 2009). We will get back to these activities later in the chapter in the context of the TOGAF ADM and our proposed integration of SOAD into TOGAF.

A particularly comprehensive result of our own guidance modeling activities is a SOA guidance model which comprises about 500 issues with more than 2500 alternatives. The exemplary SOA issues from the previous section (i.e., the strategic design issues, conceptual design issues, and platform-related design issues at PQG) appear in this guidance model in the form of issues and alternatives. Figure 4 outlines the level and layer organization of the guidance model for SOA and positions a subset of the examples from the CES case study as issues (boxes represent issues; alternatives are highlighted by question marks).

Figure 4. SOA guidance model (a.k.a. reusable architectural decision model)

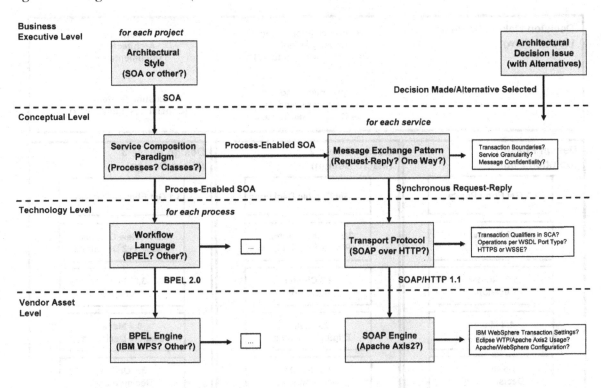

The issues in the SOAD guidance model originate from the author's project experience, input from practitioner communities, as well as the literature; they are meant to be illustrative, not normative here.

Guidance Model Tailoring and Decision Making Processes in SOAD

The tailoring of one or more reusable guidance model into the decision model for a project as well as a macro and a micro process for decision making based on guidance models are described in Chapter 7 of (Zimmermann, 2009). We summarize the essence of these two decision making processes in the following subsections.

Macro Process (Project Level)

The SOAD macro process works with a managed issue list (Zimmermann, 2009). We use the phases from the IBM Unified Method Framework (UMF) in this macro process. UMF (IBM Unified Method Framework, 1998) comprises three design phases, solution outline, macro design and micro design; these phases correspond to the RUP phases RUP inception, elaboration and construction. Figure 5 shows the activities to be conducted in these three phases (Zimmermann, 2009).

The decision making context (Hofmeister, Kruchten, Nord, Obbink, Ran., & America, 2007) includes reference information, requirements models, and documentation of the enterprise architecture as well as existing systems, e.g., legacy systems. The enterprise continuum in TOGAF is an example of a repository of such context information.

Figure 5. SOAD macro process for decision making on projects

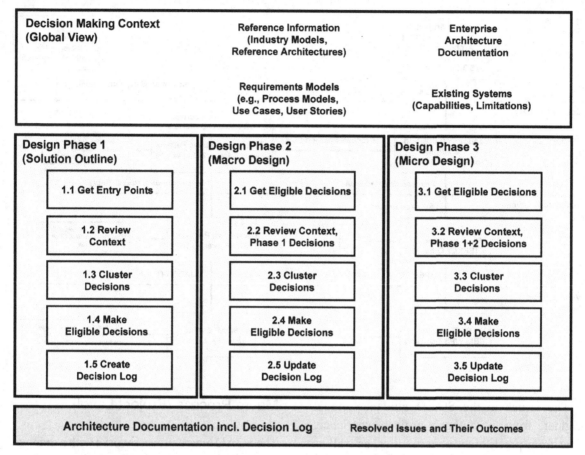

The output of the macro process is the decision log; it becomes part of the architecture documentation. As explained previously, this decision log becomes part of the TOGAF governance log.

Activity 1.1, 2.1, 3.1

Activities 1.1, 2.1, and 3.1 in our macro design process deal with the retrieval of entry points into the decision making. These activities can be approached in multiple ways. Tacit knowledge or external stakeholder input often guide the architect in the temporal ordering and prioritization of decisions; when decision dependencies between recurring issues are modeled, as suggested and made possible by the SOAD metamodel, tools can assist with this important scoping effort, which defines the focus for the following architecture design work (Zimmermann, 2009).

Activities 1.2, 2.2, 3.2

The second activity in each phase of our macro process is a review activity conducted by the architect. It includes a review of requirements and architectural documentation already available in the decision making context. In solution outline, the review includes *legacy decisions* (i.e., decisions made in another project or pertaining to a different enterprise application). The other project might have been a presales activity, the development of a legacy system a long time ago, or an enterprise architecture project. The decisions made in previous phases of the macro process are also reviewed.

Activities 1.3, 2.3, 3.3

These activities deal with decision clustering. Decisions are rarely made in isolation due to their amount and due to the many dependencies between them. However, it is not obvious how to group and order the decisions that are eligible in a particular macro process phase. Grouping decisions into clusters is typically part of the tacit knowledge of an architect; mature software engineering and architecture design methods provide related advice (Hofmeister, Kruchten, Nord, Obbink, Ran., & America, 2007; Ran & Kuusela, 1996). The actual grouping also depends on the project setup (e.g., methods adopted, human resources available) and on the architects' experience and personal preferences (bias). For instance, one of the authors' rules of thumb is "worst first" (with worst being determined by negative consequences regarding risk, cost, and flexibility).

A decision filtering concept as introduced in Section 7.1 in (Zimmermann, 2009) can be leveraged in addition to tacit knowledge about decision clustering. Due to the formalization of the SOAD meta-model, tools can give clustering advice. However, the architect drives the activity. In SOA design, a tool might suggest to assign all issues about an "ESB router" to be made in the "macro design" phase to an "integration architect". The architect may decide to follow, refine, or overrule this clustering (e.g., by splitting service consumer and provider issues and assigning them to two different integration architects).

Activities 1.4, 2.4, 3.4

These activities instruct the architect to make the decisions that were classified to be eligible in the respective phase. The micro process is launched from this activity once per issue.

Activities 1.5, 2.5, 3.5

As the last activity on the macro level, the decision log is created or updated with the outcome instances created during the execution of the micro process. It becomes part of the project deliverables and, consequently, the TOGAF governance log.

In essence, the managed issue list from SOAD implements the architecture contract required by TOGAF: open decisions form the part of the architecture contract that has not been delivered/satisfied yet (thus listing pending project obligations), whereas made decisions capture completed parts of the contract.

Micro Process (Issue Level)

Figure 6 illustrates the SOAD micro process (Zimmermann, 2009).

When performing the micro process activities, architects make use of the architectural knowledge in the guidance model and the decision model, which both are structured according to the SOAD metamodel, e.g., listing decision drivers and decision dependencies (see Figure 3).

Step A: Investigate Decision

As a first step, the information about an issue in the ADM must be analyzed; the architects can add missing information. In this step, the problem statement, defined in the SOAD metamodel (Figure 3), must be understood first; if the motivation for the issue remains unclear, the referenced background reading can be consulted (activity A.1).

Next, the decision driver attribute is studied (activity A.2). Like the problem statement, it is an issue attribute; it is reusable, but not project-specific (unless information about actual requirements has been added during tailoring). Hence, it can only list *types* of decision drivers. Still in activity A.2, decision dependencies, particularly those to and from already resolved issues (but also open ones) are investigated.

Figure 6. SOAD micro process for making single decision

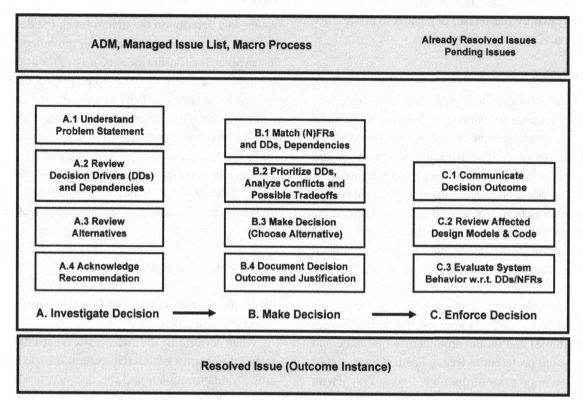

The available alternatives have to be considered next (activity A.3). The pros and cons information is particularly relevant; when studying it, the decision drivers and project requirements already considered in A.1 and A.2 are revisited.

The final investigation activity A.4 is to review and acknowledge the recommendation. This does not mean that the recommendation should always be followed. The global decision making context (Figure 5) determines whether this is possible.

Step B: Make Decision

The second step of the micro process is the actual decision making. In activity B.1, the architect matches the actual requirements on the project against the decision drivers (including architectural principles) and decision dependencies investigated in activity A.2. Both functional requirements and Non-Functional Requirements

(NFRs) are taken into consideration. Activity B.2 advises the architect to prioritize the decision drivers according to their importance and to analyze potential conflicts and tradeoffs. Before an alternative can be selected, both short term and long term consequences (implications) must be assessed. In many cases, an alternative which may appear to be suited on the micro process level cannot be selected due to certain constraints which are only visible at the macro process or enterprise architecture level (e.g., limitations of legacy systems, existing operations and maintenance procedures). Activity B.3 is to actually make the decision, based on the insight gained during the already completed step A and step B activities.

In Activity B.4, the chosen alternative and the justification for the decision are documented in outcomes. Decision drivers, pros and cons of alternatives, and the recommendation should be referenced in the justification. The justification should not only quote reusable background information such as the types of decision drivers coming from the guidance model, but also refer to actual project requirements (Zimmermann, Schuster, & Eeles, 2008).

Step C: Enforce Decision

The third step of the micro process deals with enforcing the decision. The three activities in this step are to communicate the decision outcome (Activity C.1), to review affected design model elements and code (Activity C.2), and to compare the behavior of the emerging implementations of the system under construction with the decision drivers and actual NFRs including project-specific quality attributes (Activity C.3). It is necessary to re-evaluate on the macro level, as decisions often unveil their full consequences in combination (e.g., decisions that have an impact on end-to-end scalability of the system under construction and on the system performance under heavy load from concurrent users).

Termination of Macro and Micro Process

Macro process and, in turn, micro process continue as long as architectural decision making is still required. More than three phases can be required. It may take a long time to complete the decision making; the managed issue list can even be continued to be used during system operations and maintenance (Sommerville, 1995).

SOAD-Based Decision Making in CES Project at PQG

We identified and informally presented selected design issues in the CES project earlier in this section; as discussed, they arise from the adoption of SOA patterns such as service consumer-

provider contract, ESB, and service composition (Zimmermann, 2009).

Figure 7 assigns a subset of these issues to logical components in a SOA reference model; the resulting SOA can be seen as an output of TOGAF phase C, information system architecture. The issues are shown as questions. Several of them appear multiple times, e.g., those about the ESB and those dealing with the three atomic services (customer care service, contract service, and risk management service). This is the case because the respective patterns are applied multiple times in the architecture.

The CES solution architect selects alternatives resolving the open issues based on project-specific requirements. During the SOA design and architectural decision modeling activities, (s)he captures the justifications for their decisions in outcomes, which refer to issues.

Let us assume the CES project to be in the macro design (elaboration) phase; several key decisions have already been made and documented during solution outline (inception). This becomes apparent in Figure 7, e.g., a service composition layer and two ESBs have already been introduced in the architecture.

Table 1 gives more examples for decisions already made, captured as outcomes; the table content is the result of the macro and micro decision making processes introduced in Figure 5 and Figure 6 earlier in this section. The issues and alternatives come from the guidance model for SOA. The sample justifications are specific to the case, referring or paraphrasing PQG/CES requirements.

Refining the previously made decisions, the ones in the following Table 2 proceed from conceptual to platform-specific design.

The table records the output of the partial execution of one phase of the SOAD macro process; each decision, captured in a single table row, is the result of one execution of the SOAD micro process.

Figure 7. Decision identification in PQG case study (Zimmermann, 2009)

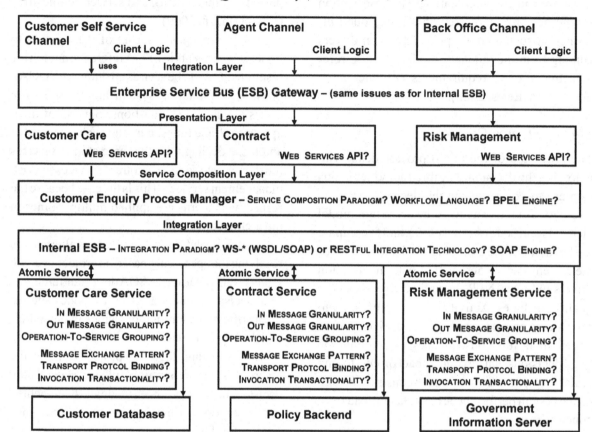

Table 1. PQG case study: Architectural decisions made already

Resolved Issue	Alternative Chosen as Outcome (and Rejected Ones)	Examples of Justifications for Decisions Made for CES (Rationale)
Architectural Style (not shown in Figure 7)	SOA Messaging File Transfer, Shared Database, RPC (Hohpe & Woolf, 2004)	Strategic initiative, cross platform integration required and desired, reliability needs
Layering (sketched only in Figure 7)	Layers in SOA Reference Architecture POEAA Layering (Fowler, 2003))	Defined by enterprise architecture team; no industry standard
Integration Paradigm	ESB (Zimmermann, 2009) Traditional EAI, Custom Code	Integration needs (legacy constraints identified in TOGAF as-is models), service monitoring required
Service Composition Paradigm	WORKFLOW (Leymann & Roller, 2000) Human User, Object-Oriented Programming	Long running process, central process manager can preserve integrity across channels (a related business rule has been stated as an architectural principle in the business architecture)
Service Registry	None (UDDI, Vendor Products) (Zimmermann, Tomlinson, & Peuser, 2003)	Only a few services, no business case for a registry yet (according to output of TOGAF ADM phases A to F)

Table 2. PQG case study: Architectural decisions made now

Resolved Issue	Alternative Chosen as Outcome (and Rejected Ones)	Examples of Justifications for Decisions Made for CES (Rationale)
Integration Technology	WS-* Web Services (Zimmermann, Tomlinson, & Peuser, 2003) RESTful Integration (Pautasso, Zimmermann, & Leymann, 2008))	Interoperability and standardization requirements (NFRs), tool support
Workflow Language	Business Process Execution Language (BPEL) (Proprietary Languages)	Standardized (to be preferred according to an architectural principle), used by BPEL Engine selected (see below)
SOAP Engine	IBM WebSphere (Apache Axis2)	Comes with BPEL Engine
BPEL Engine	WebSphere Process Server (Oracle BPEL Process Manager, Active BPEL)	Operational procedures and enterprise license agreement in place (executive decision before project start)

So far, we merely captured decisions already made and their rationale. Table 3 lists additional issues, this time issues still open at the current project stage.

More comprehensive guidance modeling and decision making examples are given in (Zimmermann, 2011), (Zimmermann, Koehler, Leymann, Polley, & Schuster, 2009), and (Zimmermann, 2009), as well as tutorials and other presentation material from the SOAD project (SOAD).

Enforcement of Decisions

In this step, the CES architects create reports about decisions made: The outcome content of Table 1 and Table 2 is exported to a decision log which becomes a part of the TOGAF governance log for the CES project. This artifact is then shared within the technical project team (e.g., other architects, developers, and system administrators) and other stakeholders (e.g., reviewers such as the PQG enterprise architect). The made decisions are executed, e.g., through procurement, installation, and configuration of the selected BPEL ENGINE and through BPEL and Java development activities.

Table 3. PQG case study: Architectural decisions still required

Open Issue	Alternatives	Decision Drivers (Guidance Model for SOA)
In Message Granularity	Dot Pattern Dotted Line Pattern Bar Pattern Comb Pattern	Structure and amount of enterprise resources to be exchanged, message verbosity, programming convenience and expressivity, change friendliness
Operation-To-Service Grouping	Single Operation Multiple Operations	Cohesion and coupling in terms of security context and versioning
Message Exchange Pattern	One Way Request-Reply	Consumer semantics and availability needs, provider up times
Transport Protocol Binding	SOAP/HTTP SOAP/JMS Plain Old XML(POX)/ HTTP	Provider availability, data currency needs from consumer's perspective, systems management considerations
Invocation Transactionality	Transaction Islands Transaction Bridge Stratified Stilts	Resource protection needs, legacy system interface capabilities, process lifetime, enterprise-level guidelines regarding system operations (e.g., regarding error handling and auditing/archiving policies)

ARCHITECTURAL DECISION MODELING AND MAKING IN TOGAF

In this section, we show how to overcome the controversy and gap between enterprise architects and solution architects, with an enterprise architect leading guidance model creation and solution architects contributing to them and using them (continuous improvement cycle).

Issues, Controversies, Problems in CES Project at PQG

The current status in the PQG case study is that the enterprise architect, following the TOGAF ADM, has established architectural principles and defined the scope for the current ADM cycle in phase A. He/she created as-is architecture models providing an inventory of existing systems and outlining to-be target architectures during the architecture development phases B to D. The output of the ADM phases E and F have triggered the CES development project.

The CES solution architecture has to meet specific project requirements to satisfy the CES project sponsor and end users, but also to adhere to the architectural principles established and enforced by the PQG enterprise architect. Several key decisions have already been made. A SOAD guidance model was not available, all issues and alternatives had to be documented by the solution architect as part of the CES project. Many of the decision outcomes referenced architectural principles in their rationale (justification attribute). This is a budget challenge for the individual project; the connection to enterprise architecture artifacts is not obvious and not tangible. Moreover, each project makes its decisions without knowing about those on other projects (past or present). Let us assume that a high-level SOA reference model has been created, which defines a layering scheme, but is not detailed enough for project development work.

To overcome the outlined governance problems, the PQG enterprise architect initiates a guidance model creation effort (project or working group), with the objective to make experience with – and knowledge about – the consolidation and modernization of enterprise applications (specifically when using the SOA style) explicit so that this knowledge can take an active guiding role on projects like CES.

Extending TOGAF with SOAD Guidance Modeling Concepts

This section presents the core contribution and novelty of the chapter, an integration of the SOAD concepts into TOGAF. Figure 8 illustrates our overall integration approach by mapping TOGAF ADM phases to SOAD guidance modeling and decision making activities.

The primary integration point with several intense interactions is TOGAF phase G, implementation governance. These interactions will be covered in more detail later in the section.

Faithful to the iterative and incremental nature of ADM, we introduce a continuous improvement cycle:

1. **Guidance Model Development (Creation and Update):** The enterprise architect provides a guidance model, with the objective to support and promote the usage of enterprise architecture models and guidelines (e.g., architectural principles) on the project level.

2. **Guidance Model Usage, Decision Model Creation and Review:** The solution architect uses the guidance model to steer the architecture design work on a project (e.g., when creating decision models/logs) and provides feedback on the relevance and consumability of the architectural knowledge found in the guidance model. The enterprise architect uses the decision model to review the evolving implementation architecture for

Figure 8. Guidance modeling and decision making in the ADM process in TOGAF

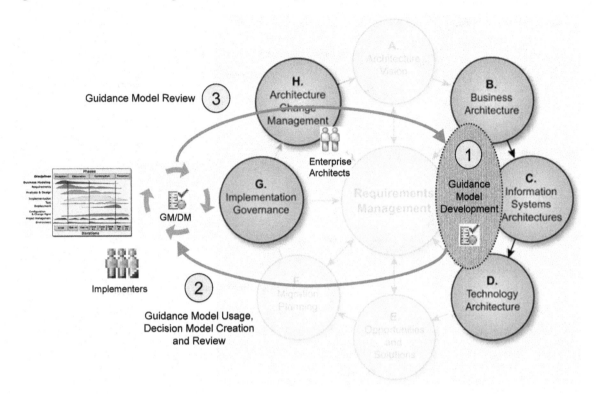

general fitness (adequateness) and compliance with the enterprise-level guidelines and constraints.

3. **Guidance Model Review:** The enterprise architect updates models and guidelines accordingly (with additional input from the solution architect community).

1. Guidance Model Development

The first integration point is guidance model creation (a.k.a. knowledge engineering or harvesting), taking place (i.e., positioned and attached to) in TOGAF phases B, C, and D. To realize this integration point (step), we propose a collaborative approach (i.e., a series of fine grained interactions between enterprise architects and solution architects). Figure 9 details this collaborative approach in the form of a UML interaction diagram.

Key initial inputs to the guidance model creation work (i.e., the early scoping activities) are architectural principles, enterprise architecture models and artifacts, enterprise blueprints and standards, reusable assets, and existing documentation of architectural decisions from implemented solutions. These inputs are ideally classified using a comprehensive taxonomy (e.g., based on the TOGAF content framework) and obtained from the organization's enterprise continuum.

Regarding depth and breadth of a guidance model, its creators have a choice between making comprehensive knowledge packs available and lightweight approaches; a basic form of an initial guidance model is a checklist with questions and possible answers for solution architects, or a simple decision tree such as the 10-node cloud buyer guide from the Open Group (Open Group, 2010).

Figure 9. Guidance model creation (knowledge harvesting in TOGAF phases B, C, and D)

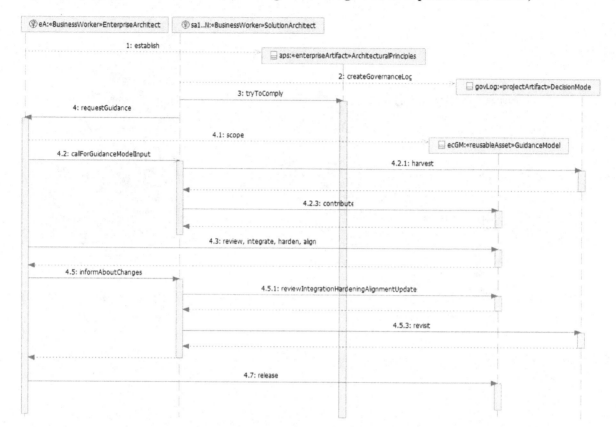

During the guidance model creation activities, enterprise architects can start with an existing guidance model such as the SOA one outlined in the previous section. Possibly, it will be required to add new levels and topic groups to adjust the structure of the guidance model for a particular enterprise. Certain fundamental issues in the guidance model may be marked with a tag like "enterprise architect involvement/review particularly important and required" (e.g., the issues for which guidance was requested in the first place, those with severe long term consequences, e.g., regarding operations and maintenance, or those with implications for multiple lines of business).

In a practical application of our TOGAF-SOAD integration concepts, each of the interactions can be supported by reusable assets such as mail templates (e.g., *callForGuidanceMod-*

elInput, release), wiki pages (e.g., *contribute*), and predefined/-populated questionnaires (e.g., *requestGuidance*). Furthermore, activity owners and activity initiation triggers should be defined to ensure timely and diligent execution.

See existing work (Zimmermann, 2009) and previous section for additional information, e.g., about our experience with the review-integrate-harden-align steps, shown as a single activity in Figure 9.

2. Guidance Model Usage

Having covered the decision harvesting activities (i.e., guidance model creation and review), the following Figure 10 focuses on decision making in TOGAF phase G (again in the form of a UML interaction diagram).

Figure 10. Decision making in TOGAF phase G (implementation governance)

The interactions in the figure detail the involvement of the enterprise architect during the SOAD macro and micro processes that we introduced in the previous section.

If solution architecture requirements have to be satisfied that require enterprise architecture artifacts (models) that do not exist yet, guidance modeling activities may be triggered (step 1). More agile approaches may also be applied, e.g., a temporary involvement of the enterprise architect on the solution development project in the form of architectural decision making workshops. The minutes (protocols) of these workshops then may serve as initial versions of future guidance models.

Our existing work and the previous section provide additional information, e.g., about tailoring (Zimmermann, 2009).

3. Guidance Model Review

The review activities have to be defined in detail when implementing the interlock between the enterprise architect and the solution architect. For instance, it has to be specified whether regular proactive/periodic reviews and content update cycles are planned.

We foresee a continuum of modes of operation and review rigor: two ends of the spectrum are a conservative process with funded design authorities and formal approvals on the one end and an opportunistic approach solely relying on volunteers (e.g., Web 2.0 crowd sourcing) on the other end. The maturity of the owning organization, amount of executive-level support and budget, and company culture are among the decision drivers for this design issue pertaining to the guidance modeling process.

The interactions during an update step are identical to those performed during guidance model creation, resulting in a new version of the guidance model (see Figure 9). During TOGAF phase H, the requirements for guidance model updates are consolidated. In the following phase A of the next TOGAF cycle, such updates (or a subset that addresses high-priority topics) may be planned to be included this cycle. They may then be implemented during the subsequent architecture development phases B, C, and D.

Initial Guidance Model Content

We propose the following candidate issues for a guidance model supporting decision making on implementation projects:

- Design, adoption, and rollout of governance and design processes as well as supporting notations and tools (e.g., UML modeling versus architecture description language versus other domain-specific language, possibly different for each stakeholder viewpoint (Küster, Völzer, & Zimmermann (2011)). Refer to TOGAF Chapter 48.3, architecture compliance reviews (The Open Group, 2009).
- Top-level functional slicings of responsibilities both in the organization and in

the IT systems, e.g., business domain concept in SOA (Krafzig, Banke, & Slama, 2005) and strategic domain-driven design (Landre, Wesenberg, & Rønneberg (2006).

- One particularly important topic group is the question when to prefer build over buy (e.g., to achieve a competitive advantage or to avoid hidden, uncontrollable integration efforts (Wesenberg, Landre, & Rønneberg (2006)), even if a general architectural principle exists to prefer software procurement and customization over custom development.
- Evaluation criteria for and selection of software packages (typically per business component or functional area) and SOA middleware whose purchase implies significant licensing cost and/or training and operations effort (e.g., workflow engine, enterprise service bus).
- Decisions about selection of open source software as well as other reusable assets (both private and public ones) and about development of company-internal solution building blocks.
- Information management decisions with an impact on the degree to which a solution adheres to relevant data privacy laws, audit compliance rules and company-internal security standards (see introduction to this chapter for examples).
- Decisions on required refactorings of existing systems to match enterprise architecture guidelines.
- For strategic system maintenance or enhancement projects, how to identify the technical debt to be reduced (and how to do so).

Note that the candidate issues are "TOGAF ADM phase G-specific" decisions; decisions about the enterprise architecture itself are not included yet. The above collection does not aim

Table 4. PQG case study; exemplary mappings from TOGAF ADM phases to SOAD activities (by role)

TOGAF Phase	Role	Activity (with Supporting Tools and Notations)
A	Enterprise architect (PQG)	Establish first version of architectural principles
	Solution architects (CES, other)	Review architectural principles
B, C, D	Enterprise architect (PQG)	Scope guidance model (SOAD tool) Call for guidance model input (via email to community, via wiki or other social networking/collaboration tool)
	Solution architects of existing applications (customer care, contract management, risk management)	Harvest decision logs from previous projects (review tool) Contribute to guidance model (via template, via copy-paste)
	Enterprise architect (PQG)	Review, Integrate, Harden, Align (RIHA) (SOAD method and tool) Inform solution architect about changes
	Solution architect (existing applications)	Review RIHA updates Revisit decision logs from projects Provide feedback to enterprise architect
	Enterprise architect (PQG)	Incorporate review feedback Release first/subsequent versions of SOA guidance model
E, F	Enterprise architect (PQG)	Identify potential projects that directly support the enterprise strategy Create a high-level roadmap and project plan for those projects Prioritize and select suitable projects Plan and prepare adoption of SOAD method and tool for selected projects
	Solution architects	n/a
G	Solution architect (CES)	Create governance log (SOAD decision model) Try to comply with architectural principles Request guidance for strategic design issues, SOA pattern selection and adoption, technology and product platform preferences Select and tailor SOA guidance model (SOAD tool) Pre-populate decision log with guidance model content Request enterprise architect participation and ongoing reviews Make and document decisions and maintain managed issue list (supported by SOAD macro and micro process and supporting tool) Update decisions according to review feedback (SOAD tool) Enforce correct implementation of decisions made
	Enterprise architect (PQG)	Review governance log/decision model (ongoing)
	Solution architect (CES)	Request final review and approval (e.g., at the inception and elaboration phase milestones of the implementation project (Kruchten, 2003)
	Enterprise architect (PQG)	Approve decisions
	Solution architect (CES)	Enforce and track resolution of review findings and reduce technical debt
H	Solution architect (CES)	Provide feedback regarding use of guidance model and additional architectural knowledge gained on CES project
	Enterprise architect (PQG)	Plan guidance model updates

at being complete; as a rule of thumb, all strategic solution decisions that require involvement of enterprise architects can/should be included eventually. In fact, all executive decisions in the taxonomy established by Kruchten, Lago and van Vliet (Kruchten, Lago, & van Vliet, 2006) benefit from enterprise-level decision making guidance.

Application of TOGAF-SOAD Integration Concepts at Premier Quotes Group

Table 4 lists the guidance modeling and decision making activities at PQG per TOGAF phase. The table also comments on notations and tools that are suited for certain activities.

FUTURE RESEARCH DIRECTIONS

Architectural Decisions and Agile Practices

An important area of future work is to investigate architectural decision making in the context of agile practices.

The literature on agile practices typically focuses on process aspects (e.g., ceremonies in Scrum (Sutherland) rather than design advice, although the original article introducing Scrum (Schwaber, 1995) mentions architecture work to be a key part of the project start phase (happening before any sprint). The notion of a sprint/iteration 0 has also been proposed (Ambler, 2009). However, it remains unclear when and how to (pre-)populate the decision backlog both for iteration 0 and for following iterations. Lean software development promotes the principle of deferring decisions until the last responsible moment (Poppendieck & Poppendieck, 2003); however, it remains unclear when this moment has come.

In our previous work, we have developed the notion of a managed issue list serving as a decision backlog (Zimmermann, 2009); this decision backlog can also be seen as a particular subset of the Scrum product backlog (featuring open design issues as a new type of backlog entry). We envision the processing of a decision backlog to steer the design work on implementation projects. Such decision backlog can highlight and prioritize the issues that have a particular relevance from an enterprise architect perspective.

Recent work by Fairbanks is particularly relevant the context of an agile governance log; he suggests an architectural haiku, a short architecture description specifically designed and compacted/comprised for agile project teams (Fairbanks, 2011). The haiku provides a short and concise syntax for capturing decision rationale:

<Driver-x> is a priority, so we chose design <Alt-y>, accepting downside <Cons-z>

The variables x and z represent instances of quality attributes or other decision drivers here, including architectural principles; y combines an issue with an alternative. We envision similar Haikus, written in the future tense, to be suited for the development of agile guidance models.

TOGAF Updates

One could also consider extending TOGAF to give architectural decisions an even more prominent place, similar to the overarching "über-phase" requirements management in the center of the ADM. Such effort would require significant changes to the existing TOGAF practices and their documentation and is therefore out our scope for the time being.

TOGAF could also provide pre-populated guidance models for particular domains such as SOA or cloud computing. Such guidance models could complement and accompany TOGAF reference models or reference architectures for these architectural styles and technical domains; they would fit into the TOGAF architecture content framework as well as the enterprise continuum.

CONCLUSION

Architectural decisions make or break a project – whether made consciously, subconsciously, or by 3rd parties like technology thought leaders (or software vendors). It is essential to identify, make, and communicate the key ones adequately; their rationale should be preserved. Capturing these decisions after the fact is a labor-intensive undertaking with many long-term, but few short-term benefits. In practice, this important documentation task is often neglected for this reason.

TOGAF is a state-of-the-art architecture framework; an architecture development method, a comprehensive collection of guidelines and techniques and the concept of the enterprise continuum are three of its key components. Tailoring TOGAF to provide tangible advice for solution architects and other technical decision makers is a challenge in practice. For instance, the structure of the content of the governance log for phase G (implementation governance) is not defined in detail and no processes or tools for creating and maintaining the log exist. Pre-defined governance log content for certain architectural styles or technology domains such as SOA or cloud computing does not exist either.

Many important decisions are encountered and solved repeatedly on multiple projects; it is therefore desirable to share related architectural knowledge between these projects. Hence, our previous SOAD work introduced guidance models as reusable assets compiling the design issues and options that will occur whenever a certain architectural style is applied in an application genre. SOAD was originally created to support enterprise application and Service-Oriented Architecture (SOA) design, but is also applicable to other application genres and architectural styles. In this chapter, we investigated how to use SOAD as governance instrument to improve the communication and knowledge exchange between enterprise and solution architects. To support this usage scenario, SOAD promotes the reuse of architectural knowledge by compiling recurring issues and options in guidance models.

The integration of SOAD into TOGAF that we presented in this chapter can be summarized as:

- Both enterprise and solution architects make decisions; solution architects expect guidance regarding a subset of their decisions from the enterprise architects. We observed this situation repeatedly on projects in various industry sectors, including financial services, telecommunications, and automotive.
- Architectural principles are established through a decision making process; once they exist, they become decision drivers and justifications for subsequent decisions.
- Guidance models may be created during TOGAF phases B to D. As reusable assets, the guidance models become part of the enterprise continuum. They are tailored into decision models and then used in TOGAF phase G (implementation governance). Requirements for guidance model updates are consolidated in phase H (architecture change management).
- The SOAD decision log becomes an integral part of the TOGAF governance log; decisions required and decisions made (maintained in the managed issue list in SOAD) form an important part of the architecture contract between enterprise architects and solution architects. The fulfillment of this contract can be monitored by observing the managed issue list and the decision log.
- The macro and micro process for decision making in SOAD is integrated into ADM phase G (implementation governance); UML interaction diagrams specify the collaborations between solution architects and enterprise architects during these processes and guidance model creation.

The result of a guidance modeling effort and a SOAD-TOGAF integration effort is a guidance model that serves as a "virtual enterprise architect" preserving formerly tacit knowledge. This relieves the real enterprise architects from routine work so that they can focus on hard design problems – or consider transitioning to implementation projects or other assignments for a certain amount of time.

We developed and evaluated the presented approach on real-world architecture consulting engagements. On these engagements, certain limitations of the presented approach became apparent. These limitations can be categorized under 1) usage prerequisites, 2) motivation issues/potential inhibitors and 3) guidance model maintenance. As for 1), we assume familiarity with and use of two rather rich and comprehensive assets, TOGAF and SOAD. At least the motivation and budget for training have to exist. Regarding 2), is has been reported that many knowledge sharing systems fail to work in practice because people feel threatened to share their knowledge; hence, architects have to be encouraged to share their knowledge within their organizations. Personal incentives are one way of doing so, e.g. tokens of appreciation (such as informal of formal knowledge management awards); ownership of or contributions to guidance models may also become a criterion that has to be met before an architect is promoted to a higher level of seniority. 3) Defining and funding a sustainable approach to guidance model management over time remains a challenge; for a more detailed discussion and solution approaches that address this governance challenge, we refer the reader to our previous publications (Miksovic & Zimmermann, 2011; Zimmermann, Koehler, Leymann, Polley, & Schuster, 2009).

Our TOGAF-SOAD integration solution allows enterprise architects and solution architects to improve their communication and the knowledge exchange between the two communities; the availability, consumability, and enforcement/acceptance issues that we observed in practice can be resolved (or at least relieved and mitigated) this way. The integrated approach allows enterprise and solution architects to share best practices recommendations in a problem-solution context:

We learn best from mistakes – but who said all these mistakes have to be our own ones?

REFERENCES

Ali Babar, M., Dingsøyr, T., Lago, P., & van Vliet, H. (2009). *Software architecture knowledge management: Theory and practice*. Springer-Verlag. doi:10.1007/978-3-642-02374-3

Ambler, S. (2009). *Agile model driven development (AMDD): The key to scaling agile software development*. Essay available online.

Ambler, S., Nalbone, J., & Vizdos, M. (2009). *The enterprise unified process: Extending the rational unified process*. Prentice Hall.

Bass, L., Clements, P., & Kazman, R. (2003). *Software architecture in practice* (2nd ed.). Addison Wesley.

Booch, G. (2009). *AoT presentation*. IBM internal.

Brown, N., Nord, R., & Ozkaya, I. (2011). *Strategic management of technical debt*. WICSA 2011 Tutorial.

Buschmann, F., Henney, K., & Schmidt, D. (2007). *Pattern-oriented software, Vol. 4 – A language for distributed computing*. Wiley.

Department of Defense. (1996). *Technical architecture framework for information management (Vol. 1)*.

Department of Defense. (2010). *The DoDAF architecture framework*, Version 2.02, 2010. Retrieved from http://cio-nii.defense.gov/sites/dodaf20/index.html

Eeles, P., & Cripps, P. (2010). *The process of software architecting*. Addison-Wesley.

Fairbanks, G. (2011). *Architecture Haiku*. WICSA 2011 tutorial. Retrieved from http://rhinoresearch.com/files/Haiku-tutorial-2011-06-24-final.pdf

Fowler, M. (2003a). *Patterns of enterprise application architecture*. Addison Wesley.

Fowler, M. (2003b). Who needs an architect? *IEEE Software, 20*(5). doi:10.1109/MS.2003.1231144

Haischt, D., & Georg, F. (2010). *Get me approved, please! Lizenzkompatibilitaet von Open-Source Komponenten. Objektspektrum, Sonderbeilage Agilitaet, Winter 2010*. SIGS Datacom.

Hofmeister, C., & Kruchten, P., Nord, Obbink, J. H., Ran, A., & America, P. (2007). A general model of software architecture design derived from five industrial approaches. *Journal of Systems and Software, 80*(1), 106–126. doi:10.1016/j.jss.2006.05.024

Hohpe, G., & Woolf, B. (2004). *Enterprise integration patterns*. Addison Wesley.

IBM. (2009). *Unified method framework: Work product description ARC 0513 (Architectural Decisions)*. IBM Corporation.

Julisch, K., Suter, C., Woitalla, T., & Zimmermann, O. (2011). Compliance by design – Bridging the chasm between auditors and IT architects. *Computers & Security, 30*(6-7). doi:10.1016/j.cose.2011.03.005

Krafzig, D., Banke, K., & Slama, D. (2005). *Enterprise SOA*. Prentice Hall.

Kruchten, P. (2003). *The rational unified process: An introduction*. Addison-Wesley.

Kruchten, P., Lago, P., & van Vliet, H. (2006). Building up and reasoning about architectural knowledge. *Proceedings of QoSA 2006, LNCS 4214*, (pp. 43-58). Springer.

Küster, J. M., Völzer, H., & Zimmermann, O. (2011). Managing artifacts with a viewpoint-realization level matrix. In Avgeriou, P., Grundy, J., Hall, J. G., Lago, P., & Mistrik, I. (Eds.), *Relating requirements and architectures*. Springer-Verlag. doi:10.1007/978-3-642-21001-3_15

Landre, E., Wesenberg, H., & Rønneberg, H. (2006). *Architectural improvement by use of strategic level domain-driven design*. OOPSLA Companion. doi:10.1145/1176617.1176728

Leymann, F., & Roller, D. (2000). *Production workflow – Concepts and techniques*. Prentice Hall.

Miksovic, C., & Zimmermann, O. (2011) Architecturally significant requirements, reference architecture and metamodel for architectural knowledge management in information technology services. *Journal of Systems and Software, 85*(9), 2014–2033, doi: http://dx.doi.org/10.1016/j.jss.2012.05.003

Pautasso, C., Zimmermann, O., & Leymann, F. (2008). RESTful web services vs. Big web services: Making the right architectural decision. *Proceedings of WWW, 2008*, 805–814. ACM. doi:10.1145/1367497.1367606

Poppendieck, M., & Poppendieck, T. (2003). *Lean software development: An agile toolkit*. Addison Wesley.

Ran, A., & Kuusela, J. (1996). Design decision trees. *Proceedings of 8th International Workshop on Software Specification and Design, International Workshop on Software Specifications & Design*, (pp. 172-175). IEEE Computer Society.

Rozanski, N., & Woods, E. (2005). *Software systems architecture: Working with stakeholders using viewpoints and perspectives*. Addison-Wesley.

Schwaber, K. (1995). Scrum development process. *Proceedings of OOPSLA '95 Workshop on Business Object Design and Implementation.*

Sommerville, I. (1995). *Software engineering* (5th ed.). Addison Wesley.

Sowa, J. F., & Zachman, J. A. (1992). Extending and formalizing the framework for information systems architecture. *IBM Systems Journal, 31*(3), 590–616. doi:10.1147/sj.313.0590

Sutherland, J. (n.d.). *Scrum blog.* Retrieved from http://scrum.jeffsutherland.com/

The Open Group. (2009). *The Open Group architecture framework,* Version 9. Retrieved from http://www.opengroup.org/togaf

The Open Group. (2010). *Cloud buyers' decision tree.*

Tyree, J., & Ackerman, A. (2002). Architecture decisions: Demystifying architecture. *IEEE Software, 22*(2), 19–27. doi:10.1109/MS.2005.27

Weerawarana, S., Curbera, F., Leymann, F., Storey, T., & Ferguson, D. F. (2005). *Web services platform architecture.* Prentice Hall.

Wesenberg, H., Landre, E., & Rønneberg, H. (2006). *Using domain-driven design to evaluate commercial off-the-shelf software.* OOPSLA Companion. Retrieved from http://dblp.uni-trier.de/db/conf/oopsla/oopsla2006c.html - Wesenberg

Zdun U., Hentrich C., & Dustdar, S. (2007). Modeling process-driven and service-oriented architectures using patterns and pattern primitives. *ACM Transactions on the Web, 1*(3).

Zimmermann, O. (2009). *An architectural decision modeling framework for service-oriented architecture design.* PhD Thesis, University of Stuttgart.

Zimmermann, O. (2011). Architectural decisions as reusable design assets. *IEEE Software, 28*(1), 64–69. doi:10.1109/MS.2011.3

Zimmermann, O., Koehler, J., Leymann, F., Polley, R., & Schuster, N. (2009). Managing architectural decision models with dependency relations, integrity constraints, and production rules. *The Journal of Systems and Software and Services, 82*(8).

Zimmermann, O., Schuster, N., & Eeles, P. (2008). *Modeling and sharing architectural decisions, Part 1: Concepts.* IBM developerWorks.

Zimmermann, O., Tomlinson, M., & Peuser, S. (2003). *Perspectives on web services: Applying SOAP, WSDL, and UDDI to real-world projects.* Springer Professional Computing.

Chapter 11
Linking Business and Application Architectures

Suresh Kamath
MetLife Inc., USA

ABSTRACT

The development of an IT strategy and ensuring that it is the best possible one for business is a key problem many organizations face. This problem is that of linking business architecture to IT architecture in general and application architecture specifically. Without this linkage it is difficult to manage the changes needed by the business and maximize the benefits from the information technology (IT) investments. Linking the two domains requires defining the two architectures using a "common language." While the application architecture domain has developed tools and processes to define and represent the architecture, the business architecture domain, however, lacks such processes and tools to be useful for linking of the two. The chapter addresses several questions dealing with the linking of the business and the application architectures. The author proposes to use category theory related constructs and notions to represent the business and information architecture and the linkages.

INTRODUCTION

How do we ensure that an IT strategy developed is the best possible one for business? This is a question that many organizations face and there is no clear cut process or approach defined to address this question. The problem is that of linking business architecture to IT architecture in general and application architecture specifically. This problem is very apparent when organizations go through mergers, acquisitions and reorganization.

Without this linkage it is it is difficult to manage the changes needed by the business and maximize the benefits from the information technology (IT) investments. Linking the two domains require that we define the two architectures using a "common language." The application architecture domain has developed tools and processes to define and represent the architecture, and use it to build the related processes and services. For example, IEEE Std. 1471-2000 (Architecture Description), ISO 15704:2000 (Requirements for enterprise-refer-

DOI: 10.4018/978-1-4666-2199-2.ch011

ence architectures and methodologies), Zachman Framework (Zachman, 1987), TOGAF (The Open Group Architecture Framework) (OpenGroup, 2007).

However, the representation of the business architecture in a way that can be linked to the corresponding IT architecture has been a challenge for a long time.

We will address a number of questions dealing with the linking of the business and the application architectures. Specifically, how do we define business architecture (useful for linking)? What level of details we need to represent? What view of the information architecture we should use for linking? How do we represent both these architectures and what "language" should we use? We propose to use Category theory related constructs and notions to represent both the business and information architecture. We would, however, point out that this work is a preliminary step towards the formalization and we intend to strengthen the framework in subsequent research.

BACKGROUND

We first review the business architecture arena, followed by the application architecture. Next we look at what has been the progress when we try to link the business and application architectures. Our focus in this review is mainly on the processes and methodology to represent the business or application architecture. We follow the TOGAF definitions (OpenGroup, 2009) to describe what we mean by the terms business and application architecture. Business architecture describes the functional aspects of the business domain. It defines the business strategy, governance, organization, and key business processes. Application architecture represents individual application systems, their interactions and relationships to the core business processes (defined in the Business Architecture) and reflects the business goals of the organization.

While the business architecture has been recognized as a key element in the overall enterprise architecture, there have been no clear cut definitions and how to represent business architecture. Reviewing the literature on business architecture we see that capability is the key word that identifies with a specific element used in defining/specifying the architecture. TOGAF defines business capability as a synonym for a macro-level business function. In deriving the business architecture a business capability assessment is used to define what capabilities an organization will need to fulfill its business goals and business drivers. TOGAF however, does not prescribe any specific set of enterprise architecture deliverables and hence there is no prescription on how to represent the business capability or how to link the business architecture with application architecture, except that the former is an input to the later.

Forrester Research, (Cameron, 2007; Scott, 2010), analyzes capability maps and provides some insights into how these maps help address improving business and IT alignment. The specifics of how this tool can be used for the linkage with IT is further discussed in (Scott, 2010b) and Cullen, 2010). The capability map is defined as a model of the firm associating the business capabilities, processes, and functions required for business success with the IT resource that enables them. Business is characterized by the capabilities required for that business to accomplish its objectives. By identifying the IT resource with the capability in the definition, a path to linking the business architecture with application architecture also gets defined. The development of a capability map and its content varies with the type of industry (e.g. manufacturing, finance) and the maturity of the organization in using business architecture - consulting groups, government agencies, and private corporations.

In the business architecture overview by the Business Architecture Working Group (BAWG, 2011), the business capability is described as the primary business functions of an enterprise and the pieces of the organization that perform those functions. This view further distinguishes between customer-facing functions, supplier-related functions, business execution, and business management functions. The recommendation is that the capabilities can be decomposed from high level to detailed level (up to level 5).

McDavid (1999), while presenting a standard for describing business architecture defines the role of business architecture as the concept in business architecture description provide a semantic framework for speaking about business concerns. The business concepts identified were "business situation," "business purpose," "business behavior," "business function" etc.

Versteeg and Bouwman (2006), discusses the creation of business architecture as well as how it can be linked to the application architecture. The high level business processes describe how the business domains and the business activities within these domains work together to achieve the organizational goals and strategies. The business activities are linked to business functions and business concepts (objects/data) to perform the activities.

The developments we have seen so far for the design and representation of business architecture has been informal. The BAWG specification (BAWG, 2011b) has provided a relational model at the conceptual level. Our focus will be to formalize this using a language that will allow us to "talk" to the application architecture and provide the mechanisms to link one to the other. We will see more on this later in this section in our review of the linkages between the business and application architecture.

Coming now to the application architecture, the ANSI/IEEE Standard 1471-2000 defines architecture as the fundamental organization of a system, embodied in its components, their relationships to each other and the environment, and the principles governing its design and evolution. Other such definitions exist - DoDAF (Defense architecture framework), TOGAF, RM-ODP.

These are mainly at the conceptual level, that is, they provide high-level guidelines. Over a period of time, various organizations have created architectural representations and supporting tools. On of the most influential development to represent any software system has been the Unified Modeling Language (UML) and is widely used to represent or describe architecture. The literature on software architecture is vast and it is beyond the scope of this paper to provide a review of this subject. We mention just the architecture description languages (ADL), which have evolved to represent the architecture that can support architecture based software development, see (Medvidovic & Taylor, 2000) for an excellent survey on the ADLs and (Medvidovic, Dashofy, and Taylor, 2007) on an update on the same. The ADLs have been analyzed from the perspective of (a) components, (b) connectors, (c) configuration and (d) tool support. Since some of these are relevant to our approach we will discuss this in detail below.

Now we are ready to look at the linkage between these two, the business and application architecture. The key question that needs to be addressed is, why we need to link the business and application architecture?

Clearly by linking the business capabilities (components of the business architecture) to IT, the resources (applications, services etc.) can be used to get a better understanding of how each capability is "enabled" within the enterprise. Once this is achieved, then we will be able to take the next steps of aligning and optimizing the resources to maximize the business benefits and build the flexibility required to address rapid changes in the business strategies and directions.

First, let us clarify what we mean by the linkage between business and application architecture. The business architecture represents the business process and tasks, see Figure 1, shown on the right hand side. The figure shows a sample linkage between the business and application architectures for account inquiry process. The logical models of these have a corresponding physical

Figure 1. Linkages between business and application (simplified)

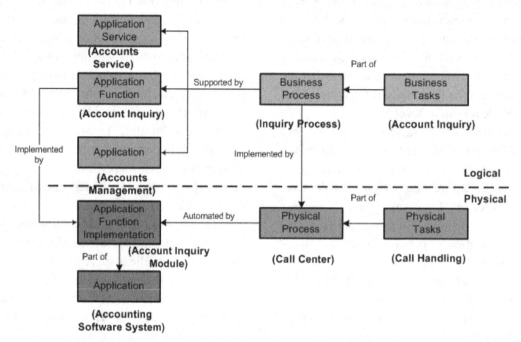

model (the upper and lower part in the diagram), for example, the logical business task could be, say, Account Inquiry. This business task is part of several steps of a business process. Within the business organization this task may be supported using a call center and the call center agent could be accessing an application that supports this task. The business process (Inquiry) will be supported by an application function (or an application service, shown on the left hand side of the diagram), please note that it is possible that an organization may have some of the business tasks manual. In the above example, the Inquiry process is linked to the Account Inquiry function on the application side. The application functions ate logically grouped into an application, e.g. Accounting System. We can also see the physical application Accounting Software System implements the various application functions and services. How do we represent the business and application architecture in a way that will allow us to address the linking is the subject matter of this chapter.

Zachman (1987) provided a framework in the area of Enterprise Architecture and is the most popular framework, Figure 2. The framework consists of rows and columns, six of each, representing different participants and their roles. He had the idea of linkage already established as can be seen from the following statement: "The cost involved and the success of the business depending increasingly on its information systems require a disciplined approach to the management of those systems "(p.267). This discipline was incorporated by having to explicitly look at every important issue from every important perspective – the rows and columns. The second row represents the conceptual enterprise model based on the role of an owner. It intersects with each of the six columns that represent the data, function etc. that facilitates abstraction of the information that is suitable for modeling purposes. Unfortunately, the practice of developing enterprise architecture based on this framework has been difficult and resulted in the creation of other frameworks such as TOGAF. Fatoli and Shams (2006) summarizes the difficul-

Figure 2. Zachman framework for the enterprise. The last row (blank) represents the actual implementation for the enterprise. For example, the How column for this row will be the object code.

	Why	How	Where	Who	Why	When
Contextual	Goal List	Process List	Material List	Organizational Unit and Role List	Locations List	Events List
Conceptual	Goal Relationship	Process Model	ER Model	Organizational Unit and Role Relationship Model	Location Model	Event Model
Logical	Rules Diagram	Process Diagram	Data Model Diagram	Role Relationship Diagram	Locations Diagram	Event Diagram
Physical	Rule Specification	Process Specification	Data Specification	Role Specification	Location Specification	Event Specification
Detailed	Rules Detail	Process Details	Data Details	Role Details	Location Details	Event Details
Functioning Enterprise						

ties. Sessions (2007) provides a comparison of several frameworks. See Gokhale (2010) for some ways on improving the effectiveness in using Zachman framework.

Henderson & Venkatraman (1993) define the strategic alignment model for "conceptualizing and directing the emerging area of strategic management of information technology." The authors argue that "no single IT application- however sophisticated and the state of the art it may be – could deliver a sustained competitive advantage Rather advantage is obtained through the capability of an organization to exploit IT functionality on a continuum basis." One of the key dimensions of the proposed alignment model is the integration of business and IT domains, the theme of this chapter. The paper goes on to consider various aspects of the strategic and operational integration between business and IT strategy.

McDavid (1999) provides "Business-to-IT concept mapping" which links the business ar-chitecture elements with the IT architecture. For example, the "business behavior" concept is linked to the architectural concepts of "component," "collaboration," and "interface." The software component is the key to implement the business behavior. Components perform and capture key information about the external and internal behavior and also support the definition of the business semantics and the interrelationships among the resources and roles within the enterprise when performing the business functions. The work presented is mostly at the conceptual level and further work is needed to take these concepts to the next level.

Versteeg and Bouwman (2006), provides the mechanism to link the business domain to the IT domain. The business domain consists of business processes, business functions, and business objects. The business process maps to the process architecture and is decomposed into procedures, activities and tasks. The function and data from the business domain are mapped to the functions and objects of the information architecture. The business processes and functions are realized through an application, which aggregates one or more functions and data objects from the information architecture (which is linked to the functions and data in the business domain). This application may be a dedicated application (e.g. CRM), a service or a component. The authors argue that because the functional decomposition of the information architecture as well as the process decomposition of the process architecture is rooted in the business architecture, these are already aligned with each other. No prescription is however provided to address the "level" of the linkage. For example, we could have a situation where in the IT function is linked to a single process/task resulting in large number of small components. The other extreme could be that a large part of the business function is "frozen" into a specific application/component.

Tian, Ding, Cao and Lee (2006) argue that a business component provide useful views and guidance for enterprise architecture design and proposes a quantitative approach using fuzzy clustering algorithm to construct business components from raw information of business activities. Business services are then identified using the communication patterns described in Geurts and Geelhoed (2004). The business component is defined as a unit of business functions that serves a unique purpose and is composed of a group of cohesive business activities supported by appropriate information system and processes.

However, a crucial step in this methodology, the assignment of "tightness" factor, i.e. internal relationships between business activities, is a manual step requiring domain experts to assign the value between 0 and 1 for every activity pair.

Aier and Winter (2009) propose an alignment architecture which replaces the direct m:n relationships between the business and IT architecture based on the decoupling mechanism found in systems theory. The alignment artifacts (enterprise services, domain, and applications) serve as a translator between the linkages between the business and IT. These artifacts are identified using a domain analysis and clustering approach. For this purpose, the business process is represented as an extended event driven process chain, which includes linkages to the various IT Systems. This model is then transformed into a graph to perform the clustering analysis.

We also have essentially tool-based approaches for linking the two architectures and we would like to cover couple of these here. ArchiMate (Open Group 2009) is an open standard architectural modeling language, recently adopted by Open Group. ArchiMate language defines three main layers to represent the organizational business process, application structure and technology used. The language offers relationships to model the link between business, application and technology layers. The relationship types are used in linking the elements between the layers, see Figure 2 for example, which illustrates the use of the relationship types "Supported by" and "Implemented" for linking the business process with the application service, application function and the physical implementation. In this case the specific business process uses the application service, which is implemented by the application function. A number of commercial modeling tools support the ArchiMate.

The Essential Meta-Model (EssentialProjectTeam 2010) is a framework independent set of semantic definitions for knowledge related to the building blocks and relationships of an enterprise. Essential Architecture Meta Model is published as open source and is available for use in any modeling tool set. A reference implementation (Essential Architecture Manager) model is provided, including some tools to capture and analyze the enterprise architecture. The Meta model has two main components - core Meta model and support Meta model. The core Meta model deals with the four layers of business, application, information and technology architecture elements and how these are linked. Within a specific layer, the model addresses elements within at the conceptual, logical and physical levels. The modeling starts with defining the business value chain, which is nothing but defining the underlying business capabilities. The business capabilities are then decomposed into business processes, business activities and business tasks. Similar process is followed to model the application, information and technology layers.

MAIN FOCUS OF THE CHAPTER

Issues, Controversies, Problems

The key issue addressed in this chapter, and also the theme of this book, is the alignment of architectures. This chapter focuses on the alignment of business and application architecture. The benefits from such an alignment can be listed as follows:

- **Focusing Future Investments:** Where and what we need to invest to improve the capabilities.
- **Outsourced Capabilities:** Those capabilities that provide no clear differentiation compared to the competition within the industry.
- **IT Strategy:** The strategy can be directly related to how one or more business capabilities can be enhanced.
- **Process Consolidation:** Consolidation of applications/services and aligning these with the business capabilities. This will lead to overall reduction in cost and maintenance.
- **Common Language:** With the linkage we will be able to express both the architectures using a common language to specify and analyze the architecture.

As we have seen there have been several efforts made to support the linkages and several frameworks and tools have been developed to address the same. These frameworks/tools require some form of manual inputs to create the mapping, capture the decision criteria, and maintain the relationships and decisions and make it persistent. The reasoning capability is limited to what has been documented. Additional tools and process may be needed to support the architecture reasoning. We believe that the introduction of formal methods will help us to address the problem of linking the two architectures efficiently and effectively, see Kamath (2011) and references therein for some details on formal methods and the role of category theory. Formal methods will allow us to systematize and introduce rigor into the specification of the linkages. More importantly, the use for formal methods will help us understand the system better and reason about its behavior in a reliable way, thus supporting the conclusions derived and decisions taken.

We propose the use of component based specification as the common "language" for representing the business and application architecture. We will augment this language with some notions from Category theory that will support the formal reasoning about the linkage framework. Rest of this section is devoted to reviewing the concepts related to component specification and category theory used later in this chapter.

The component based approach has several other advantages, Shaw and Garland (1996) and Szyperski (2002). It supports the reuse of components and it also allows for multiple representation of a business component. This is very important from an enterprise architecture point of view, where we see typically more than one application that support one or more business functions. For example, in the Insurance industry we may see similar applications addressing different product lines such as life, annuity etc. Another advantage is that the components can be replaced or adapted for reuse in different context. This flexibility is also needed when we are trying to link the business and application architectures.

Szyperski (2002) defines a software component as:

A software component is a unit of composition with contractually specified interfaces and explicit context dependencies only. A software component can be deployed independently and is subject to composition by third parties.

There is a large body of work on the formal specification and representation of components. Space constraints limit us from covering this and therefore we provide references only for a few of these selected papers and consider one in particular to show the range of formal techniques used in the research and will be the basis for our framework discussed subsequently.

With respect to formal approaches using components the following is some of the research work, Broy (1995, 2000), Padberg (2002, 2006), Filipe (2002), Mosschoyiannis (2005), the refinement calculus of object systems (rCOS) by Meng & Aichernig (2002) is based on the Unified Theories of Programming of Hoare & Jifeng (1998), Piccola – (Nierstrasz and Achermann, 2003), JavaA (Hacklinger, 2004), CoIn approach (Brim, Cerna, Varekova and Zimmerova, 2005), Fractal (Bruneton, Coupaye, Leclerq, Quema and Stefani, 2004), SOFA (Plasil, Balek, and Janecek, 1998), Components and Contracts (Pahl, 2001).

We will review the papers by Meng & Aichernig (2002), Jifeng, Liu and Xiaoshan (2003), and Jifeng, Li and Liu (2005a, 2005b, 2005c) as their work forms the basis for the proposed framework in this chapter. We will briefly look at the basics elements in the rCOS approach leading up to the definition of a component. An Interface (I) is used to specify the features provided by a component. I = (FDec, MDec), where FDec is a set of attributes (field declarations) and MDec is a set of method declarations (operations). An attribute has a type T and a method m can have input and output attributes, each of which will belong to a type U and

V. We can have more than one input attributes, but to avoid clutter we will use just one in further discussions. We will also avoid mentioning the types usually, e.g. m (in x, out y), is a method with one input attribute x and one output attribute y.

A Contract is specified as Ctr = (I, Init, Φ, Prot), where I is the interface satisfied by the contract, Init is an assignment of initial values to a set of attributes, if any. Φ is a function that maps each method of I to a specification, and Prot is an interaction protocol, which is nothing but a set of sequences of call events (e.g., m1 (x1) m2(x2)… mk(xk)). A general contract (GCtr) extends a contract Ctr with a set of private method declarations and their specifications. While the interface specifies only the syntax, a contract additionally specifies the functionality, what happens in a method. For our discussion, this specification is not really important, and for details, we refer to Liu, Jifeng and Li (2004).

A component (C) is an implementation of the interface of a general contract (called provided services). This implementation may require methods (services) provided by other components and are called required services. Formally a component C = (GCtr,InMDec), where InMDec is the set of required methods by the component, also called required interfaces.

Interfaces, Contracts and Components can be composed and using the composition of components we are ready to specify the architecture based on components. Two interfaces I1 and I2 are composable if no attribute of I1 is redefined in I2. The composition I1ΘI2 represents an interface I with the composed attributes FDec = FDec1 U FDec2 and the composed methods MDec = MDec2 (m (in:U, out:V) | m $\in$ MDec1 $\wedge$ m $\notin$ MDec2). Similarly two contracts Ctr1 and Ctr2 are composable, if I1 and I2 are composable and for any method m occurring in both I1 and I2, we have MSpec1 (m(in1:U,out1:V))=MSpec2 (m(in2:U, out2:V)). The composition is represented by Ctr1||Ctr2. for the general contracts we have GCtr1||GCtr2. In this case the required interfaces are a union of the required interfaces. For components we have two types of compositions, (i) chaining (C1>>C2), and (ii) disjoint composition (C1ΘC2).

An example of a component representation using UML 2.0 is shown in Figure 3. The component **AccountManager** has three provided interfaces, **IGetAccount**, **IUpdateAccount**, and **IPrintStatement**. The component requires two interfaces, **IPrintService** for the printing of statements and **IPersistAccount** for saving the account information.

A concrete example of composition is shown in Figure 4. We show the composition of **Ac-countManager** component with the **Statement-Printer** component, the later one implements the required interface **IPrintService** of the **Accout-nManager**.

Next we will review some of the basic constructs we need from category theory. Due to lack of space, we only provide some of the definitions that will be used later in this section. Category theory is a comparatively new mathematical tool and appeared first in the area of topology about 70 years ago. Category theory deals with objects and their interrelationships. Morphisms, that is, the connection between objects are used to characterize an object, than the internal structure of the object (MacLane, 1998).

Figure 3. Component in UML notation. The left side of the diagram shows the required interfaces and the right side shows the provided interfaces.

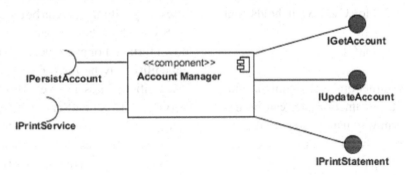

Figure 4. Component composition in UML notation. The required interface IPrintService is now provided by the statement printer component.

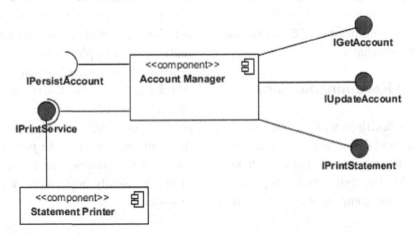

A Category C is a collection of things called objects (Obj(C)) and things called arrows or morphisms (Mor(C)), which represent the relationships between the objects A, B $\in$ Obj(C). Additionally it contains:

- If A and B are objects in a category C, then f: A $\rightarrow$ B represents a relation between A (domain of f) and B (codomain of f).
- For all A,B,C $\in$ Obj(C) a mapping Mor(C) (B,C) x Mor(C) (A,B) $\rightarrow$ Mor(C) (A,C) called composition (denoted by $\circ$).
- For all A $\in$ Obj(C) a distinguished morphism idA $\in$ Mor(C) (A,A) called identity morphism for A.
- For all A, B, C, D $\in$ Obj(C) and f $\in$ Mor(C) (A,B). g $\in$ Mor(C)(B,C), and h $\in$ Mor(C) (C,D) it holds that h $\circ$ (g $\circ$ f) = (h $\circ$ g) $\circ$ f.
- For all A, B, C $\in$ Obj(C) and f $\in$ Mor(C) (A,B). g $\in$ 2 Mor(C)(C,A) it holds that f $\circ$ idA = f.
- idA $\circ$ g = g $\in$ Obj(C).

Many other constructions such as union, sum, products, quotient, conjunction etc. can be described in a uniform way using category theory. However, we need only one additional concept (Functor) for our purpose.

The concept of morphism can be extended from objects within a category to categories whose objects are categories. This morphism is called a functor. A functor F: C $\rightarrow$ D is given by two mappings, one for the objects in C and D, and the other for the morphisms of C and D, see MacLane (1998) for details.

Solutions and Recommendations

We start from the description of software architecture, which we will define as a set of software components and the relationship between them. Our goal is to (i) define and formally represent software and business components, (ii) describe the relationship between the business components and software components, and finally (iii) represent architecture as a set of components. The last step will achieve the desired result of linking of the business and application architecture.

We will use examples from the Insurance domain for further discussion in this chapter. Business capabilities are services that a business or enterprise offers or requires (what). The business capabilities are realized by the business processes. The business capability itself can be broken down into supporting capabilities. The business capabilities also can be ordered based on how the business value chain is defined.

For example, in the Insurance Industry (see Figure 5), the high level capabilities may consist of Product Development (PD), Policy Administration (PA), and Sales and Services (SS). Based on how the value gets added within the organization. These capabilities also can be ordered as PD $\rightarrow$ PA $\rightarrow$ SS. Each of these capabilities may be broken down further. For example, the Sales and Service capability may be further broken into: Channel Acquisition, Sales and New Business, Customer Service, and Channel Servicing. Customer Service can be broken further into Customer Inquiry $\rightarrow$ Customer Changes $\rightarrow$ Customer Claims.

We observe that the business capabilities may consists of other capabilities or may be realized by one or more business processes. A business process represents a specification of how a process should be performed to meet the services. A business process in turn may contain one or business activities and other business processes, or may be realized by an application. The business activity is realized by a set of business tasks (or other activities) or may be realized by an application. The business task is the lowest level of representation. *Please note that all business tasks may not be automated and may be performed manually, e.g. mail the invoice.* The business activity and tasks are usually performed by a single person or system.

Figure 5. Business capability definition: Insurance business unit. The diagram shows capabilities up to 4 levels for the sales and service capability (level 1), customer service (level 2), customer inquiry (level 3), and account inquiry (level 4).

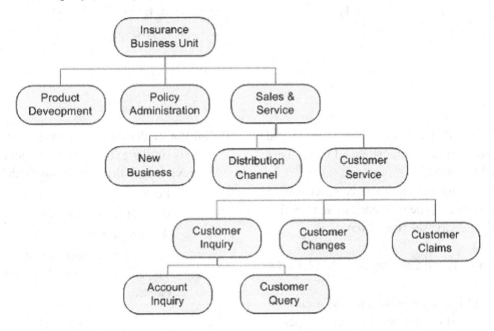

The key assumption for our framework (discussed next) is that in the context of the business architecture:

1. We have a list of business capabilities, processes, activities and tasks available.
2. For each of these capabilities and processes, etc.:
    a. At a logical level, we know the business classes (e.g. Account, Client) involved.
    b. Methods supported by these classes are known.
    c. The attributes that are used (input as well as output) to perform the activities and tasks are also known (methods).

We will use the example capabilities shown in Figure 5 throughout the rest of this chapter to illustrate the approach. We will focus on the **CustomerService** capability and the related capability **CustomerInquiry**, which again contains **AccountInquiry** and **CustomerQuery**. For the purposes of discussion, we consider Customer Service as an Interface that contains both **AccountInquiry** and **CustomerQuery**.

Representing Business Architecture

The basic idea in representing business architecture is to use the concept of interface described earlier to capture the basic services provided by a single business task or a business process. In this context it is also possible to extend an interface to add additional methods. The composition of interfaces will be used to represent the aggregate entity called the business capability.

Consider the structure shown in Figure 6; we have a number of interface specifications represented as Ii, where i range from 1 to 7. The relationships between interfaces are indicated as labeled arrows (please note that we follow the category theory notations to represent the relation rather than the UML convention here). For example I1 → I2 represents the type extension,

Figure 6. Interfaces and their representation. In the notation we follow an arrow of type "ext" from I_1 to I_2 means I_2 extends I_1.

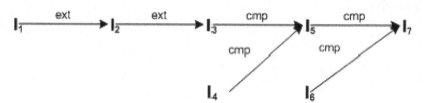

where I2 extends I1. Similarly the I3 → I5 and I4 → I5 are of type "composition," I3 and I4 are composed to form I5.

We will show that the interface specification in Figure 5 forms a typed category. First we define the typed category, see (Lu, 2005):

Definition 1: Typed Category K = (O, M, G, T), where:

1. O is a class of objects, M a class of typed morphisms, G a set of types, T a set of type composition rules.
2. M = {M (a, b, t) | a, b ∈ O, t ∈ G}, is the disjoint union of morphism sets, where each M(a,b,t) is a set of morphisms from a to b.
3. There is a unit type u ∈ G such that for any x ∈ O, we have M(x, x, u) = {Id_x: x $\underset{u}{\to}$ x}
4. T: G x G → G, is a partial mapping, assigning to any (t, s) ∈ dom(T) a type w = t x s called the composition types.

For specifying the business architecture with O as the objects Ii (interface specifications) and types as the "set {ext, cmp}" (see Figure 6), consider the case of f: I2 $\underset{t}{\to}$ I3, g: I3 $\underset{s}{\to}$ I5. We do not have a composition rule with ext x cmp types, so the conditions required by the typed category are not satisfied.

We will use the notion of pseudo-category; see (Lu, 2005).

Definition 2: Pseudo Category K = (O, M, G, T) is similar to the Typed Category defined previously, with the following modifications:

1. For morphisms f: a $\underset{t}{\to}$ b, g: b $\underset{s}{\to}$ c, the product t x s does not necessarily exist. A third morphism h = g°f = a $\underset{txs}{\to}$ c does not necessarily exist.
2. The composition f°Id_a = f and Id_u°g=g exists.

Now we are ready to define the business architecture, which is nothing but a collection of the interface specifications I_i.

Definition 3: Business Architecture is a collection of interfaces Ii, with 1 ≤ I ≤ M, is a pseudo-category BA = (I, M_1, G_1, T_1), where:

1. I is a set containing the interface containing the interface specifications I_i.
2. M_1 contains the morphisms f: I_i $\underset{t}{\to}$ I_j, IJ, where t = {ext, cmp}.
3. The set G_1 is {ext, cmp}.
4. The set T_1 contains ext x ext → ext and cpm x cmp → cmp.

Given that I_2 extends I_1 ((I_1 $\underset{ext}{\to}$ I_2) and I_3 extends I_2 (I_2 $\underset{ext}{\to}$ I_3), we can see that I_3 extends I_1 (I_3 $\underset{ext}{\to}$ I_1). The same applies for the **cmp** (composition) relation. If, for example, I_2 has I_1 in its composition and I_3 has I_2 in its composition, then I_3 also has I_1 in its composition.

Using the example provided in Figure 5, we have the interface **CustomerInquiry** composed of two other interfaces, **AccountInquiry** and **CustomerQuery**. Here **CustomerQuery** will contain the methods, say, getOwner(), getInsured(), getMailingAddress(). The **AccountInquiry** on the other hand will contain methods to support getAccount(), printStatement(). To keep the notations simple we do not use any attributes in this example and this in no way impacts any arguments presented.

Using the notations explained above, the relationship can be expressed as **CustomerQuery** *cmp* **CustomerInquiry** and **AccountInquiry** *cmp* **CustomerInquiry**. These interfaces defined by the business architecture will have an implementation at the application architecture level. We will see this in the next section. Essentially business architecture is presented as a set of interfaces that specifies a contract for each of these interfaces. The interfaces can be composed to form "larger" interfaces, for example, a business process is a larger interface that is composed of other interfaces that are either business activities and/or tasks.

Representing Application Architecture

We will use the component specifications as the objects for representing the application architecture. The application architecture is a pseudo-category with the morphism types **use**, **cmp**. The **use** stands for the chaining and the **cmp** stands for the disjoint composition.

Definition 4: Application Architecture is a collection of the component specifications Ci, with $1 \leq I \leq N$, is a pseudo-category AA = (C, M_C, G_C, T_C), where:
1. C is a set containing the component specifications C_i.

2. M_c contains the morphisms f: C_i C_j, $i \neq j$, where t $\in$ {**use,cpmg**}.
3. The set G_c is {**use,cmpg**}.
4. The set T_c sontains use x use *uses* use and cmp x cmp *uses* cmp.

Given that C_2 uses C_1 (C_1 C_2) and C_3 uses C_2, (C_2 *uses* C_3), we can see that C_3 uses C_1 (C_3 *uses* C_1). The same applies for the cmp (composition relation. If, for example, C2 has C1 in its composition and C_3 has C_2 in its composition, then C_3 also has C_1 in its composition.

Using the example of Figure 5, the application architecture may support the following applications, a Portal (where the customers interact) and another application, say, Customer Management System that actually implements various components to support the customer interaction through the Portal. One of the components of the Customer Management System is the **AccountManager** (shown in Figure 4). This component implements **IGetAccount()**, **IUpdateAccount()**, and **IPrintStatement()**. To implement IUpdateAccount(), it requires the service **IPersistAccount()**, and to implement the **IPrintStatement()**, it requires **IPrintService()**.

There is also a CustomerManager component that supports the interfaces IgetOwner(), IgetInsured() etc. (not shown in the diagram referred to). How this is linked with the business interfaces will be discussed next.

Linking the Two Architectures

We will use the concept of a functor, which is a morphism between categories, to link the business and application architectures. First we will define the typed functor, and then we will modify this definition to be applicable in the case of pseudo-categories (pseudo functor), see (Lu, 2005).

Definition 5: A typed functor F between two typed categories K1 = (O1; M1;G1; T1) and K2=(O2;M2;G2; T2) is defined as follows:

1. F associates each object x in O1 with an object Fx in O2.
2. F is a homomorphism from G1 to G2.
3. F is a homomorphism from M1 to M2:
   a. F associates each morphism f in M1(x; y; t) with a morphism Ff in M2(Fx; Fy; Ft).
   b. For each x in O1; $FId_x = Id_{Fx}$.
   c. $F(f \circ g) = Ff \circ Fg$, where $\circ$ stands for morphism composition.

Definition 6: A pseudo functor F between two pseudo-categories K1 and K2 is the same as Definition 5 with modification: Replace 3(c) of Definition with: $Fh = Ff \circ Fg$ for all $f \in M(x, y, t)$, $g \in M(y, z, s)$ and $h = f^\circ g \in M(x; z; t \times s)$.

We can interpret the functor as a mechanism that links the interface specification to an implementation.

For example, if I1 in the pseudo-category BA is linked to Cj in the pseudo-category AA, it means that Cj implement Ii. There are several possibilities when we look at such mappings:

- Multiple components may implement the same interface. Please note that within the enterprise applications get developed over a period of time within different organizational units, sometimes independently, re-

sulting in multiple applications supporting the same functionality.

- There could be inconsistencies in the usage of components by different applications, which will get reflected in the violation of the rules for a functor, illustrated later in this section.

- The structure of the interfaces such as the extension and composition may also reveal duplication of functionality and/or inconsistencies in the component usage.

For the example discussed Figure 7 shows the linkage between the business interfaces and application components. In this diagram, the business component **AccountInquiry** is implemented by the application component **AccountManager** using the arrow type "imp." Please note that **CustomerInquiry** is not mapped to any specific component. It is possible that there are other interfaces in **CustomerInquiry** that gets mapped to other application components or there are interfaces that may not map to any application/component – for example, manual tasks in the business process. The **CustomerManager** "uses" **AccountManager** component.

We can clearly see the advantages of having the linkages, due lack of space we will provide two examples below. The first example will show how we can assess a proposed change in the business functionality and the second example will show how inconsistencies can be spotted.

Figure 7. Linking the two architectures

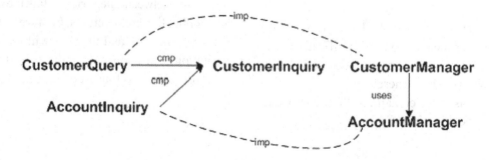

Consider the case where the business wants to provide customers with the capability of creating and managing their own portfolios (of accounts). The new contracts will include a new interface, ManagePortfolio that will support methods to create and manage portfolios, add/delete additional accounts, and transfer accounts, see below:

```
Interface ManagePortfolio{
createPortfolio();
addAccount();
removeAccount();
transferAccount();
}
```

On the application architecture side, we will have to build components to provide this capability as there is no support exists. The decision could be to build an additional component that implements the contract required for **ManagePortfolio**. So we may build a **PortfolioManager** component that can address the required functionality, see Figure 8. Here we can see the modifications; The **ManagePortfolio** is implemented by the **PortfolioManager** on the application side.

The application Customer Management System is composed of the components, **CustomerManager**, **AccountManager**, and **PortfolioManager**.

The example in Figure 9 shows the inconsistencies because of duplicate functionality and the way the interfaces are required to be composed as per the business architecture. We show a fragment of the mapping. Also we only show the object mappings (dashed lines) and not the edge mappings.

Using the functor mapping conditions, we need to satisfy Definition6 3(c).Let us consider the following:

- Consider f: $I_3 \xrightarrow{cmp} I_5$ and g: $I_5 \xrightarrow{cmp} I_7$.

- We have f°g: $I_3 \xrightarrow{cmp} I_7$, with cmp x cmp= cmp.

- We need to compute Ff°Fg. This can be done by looking at the objects $F(I_3)$, $F(I_5)$, and $F(I_7)$ and the mapping between them. These objects in AA correspond to C_2, C_3, and C_5 respectively. So we have Ff: $C_2 \xrightarrow{cmp} C_3$ and Fg: $C_3 \xrightarrow{cmp} C_5$. However, the composition of *cmp* x *use* does not exist, resulting in the invalid functor.

The inconsistency can be seen based on the following: We have C5 implement I6 and I7 as per the mapping (Figure 9). However, I7 is composed of I5 and I6, and in turn I5 is composed of I3 and I4. This means that the component C5 meets the specifications of I3, I4, I5 and I6. So it

Figure 8. Managing portfolio - realization

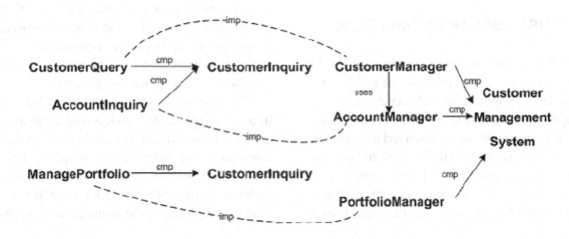

Figure 9. Inconsistency when mapping BA to AA. The composition cmp x use between C2, C3 and C5 does not exist.

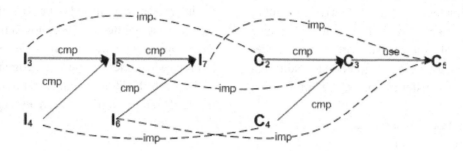

does not need to "use" the component C3, which meets the specifications of I3 and I4 and is already there in C5.

From the example above we can see the benefit of this approach, first is the ability to link the business and application architecture, and second is the ability to identify the inconsistencies and duplication that exists in the existing application architecture. The linkage discussed in this paper however is based on the manual process, which involves (i) creating the business architecture specification and expressing it as the category BA, (ii) identifying the application architecture components in the enterprise and expressing it as the category AA, and finally (iii) creation of the functor that maps the objects and arrows between these two categories. Mechanization of these processes with appropriate tool support will be dealt with in future work.

FUTURE RESEARCH DIRECTIONS

There are many challenges ahead to achieve the goal of an automated process that will link the business and application architecture. One of the approaches could be to derive the contract based on the component specification and match it with the specified contract in the business architecture, see Zhan, Kang and Liu (2010) wherein the concept of calculating the required contract from a component is dealt with. Ko, Gschwind, Kuster,

Volzer, and Zimmermann (2008) propose a "business compiler" that takes the business process specification as input and compiles them into executable IT systems. The focus of their research is in the area of business process management (BPM) and service-oriented architecture (SOA), but easily can be adapted to the problem we are dealing with.

CONCLUSION

This paper presents our results from the investigation to develop a framework to represent the business and application architecture and the linkages between the two. As we have seen this linkage is crucial for organizations to manage it investments and aligning the IT infrastructure with the evolving business strategies. Category theory was proposed as the formal language to unify the business and it worlds with the ability to represent the concepts and relations between the two in a unified way. We presented the rCOS as the underlying model for the specification of interfaces, contracts, and components.

The concept of pseudo-category is then utilized to represent the business and application architecture specifications and the relationships contained within and a pseudo functor is defined to capture the "implementation" linkages between the business and application architecture. We have shown examples using the insurance domain and were also able to illustrate the usefulness of this approach in identifying duplication and inconsistencies within an existing application architecture. The linkage discussed in this paper however is based on manual processes.

We intend to explore the contract matching as a mechanism to match the interfaces with the components so as to automate the process.

REFERENCES

Aier, S., & Winter, R. (2009). Virtual decoupling for IT/business alignment- Conceptual foundations, architecture design and implementation example. *Business and Information Systems Engineering, 2,* 1–13.

Brim, L., Černá, I., Vařeková, P., & Zimmerova, B. (2005). Component-interaction automata as a verification-oriented component-based system specification. *SIGSOFT Software Engineering Notes, 31.*

Broy, M. (1995). Advanced component interface specification. In T. Ito & A. Yonezawa (Eds.), *Theory and Practice of Parallel Programming* (*Vol. 907,* pp. 369–392). *Lecture Notes in Computer Science* Berlin, Germany: Springer. Retrieved from. doi:10.1007/BFb0026580doi:10.1007/BFb0026580

Broy, M. (2000). Algebraic specification of reactive systems. *Theoretical Computer Science, 239*(1), 3–40. doi:10.1016/S0304-3975(99)00212-1doi:10.1016/S0304-3975(99)00212-1

Bruneton, E., Coupaye, T., Leclercq, M., Quema, V., & Stefani, J.-B. (2004). An open component model and its support in Java. In I. Crnkovic, J. A. Stafford, H. W. Schmidt, & K. Wallnau (Eds.), *Component-Based Software Engineering* (*Vol. 3054,* pp. 7–22). *Lecture Notes in Computer Science* Berlin, Germany: Springer. doi:10.1007/978-3-540-24774-6_3doi:10.1007/978-3-540-24774-6_3

BAWG. (2011). *Business architecture overview.* Retrieved August 5, 2011, from http://bawg.omg.org/.

BAWG. (2011b). *Business architecture working group.* Retrieved August 5, 2011, from http://bawg.omg.org/business architecture overview.htm

Cameron, B. (2007). *Capability maps anchor business complexity.* Forrester Research. Retrieved January 8, 2012, from http://www.forrester.com/rb/Research/capability_maps_anchor_business_complexity/q/id/43049/t/

Crnkovic, I., & Larsson, M. (2002). *Building reliable component-based software systems.*

Cullen, A. (2010a). *Sample business capability map: Insurance.* Forrester Research. Retrieved January 8, 2012 from http://www.forrester.com/rb/Research/sample_business_capability_map_insurance/q/id/56540/t/2

Cullen, A. (2010b). *Using business capability maps to guide IT investment governance.* Forrester Research. Retrieved January 8, 2012, from http://www.forrester.com/rb/Research/using_business_capability_maps_to_guide_it/q/id/56376/t/2

Ehrig, H., Orejas, F., Braatz, B., Klein, M., & Piirainen, M. (2002). A generic component framework for system modeling. In R. D. Kutsche & H. Weber (Eds.), *FASE* (pp. 33–48). Berlin, Germany: Springer. doi:10.1007/3-540-45923-5_3doi:10.1007/3-540-45923-5_3

EssentialProjectTeam. (2010). *Essential metamodel.* Retrieved August 8, 2011, from http://www.enterprise-architecture.org/about/35-essential-meta-model

Filipe, J. K. (2002). A logic-based formalization for component specification. *Journal of Object Technology, 1*(3), 231–248. doi:10.5381/jot.2002.1.3.a13doi:10.5381/jot.2002.1.3.a13

Geurts, G., & Geelhoed, A. (2004). Business process decomposition and service identification using communication patterns. *Mirosoft Architecture Journal, 1*, 18–27.

Gokhale, A. (2010). *Increasing effectiveness of the Zachman framework using the Balanced Scorecard.* Unpublished Master's thesis, Purdue University, Indiana

Hacklinger, F. (2004). Java\A - Taking components into Java. In W. Dosch & N. Debnath (Eds.), *Proceedings of the 13th ISCA Conference, Intelligent and Adaptive Systems and Software Engineering.*

Henderson, J. C., & Venkatraman, N. (1993). Strategic alignment: Leveraging information technology for transforming organizations. *IBM Systems Journal, 32*, 472–484. doi:10.1147/sj.382.0472doi:10.1147/sj.382.0472

Hoare, C. A. R., & Jifeng, H. (1998). *Foundations of component-based systems.*

Jifeng, H., Li, X., & Liu, Z. (2005a). *Component-based software engineering -The need to link methods and their theories.* The United Nations University.

Jifeng, H., Li, X., & Liu, Z. (2005b). *rCOS: A refinement calculus for object systems.* The United Nations University.

Jifeng, H., Liu, Z., & Li, X. (2005c). *Reactive components.* The United Nations University.

Jifeng, H., Liu, Z., & Xiaoshan, L. (2003). *Contract-oriented component software development.* The United Nations University.

Kamath, S. (2011). Capabilities and features: Linking business and application architectures - I. *International Conference on Information Science and Applications*, (pp. 1-7). Retrieved from doi:http://doi.ieeecomputersociety.org/10.1109/ICISA.2011.5772351

Koehler, J., Gschwind, T., Kuster, J., Volzer, H., & Zimmermann, O. (2011). Towards a compiler for business-IT systems- A vision statement complemented with a research agenda. In Z. Huzar & M. Koci (Eds.), *Springer (Vol. 4980). Lecture Notes in Computer Science.*

Liu, Z., Jifeng, H., & Li, X. (2004). *Component-oriented development of component software.* Macau: The United Nations University.

Lu, R. (2005). Towards a mathematical theory of knowledge—Categorical analysis of knowledge. *Journal of Computer Science and Technology, 20*(6), 751–757. doi:10.1007/s11390-005-0751-4doi:10.1007/s11390-005-0751-4

MacLane, S. (1998). *Categories for the working mathematician: Graduate texts in mathematics* (2nd ed., *Vol. 5*). Springer-Verlag.

McDavid, D. W. (1999). A standard for business architecture description. *IBM Systems Journal, 38*, 12–31. doi:10.1147/sj.381.0012doi:10.1147/sj.381.0012

Medvidovic, N., Dashofy, E. M., & Taylor, R. N. (2007). Moving architectural description from under the technology lamppost. *Information and Software Technology, 49*, 12–31. doi:10.1016/j.infsof.2006.08.006doi:10.1016/j.infsof.2006.08.006

Medvidovic, N., & Taylor, R. N. (2000). A classification and comparison framework for software architecture description languages. *IEEE Transactions on Software Engineering, 26*, 70–93. doi:10.1109/32.825767doi:10.1109/32.825767

Meng, S., & Aichernig, B. K. (2002). *Component-based coalgebraic specification and verification in RSL.* The United Nations University.

Nierstrasz, O., & Achermann, F. (2003). A calculus for modeling software components. In F. S. de Boer, M. M. Bonsangue, S. Graf, & W.-P. de Roever (Eds.), *Formal methods for components and objects, LNCS 2852*. Springer. doi:10.1007/978-3-540-39656-7_14doi:10.1007/978-3-540-39656-7_14

OpenGroup. (2007). *The open group architecture framework (TOGAF) version 8.1.1*, enterprise edition. Retrieved August 5, 2011, from http://www.opengroup.org/

OpenGroup. (2009). *Archimate 1.0 specification*. Retrieved August 5, 2011, from http://www.opengroup.org/

Padberg, J. (2002). Integration of categorical frameworks: Rule-based refinement and hierarchical composition for components. *Applied Categorical Structures*, 333–364.

Padberg, J., & Ehrig, H. (2006). Petri net modules in the transformation-based component framework. *Journal of Logic and Algebraic Programming*, *67*(1-2), 198–225. doi:10.1016/j.jlap.2005.09.007doi:10.1016/j.jlap.2005.09.007

Pahl, C. (2001). *Components, contracts, and connectors for the unified modeling language*. FME, LNCS 2021 (pp. 259–277). Berlin, Germany: Springer.

Plasil, F., Balek, D., & Janecek, R. (1998). SOFA/DCUP: Architecture for component trading and dynamic updating. *Fourth International Conference on Configurable Distributed Systems* (pp. 43–52). IEEE CS Press.

Scott, J. (2010). *The anatomy of a capability map*. Forrester Research. Retrieved January 8, 2012, from http://www.forrester.com/rb/Research/anatomy_of_capability_map/q/id/55972/t/2

Scott, J. (2010b). *Building capability maps for business-IT alignment*. Forrester Research. Retrieved January 8, 2012, from http://www.forrester.com/rb/Research/building_capability_maps_for_business-it_alignment/q/id/56405/t/2

Sessions, R. (2007). *A comparison of the top four enterprise-architecture methodologies*. Retrieved August 2, 2011, from http://msdn.microsoft.com/en-us/library/bb466232.asp

Shaw, M., & Garlan, D. (1996). *Software architecture: Perspectives on an emerging discipline*. Prentice Hall.

Stafford, J. A., & Wolf, A. L. (2001). Software architecture. In G. T. Heinman & W. T. Council (Eds.), *Component-based software engineering* (pp. 371–387). Addison Wesley.

Szyperski, C. (2002). *Component software: Beyond object-oriented programming*. Addison-Wesley.

Tian, C., Ding, W., Cao, R., & Lee, J. (2006). *Business componentization: A principle for enterprise architecture design*. IBM.

Versteeg, G., & Bouwman, H. (2006). Business architecture: A new paradigm to relate business strategy to ICT. *Information Systems Frontiers*, *8*, 91–102. doi:10.1007/s10796-006-7973-zdoi:10.1007/s10796-006-7973-z

Zachman, J. A. (1987). A framework for information system architecture. *IBM Systems Journal*, *26*(3), 276–292. doi:10.1147/sj.263.0276doi:10.1147/sj.263.0276

Zhan, N., Kang, E., & Liu, Z. (2010). Component publications and compositions. In A. Butterfield (Ed.), *Unifying Theories of Programming* (*Vol. 5713*, pp. 238–257). *Lecture Notes in Computer Science* Berlin, Germany: Springer. doi:10.1007/978-3-642-14521-6_14doi:10.1007/978-3-642-14521-6_14

ADDITIONAL READING

Cheesman, J., & Daniels, J. (2001). *UML components: A simple process for specifying component-based software*. Addison-Wesley.

Fiadeiro, J. L. (2005). *Categories for software engineering*. Berlin, Germany: Springer.

Gerken, M. J. (1995, March). *Formal foundations for the specification of software architecture*. Wright-Patterson AFB, OH: Air Force Institute of Technology.

Huschens, J., & Rumpold-Preining, M. (2006). IBM insurance application architecture (IAA) - An overview of the insurance business architecture. In P. Bernus, K. Mertins, & G. Schmidt (Eds.), *Handbook on architectures of information systems* (pp. 669–692). Berlin, Germany: Springer. doi:10.1007/3-540-26661-5_28doi:10.1007/3-540-26661-5_28

Leavens, G. T., & Sitaraman, M. (2000). *Foundations of component-based systems*. Cambridge, UK.

KEY TERMS AND DEFINITIONS

Application Architecture: How the information technology is organized to supports one or more business capabilities.

Business Architecture: How business processes and tasks are organized to deliver the services.

Business Capability: Primary business functions, processes and the organization to perform these functions.

Category Theory: Study of mathematical structures and objects and the relationship between them.

Component: Encapsulation of a business function or process (business component) or its implementation using information technology (application component).

Formal Methods: In the context of software, techniques for systematize the specification and development of software.

Specification: A detailed and explicit statement of requirements to be satisfied by a process of service that is being designed, when formalized is also called formal specifications.

Section 4
Industrial Case Studies and Practices

Chapter 12
Software Architecture Practices in Agile Enterprises

Veli-Pekka Eloranta
Tampere University of Technology, Finland

Kai Koskimies
Tampere University of Technology, Finland

ABSTRACT

This chapter is based on the results of a survey carried out in 11 IT companies in Finland in Fall 2010. In this survey, the existing practices regarding software architecting work in agile enterprises using Scrum are mapped out. Four main practices to cope with software architecture in Scrum are identified and analyzed. The adoption of these practices is discussed in relation with the characteristics of the teams and project types. Further, the interaction of these practices and Scrum patterns is analyzed. The results indicate that most of the found practices are in conflict with Scrum. The analyzed relationships between Scrum patterns and the identified architecture practices help to understand how software architecture work is aligned with Scrum in real life, as well as the problems of the practices from the Scrum point of view.

INTRODUCTION

During the last decade, software industry has widely embraced agile approaches in the development of software systems. Today, the most popular agile approach applied in industrial software development projects is Scrum (Nord & Tomayko, 2006); according to a recent survey (VersionOne, 2010) Scrum has 78% market share of agile methods in software industry. Even though

Scrum is not particularly intended for software development, it has proved to be very suitable for this kind of production work, improving the quality of the products as well (e.g. Huo, Verner, Zhu, & Babar, 2004; Korhonen, 2010). Scrum combines agile principles (Agile Alliance 2001) with lean manufacturing philosophy (Poppendieck & Poppendieck, 2006). Essentially, Scrum defines how the work is decomposed into tasks, how the tasks are ordered, managed, and carried out, which are

DOI: 10.4018/978-1-4666-2199-2.ch012

the roles of the project members, and how persons in these roles interact during the development process. A central concept of Scrum is a sprint, a working period during which the team produces a potentially shippable product increment.

In software engineering, agile approaches are often contrasted with plan-driven approaches. This is sometimes misinterpreted to imply that planning is not required in agile software development. Obviously, careful planning is required in most industrial software development projects involving tens, hundreds, or even thousands of persons. However, instead of a rigid, detailed pre-existing work plan enforced during the entire process, in agile development there is typically only a fairly loose up-front project plan, and the plan is allowed to evolve and become more precise during the process.

Software architecture is traditionally defined as the high-level organization of a system (e.g. Bass, Clements & Kazman 2003; "ISO/IEC 42010", 2011). However, from the viewpoint of a software development project, software architecture is a plan of a new software system, in the same sense as a blueprint is a plan of a house. This creates certain tension between software architecture and non-plan-driven agile philosophy. Indeed, the role of software architecture design was questioned by the early advocates of agile approaches, claiming that software architecture emerges without up-front design efforts. Later, the role of software architecture in agile projects has been studied (Abrahamsson, Babar & Kruchten, 2010; Kruchten, 2010; Nord et al., 2006), but there is still considerable variation among practitioners concerning the ways architecture is involved in agile development. This is particularly visible in Scrum, which itself does not give any advice specifically regarding software related activities, like software architecture work. Lack of up-front planning is one of the main concerns about adopting agile and barriers for further adoption (VersionOne, 2009).

In the following, we will limit the discussion to Scrum. The main aim for this work is to identify the ways of working that architects have taken while using Scrum. Furthermore, we want to investigate to what extent architecture work practices are in conflict with Scrum. In addition, we wanted to find out if there are correlations between these practices and the characteristics of the companies and teams running the projects. To analyze the Scrum conformance of these practices in more detail we used a set of core Scrum patterns (Scrum Pattern Community, 2011) as a reference and analyzed the potential problems arising for each practice/pattern pair. Presenting Scrum as an extendable pattern language has been recently adopted as a preferred policy in the Scrum community (Scrum.org, 2012).

In this study, the term architecture work refers mainly to architecture design, which is the most time-consuming and critical phase related to software architectures. Some practitioners consider architecture documentation as part of architecture design, and therefore documentation activities may be counted as architecture work in this study as well. However, architecture evaluation activities are explicitly excluded.

This work is based on an analysis of the results of a survey concerning the use of Scrum and the role of software architecture related work in Scrum, carried out in Finnish software industry in fall 2010. The target companies (11) ranged from small to large global companies, developing both embedded systems and more traditional business applications. The survey was carried out by conducting on-site interviews with project managers, product managers and software architects.

The chapter is structured according to the research setup given above. We will first briefly discuss existing work on the role of software architecture in agile development. We continue with an account of the survey and its results concerning the Scrum maturity in the target companies. The results related to the architecture work practices are discussed next, leading to the identification of four basic practices. The correlations of the Scrum maturity and the practices are also discussed in this context. Next, we review existing core Scrum patterns from the perspective of software architecture work and especially map out the potential problems arising from the conflicts between these patterns and the practices identified earlier. Finally, the chapter is concluded with a summary of the lessons learned.

SCRUM

Scrum is an iterative, incremental framework for project management in agile software development. Scrum can be described in sets of three (Sutherland & Schwaber, 2011). There are three roles within a Scrum team: Product Owner, Scrum Master and the development team. There are three meetings: sprint planning meeting, daily Scrum and sprint review (and retrospective) meeting. Finally, there are three artefacts: product backlog, sprint backlog, and impediment list. In the following subsections, each of these concepts is described in more detail.

Scrum Roles

The responsibility of Product Owner (PO) is to establish and communicate the product vision. PO creates the product backlog containing enabling specifications for the development team. PO orders the product backlog so that items in the top maximize the return on investment (ROI). However, the dependencies between items must be taken into account. Product owner also reviews the results of the sprint and makes release readiness decisions.

Scrum Master (SM) owns the Scrum process and makes sure that everybody follows the agreed process. SM also manages the definition of *done,* defining when a task can be considered as finished. The main responsibility, however, is to shield and

help the team to develop the product. SM keeps track of impediments and tries to remove them.

The development team estimates, selects and develop work items. The development team commits to deliver selected work items in time-boxed development iteration (sprint). The development team should be cross-functional meaning that it has enough expertise to build a potentially shippable product increment in a sprint. In addition, the development team should work in self-organized fashion, meaning that team members should select themselves work items they want to work on.

Scrum Meetings

The goal of a sprint planning meeting is to make sure that the development team members understand requirements well enough, so that they can implement them. On the other hand, PO needs to get sufficient understanding on the development costs to manage the risks.

During the sprints development team gathers daily to a 15 minute daily Scrum meeting. The purpose of this meeting is to synchronize activities and to create a plan for the next 24 hours. In the meeting each development team member explains what (s)he has been doing since the last meeting, what will be done before the next daily scrum, and what obstacles are in the way.

Sprint review meeting is organized in order to review the results of a sprint and to get feedback on the results. Meeting lasts from two to three hours and maximum of 30 minutes is used for preparation. In the meeting the development team presents potentially shippable increment of product functionality to PO who accepts (or rejects) the result. In addition, key learnings from the sprint are discussed in the meeting.

Scrum Artefacts

Product backlog is an ordered list of everything that might be needed in the product. PO owns product backlog and is responsible for keeping it up-to-date. Product backlog changes constantly as new information (or requirements) become available. The items in the backlog are called product backlog items (PBI), which contain description, order and work estimate for the item. The ordering of PBIs can be done according to value (Return On Investment), risk priority and necessity. Typically, the items on top of the list are well-defined and more detailed than items which are lower on the list. Development team estimates the items, and if multiple teams are working for the same product they all take items into the sprints from the same product backlog.

Sprint backlog is a set of PBIs selected for the sprint plus a plan for delivering the product increment. Sprint backlog should contain all the work the team is going to do in a sprint. Sprint backlog is created during sprint planning meeting by development team.

Impediment list is a tool for SM. It is a list of obstacles and impediments that SM needs to remove in order to enable development team to work as efficiently as possible. Some of the impediments may require actions from the team and if this is the case these impediments can be added to sprint backlog during sprint planning meeting.

SURVEY AND TARGET COMPANIES

Target Group

The target group of the survey constituted of 13 teams in 11 Finnish companies. Approximately half of the companies were developing embedded real time machine control systems, while the rest of the companies were more traditional IT companies working on business and desktop applications. The survey was conducted as interviews of software professionals who had attended Scrum trainings at Tampere University of Technology. This guaranteed that the participants had roughly the same knowledge and understanding of Scrum, which the interviews and questions could rely on.

A typical title of a person being interviewed was development manager, but also developers, Scrum Masters and architects participated in the survey.

Execution of the Survey

The survey was executed with a series of semi-structured interviews (Seaman, 2010) of the teams in the target companies. Semi-structured interviews consist of a mixture of open ended and specific questions, which allowed us on one hand to map out data concerning facts that were known beforehand (e.g. questions related to the characteristics of the company), and on the other hand to recover unforeseen information (e.g. architecting practices and issues related to them). In addition to the questions related to architecture work, another aim of the interview was to explore the advantages and problems the teams had discovered in the use of Scrum practices in general. However, the latter part of the interviews is not covered in this paper.

The questions in the interview were divided into three different sections: background questions, questions related to the level of adopting Scrum, and questions related to architecture work. Background questions were intended to clarify the company size, experience in Scrum, the domain they are working on, etc. The Scrum related questions aimed at rating the company according to the so called Nokia test (Sutherland, 2010), profiling the company with respect to the Scrum adoption level. By using the Nokia test questions, we wanted to make sure that the company is truly using Scrum, rather than just claiming to be agile. In order to be included in the study, the company has to have adopted at least the most fundamental Scrum practices. Additionally, using the Nokia test we could gain valuable input for the analysis of the interplay of Scrum patterns and architecture work practices.

The questions related to architecture work constituted the core of the interview regarding the objectives of this paper: we asked specific questions related to the practices the teams have used with respect to software architectures, and the problems the teams have experienced in exercising these practices. The interview included questions clarifying the role an architect, the contents of that role, and the way architects work. Adopted architecture work practices were identified in the answers to these questions. For a complete list of the questions, see (Eloranta, 2011).

Nokia Test Results of the Target Companies

The idea of Nokia test was originally introduced in 2005, when Bas Vodde was coaching teams at Nokia Networks (now Nokia-Siemens Networks) in Finland and developed the first Nokia test focused on agile practices. He had hundreds of teams and wanted a simple way to determine if each team was doing the basics (Sutherland, 2008). Nokia test cannot be taken as a scientific method for evaluating how agile organization is or how well they are implementing Scrum. Even so, it has some value as it gives a rough estimate on how Scrum is implemented. The results of each company are comparable to other companies, as the grading for each question is carried out by the

same person and with the same criteria. However, the results are not repeatable by other persons as the judging criteria may differ.

Nokia test consists of nine questions that investigate different aspects of Scrum: sprint length, concept of done, enabling specifications, Product Owner, product backlog, work estimates, sprint burndown charts, team disruption and team self-organization. Each question is given 0-10 points, and the average value of these points describes the company's agile performance in Scrum (Sutherland, 2010). According to Jeff Sutherland (2010), at the end of a typical Scrum Certification course, in average, participants think they can get their teams to score 6 out of 10.

Scoring of each question was carried out by two persons separately. Afterwards scoring results were discussed and differences of two or more points in scoring were discussed and resolved. In this way, misinterpretations of answers could be avoided. Summarized results of the Nokia test are illustrated in Figure 1, giving the average scores of all questions for each company.

The results show that there are 4 companies which are below 5, and 7 companies above 5. The overall Scrum adoption level shown in Figure 1 is rather typical for companies that have ex-

Figure 1. Results of Nokia test conducted during the interview survey

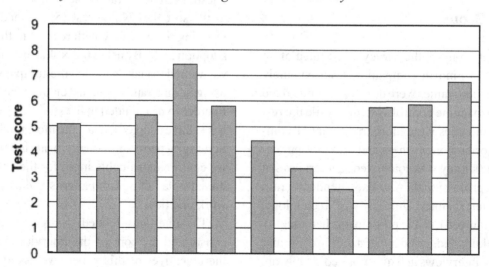

ploited Scrum work practices for some time, but that are not committed to full adoption of Scrum.

Limitations

As a method for collecting qualitative data, semi-structured interviews are widely used, but also sensitive to various sources of errors (Seaman, 2010). If the interview includes codifying, the results should be confirmed with the target persons to avoid misinterpretations. This was done in the context of the Nokia test. For the information regarding the architectural practices, possible misinterpretations were tried to be resolved during the interviews as much as possible, and the final report was sent to the attendees of the interviews for checking. Still, misinterpretations cannot be fully ruled out. To minimize the risk of missing or misinterpreted data we used several interviewers who were familiar both with Scrum and with software architectures.

Another threat to the validity of the results is the relatively small number of teams that were interviewed. As far as the quantitative data are concerned, the number is too small to allow statistical analysis. However, regarding the identified architectural practices in Scrum we argue that this study provides a reasonably covering picture of the ways practitioners perform architecture work in Scrum, given that the found four practices emerge consistently in the survey, and that theoretical considerations support the findings. On the other hand, more detailed observations extracted from the data may have only anecdotal evidence.

Since the companies in this survey represent different sizes and domains, the qualitative results are not expected to be biased towards certain kinds of companies. Still, the quantitative results may be affected by the relatively large number of machine manufacturers in the target companies.

SOFTWARE ARCHITECTURE PRACTICES IN SCRUM

As stated in (Abrahamsson et al., 2010), architecture and Scrum do not go very well together, as there is no natural place for architecture work in Scrum. Yet, in the real world architecture work is carried out in one way or another. Whatever way is chosen, practitioners will probably face challenges in merging architecture work with Scrum. In this section we first analyze the topic theoretically and then briefly outline the practices for architecture work we have identified in the survey.

Theoretical View

In principle, software architecture work can appear in different places of the Scrum work flow. First, the architecture can be created either before the actual Scrum sprints start, or during the sprints. In the latter case the architecture can be created either within the sprints, or as a simultaneous activity outside the sprints. If the architecture is created within the sprints, there are again two options: the architecture can be either created in one or more sprints that precede the actual implementation sprints, or it can be created incrementally as needed in any sprint.

This analysis suggests that there are basically four options to place software architecture work in Scrum: before sprints, simultaneously outside sprints, in the first sprint(s), and along all the sprints. Intuitively, the last approach is closest to the Scrum philosophy, while the other approaches are less aligned with Scrum. If the architecture is designed up-front or in a separate simultaneous process, it becomes a plan which is given to the Scrum team from above, which is clearly against the self-organizing philosophy of Scrum. Furthermore, Agile Manifesto (Agile Alliance, 2001) suggests to value response to change over following a plan. If the architecture is designed in a dedicated sprint, the sprint does not produce a potentially shippable increment to the software, as required in Scrum.

In the following subsection we explore the actual practices to incorporate software architecture work in Scrum based on empirical data. The theoretical analysis above stems from that data: the analysis was carried out to provide further confidence that the four practices identified in the survey data indeed cover the major options to relate software architecture work with Scrum.

Observed Practices

From the interviews, four different strategies for architecture work were discovered:

1. Big up-front architecture created during the analysis phase before starting the development in sprints (BUFA).
2. Sprint zero (Rawsthorne, 2007) where the team created the architecture in the first planning sprint (SPR0).
3. Designing architecture when needed in normal sprints (SPR*).

4. Separate architecture process where architecture is designed outside Scrum process when necessary (SEPA).

The boundaries between different approaches are not clear cut, but we analyzed the work practices in each team and selected the approach that had the closest correspondence with the practice that was used in the team.

Figure 2 shows how many teams were using each approach. Note that the number of interviewed teams was larger than the number of companies. In the following subsections we describe each approach in more detail, based on the information obtained in the interviews.

Big Up-Front Architecture (BUFA)

BUFA is typically used in companies that are building very complex real-time embedded control systems. The common factor is that the systems are huge in terms of lines of code. This kind of companies typically has a proprietary platform that is used to build specific products and work-

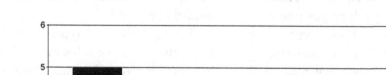

Figure 2. Number of teams using each architecture work approach in Scrum

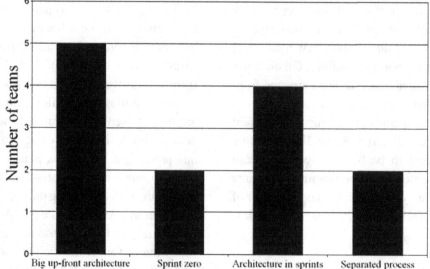

ing machines. However, the hardware part of the system is significant and has its specific requirements. In many cases, there is a long analysis phase where requirements are gathered and architecture is designed. Even though the platform provides the most common features, the product architecture needs serious design effort. The analysis phase might last for six months.

Once the most of the architecture is in place, the development starts. In this phase the architecture still changes when emergent requirements come in or when new information has come up in the development sprints. The platform changes may also require architectural changes. The changes are typically handled by the same architect or architecture team that designed the original architecture up-front. So the Scrum teams do not make architectural decisions at any stage.

According to interviews, this approach was taken in use as it is hard to describe features in product backlog so that they are small enough. Teams reported that typically the features are so big that it is almost impossible to implement them in one sprint, even if there were multiple teams working on them. If architecture is designed up-front; it becomes easier to divide the features into smaller items in product backlog.

Interviews also revealed that some companies did prototyping as well in the up-front design phase. They experimented with different approaches and technologies, and implemented the basic building blocks of the architecture. Especially if the architects take part in coding, this comes close to the architecture in sprints approach.

Sprint Zero (SPR0)

Two of the interviewed companies used SPR0. It means that they had one sprint before actual development sprints where they built product backlog and the architecture. Typically this sprint was about the same length as the other sprints, i.e. from one to four weeks. In this sprint the main designer (or several designers) worked with the

development team(s) and designed the initial architecture. Many companies reported that later in the development sprints the architecture changed as the knowledge about the system increased. If this was the case, then typically the development team made the architectural changes within sprints. The most critical parts of the architecture usually persisted without changes but the rest of the design evolved during the sprints.

The main difference to BUFA is that the architecture is essentially designed by the development team itself and not by an architect who is a separate person from the team. Furthermore, the length of the sprint zero is shorter than the length of the up-front architecture design phase. When there is an up-front design phase, it might last up to six months, but sprint zero is four weeks at maximum and typically less.

Architecture in Sprints (SPR*)

Four teams reported that they do not have separate analysis or architecture phase: they just start doing sprints and developing the system. The goal with this approach is to produce the initial architecture during the first sprint while implementing potentially shippable features. The architecture is designed in detail only for the features that are shipped after the current sprint. For other parts, there is just a rough vision of what the architecture will look like. In every sprint, the architecture concerning potentially shippable features is refined and already implemented parts are refactored when necessary. This process goes on and the architecture is designed piece by piece during the sprints until it is finished. The approach increases the amount of required architectural refactoring as architecture is designed incrementally.

In some cases, the design was guided by one or more persons in the team that had the most experience on the domain. Other team members then built features on top of the design. One team reported that the designer is an emergent role within the team and changes from sprint to sprint. The same team also stated that anyone in the team is privileged to do architecturally significant decisions.

The common nominator in this approach is that the teams were experienced in the domain. One company reported that they have had bad experiences with this approach when the team was new to the domain. The team did not know how to proceed with the design and as there was no up-front architecture, the result was a failure. The architecture just did not correspond to requirements and it had to be refactored all the time. Finally, they had to do it again from the scratch.

Separate Architecture Process (SEPA)

The fourth way to carry out architecture work in Scrum was to have it as a separate process. In this approach architecture is created by a separate team that may have members from the development team(s) but is organizationally completely separated from the development team(s). Members of the architecture team might do architecture work part time, meaning that they are working also in the development team, or they can be working only for the architecture team. The architecture team has checkpoints or milestones when a certain part of the architecture must be ready. Typically there is one checkpoint for each release of the architecture team (i.e., a new version of the system's architecture that contains support for new features for the next product release). In the interviewed companies, the checkpoint cycle was three months as their release cycle was four times a year.

In the checkpoint meeting, the architecture team provides the architecture (or possibly several alternative architectures) for evaluation. Members of the development team, PO, SM, team lead, and possibly customers participate in the meeting. Once all the participants are satisfied by one of the competing proposals, they select it as a basis of the design.

It was interesting to notice that the motivation for the companies to use this approach was to make sure that "they don't mess up the Scrum process in any way". The separate architecture process is connected to the Scrum process essentially via the product backlog: the architecture process produces items to the product backlog.

Team Characteristics and Architecture Practices

After the interview sessions, we analyzed the ways of working and as we saw that the way of working clearly stood out from the ways we had observed earlier, we added a new approach as an observed work practice. After having four different approaches identified, it turned out that all new interviewed companies could be classified using these four categories. Since the same practices repeated themselves from one interview to another, we are confident that these are the main practices which are used to carry out software architecture work in Scrum in general, in spite of the relatively small number of interviewed teams. This conclusion is supported by the theoretical analysis as well. Interestingly, all the possible options revealed by the theoretical analysis are actually used in the companies. However, the boundaries are not always clear cut, and the practices emerge in different variations.

We compared the used architecture work approaches to team's characteristics such as agile experience, domain and project type. Table 1 shows the relationship between the used architecting practice and the experience of the team in agile methods. In the table, the numbers indicate how many teams in a particular experience category (columns) were using a particular practice (row).

As Table 1 shows, teams that have been using Scrum for more than three years relied on the BUFA approach. Interestingly, teams that have a couple of years experience on Scrum seem to try out different approaches without clear prefer-

Table 1. Team's Scrum experience in years and the architecture work approach they used

Approach Used	Less than 1 Year	1-2 Years	2-3 Years	Over 3 Years
BUFA	1	2	0	2
SPR0	0	0	2	0
SPR*	0	1	3	0
SEPA	0	1	1	0

ences. A possible interpretation of these numbers is that inexperienced teams start with BUFA, which is probably the easiest to understand and manage, and the most experienced teams resort back to this practice after trying out other approaches.

Next we compared the architecture work approaches to the project types the teams reported to be working on. Projects were divided into two categories: customer projects and product projects. Customer projects were identified as projects where customer has ordered something and team was creating that artefact or the team was subcontracting for a product manufacturer. Product projects are projects where the team is building a product that the company will sell to its customers.

Table 2 shows how many teams used particular architecture work practices for particular project type. As can be seen from the results, both the customer projects and product projects used all architecture work practices, with the exception that SPR0 was used only in product projects. It seems that the project type has less influence on

the chosen practice. The results are not surprising as some of the interviewed teams mentioned that they used the same way of working regardless of the project.

Finally we wanted to see if the nature of the domain of the company had any influence on the chosen practice. The interviewed companies and teams can be roughly divided into two categories: teams that work on embedded systems and teams that work on more traditional software systems. Former typically in this context are embedded control systems for work machines whereas the latter are software systems running on a web server or locally on a workstation.

Table 3 shows the results. A clear tendency can be seen in the figures: companies that are developing embedded systems use more BUFA, whereas companies developing traditional workstation systems are more willing to integrate architecture work with Scrum more tightly. A possible explanation is that in the case of embedded systems, the software architecture has to be designed in concert with the hardware architecture, and hardware (electronic, hydraulics and mechanical) designers are seldom comfortable with Scrum. Obviously, using BUFA the conflict of agile and non-agile practices can be avoided, or at least reduced. In this study we have not analyzed the impact of non-agile teams on Scrum teams in more detail, but we have identified this as an interesting topic for future research.

However, these figures should be taken with a grain of salt. It seems that the social value of

Table 2. Team's project type and the architecture work approach they used

Approach Used	Product Project	Customer Project
BUFA	2	3
SPR0	2	0
SPR*	2	2
SEPA	1	1

Table 3. Domain the team is working on and the architecture work approach they used

Approach Used	Embedded Systems	Traditional Software Systems
BUFA	3	2
SPR0	1	1
SPR*	1	3
SEPA	1	1

the team is more dominant than any other factor. During the interviews it was noticed that some teams have embraced agile values and methods more deeply than others even it might not have shown in the Nokia test. This probably affects also the architecting work practice choice. The teams that appreciated agile values typically used architecture in sprints approach or let the team choose whatever approach they wanted. In companies which favored more traditional methods, the work approach was usually given to the developers from above. However, since the number of interviewed teams is relatively small, this can be regarded only as anecdotal evidence.

SCRUM PATTERNS AND ARCHITECTURE PRACTICES

In the previous section it was argued that some of the identified architecting practices are more in line with Scrum than others. To place that argumentation on a more firm basis, we have analyzed how the Scrum patterns, available at Scrumplop. org (Scrum Pattern Community, 2011), resonate with the practices. Scrum patterns describe Scrum practices and experiences from practice in a pattern format. They look like design patterns but instead of creating an architectural artifact, Scrum patterns build organization structure, social value and software engineering process that uses Scrum. Scrum patterns are divided into separate pattern languages, each building a certain element of the Scrum framework. Scrum patterns are also recognized as an extension mechanism to the Scrum framework (Scrum.org, 2012). Practitioners can provide their insights and extensions to Scrum in a pattern format using this extension mechanism.

Since there are numerous Scrum patterns available at Scrum Pattern Community (2011), we have limited our study to the most central Scrum patterns to facilitate the analysis. We selected patterns from the Scrum core pattern language and the value stream pattern language for this study, both available at Scrum Pattern Community, for this analysis. Advanced topics such as scaling Scrum and distributed Scrum were ruled out.

While Scrum patterns do not mention software architecture, or directly concern architecture work, they may still indirectly affect the way architecting work is done, and in that way resonate with the identified work practices. In the following, we discuss each pattern, and how it resonates with the four identified practices. The patterns are divided into four major groups according to the purpose of the patterns: patterns that concern the meetings, patterns that concern the artifacts, patterns that concern the Scrum roles, and finally patterns belonging to the value pattern language. The subsections follow this structure.

To give a general overview of the results of the analysis for each pattern category, we use a table in which each row corresponds to a pattern and each column corresponds to a practice. The extent to which the practice conflicts with the pattern is expressed with symbols -, 0, +, denoting "practice potentially problematic with the pattern," "no resonance," "can be used together," respectively. If the pattern is found problematic it means that the practices described in the Scrum pattern are conflicting with the architecture work approach, or the pattern makes it harder to use that approach (indirect conflict). No resonance means that the Scrum pattern and the architecture work approach do not share anything in common, i.e. the pattern does not suggest anything that has an effect on the architecture work while using the specific approach. If the pattern and the approach can be used together, it means that the pattern supports the way of carrying out architecture work. The argumentations why a pattern either supports or is in conflict with the architecture work approach are based on the data gathered in the interviews. The final judgment is, however, the authors' own conclusion on the topic.

Scrum Meeting Patterns

Scrum meeting patterns describe different kinds of meetings that are organized in Scrum. Table 4 summarizes the analysis of the patterns in this category.

Backlog grooming meeting describes a meeting where product backlog is cleaned up. This meeting is arranged approximately once a week. The whole development team usually attends these meetings. Backlog grooming meeting is optional and it is not a part of the Scrum core. It is not a problem for any of the architectural work practices, even though it is only applicable if SPR0 or SPR* is used. In two other work approaches, this pattern does not have an influence as the work is not accounted for in the product backlog.

Daily Scrum describes daily Scrum meeting where developers meet and tell what they have done, what they will do and which problems they have encountered. If the architecture is created using SPR0 or SPR*, architectural issues can be discussed in this short meeting daily. If the architecture is created using SEPA, then someone from the architecture team should be present in this meeting, even though they are probably not allowed to talk as they are so-called "chickens." If BUFA is used and architecture-related issues emerge in developers' work, problems may arise. Architecture might need to be changed, but who

is the person who will change it? Is it the architect or someone from the team? The architect may be already working on a new project or with the next version of the system and therefore unavailable. If the architect is not present in daily Scrum meeting, this might be a problem. The main problem here is, however, that the up-front architecture might get changed - even radically - as new information emerges. This increases the amount of wasted work. The same applies for the SPR* approach.

Release planning meeting describes a meeting where the goal and the vision of a release is established, and the initial version of product backlog is created. It affects all architecture work approaches, but does not conflict with any of them.

Sprint planning meeting describes an 8 hour meeting where the Product Owner presents the ordered product backlog to the team. The team then selects and negotiates with PO the work to be done in the sprint. This pattern can be applied to architecture work (and is not in conflict) if SPR0 or SPR* is used. The pattern is not applicable to other approaches as the work is not done in sprints.

Sprint retrospective describes a meeting after sprint review but before the next sprint planning meeting where the team discusses its development process and improves it, both to make it more effective and enjoyable. It has no direct relationship to the architecture work. However, the discussion in the meeting may concern the architecture work approach selected and if it should be changed.

Sprint review describes a meeting at the end of each sprint where the results of a sprint are reviewed and discussed. From the perspective of architecture work this pattern is in line with all approaches but BUFA. Here again the problem is that once the architecture is designed up-front there is no feedback loop. Sprint review is essentially a feedback event, and it might generate architectural tasks that have to be done. Of course, observed problems with the architecture can still be fixed, but the feedback loop becomes quite long, which is against the main idea of sprint reviews. Even if SEPA is used, those emerging tasks can be dealt

Table 4. Scrum meeting patterns and architecture work approaches

Pattern	BUFA	SPR0	SPR*	SEPA
Backlog grooming meeting	0	+	+	0
Daily Scrum	-	-	+	+
Release planning meeting	+	+	+	+
Sprint planning meeting	0	+	+	0
Sprint retrospective	0	0	0	0
Sprint review	-	+	+	+

with, as those tasks are input for the architecture team. However, BUFA does not support this as the architecture is already fixed. The team or the architect can make the required changes, but again this can be interpreted as extraneous work.

Scrum Patterns Generating Scrum Artifacts

Scrum patterns generating Scrum artifacts describe what kinds "tools" are used in Scrum process. For example, sprint or product backlog are typical tools used in the Scrum methodology. Table 5 summarizes the analysis of this pattern category.

Product backlog pattern solves the problem that everyone should agree to what needs to be done next at any given time, and that the agreement should be visible. The solution is to create a single ordered list of all deliverables, called Product Backlog Items (PBIs). The list is ordered by delivery date. However, if the architecture is done with BUFA, the architecture is not on this single list as it is already designed when starting the sprints. This creates a problem: how is the architectural knowledge transferred to the team? Furthermore, how can the team commit to PBIs (that are taken into the sprints) as the architecture is created by someone else? Furthermore, the development team should be able to estimate PBIs, but as the architecture design is ready-made by someone else, it will hard to estimate PBIs, at least for a couple of first sprints. This problem

does not exist in approaches where the architecture is created in sprints (including SPR0) as then the development team designs the architecture. If SEPA is used, the team gets the architecture given to them, but they have a chance to influence it during a checkpoint meeting. Furthermore, the architecture team can work on the same product backlog as the team, so they can collectively commit to that.

Release burndown pattern instructs to create a burndown chart for the work remaining to complete the release. This has no effect on BUFA. If the architecture is designed in sprints (SPR0 or SPR*), architecture work is also accounted for in this chart. Release burndown is especially useful in SEPA: from the release burndown the architecture team sees when the architecture for the next release has to be ready.

Sprint pattern states that the work should be time-boxed in periods called sprints. The pattern is not applicable to BUFA as the architecture is created before the sprints start. The pattern is not applicable to SEPA, either. However, it does not conflict or cause problems for any of the architecture work approaches.

Sprint backlog is a selected portion of the product backlog transformed into tasks in a sprint backlog. The pattern also instructs to let the developers choose what tasks they want to be responsible for, while making sure they are collectively capable of completing the work selected for the sprint backlog. This is not a problem from the architecture design point of view if the architecture is created in sprints (SPR0 or SPR*). In BUFA or SEPA, the developers cannot work on the architecture tasks as the architecture is given to them as a ready-made design. If SEPA is used, the developers can affect the design in checkpoints, but they cannot work on architecture tasks if they are not part of the architecture team. This reduces the benefits of the self-organization aspect of Scrum as the team is not self-organizing when it comes to tasks related to the architecture. In addition, the Scrum team has to commit to the architecture design that is out

Table 5. Scrum artefact patterns and architecture work approaches

Pattern	BUFA	SPR0	SPR*	SEPA
Product backlog	-	+	+	+
Release burndown	0	+	+	+
Sprint	0	+	+	0
Sprint backlog	-	+	+	-
Sprint burndown	0	+	+	0

of their hands. This is against the principle that the team should be cross-functional and have all skills required to produce the system. Of course, some architectural refactoring is done in sprints (especially if the architecture is designed up-front). Usually this means that the team refactors some parts of the system and updates the architecture documentation. But the negative effect of losing cross-functionality and self-organization makes this pattern incompatible with SEPA and BUFA.

Sprint burndown pattern suggests that burndown charts should be used to provide overall status of the team in the sprint. The pattern is not applicable to BUFA and to SEPA (unless the architecture team uses burndowns to show their progress). As there is no burndown used in these approaches, it might reduce the visibility that is a central theme in Scrum. Other approaches are in line with the pattern.

Scrum Patterns Generating Scrum Roles

Scrum patterns generating Scrum roles describe the three Scrum roles in a pattern format. Table 6 summarizes the analysis of this pattern category.

Product Owner is responsible for the product backlog and the vision of the product. In BUFA, the architecture is created either by a separate architect, or by PO (or both). Since PO should be a business oriented person, she might need help in the architecture work. SPR0 and SPR* also do not conflict with the PO role. However, it might be hard for PO to see the value of architecturally

Table 6. Scrum role patterns and architecture work approaches

Pattern	BUFA	SPR0	SPR*	SEPA
Product owner	+	+	+	+
Development team	-	+	+	-
Scrum master	0	+	+	0

significant items in the product backlog. This might result in a situation where architectural refactoring is not getting done as PO does not see enough value in it. Consequently, this leads to increased technical debt. SEPA does not conflict with this pattern, either, especially if the architecture team works on the same product backlog as the development team(s). If the separate architecture team works on its own product backlog, it should have its own PO.

Development team pattern states that there should be a cross-functional, self-organizing team that has enough combined competencies to accomplish the project. However, if the architecture is designed up-front by the architect or as a separated process by an architecture team, then the team probably does not have enough competence to create the architecture. On the other hand, as the development team members may be working in the architecture team, it might not be a problem. If the architecture is given to the team by the architect or by the separate architecture team, it is possible that the team might not understand all the forces that have affected the design. In addition, as the architecture design is handed over from outside, it might take a lot more communication to transfer the architectural knowledge.

Scrum Master is responsible for the Scrum process. As BUFA and SEPA are outside Scrum, the pattern is not applicable to them. However, these approaches also miss the benefits of having Scrum Master removing impediments. The other two architecture work approaches are in line with the pattern.

Value Pattern Language

Value pattern language describes very central principles of Scrum as patterns, for example, that every sprint should produce potentially shippable increment of the product. Table 7 lists all Scrum value stream pattern language patterns.

All work needs to be accounted for if PO wants to use velocity of the team(s) for release planning.

Table 7. Value pattern language and architecture work approaches

Pattern	BUFA	SPR0	SPR*	SEPA
Fixed work	0	-	-	+
Regular product increment	0	-	+	0
Release plan	+	+	+	+
Visible status	-	+	+	+
Vision	-	+	+	-

Fixed work pattern suggests to "compartmentalize the planning work for long-running high-risk business items into periodic meetings that are outside the sprint budget." Architecture work can be recognized as planning work for long-running high-risk business items as the architecture should address multiple quality requirements that are directly derived from the business goals. With this interpretation, Fixed work basically suggests that architecture work should be isolated as a separate process that is not counted in the sprint work budget, thus encouraging SEPA rather than SPR0 or SPR*. The pattern does not resonate with BUFA as in that approach the amount of architecture work carried out in sprints is minimal.

Regular product increment pattern says that in every sprint the team must work together to create a regular product increment in a short time box. If every sprint should produce potentially shippable product increment, it means that SPR0 is in conflict with this pattern. In the sprint zero, development and testing environments are set up and the architecture is designed. However, this is not a shippable result as it does not provide any value to the customer. If the zero sprint produces usable features, too, the approach is not pure SPR0 any more. SPR* does not conflict with this pattern as in that approach each sprint produces potentially shippable product increment. In other approaches this pattern is not applicable as there are no sprints involved.

Release plan also known as product roadmap describes how PO should select features for each release and basing on velocities of the team(s) calculate the release date for each release. This pattern is applicable to all four approaches to architecture work. Furthermore, it is especially suitable for a separated architecting process, as the architecture team sees the future release dates and features that the releases contain and can plan their work based on the roadmap. Without this pattern applied, it might even be impossible to use that approach. This pattern can be also used with up-front architecture for the same reasons.

Visible status pattern promotes Scrum core value, visibility, by saying that the statuses of teams should be posted on the walls in the organization. One could use sprint burndowns, release burndowns or other approaches. In approaches where the architecture is designed in sprints, this pattern is easy to apply. Even in SEPA, visibility of the architecture team can be supported by this pattern, if the architecture work proceeds in clear increments. However, in BUFA the visibility of the architecture work has less value, and it might be hard to say reliably which percentage of the design is completed.

Vision pattern describes the vision as a description of the desired future state the team is going to create. Furthermore, unlike many corporate visions, this vision needs to be something that can be created. The product backlog items should describe how PO thinks the vision will realize. If interpreted loosely, this means that PO should have a vision of the system and its architecture and the team means basically everybody else that is involved in creating the vision - including the architect. If that is the case, this pattern is in line with all the architecture work approaches. If interpreted more strictly, the team meaning development team, this pattern is in conflict with the BUFA and SEPA.

Summary

To summarize the analysis on Scrum patterns and architecture work practices, it seems that the SPR* approach is compatible with all the patterns but one. Both SPR0 and SEPA have conflicts with few patterns, but both seem to be mostly in line with Scrum. On the other hand, Scrum guide (Sutherland et al. 2011) clearly states that each sprint should produce potentially shippable product increment. If the architecture is created in the first sprint, it might be the case that the product of that sprint is not potentially shippable. Incremental architecting required by SPR*, although well aligned with Scrum, is challenging since it requires exceptionally skillful and knowledgeable development team, both in terms of software architectures and the domain. BUFA is both most popular, and most in conflict with Scrum, with 7 Scrum pattern conflicts. Still, even this practice is aligned with Scrum patterns in 3 cases and has no resonance in 9 cases, which gives some rationale why even this practice seems to work, at least with partial Scrum.

As a conclusion, aligning architecture work and Scrum is possible but challenging. For example, it can be difficult to develop a large embedded system without big up-front design. It may be sensible for a company to apply architecting practices which are less aligned with Scrum, because the loss of some of the benefits of agile methods may be compensated by better alignment with the organization. Architecture could also be built in sprints, but then to be successful, the team must have strong domain knowledge or the project has to be small enough. SPR0 or SEPA could be a feasible choice if the company is not deeply committed to Scrum values. SEPA might work for both large and small systems, but it requires coordinated communication between the architect and the development team. Ergo, a company should choose pragmatically an approach which fits the characteristics of the project and the desired level of agility, without forgetting to continuously improve the process.

RELATED WORK

Even though incompatibility of Scrum and software architecture is often used as an argument against Scrum, there are surprisingly few studies made on the topic. Babar (2009a) has studied architectural practices in agile software development, based on interviews and focus groups. The interviews were carried out in a company developing systems for financial services. This study was not specifically focusing on Scrum. Babar's analysis was based on different architectural activities, like architectural analysis, synthesis and evaluation, rather than on overall approaches to integrate software architecture work with agile. In this sense we see our work as complementary to Babar's work. The key challenges found in this research were incorrect prioritization of user stories, lack of time and motivation to consider design choices, and unknown domain and untried solutions. Especially the last two challenges are quite obvious if software architecture design is carried out in the most Scrum-like way, SPR*. This may be one reason why so many experienced Scrum teams had chosen BUFA in our study.

Schougaard et al (2008) have carried out field studies on software architecture and software quality in four Danish software companies. In their study they say that all architects in studied companies reported having problems in fitting their work to the Scrum framework. Schougaard et al (2008) also say that it seems that there is a need for a parallel process or an addition to Scrum that takes the special characteristics of software architecture work into account. This is in line with our observation that some of the interviewed companies used a separate process for the architecture work (SEPA).

Babar, Ihme & Pikkarainen (2009b) present an industrial case study of exploiting product line architectures in agile software development. In the case study they describe software architecture process of a software company. They also present a lot of day-to-day practices such as how architecture is documented and how daily meetings are carried out. However, they also report on a practice where the company uses separate development process for the baseline architecture and new features are tried out in a research process. Both of these processes use Scrum. The research process results are integrated (if necessary) to baseline architecture which is developed in the development process. The research project approach described by Babar et al. (2009b) has some similar characteristics to what we have observed in SEPA.

Baskerville, Pries-Heje & Madsen, (2010) have conducted four studies over 10 years. They have observed a two-stage pattern where changes in the market cause a disruption of established engineering practices. Baskerville et al. (2010) conclude that the next arising problem could be the organizational issue created by the boundaries between agile and plan-driven teams. This issue is a root cause for the problems studied in this paper, as architectural practices mainly originate from the plan-driven approaches. This issue was also observed in the cases where agile Scrum teams had to co-operate with non-agile hardware design teams.

Isham (2008) describes how monolithic re-design of software architecture leads to a failed project. In this work, the architecture was then re-designed using Scrum. The success story presented by Isham (2008) was accomplished by setting a vision and a roadmap in place in the beginning of the project, and changing the course as new information became available. This approach resembles the SPR* approach that we observed in our study. This experience also speaks against BUFA.

Cockburn (2006) suggests starting with a simple architecture that handles the most critical cases. Then it can be developed and refactored to tackle the special cases and new requirements. However, it should not be an objective itself to get the architecture at the end of the project. This approach is similar to what we have observed in companies which use the SPR* approach.

Coplien & Bjørnvig (2010) describe a lean approach to software architecture. Lean architecture means just-in-time delivery of functionality and reducing the waste. Coplien et al. (2010) also state that rework in production is waste. However, in design rework is not waste, rather it creates value as it saves more expensive work in the production phase. In order to achieve this, Coplien et al. (2010) encourage to engage all stakeholders together as early as possible. They continue that architectural decisions should be made at the responsible moment - that moment after which the foregone decision has a bearing on how subsequent decisions are made, or would have been made. Furthermore in lean architecture approach there is strong emphasis on collaboration between people during the design phase and utilization of domain knowledge. Domain knowledge is recognized as an essential part, in order to capture the end user mental model. Regarding the practices we have identified, the lean architecture concept seems to advocate the SPR* approach.

CONCLUSION

In this study, we have identified four approaches to integrate Scrum with software architecture work in 11 companies. Although there may be different variants of these practices, it seems reasonable to expect that they represent main Scrum practices in the industry. This belief is also grounded by an analysis of the possible (sensible) choices there are for arranging architecture work in Scrum: the identified practices cover those choices.

The practices were studied both from the viewpoint of the data revealed by the interviews, and from the viewpoint of their potential conflicts with actual Scrum practices, as concretized by Scrum patterns. The most popular practice appearing in the interviews was also found to be the most problematic in terms of the Scrum patterns. On the basis of the analysis on the interplay between Scrum patterns and architecture work practices, we conclude that BUFA (big up-front architecture) and SEPA (separate architecture process) approaches are the most conflicting approaches when using Scrum. However, in interviews it was discovered that the other two approaches are not without problems, too. SPR* (architecture in sprints) approach can lead to a failure of the project if the team does not have enough domain knowledge. In turn, SPR0 (sprint zero) approach is in conflict with one of the most fundamental concept of Scrum: delivering a potentially shippable product increment in every sprint. In general, it seems that there are strong forces which discourage practitioners to design software architecture in the ways aligned with Scrum.

We see that our study can serve practitioners in several ways. First, the study presents a covering set of practices for architecting that has been tried in industry. These practices work at least in some environments, but the study illuminates the problems associated with each of the practices. Second, the study helps to understand which practices are less problematic, given a certain set of Scrum patterns that have been adopted in the company. Third, if the company has already adopted one of the four architecting practice, and is considering to increase the level of agility by imposing new Scrum patterns, the study shows the possible management risks arising from conflicts between the new Scrum patterns and the adopted way of architecture work.

REFERENCES

Abrahamsson, P., Babar, M. A., & Kruchten, P. (2010). Agility and architecture: Can they coexist? *IEEE Software*, 27(2), 16–22. doi:10.1109/MS.2010.36

Agile Alliance. (2001). *Manifesto for agile software development.* Retrieved January 10, 2012, from http://agilemanifesto.org

Babar, M. A. (2009). An exploratory study of architectural practices and challenges in using agile software development approaches. In *Proceedings of the European Conference on Software Architecture (ICSA/ECSA 2009)*, (pp. 81-90). IEEE.

Babar, M. A., Ihme, T., & Pikkarainen, M. (2009). An industrial case of exploiting product line architectures in agile software development. In *SPLC '09 – Proceedings of the 13th International Software Product Line Conference*, (pp. 171-179). Pittsburgh, PA: Carnegie Mellon University.

Baskerville, R., Pries-Heje, J., & Madsen, S. (2010). Post-agility: What follows a decade of agility? *Information and Software Technology*, 53(5), 543–555. doi:10.1016/j.infsof.2010.10.010

Bass, L., Clements, P., & Kazman, R. (2003). *Software architecture in practice* (2nd ed.). Addison-Wesley.

Cockburn, A. (2006). *Agile software development: The cooperative game* (2nd ed.). Addison-Wesley.

Coplien, J., & Bjørnvig, G. (2010). *Lean architecture for agile software development.* Wiley.

Eloranta, V.-P. (2011). *Scrum and architecture work survey – Interview questions.* Retrieved, January 10, 2012, from http://www.cs.tut.fi/~elorantv/interview_questions.html

Huo, M., Verner, J., Zhu, L., & Babar, M. A. (2004). Software quality and agile methods. In *Proceedings of the COMPSAC 2004.* IEEE Computer Society.

Isham, M. (2008). Agile architecture is possible – You first have to believe! In *Proceedings of Agile 2008 conference*, (pp. 484-489). IEEE Computer Society.

ISO. IEC 42010 CD1. (2010). *Systems and software engineering –Architectural description*, draft. Retrieved August 30, 2011, from http://www.iso-architecture.org/ieee-1471/docs/ISO-IEC-IEEE-latest-draft-42010.pdf

Korhonen, K. (2010). Evaluating the effect of agile methods on software defect data and defect reporting practices - A case study. In *Proceedings of the 7th International Conference on the Quality of Information and Communications Technology*, (pp. 35–43). IEEE Computer Society.

Kruchten, P. (2010). Software architecture and agile software development: A clash of two cultures? *Proceedings of ICSE, 2010*, 497–498. Cape Town, South Africa: ACM.

Nord, R. L., & Tomayko, J. E. (2006). Software architecture-centric methods and agile development. *IEEE Software, 23*(2), 47–53. doi:10.1109/MS.2006.54

Poppendieck, M., & Poppendieck, T. (2006). *Implementing lean software development from concept to cash*. Addison-Wesley.

Rawsthorne, D. (2007). *Collabnet Scrum and agile blog: Sprint zero*. Retrieved, August 30, 2011, from http://blogs.danube.com/sprint-zero?q=blog/dan_rawsthorne/sprint_zero

Schougaard, K., Hansen, K., & Christensen, H. (2008) Sa@work: A field study of software architecture and software quality at work. In *Proceedings of the 15th Asia-Pacific Software Engineering Conference APSEC 2008*, (pp. 411-418). IEEE.

Scrum Pattern Community. (2011). *Published patterns*. Retrieved August 10, 2011, from http://sites.google.com/a/scrumplop.org/published-patterns/

Scrum.org. (2012). *Scrum extension library*. Retrieved, January 2, 2012, from http://www.scrum.org/scrum-extensions/

Seaman, C. B. (2010). Qualitative methods in empirical studies of software engineering. *IEEE Software, 27*(2), 16–22.

Sutherland, J. (2008). *Nokia test: Where did it come from?* Retrieved November 19, 2011 from http://scrum.jeffsutherland.com/2008/08/nokia-test-where-did-it-come-from.html

Sutherland, J. (2010). *Scrumbut test aka the Nokia test*. Retrieved November 19, 2011, from http://jeffsutherland.com/scrumbutttest.pdf

Sutherland, J., & Schwaber, K. (2011). *The Scrum guide – The definitive guide to Scrum: The rules of the game*. Retrieved September 9, 2011, from http://www.scrum.org/storage/scrumguides/Scrum_Guide.pdf

VersionOne. (2009). *4th annual state of agile survey*. Retrieved December 30, 2011, from http://www.versionone.com/pdf/2009_State_of_Agile_Development_Survey_Results.pdf

VersionOne. (2010). *5th annual state of agile survey*. Retrieved December 30, 2011, from http://www.versionone.com/pdf/2010_State_of_Agile_Development_Survey_Results.pdf

KEY TERMS AND DEFINITIONS

Agile Principles: A set of software development principles described in agile manifesto.

Embedded System: A software system running as part of a larger device intended to control the functionality of the device.

Pattern: Systematically documented solution to a frequently occurring problem in a context.

Pattern Language: Organized collection of patterns for a particular field of expertise.

Scrum: Iterative and incremental framework for project management in agile software development.

Software Architecture: The high level organization of a software system.

Software Architecture Practice: A way of working to accomplish the architecture of a software system.

Software Development Process: The structured activities required to produce a software product.

Chapter 13
Contexts and Challenges:
Toward the Architecture of the Problem

Charlie Alfred
Foliage, Inc., USA

ABSTRACT

Historically, architecture has been about the structure of the solution, focused on the components that make up a system and the connectors which enable their coordinated interaction. Given this solution focus, systems, enterprise, and software architecture evolved in different directions. During the past 15+ years, architectural theory and practice have been undergoing a gradual, but significant, shift in focus. Five trends which highlight this shift are: decision rationale, challenges vs. requirements, systems-of-systems, contextual analysis, and design cognition. Each of these trends facilitates a necessary shift from the architecture of the solution to the architecture of the problem. In addition to enabling a clearer link between the problem and solution, these trends also help to unify systems, enterprise, and software architecture by providing a common foundation for collaboration on complex problems.

INTRODUCTION

This chapter discusses an evolution in architectural thinking which has been taking place over the past 20 years. The first section, titled Background, discusses trends in five areas of activity. The common denominator for these areas is the focus on a solution – on the creation of a solid architectural definition that can serve as the backbone of a system. None of these areas: decision rationale, design concerns, systems-of-systems, contextual analysis, and design cognition are considered revolutionary. However, when combined, they shift architectural focus from the solution to the problem. The second section, titled Synthesis, discusses the synergy that results from the combination of these areas. Finally, the chapter concludes with discussions of Issues and Problems, Future Research Directions and Conclusions.

Two concepts are fundamental to this shift: context and challenges. In this chapter, the term context refers to a collection of stakeholders who share a similar set of perceptions, priorities, and desired outcomes and are subjected to a similar

DOI: 10.4018/978-1-4666-2199-2.ch013

set of forces. Challenge refers to a situation where one or more limiting factors make it more difficult to satisfy one or more value expectations.

These two concepts, in turn, lead to three important considerations. First, because value (unlike benefit) is subjective, challenges, priorities, risks and tradeoffs are inherently contextual, and the architect must treat context as a first-class concern. Second, the priority of challenges within a context needs to drive architectural decision making. Addressing the highest priority challenges first improves the quality tradeoffs and increases degrees of freedom. Third, while different contexts may pose similar challenges, frequently, the priorities of challenges vary among contexts. Tradeoffs between challenges in a context are often subordinate to tradeoffs between similar challenges across contexts.

The architecture of the solution is largely about resolving forces within a system. The architecture of the problem is about understanding contexts deeply and balancing the solution to overcome challenges both within and across contexts. While in theory, this may sound like a simple shift, in practice the impact is much more significant.

BACKGROUND

For over 20 years, enterprise, systems, and software architecture each have been making significant contributions to the development of complex systems that enrich our lives every day. These three disciplines share a similar mission, as evidenced by their common adoption of the architecture definition in IEC 42010 (2007, pg. 10), "the fundamental organization of a system embodied in its components, their relationships to each other, and to the environment, and the principles guiding its design and evolution."

While these disciplines share a common mission, their focus and practice differ in important ways. Maier (2009, pg. 425) defines a system as "a collection of things or elements that, working together, produce a result not achievable by the elements alone."

These definitions of system and architecture lead to a broad view of systems architecture, as shown in Figure 1.

With its focus on managing business information and enabling business processes, enterprise architecture is a specialization of systems architecture according to problem focus. By contrast, with its focus on manipulating computational abstractions which represent real world entities, software architecture is a specialization of system architecture on a different axis: solution mechanism.

Software, systems and enterprise architecture intersect in the region where computational abstractions manage the storage and flow of business information and model the behavior of business processes and workflows. Realtime control systems, such as medical devices, automotive and avionics are areas where software and systems architecture overlap, with a somewhat lesser concern for enterprise architecture. However, all one need do is step outside the boundary of a medical device and strong evidence of electronic medical records and hospital information systems (enterprise architecture) will be present. Virtually the same statement can be made for any other realtime control system.

Areas where enterprise and system architecture overlap with a lesser influence of software architecture are more difficult to find. Complex networks, which on the surface, appear to be composed entirely of radio transmission, bundles of wire enclosed in cable, and computer hardware have significant amounts of software controlling transmission, routing, service provisioning, and error recovery. Similarly, the racks of server blades and RAID drives that make up most compute centers require complex operating system and device driver software to run.

So what this strongly suggests is that enterprise, systems, and software architecture are more alike and interdependent than it might seem. Yet, the

Figure 1. Enterprise, systems, and software architecture domains

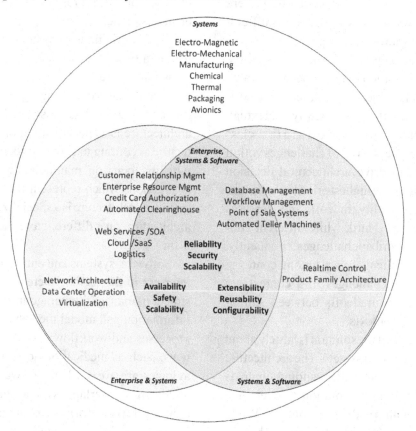

practice of architecture in these fields has diverged. One possible explanation is that, in practice, architecture has evolved into a discipline that is as much (or more) about its application than its principles and methods.

An enterprise architect without deep subject matter knowledge in large scale relational databases, replication, data warehousing, predictive analytics, Web Services, Cloud services, routers, firewalls, server scalability and encryption is going to have a difficult time functioning on the job. A systems engineer lacking knowledge of strength and flexibility of materials, electro-magnetic interference, vibration, manufacturing systems, or supply chain management is at a severe disadvantage. A software architect lacking deep knowledge of J2EE or.NET, Apple iOS and Android, SOAP and REST, object-relational modeling, multi-core

CPU's, and multi-threaded programming will be similarly handicapped.

Given these realities, the observations of Maier (2009, pg. xvii) about the inherent difference between architecture and engineering are quite compelling:

Generally speaking, engineering deals almost entirely with the measurable, using analytical tools derived from mathematics, and the hard sciences; that is, engineering is a deductive process. Architecture deals largely with unmeasurables using non-quantitative tools and guidelines; based on practical lessons learned; that is, architecture is an inductive process...

There is a very important message here. Current commercial practice in architecture continues to be very focused on "the architecture of the solution." The roles and responsibilities of most enterprise, systems, and software architects is to transform requirements specified by others into suitable system structures which will best utilize the available selection of off-the-shelf technologies and frameworks. Experience and know-how with these 3rd party solution enablers is frequently perceived as more valuable than the ability to synthesize the right problem. One consequence is that the varying specialties in the fields of enterprise, systems, and software architecture are causing the skill sets of qualified architects to drift further apart.

On the other hand, several journal articles published during the past decade indicate that architecture research is moving away from "the architecture of the solution." In particular, five topics, which are an important part of this evolution, will be discussed here:

1. Focus on the solution structure to an emphasis on the set of decisions, including rationale.
2. Requirements as a definitive problem statement to goals, constraints, and challenges.
3. Emerging recognition of problem-solution co-evolution techniques.
4. Role-based view of stakeholders in homogenous environments to contrasting contexts.
5. Expansion of scope from one system into a system-of-systems.

These five trends have an important cumulative effect, which I refer to as the "architecture of the problem" and will explore in more detail in the body of this chapter. This effect is more than just a recognition that systems architecture and development occurs in a broader context than the target system. It is a recognition that the architecture of this broader system, including the alignment and interaction of the pieces has as much, if not more, to do with creating value as the architecture of the system under development.

Specifically, here is an overview of the synergy between these five trends:

1. The environment where a complex system is deployed is a system-of-systems. For example:
   a. When a Hospital Information System (HIS) is deployed in a hospital, this environment includes: hospital staff (physicians, clinicians, IT), patients, insurance companies, the HIS supplier, and other systems the HIS is connected with.
   b. When the system is a product that can be used in many ways, such as an automobile or a cellular network, this environment takes the form of several partially overlapping systems-of-systems.
2. Embedded within the system development organization is another system-of-systems. The development of any complex system, whether enterprise or product, requires integration of, both within and across each of the following areas:
   a. Interdependent teams from marketing, project management, engineering, testing, quality, and production (e.g. manufacturing for product or infrastructure for IT).
   b. Interrelated processes, including requirements, risk management, project planning, architecture, development, and testing.
   c. Interdependent technologies, including hardware, networks, frameworks, libraries, and tools for requirements, design, development, configuration management, defect tracking, and testing.
3. As system complexity increases, it is highly unlikely that any individual will be fully knowledgeable about the problem scope or the set of processes and solution tech-

nologies across these system-of-systems. Effectiveness depends on the architecture of these systems-of-systems, which in turn depends on understanding the context for each of these component systems – how perceptions of benefits and priorities are affected by conditions and situations.

4. Within every context, there are numerous challenges which must be overcome in order to generate value. In an ideal world, these challenges would all be static, free of uncertainty and compatible with each other. Unfortunately, none of us live in this world, and change, uncertainty and tradeoffs are unavoidable. In this chapter, the term "challenge" is used to refer to a particular fine-grained concern, while the term "problem" is used more broadly, to refer to the aggregation of challenges which must be addressed by a system. Architecture is directly concerned with how well these challenges are understood and prioritized and how effectively tradeoffs are made.

5. As problem complexity expands, there is increased risk that a partial solution will conflict with an unforeseen part of the problem. Prior experience and reference models become less likely to yield a complete solution. The use of problem-solution co-evolution techniques becomes an increasingly important way to prioritize and test partial solutions to challenges.

Architectural decisions must be implemented by many people to overcome challenges and create value. As a general rule, the effectiveness of architecture decisions is limited by how effectively their rationale (i.e. why this decision, tradeoff, or priority was chosen) is communicated and understood.

Architecture as Solution Structure

During the late 1970's, the development life cycle was seen as a progression from requirements to design, implementation, and test. As technology grew more powerful, solutions to more complex problems became possible. Brooks (1987, pg. 10-11) observed that complexity has two sides:

- **Essential:** Complexity which is inherent in the problem itself.
- **Accidental:** All complexity introduced by a particular solution.

The original mission of architecture was to help to contain solution complexity. Garland and Shaw (1994, pg.2) wrote:

As the size and complexity of software systems increases, the design problem goes beyond the algorithms and data structures of the computation: designing and specifying the overall system structure emerges as a new kind of problem. Structural issues include gross organization and global control structure; protocols for communication, synchronization, and data access; assignment of functionality to design elements; physical distribution; composition of design elements; scaling and performance; and selection among design alternatives. This is the software architecture level of design.

Experts in other architecture disciplines expressed very similar ideas. In the field of systems architecture, Maier (2009, pg. 414) described architecture as "the structure – in terms of components, connections, and constraints - of a product, process, or element. It includes all elements of a system that determine its form and function." In the field of enterprise architecture, Fowler (2002, pg. 1) described architecture as "the highest-level breakdown of a system into its parts; the decisions that are hard to change."

This view of architecture as a description of solution manifested itself as a convergence of both principles and practice. UML 2.0 (including SysML extensions) has been widely adopted in systems, enterprise, and software disciplines as the de facto notation for architecture diagrams.

Beginning in the early 2000s, the primary emphasis for architecture began to shift from the description of the solution structure toward the decisions and rationale that gave rise to them. (Kazman et al, 2000, pg. 13) wrote "[architectural] design decisions are critical; they have the most far-reaching consequences and are the most difficult to change after a system is implemented." They went on to argue that the suitability of an architecture should be evaluated according to how well it satisfies the highest priority quality attribute scenarios. Kruchten (2004, pg. 54) wrote:

Representations of software architecture were centered on views, as captured by the IEEE-1471 standard, or usage of an architecture description language. But doing so, we lose some of the knowledge that is attached to the decision itself, and to the decision process: rationale, avoided alternatives, etc.

Jansen and Bosch (2005, 109) concur, writing:

Currently, almost all the knowledge and information about the design decisions the architecture is based on are implicitly embedded in the architecture, but lack a first-class representation. Consequently, knowledge about these design decisions disappears into the architecture.

Insights such as these have provided the impetus to move architecture practice toward focusing on formulating and capturing the rationale for high-leverage decisions. At the conceptual level, this shift has occurred across systems, enterprise and software disciplines. Several research efforts have focused on specifying a mechanism for capturing architecture decisions. Bu et al (2009) describe nine of them. Currently, none of these mechanisms has emerged as a standard. Unlike the notation for architecture diagrams, capturing and documenting the rationale for architecture decisions relies largely on text documents using locally-defined templates.

Architecture and Requirements

As architectural practice shifted from solution structure to decision rationale, friction with requirements engineering was inevitable. SWEBOK (the Software Engineering Body of Knowledge) (2004) decomposes the requirements knowledge area is decomposed into: process, elicitation, analysis, and specification and validation sub-areas. The description of the Requirements Analysis sub-area articulates the perception of the role played by architecture in the systems definition process:

[...] the process of analyzing and elaborating the requirements demands that the components that will be responsible for satisfying the requirements be identified. This is requirements allocation–the assignment, to components, of the responsibility for satisfying requirements. Allocation is important to permit detailed analysis of requirements.

Earlier, we discussed the view that architecture is essentially about defining and describing the structure of the system. The SWEBOK description is consistent with this perception, adding the notion of a layered process which is called functional decomposition:

1. Requirements are defined and analyzed.
2. Next architecture uses these requirements to identify components and connectors.
3. Then requirements are defined for the high-level components.

4. Then the largest and most complex components are decomposed into finer-grained components and connectors, etc.

This approach is widely adopted in industry, largely because it is so familiar to so many people. Hierarchical organizations are based on principles of "divide and conquer" and hiding unnecessary details (encapsulation). In addition, hierarchical organizations permeate our daily life and are very familiar to all. Corporate organizations, government agencies and department stores are but a few examples.

However, functional decomposition and hierarchical organizations can have some important drawbacks. These approaches make a simplifying assumption that the components have loose coupling. They also tend to make the assumption that the system has a single point of control. In other words, components of the system do not concurrently assess the external environment and make independent decisions about behavioral responses.

As systems become more complex, architecture becomes less about functional decomposition, and more about the systemic nature of the relationships among the elements, and between the elements and the external environment. Augmenting a functional view of a system with other complementary viewpoints, such as concurrency, dependency and variability viewpoints broadens understanding considerably.

Waldo et al (1994, 1) make this point very clearly regarding Sun Microsystems' effort to develop the Network File System (NFS):

We argue that objects that interact in a distributed system need to be dealt with in ways that are intrinsically different from objects that interact in a single address space. These differences are required because distributed systems require that the programmer be aware of latency, have a different model of memory access, and take into account issues of concurrency and partial failure.

In other words, access to a local file system is inherently different from access to a file system on a remote computer. A simple set of requirements which specify how to open, close, read, write and seek in files and directories, might be atomic, clear and verifiable, but they cannot be determined to be consistent and complete without knowledge of whether the file system is local or remote to the client application.

Another important issue with requirements is their dual purpose. First, requirements have been used to drive system definition. Second, requirements have been used to verify acceptance criteria, and validate that the system as built serves its intended purpose. While the strategic purpose of these two goals is consistent (build a system that addresses the problem), there is a significant tension between them.

The system definition process is inherently about discovery: of stakeholder needs and feasible solutions. This process is performed in a space populated with uncontrollable forces, which give rise to uncertainties, constraints, and dependencies. Flexibility, adaptability, and the ability to make effective tradeoffs and manage risks are essential here. The system verification and validation process are inherently about testing hypotheses. By contrast, this process requires clarity and specificity. Does the system do what it is supposed to, or not?

The dual responsibility to drive architecture and verification creates a tension. In order to specify requirements that are atomic, identifiable, clear, and precise, it is necessary to make decisions about the nature of the solution. The fuel economy of an automobile depends on its weight and aerodynamics, as well as the type and octane level of the fuel it uses.

In most cases, consistency is determined by factors outside the requirements, such as the architecture or environment. Aerodynamics can be used to show that an aircraft with a given weight, engine thrust, and wing shape cannot fly. While verification of completeness is an admirable although unreachable goal, its pursuit requires system-level testing of requirements, plus a thorough evaluation of the architecture, as discussed in (Kazman et al, 2000).

In summary, as system complexity increases relative to functionality, there has been a shift in emphasis both from "architecture as solution structure" to "architecture as the rationale for critical decisions," as well as from requirements to architectural challenges.

Problem-Solution Co-Evolution

As enterprise, systems, and software architecture problems become more anomalous and complex, prior solutions and reference architectures become less effective. Reusing a good solution to a related problem can conflict with other challenges in a larger or different problem. As a result, over the past 20 years, there has been significant research into design cognition – or the study of how people think about and solve design problems.

Kruger and Cross (2006) conducted protocol studies of nine experienced industrial designers and identified four different cognitive strategies: problem-driven, solution-driven, information-driven, and knowledge-driven. Designers using a solution-driven strategy tended to have lower overall scores on solution effectiveness, but scored higher in the creativity of their approach.

Several design cognition researchers have noted patterns involving some degree of co-evolution of problem and solution. Dorst and Cross (1999, pg. 435) in a study of industrial designers observed:

Our observations confirm that creative design involves a period of exploration in which problem and solution spaces are evolving and are unstable until (temporarily) fixed by an emergent bridge which identifies a problem–solution pairing.

Tang et al (2010, pg. 630-640) studied two teams of software designers working independently on a traffic light simulation problem. Among their conclusions were:

1. When the designers are at the exploratory stage, all related problems are explored to gain a better understanding of the problem space. At this stage, few solutions are provided. When all the design issues are well understood, designers would then hone in on a single design issue and proceed to creating a design with problems and solutions co-evolution.
2. When designer familiarity with the problem domain is lower, reasoning approaches, such as problem-solution co-evolution, permit better problem space exploration than more intuitive decision-driven approaches.

Boehm and Ross (1989, pp. 902-16) discuss Theory W as a means to negotiate mutually-acceptable solutions among key stakeholders in a system development effort. Theory W is based on findings of the Harvard Negotiation Project (Fisher et al, 1991, pg. 11-12) which stresses the following principles for successful negotiation:

1. Separate the people from the problem.
2. Focus on interests, not positions.
3. Invent options for mutual gain.
4. Insist on using objective criteria.

Applying these principles to architecture formulation leads to a form of solution-driven evolution. When conflicts are detected between stakeholders' win positions, win-win solutions often can be discovered by examining commonalities in the underlying interests.

Another useful technique is to discover the underlying challenges which are at the heart of the conflict. This approach can be an effective way to transform solution statements (objectives) into problem statements, enabling all participants to uncover suitable ways to overcome them, without being tethered to one particular outcome.

Contextual Analysis

Early systems development activities primarily took a functional perspective. For example, airline reservations systems concentrated on flight reservations, seat assignment, check-in, and passenger boarding. When different types of users exercise different features of a system, a role-based view of the system typically is taken. In the airline reservations system, Passenger, Reservations Agent and Gate Agent are common roles, and they appear as actors in use case scenarios.

Boehm and Ross (1989) emphasize the importance of incorporating the win conditions of all significant stakeholders. In the process, they stress the importance of "not projecting your own interests into another stakeholder's win conditions". They use the example of a project manager assuming that all engineers want to be promoted into management. Another example is where an architect concludes that business stakeholders want the most robust, extensible, longest-lasting solution, when it is possible that all they are seeking is a short term bridge to buy time to design the long term solution.

Tang et al (2010, pg. 631) describe contextualization as "the process of attaching a meaning and interpreting a phenomenon to a design problem. Well-reasoned arguments state the context of the problem, i.e. what and how the context influences the design."

In many environments, especially those involving families of related products, contextualization becomes an extremely important activity. In these areas, reuse of common components across multiple products is a key driver for increasing return on investment. At the same time, it is essential to identify and actively manage variabilities between products in order to achieve this ROI.

The Software Engineering Institute (2011, pg. 1) writes:

A software product line is a set of software-intensive systems sharing a common, managed set of features that satisfy the specific needs of a particular market segment or mission and that are developed from a common set of core assets in a prescribed way.

Van der Linden et. al: (2007, pg. 8) wrote:

Software product line engineering aims at supporting a range of products... As a result, variability is a key concept in any such approach. Instead of understanding each individual system all by itself, software product line engineering looks at the product line as a whole and the variation among the individual systems.

Careful management of variability points is critical in a product family. Variability points represent places in the product architecture where a specific range of variability options are permitted. Interdependencies among variability points (as well as interdependencies among options) make component configuration a very important architectural concern. For example, selection of one variability option may require or preclude a specific option in another variability point.

For product families to be effective, the needs of key market segments, product features, platform capabilities, and business strategy must be aligned. A platform with incomplete variability points or the wrong set of options will be hampered in its ability to create products that appeal to market segments. While some members of the product family may be good fits for their market segments, others may be lacking important features or may cost too much.

Systems of Systems

The preceding sections have implied that architecture is concerned with early design decisions and solution structure for a system. During the 1980s, the systems architecture communities began to recognize a systems-of-systems concept. During the late 1990s and early 2000s, the systems family engineering approach addressed the solution structure of several systems at once.

Maier (1998, pg. 268) identifies five principal characteristics are useful in distinguishing very large and complex but monolithic systems from true systems-of-systems.

1. Operational Independence of the Elements
2. Managerial Independence of the Elements
3. Evolutionary Development
4. Emergent Behavior
5. Geographic Distribution

Lane and Valerdi (1998, pg. 197) discuss four forms of systems-of-systems, depending on the existence of a central system-of-systems engineering team and its level of authority:

- **Virtual:** No central system-of-systems engineering team and constituent systems do not typically know about each other (little to no authority or responsibility).
- **Collaborative:** No central system-of-systems engineering team, but constituent systems have responsibility to collaborate for crosscutting issues and needs.
- **Acknowledged:** A central system-of-systems team with responsibility, but limited authority over the constituent systems.
- **Directed:** A central system-of-systems team exists and has both responsibility and considerable authority over the constituent systems.

SYNTHESIS

In commercial practice, the five subjects discussed in the Background section are frequently performed independently or in small groups. This occurs commonly when architecture is focused on the solution. However, when these five subjects are fully integrated, the focus of architects is shifted to the problem, and significant synergy results from the combination.

Ackoff (1999, pp. 8-24) highlighted two modes of thought identified by the ancient Greek philosophers:

- **Analysis:** The act of decomposing bigger things into smaller pieces to understand how they fit together, has been the dominant mode of thinking since the Industrial Revolution.
- **Synthesis:** Shifts attention to the containing system to grasp why things are the way they are, and what forces and cycles hold them in place.

For most of its development, architecture has been dominated by analytical thinking. With a few exceptions, the vast majority of effort has been solution-focused. This is not meant as a criticism. Progress in the field of architectural analysis has been exceptional and great value has emerged from the work. However, it does mean that a great deal of opportunity exists in the area of synthesis. Systems of systems, contexts, and system dynamics play an extremely important role here. A much better understanding of how architecture and requirements co-exist is also important.

Architecture Rationale

Kazman et al (2000) describe a method called ATAM, which is used to evaluate the architecture of a software-intensive system. This method focuses on how well the key architecture decisions satisfy the prioritized system quality attributes and core architectural capabilities, such as workflow management or task scheduling. Scenarios, which describe stimuli, conditions and expected outcomes, are used to analyze the suitability of the architecture decisions under a variety of input stimuli and environmental conditions. Properly chosen scenarios help to identify risks, tradeoffs, and the sensitivity of outcomes to variations in inputs can be assessed.

While this method does not directly address how to represent rationale for architecture decisions, it indicates the rationale that architects must provide for their decisions in order to support an architecture evaluation. In particular this rationale must:

- Trace decisions to the quality attributes they support, and justify why they are suitable.
- Identify tradeoffs imposed by the decisions on competing quality attributes, and show how the decisions favor the higher priority quality attributes.
- Identify the uncertainties present in these decisions and characterize the resulting risk exposure.
- Show how the selected decisions are superior to the alternative options considered, in terms of better support for quality attributes, lower impact of tradeoffs, and lower risks.

But perhaps the most important element of rationale is showing how and why the particular decision helps to overcome opposing forces which the environment imposes on the system. It is precisely the force of gravity that makes an airplane's wings and propulsion system necessary, and, along with the size and purpose of the aircraft, determines the suitability of these decisions.

Challenges

Alfred (2005, pg. 37) writes: "A challenge is a situation where one or more limiting factors make it more difficult to satisfy one or more value expectations. Simply put, an architecture challenge is an obstacle or barrier that the system must overcome to provide value."

A limiting factor might be a physical or logistical constraint which prevents or reduces a desired outcome, or an uncertainty which creates a complication or poses a threat of loss. In either case, the architect's responsibility is to understand the impact of the challenge and make one or more decisions to neutralize or mitigate this impact.

Alexander (1979, pg. 247) describes patterns for building architecture as: "Each pattern is a three part rule, which expresses a relation between a certain context, a problem, and a solution." Challenges straddle problem and context in this definition. Limiting factors posing obstacles to a goal represent the problem aspect. The impact on value expectations, the subjective perception of what makes outcomes better or worse, is inseparable from the context in which the factors and outcomes occur.

For example, a vital signs monitor is used to capture blood pressure, heart rate, oxygen saturation and other physiological measurements from a patient. These monitors are often used to capture vital signs for patients in hospital medical-surgical wards and are often equipped with a network connection to report patient vital signs readings to a medical information system. Network loads and wireless interference can interfere with latency. Low latency is extremely important for patients who have just been released from surgery and are recovering from anesthesia, but is less critical for those who are awaiting surgery or are recuperating after successful recovery from anesthesia. The same monitor, deployed in the same medical setting poses different challenges for different types of patients.

Figure 2 illustrates the relationship between Challenges, Value-Drivers, Quality Attribute Scenarios and Architecture Decisions.

Quality attribute scenarios, as discussed by Kazman et al (2000) are similar to but subtly different from challenges. Quality attribute scenarios are used in ATAM as test cases for verifying an architecture. Each challenge, on the other hand, represents a key impedance condition, something that the architecture must overcome to deliver value. There is a many-to-many relationship between challenges and quality attribute scenarios. More than one challenge may need to be addressed to achieve a quality attribute scenario, and the same challenge might be a barrier to several scenarios.

Challenges are also similar to requirements, but again have an important difference. Greenfield and Short (2004, pg. 96) write, "We tend to think in terms of solving a specific problem, but in practice, we are usually interested in solving a family of related problems." In other words, requirements are all too often not statements about the problem; they are statements made by a stakeholder about a preferred solution. De Boer and van Vliet (2008,

pg. 546) assert "architectural design decisions and architecturally significant requirements are really the same; they're only being observed from different directions."

A challenge is neither a requirement nor an architecture design decision. A challenge is a statement about the problem. It represents an obstacle or risk which exists, and if left unaddressed is very likely to decrease the value the system is able to provide. Requirements and architecture design decisions, like quality attribute scenarios, can and should be traced to challenges.

While multiple requirements (or multiple architecture design decisions) may conflict with each other and need to be restated to be consist, multiple challenges are additive. Consider different challenges involved in monitoring patient vital signs (heart rate, blood pressure, sperometry, etc.):

- Patients in the medical/surgical ward who have been out of surgery for several hours need to have their vital signs checked periodically. Challenges here include: the ability to precisely measure each vital sign, as

Figure 2. Challenges, value drivers, quality attribute scenarios and architecture decisions

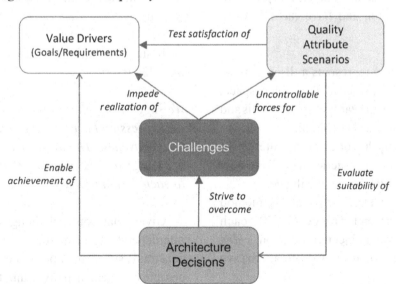

well as managing the capital investment of monitoring devices/patient.

- The medical/surgical ward of a hospital cares for patients who have undergone major surgery. Some of these patients have just been released from surgery and are recovering from anesthesia. These patients must receive immediate medical attention if any respiratory or heart problems are detected. Challenges here include: the ability to precisely measure each vital sign, the ability to do it continuously, the ability to set alarm limits, and the ability to deliver alarms immediately.

- The intensive care unit cares for patients who have undergone recent surgery for life-threatening conditions, such as heart bypass surgery. These patients need continuous monitoring of their vital signs, but also need to walk around periodically for exercise. Challenges here include all of the challenges in the prior example, and the need to measure vital signs while the patient is mobile.

Problem-Solution Co-Evolution

Challenges are a useful enabler for problem-solution co-evolution, and have the following properties:

1. Each challenge represents a discrete issue or concern discovered in the problem space.
2. Challenges are traceable to system goals and externally imposed constraints.
3. Each challenge has one or more alternative solutions, where "no action taken" is a possible alternative for any challenge.
4. Based on the Decision Analysis method from Kepner and Tregoe (1977), each challenge has an objective function: *value = f(outcome)*, used to evaluate alternative approaches.

5. The solution chosen for a challenge can, and most likely will, constrain the viable solutions to subsequent challenges.
6. Challenges may depend on other challenges, independent of the particular solution chosen for the independent challenge. For example, the aerodynamic challenge of an airplane wings may depend on the safety challenge to have engine redundancy, regardless of the type of engine.
7. Challenges can be prioritized relative to other challenges, based on an assessment of importance, difficulty, and impact on other challenges (e.g. dependency).

An important hypothesis can be derived from this set of properties: architecture should focus first on the highest priority challenges. This hypothesis has the following corollaries:

- It is valuable to discover many challenges before trying to address any of them. This does not mean that all challenges must be identified. Some challenges only emerge after trying to analyze and formulate solutions.
- It is valuable to assess challenges, compare them with each other and try to prioritize them.

In support of this hypothesis, Tang et al (2010, pg. 622) assert:

We suggest that the decisions on how to plan a design session have bearings on the results and its effectiveness. The considerations are the scope of a design and the priorities that should be given to each design problem.

Given that some challenges are inherently interdependent and the solution for one challenge constrains subsequent ones, the architecture of a complex system usually cannot be formulated in a linear fashion. For example, the solutions chosen for the three highest priority challenges may leave the sixth challenge without any viable options. In this case, it would be necessary to reconsider the three high priority challenges. An alternate solution to one of them might only sacrifice a small amount of value, while opening up a viable alternative for the sixth challenge. A similar example is where the "best" option for the highest priority challenge results in a much larger negative tradeoff by constraining several other downstream challenges.

Tang et al (2009) discuss the relationship between design concerns, decisions, and outcomes. Apart Figure 3 illustrates a similar notion: the circular relationship between challenges, architecture decisions, and requirements derived from these architecture decisions. While challenges and design concerns are related, challenges are more focused on external goals and environmental influences. Design concerns are a more general concept that might represent solution concerns

(e.g. tradeoffs, dependencies or 3rd party technology). The example immediately following the diagram describes several challenges facing a medical device and their implications on its system architecture.

Let's consider a medical imaging example to illustrate how challenges and problem-solution co-evolution interact. A medical imaging device uses optical imaging techniques to capture high resolution 3D images of an area of interest in the patient's internal anatomy. Remote diagnostic collaboration is a very important goal, with significant potential benefits for patients, physicians, and health care institutions. Time constraints on physician and pathologist interaction, the need for very high resolution images to support accurate diagnosis, image size, and network transfer speeds combine to create a serious challenge. Several challenges emerge from this short problem description:

Figure 3. Challenges, external and derived requirements, and architecture decisions

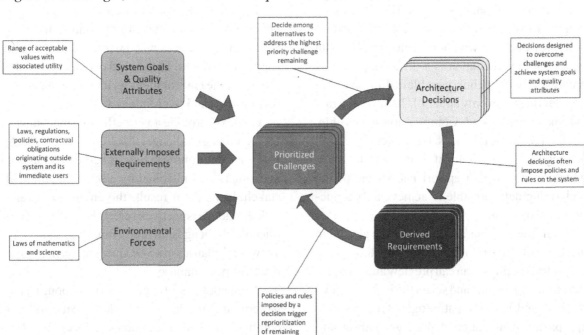

1. Acquiring the optical imaging signal to achieve 20 micrometers of resolution with 3-4 millimeters of tissue depth.
2. Minimizing the noise level in the optical imaging signal, either at acquisition time or by using post-processing techniques.
3. Performing the analog to digital signal processing fast enough to keep up with data acquisition.
4. Performing lossless compression of 7-10GB of examination data with latency of 2 seconds or less.
5. Performing image analysis to recognize patterns in diseased tissue, minimizing both false positives and false negative error conditions.
6. Sharing video/image data between the examination room and remote physician using broadband Internet connections within 10 minute of exam completion.

While the optical and mechanical challenges of this new imaging technology are daunting, one challenge is noteworthy. Modern graphics display technology is able to quickly render 7-10GB of examination data as a 3D video on the graphic display connected to the local workstation. However, presentation of the graphic data on a remote workstation is a different matter. A broadband network link, capable of 40Mb/second transfer rates, can only stream 1/2000th of the raw 3D image per second. Compression is possible, but for diagnostic purposes, lossless compression is a regulatory requirement. Current techniques, which do not exploit apriori knowledge of the underlying data, are able to achieve a 2x reduction in data volume.

Realtime collaboration between the physician in the examination room and a remote pathologist is possible if the physician can preview and interpret the 3D image display and select the image regions to be shared with the pathologist. One possible approach is using automated image analysis and pattern recognition techniques to scan the full 3D image and identify regions of interest for the examination physician to preview. The unknowns with this approach are image analysis speed, the accuracy of pattern detection (false positives and false negatives), and the effort/time needed for development.

What this example illustrates is how the evaluation of a critical challenge for a very important system goal can lead to exploration (or acceleration) of new functionality, with major implications to the system architecture. When this exploration is complete, the result is likely to be a more stable system offering valuable benefits, both short and longer term.

Contexts

Alfred (2009, pg. 26) identifies a context as a first-class abstraction in architecture formulation:

A context is a collection of stakeholders who share a similar set of perceptions, priorities, and desired outcomes and are subjected to a similar set of forces, in the form of conditions and situations.

The first part of this definition deals with perspective: what a stakeholder wants, and how the benefits they seek and the priorities they have shape those wants. The second part deals with the impact of the environment, as it varies over space (conditions) and over time (situations).

Contexts provide a very effective mechanism for organizing challenges. Each context represents a similar environment (e.g. range of conditions and situations) inhabited by a set of likeminded stakeholders. As a result, the environment and stakeholder perspectives select the subset of applicable challenges, in pretty much the same way as "where" clauses in a SQL query select matching rows from a database.

Alexander (1979, pg. xi) writes about living pattern languages, a network of patterns that combine to resolve the forces in a context. The collection of challenges in a context capture the forces that matter in that context and the way they inhibit (or enhance) the perception of value. The architectural approaches to overcome these challenges balance tradeoffs and manage risks to form the pattern language.

The relationship of contexts to challenges is many-to-many. Some challenges appear in many contexts. Other challenges appear in one (or even none). On the other side, each context typically includes several challenges. However, the important aspect here is that the challenges are not equal within a context. The perceptions of the stakeholders prioritize them, according to importance, difficulty, and dependency.

Consider the following example. A scanning electron microscope (SEM) is a type of electron microscope that images a sample by scanning it with a high-energy beam of electrons in a raster scan pattern. The electrons interact with the atoms that make up the sample producing signals that contain information about the sample's surface topography, composition, and other properties such as electrical conductivity.

In the most common or standard detection mode, secondary electron imaging or SEI, the SEM can produce very high-resolution images of a sample surface, revealing details less than 1 nm in size. Due to the very narrow electron beam, SEM micrographs have a large depth of field, yielding a characteristic three-dimensional appearance useful for understanding the surface structure of a sample.

Provided below are summaries of two contexts which need scanning electron microscopes:

Context 1. Specialized Electro-Physics and Chemistry Labs: These labs run short-duration experiments with frequent changes in system setup. There is a very strong desire for flexibility. The microscope is used by PhD scientists who are very acquainted with the principles of non-linear physics needed to properly tune the electron beam.

Context 2. Semiconductor Fabrication: Fabs use metrology to measure the surface of a wafer to verify that the circuitry position and size are within critical dimensions. Long production runs of identical circuit patterns are common, frequently 4-6 weeks or longer. Fabs have a strong desire for reliability and repeatability. Typical users are high-school educated operators lacking the required skills to tune the electron beam. Beam setup is done by qualified scientists and tested carefully before each new production run, and is not modified once setup.

Both of these contexts require the precision of a scanning electron microscope and neither has many other satisfactory alternative solutions to achieve this. However, beyond the need for sub-nanometer level measurement precision, the benefits required by the two contexts diverge. While both contexts need to have the operator be able to control all setup parameters, the two contexts have very different perspectives about how to do this. Labs see this as a feature that must be enabled for all users. Fabs see this feature being limited to engineers, and never exposed to operators. Furthermore, fabs insist that each SEM undergo a thorough set of qualification tests after its setup has been reconfigured, before it can be put back onto the factory floor. The economic risk of a drift in measurements over time is too high. Labs also require small sample testing before the SEM is used in measurements. However, because of the short duration experiments, the risk of measurement drift is inherently low.

In summary, this example highlights the importance of contexts, as manifested by how both architecture and demand for capabilities is altered by differences in value expectations and priorities of challenges.

Systems of Systems

As mentioned above, a system-of-systems involves collaboration between systems that are geographically distributed, operate and evolve independently and generate emergent behavior. The systems development process, itself, is a good example of system-of-systems, at multiple levels.

At the top-level, whether the system is a product or is used to provide a service, the consumer of that system uses it as a component to help fulfill a larger purpose in their context. For example:

- Semiconductor fabricators use products to manufacture chips, such as factory automation systems, robotic material handlers, and laser, deposition, implantation, and metrology tools.
- Investment management organizations rely on systems for reference data management, portfolio management, trade execution and settlement, compliance, accounting and customer reporting.
- Hospitals use hospital information systems (HIS) for maintaining patient electronic medical records, admissions, discharges, and transfers, and insurance claims processing. In addition, the HIS integrates with departmental systems for image management, radiology, laboratory, etc.
- Transportation companies use customer-facing systems to accept pickups and record deliveries, and use internal systems to dispatch vehicles, drivers, and freight, track shipments en-route, and manage sorting and dock operations.

In each of these examples, complex products and IT applications play particular roles and interoperate with many other systems, to help to automate and manage larger, more complex systems.

At the next level down, the systems development process itself is a system-of-systems. Large-scale system development requires collaboration across many functional areas, including:

- Knowledge management
- Product/service marketing
- Requirements engineering
- Electrical, mechanical and software engineering
- Systems architecture
- Risk management
- Configuration management
- Resource/schedule planning
- Testing and defect tracking
- Service and support

Successful collaboration requires careful integration of teams, processes and tools across these functional areas. Tool integration is needed to trace architecture decisions, requirements, tests and defects. Automated test systems are integrated with configuration management and build control systems to provide continuous integration and test capabilities. In addition, tools and processes need to align, and integrated with the workflows of the teams which use them.

Significant systems-of-systems complexity is evident in various aspects of system development. Processes, tools, and teams often change independently. As with any other system, the "architecture of system development" will have an impact on the effectiveness of these efforts. The magnitude of this impact depends largely on how complex and challenging the system under development is.

Table 1 lists several characteristics which affect whether the development process described by SWEBOK (2004) is appropriate, or whether a process consistent with the "architecture of the problem" is justified. If one or more of the conditions in the right hand column are present, then there is likely to be enough risk present to war-

Table 1. System characteristics affecting whether "architecture of the problem" approach is warranted

System Characteristic	"Architecture of the Solution" Approach is Still Appropriate	"Architecture of the Problem" Approach is Warranted
Capability Innovations	System uses well-known capabilities	System relies on major technology or operational innovations
Workflows or Job Responsibilities	System relies on familiar workflows and job responsibilities	System makes significant alterations to workflows or job responsibilities
Impact on Interfaces to Existing Systems	System uses existing data models, services, and messaging mechanisms	System requires extensive changes to existing data models, services, or messaging mechanisms
Developer Familiarity	System developers have solid prior experience with solution technologies	Solution technologies are new, and there are few reference models for successful application.
Degree of Safety Criticality	System does not pose a significant risk to life or an irreversible loss of serious health capability.	System poses a significant risk to life or irreversible loss critical health capability, before or after mitigation
Degree of Business Risk	System failure can cause a temporary business interruption, with minor disruption and/or financial loss.	System failure can cause a significant financial loss or damage to business reputation.
Sophistication of Algorithms	System uses simple or well-known algorithms for decisions	System relies on complex or experimental algorithms for its success.
Performance/Precision	Expectations for throughput, response time, and precision are easily achieved by known solutions.	System has requirements for performance and/or precision that far exceed existing approaches
Scalability	System scale is well within the capabilities of existing technology and should be stable over time	System scale pushes the envelope of existing technology, or is expected to grow exponentially
Contextual Variability	Value expectations and environmental conditions are very consistent across stakeholders.	Stakeholders experience different environmental conditions and have different value expectations.

rant a development process based on challenges, contexts, and problem-solution co-evolution:

- Specify the system's goals to expand degrees of freedom and facilitate important tradeoffs:
  - Reduce the use of invariant constraints (i.e. hard requirements) through set-based design and late decision making.
  - Express goals as ranges of acceptable outcomes with associated utility functions.
  - Identify contexts and prioritize them based on relative importance.
  - Vary goals by context where appropriate.
- Identify challenges and prioritize them within each context.
- Address the highest priority challenges first, assess the impact of alternative approaches on subsequent challenges, and reassess challenge priorities after making decisions.
- When solutions to challenges are uncertain, use simulations and prototypes to reduce risk.

Issues, Controversies, and Problems

While there are many challenges to overcome in complex system development, experience has shown that five of the more significant are:

1. As a general rule, system-of-systems rarely, if ever, present a "clean slate" problem. Evolution is almost always a necessity. The current state and degrees of freedom available to change any system and its connections are critical.

2. "Customers" of a system reside in different contexts. As a result, they often experience different pressures, demand different benefits, and prioritize these demands differently. Sometimes the span across these variations is small enough that one solution can be customized to fit all. Other times (as with the fabs and labs example above) this approach is not viable.

3. Alignment of problem domain knowledge with decision making authority is difficult, especially as the breadth and complexity of the problem expands. Regardless of how well knowledge is articulated, communication is not effective unless the intended audience understands the message.

4. Premature debate or negotiation of solutions, before adequate understanding of the problem exists is often a serious limitation on the effectiveness of the process.

5. Lack of decision rationale makes it very difficult for individual participants to align behind a solution. When decision makers present decisions without a clear articulation of the problem or a compelling set of reasons to support the decision, people are forced to "fill in the blanks" with their own version of the problem and rationale. When forced to do this, they often fail to connect the dots, or they connect the dots differently than the people with whom they must collaborate.

In addition, two other factors tend to pose additional obstacles to change:

1. Innovative processes such as architecture, agile methods and continuous integration often meet with impedance, in the form of initial resistance to change, before becoming widely adopted.

2. Information overload, compounded by the ubiquity of the Internet, electronic mail, text messaging and cellular phones, makes it more difficult for people to absorb and comprehend complex information.

Solutions and Recommendations

In any complex system, two drivers of effectiveness are an appropriate strategy and properly-aligned components. These drivers work in combination. Well-aligned components with a poor strategy work efficiently, but in the wrong direction. Similarly, misaligned components cannot execute a brilliant strategy efficiently. Only a fraction of the combined effort is directed toward the system's purpose, as much of the energy is lost to friction.

Brooks (1995) uses the biblical story of the Tower of Babel as a metaphor for today's challenges with complex systems development. Language barriers between the workers led to frustration, conflict and eventual failure of the overly ambitious project. Modern engineering has conquered the challenges of massive skyscrapers, only to run into similar barriers in other complex endeavors. Sessions: (2009, pg.1) estimates the worldwide cost of IT failures at $500 billion per month.

Effective strategy is a function of a very well-understood problem, knowledge about what resources are needed to address that problem and how to organize them properly. Effective alignment and execution depend on communication, organization, and coordination. As scale and problem complexity grow, problem-comprehension and communication are often the limiting factors.

As the scope and complexity of the problem exceed the knowledge and experience of a few individuals, success depends on multiple people efficiently aggregating their level of understanding. Senge (1999, pg. 191-257) refers to this process as shared vision and team learning. At its core, this process depends on strong bi-directional communication. Bi-directional is the operative word here, since effective transfer of knowledge among parties is necessary to leverage the insights of all contributors.

We conclude that two focal points (and skills) are necessary to enable this level of communication:

1. **Focus on understanding challenges before pursuing solutions.** Partial understanding of the problem space is a risk that expands with scope and complexity, and is a root cause of sub-optimal solutions. While solution conjectures can be useful ways to explore the problem, it is important that these conjectures be regarded as temporary hypotheses. Premature attachment to solutions frequently turns into either-or debates about solutions. Conversely, conversations about the problem are more likely to "fill in the gaps" and expand the comprehension of all parties.

2. **Keep context in the forefront.** Few observations or conclusions are truly universal. Yet many discussions in systems development gravitate toward generalization and abstraction. It is vital to keep the context of a discussion, the conditions and situations which motivate point of view and behavior, in the forefront. This is one of the drivers behind (Clements et al, 2001) use of quality attribute *scenarios* as the vehicle for architecture evaluation instead of quality attributes. The former preserves essential information about context which the latter loses in generalization.

Sense of urgency is the primary opposing force for better understanding of context and challenges. A strong perception exists that significant time savings are possible by moving quickly through the problem comprehension stage. This perception exists because there are many places where this is true. When today's problem is very similar to yesterday's problem and viable solution, an incremental solution is often valid. We don't need to relearn how to drive the car every day.

Yet, when the problem context or challenges change, these assumptions can break down. A U.S. citizen, used to driving a car with automatic transmission on familiar roads may discover that they need to drive a car with manual transmission on unfamiliar roads in England. Driving to the left side of a busy roundabout, operating the clutch with their left foot while shifting with their left hand might be just enough of a problem shift to lead to a significant increase in risk.

So how do you know? The answer lies in a lesson we all were taught as children by our parents: "Look both ways before crossing." When facing a new systems development engagement, it is better to treat it initially as complex and dangerous (and take some time to identify contexts and challenges) before concluding that the problem is straightforward and tractable. In general, there can be a lot more pain and suffering involved in not looking both ways before crossing and being wrong.

FUTURE RESEARCH DIRECTIONS

There are a number of areas of future research which are motivated by a systems development approach based on "the architecture of the problem." First, much of the current problem-solution co-evolution research is focused on smaller scale design problems. A significant sample size of research subjects is needed for valid comparative analysis, and the protocol method calls for detailed observation of these subjects. However, it is unclear whether the findings from studying smaller scale problems necessarily scale to larger design problems. In smaller problems, there may be a greater likelihood that the subject(s) will intuitively recognize solutions from prior experience which fit the problem.

Second, more research is needed to validate the relationships between goals, challenges, requirements and architecture decisions. Historically, requirements engineering translates system goals into functional requirements, while architecture focuses on the non-functional requirements. However, as de Boor and van Vliet (2008, pg. 549) assert, there is no essential difference between architecturally significant requirements and architectural design decisions. Research is needed into how decisions derived from functional and non-functional requirements should get reconciled. Challenges potentially are a unifying force, which enable requirements and architecture decisions to be resolved in a way that is more consistent with the system and its contexts.

Third, Beck (2002) describes Test-Driven Development (TDD) as a change to the software development process in which tests for features are designed and implemented before the features themselves. Beck asserts that this approach increases quality in two ways: a) complete and valid tests are defined for all features, and b) it forces developers to think through how consumers see the interface to a capability. ATAM, as described by Kazman et al (2000) is a method for using quality attribute scenarios to evaluate the suitability of an architecture. In commercial practice, ATAM is most commonly used as a method for evaluating an architecture for an implemented system, or a nearly-completed architecture for a new system. In both cases, the highest impact architecture decisions have been hardened, and several downstream decisions either depend, or are constrained by them. As a result, significant

issues uncovered by the ATAM process are often difficult, expensive or risky to correct. For software development, TDD introduces the notion of "specifying tests before development" then using early and continuous testing to improve quality. An equivalent approach for incrementally validating architecture decisions would help to find flaws with early decisions while it is still economical to correct them. The critical challenge with this notion is the fact that architecture decisions typically have more cross-dependencies than development, and this makes incremental verification of partial architectures more difficult.

Finally, current approaches to architecture focus primarily on a static view of the system with respect to its environment. Dynamic modeling currently tends to focus on internal behavior, such as timing and finite state models. Senge (1990) wrote:

Systems thinking teaches us that there are two types of complexity - the 'detail complexity' of many variables, and the 'dynamic complexity' when 'cause and effect' are not close in time and space and obvious interventions do not produce expected outcomes.

Given the emergence of systems-of-systems architecture, the importance of understanding the sensitivity of a particular system's architecture to the contexts in its external environment would be useful.

CONCLUSION

Traditional system development calls for architecture to focus on the solution: what the key components are and how they collaborate to satisfy stated requirements. This approach is effective when the problem complexity is manageable and well-understood reference architectures or suitable prior solutions to these types of problems are readily available. However, as problems grow in scope and complexity, the risks associated with this approach increase.

Five themes, which have appeared in the architecture literature during the past 10 years, combine to create a new approach to architecture. These themes include: architecture rationale, challenges, problem-solution co-evolution, contexts, and systems-of-systems. Figure 4 shows an object diagram which illustrates the relationships among these themes.

Together, these five themes emphasize synthesis and push architecture's primary focus outside of the scope of the system being developed. As Russell Ackoff emphasized, they view the system as a component part which is called on to overcome obstacles and create value in its containing contexts. This shift in focus is equally significant and valid for enterprise, systems, and software architecture.

We refer to this shift as "the architecture of the problem" because of its primary emphasis on understanding the obstacles, risks, tradeoffs, and value perceptions within the contexts where the target system will live. This is beyond business analysis and requirements engineering. Like business analysis, it lives in the problem domains. Like requirements engineering, its focus is on formulating the critical decisions which will drive systems development. But to supplement both, it focuses on challenges in the contexts where they matter. It forces comprehension and prioritization of these challenges to ensure that the earliest architecture decisions address and tradeoffs favor the most significant challenges.

Figure 4. Architecture of the problem object model

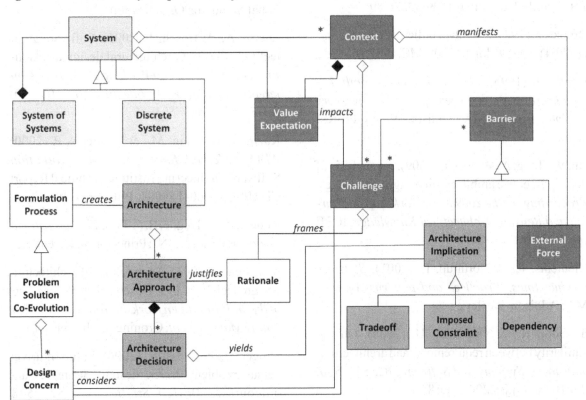

REFERENCES

Ackoff, R. (1999). *Ackoff's best: His classic writings on management*. Marblehead, MA: John Wiley & Sons Publishing.

Alexander, C. (1979). *A timeless way of building*. New York, NY: Oxford University Press.

Alfred, C. (2005). Product strategy and architecture. *Microsoft Architecture Journal, 5*, 33–39.

Alfred, C. (2010). Multiple-context systems: A new frontier in architecture. *Microsoft Architecture Journal, 23*, 26–31.

Beck, K. (2002). *Test driven development: By example*. Boston, MA: Addison-Wesley Professional.

Boehm, B., & Ross, R. (1989). Theory W: Software project management: Principles and examples. *IEEE Transactions on Software Engineering, 15*(7), 902–916. doi:10.1109/32.29489

Brooks, F. (1987). No silver bullet. *IEEE Computer, 20*(4), 10–19. doi:10.1109/MC.1987.1663532

Brooks, F. (1995). *The mythical man-month: Essays on software engineering, (2nd anniversary edition)*. Boston, MA: Addison-Wesley Professional.

Bu, W., Tang, A., & Han, J. (2009). An analysis of decision-centric architectural design approaches. *Proceedings of the 2009 ICSE Workshop on Sharing and Reusing Architectural Knowledge*, ICSE (pp. 33-40).

Clements, P., & Northrup, L. (2001). *Software product lines: Practices and patterns*. Boston, MA: Addison-Wesley.

de Boor, R., & van Vliet, H. (2008). On the similarity between requirements and architecture. *Journal of Systems and Software, 82*, 544–550. doi:10.1016/j.jss.2008.11.185

Dorst, K., & Cross, N. (2001). Creativity in the design process: Co-evolution of problem-solution. *Design Studies, 22*, 425–437. doi:10.1016/S0142-694X(01)00009-6

Fisher, R., Ury, W., & Patton, B. (1991). *Getting to yes: Negotiating agreement without giving in* (2nd ed.). New York, NY: Penguin Books.

Fowler, M. (2002). *Patterns of enterprise application architecture*. Boston, MA: Addison-Wesley.

Garland, D., & Shaw, M. (1994). An introduction to software architecture (pp. 1-39). Carnegie Mellon University Technical Report, CMU-CS-94-166.

Greenfield, J., Short, K., Cook, S., & Kent, S. (2004). *Software factories: Assembling applications with patterns, models, frameworks, and tools*. Indianapolis, IN: Wiley.

ISO. IEC 42010. (2007). *Systems and software engineering: Architectural description*. International Standards Organization.

Jansen, A., & Bosch, J. (2005). Software architecture as a set of architectural design decisions. *Proceedings of the 5th Working IEEE/IFIP Conference on Software Architecture*, (pp. 109-120). IEEE Software.

Kazman, R., Klein, M., & Clements, P. (2000). *ATAM: Method for architecture evaluation*. Software Engineering Institute Technical Report, CMU/SEI-2000-TR-004, Pittsburgh, PA.

Kepner, C., & Tregoe, B. (1981). *The new rational manager*. Princeton, NJ: Princeton Research Press.

Kruchten, P. (2004). An ontology of architectural design decisions. In J. Bosch (Ed.), *Proceedings of the 2nd Groningen Workshop on Software Variability Management*, Groningen, NL, (pp. 54-61).

Kruger, C., & Cross, N. (2006). Solution driven versus problem driven design: Strategies and outcomes. *Design Studies, 27*, 527–548. doi:10.1016/j.destud.2006.01.001

Lane, J., & Valerdi, R. (2010). Accelerating system of systems engineering understanding and optimization through lean enterprise principles. *4th Annual IEEE Systems Conference* (pp. 196-201). San Diego, CA: IEEE Systems.

Maier, M. (1998). Architecting principles for systems-of-systems. *Systems Engineering*, *1*(4), 267–284. doi:10.1002/(SICI)1520-6858(1998)1:4<267::AID-SYS3>3.0.CO;2-D

Maier, M., & Rechtin, E. (2009). *The art of systems architecting* (3rd ed.). Boca Raton, FL: CRC Press.

Senge, P. (1990). *The fifth discipline: The art & practice of the learning organization.*

Sessions, r. (2009). *The it complexity crisis: danger and opportunity.* Retrieved September 3, 2011, from http://www.objectwatch.com/whitepapers/ITComplexityWhitePaper.pdf

Software Engineering Institute. (2011). *Software product lines.* Retrieved October 30, 2011, from http://www.sei.cmu.edu/productlines/

SWEBOK. (2004). *The software engineering body of knowledge* (Abran, A., Moore, J., Borque, P., & Dupuis, R., Eds.). Los Alamitos, CA: IEEE Computer Society.

Tang, A., Aleti, A., Burge, J., & van Vliet, H. (2010). What makes software design effective. *Design Studies*, *31*, 614–640. doi:10.1016/j.destud.2010.09.004

Tang, A., Han, J., & Vasa, R. (2009). Software architecture design reasoning: A case for improved methodology support. *IEEE Software*, *26*, 43–49. doi:10.1109/MS.2009.46

van der Linden, F., Schmidt, K., & Rommes, E. (2007). *Software product lines in action: The best industrial practice in product line engineering.* Berlin, Germany: Springer.

Waldo, J., Wyant, J., Wolrath, A., & Kendall, S. (1994). *A note on distributed computing.* Sun Microsystems Laboratories Inc., SMLI TR-94-29, 1994. Retrieved July 9, 2011, from http://citeseerx.ist.psu.edu/viewdoc/download?doi=10.1.1.48.7969-&rep=rep1&type=pdf

KEY TERMS AND DEFINITIONS

Analysis: One of two complementary techniques for understanding a system; it is the act of decomposing bigger things into smaller pieces to understand *how* they fit together, has been the dominant mode of thinking since the Industrial Revolution. Taking an automobile engine apart will show how the pistons, valves, and spark plugs are connected, but will not explain why they are connected that way.

Architecture of the Problem: A process which applies synthesis to view systems development of complex systems with large scope as a system-of-systems which includes the consumers of the system under development, 3rd party supplies of components, regulatory agencies, and the tools, teams, and processes of the system developer. It sees the architecture of this larger system as inseparable from the architecture of the system being developed. In particular, architectural challenges in the context of the larger system are inseparable from the architecture challenges which drive the system being developed.

Architecture of the Solution: A systems development process for defining the components that make up a system, how they are organized, how they behave, and how their behavior is coordinated. This process is driven by the functional and quality requirements previously defined for the system.

Challenge: A situation where one or more limiting factors make it more difficult to satisfy one or more value expectations. Simply put, an architecture challenge is an obstacle or barrier that the system must overcome to provide value.

Context: A collection of stakeholders who share a similar set of perceptions, priorities, and desired outcomes and are subjected to a similar set of forces, in the form of conditions and situations.

Decision Analysis: A method for making decisions, defined by Charles Kepner and Benjamin Tregoe, which organizes objectives into two groups: *musts* are binary objectives used to efficiently disqualify unsatisfactory alternatives, and *wants* are expressions of utility which identify how well each qualifying alternative satisfies each want objective. This method is especially useful in groups, as it does a very good job of providing transparency for the underlying rationale for the decision.

Problem-Solution Co-Evolution: A problem solving technique where a larger problem is initially broken into a set of sub-problems (or challenges), which are addressed individually or in small groups. During the process of finding solutions for specific problems, additional problems are discovered.

Synthesis: One of two complementary techniques for understanding why a system is the way it is. It starts with the system and expands outward to include other systems which include this system, then studies how the target system contributes to these broader systems with a focus on why it has these roles and responsibilities.

System-of-Systems: A collection of complete and independent systems which collaborate indirectly and depend on each other to create emergent value. Inter-bank electronic funds transfer and credit card authorization and settlement networks are common examples of systems-of-systems.

Variability Management: A process of comparing and contrasting expectations and environmental forces across contexts in order to define the similarities and differences in capabilities needed to efficiently deliver sufficient value to each context.

Chapter 14
Using Obstacles for Systematically Modeling, Analysing, and Mitigating Risks in Cloud Adoption

Shehnila Zardari
University of Birmingham, UK

Funmilade Faniyi
University of Birmingham, UK

Rami Bahsoon
University of Birmingham, UK

ABSTRACT

In this chapter, the authors motivate the need for a systematic approach to cloud adoption from the risk perspective. The enormous potential of cloud computing for improved and cost-effective service delivery for commercial and academic purposes has generated unprecedented interest in its adoption. However, a potential cloud user faces numerous risks regarding service requirements, cost implications of failure, and uncertainty about cloud providers' ability to meet service level agreements. Hence, the authors consider two perspectives of a case study to identify risks associated with cloud adoption. They propose a risk management framework based on the principle of GORE (Goal-Oriented Requirements Engineering). In this approach, they liken risks to obstacles encountered while realising cloud user goals, therefore proposing cloud-specific obstacle resolution tactics for mitigating identified risks. The proposed framework shows benefits by providing a principled engineering approach to cloud adoption and empowering stakeholders with tactics for resolving risks when adopting the cloud.

DOI: 10.4018/978-1-4666-2199-2.ch014

1. INTRODUCTION

The ever increasing need for data processing, storage, elastic and unbounded scale of computing infrastructure has provided great thrust for shifting the data and computing operations to the cloud. IBM advocates cloud computing as a cost efficient model for service provision (IBM, 2008). The adoption of cloud computing is gaining momentum because most of the services provided by the cloud are low cost and readily available. The pay- as-you- go structure of the cloud is particularly suited to Small and Medium Enterprises (SME) who have little or no resources for IT services (Biggs, Vidalis,2009).

The growing trend of cloud computing has led many organisations and even individuals to move their computing operations, data, and/or commissioning their e-services to the cloud. Moving to the cloud has reduced the cost of computing and operations due to resource sharing, virtualization, less maintenance cost, lower IT infrastructure cost, lower software cost, expertise utilization and sharing etc. (Miller, 2008). For example, the New York Times managed to convert 4TB of scanned images containing 11 million articles into PDF files, which took 24 hours for conversion and used 100 Amazon EC2 Instances (Gottfrid, 2007). Such relatively quick conversion would be very expensive if done in-house. The term cloud computing may simply refer to different applications over the Internet or the hardware shared between different users (Armburst et al, 2010). Buyya et al have defined cloud:

A Cloud is a type of parallel and distributed system consisting of a collection of inter-connected and virtualized computers that are dynamically provisioned and presented as one or more unified computing resources based on service level agreements established through negotiation between the service provider and consumer (Buyya et al, 2008).

In a cloud, hardware/software are shared and utilized as services at lower cost. Many services are now offered in the realm of cloud computing. These are:

- **Infrastructure as a Service (IaaS):** A model in which an organization outsources the equipment required to perform operations like storage, hardware, servers etc. Cloud service provider provides all the hardware needed for operations and is responsible for maintaining it. The client pays for what he uses. Amazon's Elastic Compute is an example of such a service.
- **Platform as a Service (PaaS):** Cloud Service Provider provides a platform to the user on which a user can develop an application. The applications are delivered to the users through cloud service provider's infrastructure. Coghead and Google App Engine are examples of PaaS.
- **Software as a Service (SaaS):** Delivers a single application through the browser to thousands of users. Users are not required to invest on purchasing servers or software licensing. Payment is made on the basis of the data transferred and some fixed rent. Google App Engine is a representative example of SaaS.

This chapter is structured as follows. We motivate the need for a requirements engineering framework for cloud adoption in Section 2. Risks that were identified from different cloud service providers' SLAs are presented in Section 3. Section 4 introduces goal-oriented requirements engineering for the process of cloud adoption. We define obstacles in Section 5 and argue that obstacle analysis should be part of the lifecycle for cloud adoption process. We have modelled a case study with two different perspectives (user and cloud service provider) using goal-oriented approach in Section 6. We have proposed some obstacle resolution tactics which could help in mitigating the risks associated with cloud adoption in Section 7. In Section 8, method for prioritizing goals using the utility theory is explained. Section 9 provides some insight into the related work. We discuss the open problems in Section 10. Section 11 concludes the chapter.

2. BACKGROUND AND MOTIVATION

We looked at a case study of a leading cloud service provider- referred to as *Indus* throughout this paper. The case study revealed that there are many risks associated with cloud adoption. Since the cloud is perceived as a "black box", a user has little or no control over the promises set by cloud's SLAs. For instance, the user mostly cannot negotiate the SLAs with the cloud service provider and hence has to agree with the set terms and conditions.

As an example, Indus sufficiently describes their security mechanisms in the agreement accompanying their SLAs "Indus Web Services Customer Agreement." Interestingly enough, Indus mentions that the nature of communication over the Internet is unpredictable and largely insecure. Given the vulnerability of the Internet, Indus cannot guarantee the security of user's content. While Indus strives for a secure environment, the security responsibility and accountability lie solely on the users and the organisation using the services. In the event of any breach in security requirements, Indus is not entirely liable to the user for any unauthorized access, use, deletion, corruption or destruction of user's contents. The service provider has attempted to win the confidence and trust of the users by publishing the agreement, yet it has failed to ascertain the individual needs of different users. Indus has a shared responsibility environment for the safety of user's contents, where one of the inherent problems with such "joint" responsibility is that it

makes accountability difficult. Referring to SLAs terms and conditions, Indus absolves itself of any responsibility in the wake of anything goes wrong. For instance, Indus recommends customers to encrypt data transferred over the network. There are tradeoffs involved with large data encrypted over the network: this will lead to higher processing time, which might affect cloud performance and consequently violate the promises set in the SLA. In fact, sending a disk containing the encrypted data by post has been stated to be more effective when the data volume is large (Ambrust et al, 2009). Such transfer of disks through post involves a lot of human efforts and therefore the system cannot be termed as automated. Despite the promised dynamic elasticity of cloud architecture, resources continue to be scarce. E.g. enhancing security provision may cause performance bottleneck. As a result, the promised Quality of Service (QoS) can't be often met as the SLA terms and conditions stipulate.

We call for a novel requirements engineering methodology for cloud adoption, which could assist businesses in screening, selecting cloud service providers and negotiating their services and qualities of provision. The framework aims at helping businesses screen, match, and negotiate their requirements against cloud services' provision. The framework will also assist in the problem of managing the tradeoffs associated with matches and mismatches of users' requirements against cloud's provision. Such provision aims at objectively evaluating the strategic decisions, satisfaction of the technical and operational goals, cost and value of such decisions and the tradeoffs involved in moving to the cloud. Despite rapid growth of cloud use, there is a general lack of systematic methodologies aiming at its adoption. Decisions regarding the selection of cloud service providers are made on ad hoc basis based on recommendations or on the reputation of the service provider. The lack of such methodologies exposes businesses considering the cloud to unpredictable risks. It would be expensive to get "locked in" with a wrong cloud. Evaluating pre adoption choices at early stages is cost-effective strategy to mitigate risks of probable losses due to wrong or unjustified selection decisions. Furthermore, the framework aims at assisting users in assessing their requirements against cloud provision. Due to the dynamic evolution of the cloud, mismatches may occur between what is required by the user and what is provided by the cloud provider. The framework will assess the suitability of cloud service providers by exploring mismatches, managing risks, and suggesting possible tradeoffs. We use goal-oriented approach for modelling cloud provision. The expected beneficiaries of the work are small to large businesses, educational institutes and even individuals, who wish to exploit the cloud. Such work is novel and bridges an important gap in making the process of cloud adoption more transparent, systematic and user oriented. It would be worth noting that ongoing research on cloud selection has addressed the problem of dynamic selection of the cloud services with respect to QoS (Goscinski, Brock, 2010). (Khajeh-Hosseini et al, 2010) is a recent research to facilitate users in cloud migration but this research doesn't involve refining and elaborating user requirements. We proposed a lifecycle based on goal-oriented requirements engineering for cloud adoption in (Zardari, Bahsoon, 2011). This book chapter is an extension of our previous work. We have refined the cloud adoption lifecycle and have introduced the notion of obstacles. We have also defined some concrete and abstract obstacle resolution tactics.

3. RISKS IDENTIFIED FROM DIFFERENT CLOUDS AND THEIR IMPLICATIONS

Risks that were identified by looking at the SLAs of different cloud service providers are shown in Table 1. The information presented in Table 1 has been collected after inspection of SLAs and white papers of several leading cloud providers such as Amazon Web Services, Google App Engine and Microsoft Azure. Risks could be classified into various areas of concern (e.g. network, environment etc). For each identified risk, we provide an impact assessment of the occurrence of the risk. We believe that the identified areas, potential risks and impact assessment is representative of the state-of-the-art in cloud service provision.

Although, cloud service providers have tried to win the confidence of the users by either publishing their whitepapers, web service agreements or by providing the details regarding their cloud service on their website yet most of the cloud service providers have failed to take the responsibility of the users' contents in case of provider's inability to live up to promises to the user. SLAs of most of the cloud service providers absolve them from any responsibility should anything happen to users' contents. Signing a contract with such cloud service providers can be a risky business. It is evident from Table 1 that many risks will eventually lead to financial losses for a business. To minimise the risk of being locked-in with a cloud provider who is unable to meet the needs of the users; the proposed framework informs cloud provider selection on a systematic and sound framework.

4. CLOUD- BASED GOAL ORIENTED REQUIREMENTS ENGINEERING

The specification of users' requirements is the first step towards selecting an appropriate cloud service provider. Boehm estimates that the late corrections of requirements errors could cost 200 times as much as corrections during requirements engineering phases (Boehm, 1981). Though the Boehm's argument is related to the case of projects and software developed for relatively defined set of requirements, it would be argued that late rectification of unwise selection may lead

Table 1. Risks identified from cloud service providers SLAs

Area	Description of Risk	Impact Assessment
Network	IP spoofing Port scanning Packet sniffing	Data leakage Financial losses Customer trust
Environmental	Fire Electrical Failure Temperature inside the data centre	Hardware damage Service delivery Customer trust Business reputation Huge financial losses
Technical	Integration Risk Insecure interfaces and APIs Shared technology issue Weak encryption of data in transit Incomplete data deletion Resource exhaustion	More investment on company's infrastructure Huge financial losses Data leakage Company's reputation Customer's trust Service delivery
Physical Access	Unauthorized access to the data centre Malicious insider	Financial losses Customer's trust Business reputation Data leakage Hardware damage
Business Risks	Compliance challenges Natural disasters Data Loss or leakage Unknown risk profile Malicious insiders SLA clauses containing business risks Incomplete data deletion Long term viability Interoperability Resource exhaustion	Industry certifications Company reputation Customer trust Closure of business High financial losses Going bankrupt Company's secret made public Financial losses Service delivery
Legal	Risks from change of jurisdiction SLA clauses containing business risks Loss of governance Unknown risk profile Data Recovery and investigation	Financial Losses Customer trust Business reputation Service delivery

to higher cost, which could be disproportional to the benefits of using the cloud and will place such investment into risk.

Our approach starts with high-level goals. Initially when any organization decides to move to the cloud, the goals are general expression of the requirements, whether these are strategic requirements, functional and/or non-functional. The higher level goals (such as secure payment transactions) are more stable than low level ones (such as Secure Socket Layer (SSL) Technology). Defining goals is the first step of requirements elicitation in software engineering. Pamela Zave in her research defines requirements engineering

as something which is "concerned with the real world goals for functions of and constraints on software systems" (Zave, 1997). A goal is a target that a system must achieve. Goals are generally more stable than the requirements to achieve them (Anton et al, 1994). Goals cover different types of issues - both functional and non-functional. The functional goals can be associated with the services to be provided whereas non-functional goals can be associated with the quality of service e.g. security, reliability, availability etc (Lamsweerde, 2001). Goals represent the roots for detecting conflicts among requirements and for resolving them in time (Lamsweerde et al, 1998). GORE uses goals for eliciting, elaborating, analysing, documenting, modifying and refining the requirements (Lamsweerde, 2004). We specify the requirements of the stakeholders in the form of goals.

To make a sensible decision for selecting a cloud service provider, businesses require a methodology which could help them make a choice. In conventional software development, the requirements engineering basically consists of eliciting stakeholders' needs, refining the goals into non-conflicting requirements, followed by validating these requirements with stakeholders (Nuseibeh, Easterbrook, 2000). The main objective of the requirements engineer is to ensure that the requirements specifications meet stakeholders' needs and represent a clear description of the cloud services that are to be adopted. Stakeholders' requirements play a deciding / leading role in cloud service provider's selection.

5. OBSTACLES FOR MITIGATING RISKS IN CLOUD ADOPTION PROCESS

We recently proposed a methodology which could help users to adopt cloud services (Zardari, Bahsoon, 2011). The methodology is grounded in Goal-Oriented Requirements Engineering. The initial work did not provide the means to resolve obstacles for achieving goals. Requirements engineering is concerned with elicitation of high-level goals that are to be achieved by the system-to-be. The high-level goals are refined into low level goals which can be operationalised. Classically in GORE we operationalise goals by assigning them to the agents such as humans, devices and software (in our case, the agent can be either cloud service provider or any particular service). Sometimes the requirements engineering process results in goals and assumptions about the agent behaviour which is too ideal; some are unlikely to be satisfied by the system. We present techniques to resolve the obstacles in achieving goals. We are defining a

number of abstract and concrete techniques for resolving obstacles which could mitigate risks in the cloud adoption process.

5.1 Obstacle Analysis

First sketch of goals tend to be too ideal (Letier, Lamsweerde, 2004). Such over ideal goals can be violated from time to time due to unexpected behaviour of agents. In KAOS, such exceptional behaviours are called obstacles to goal satisfaction. Obstacles were first proposed by Potts in (Potts, 1995). He identified obstacles for a particular goal by asking different questions. For example: "Can this goal be obstructed, if so, how?" According to Anton (Anton, 1996) while obstacle denote the reason why a goal failed, scenarios determine concrete circumstances under which the goal may fail. KAOS provides well-developed methods for identifying and resolving obstacles (Lamsweerde, Leiter, 2000). Lamsweerde et al recommend that obstacles be identified from leaf-level goals Once identified obstacles can be refined like goals (by AND/OR decomposition). Obstacles can lead to risks. Obstacle resolution will eventually result in minimising potential risks.

5.2 Obstacles in Requirements Engineering Process for Cloud Adoption

We found that there are some obstacles in achieving goals. We have therefore refined the lifecycle for cloud adoption (Zardari, Bahsoon, 2011) by introducing obstacle identification and resolution in the lifecycle (see Figure 1). During the Specify Goals phase the goals are refined and obstacles are generated. Obstacles can be repeatedly refined. The generated obstacles are resolved which result in updating goals. New goal specification may result in new iteration of goal refinement and obstacle identification. It can therefore be said that obstacles analysis and resolution has to be a continual process. Figure 1 shows the life cycle for

Figure 1. Lifecycle for cloud adoption

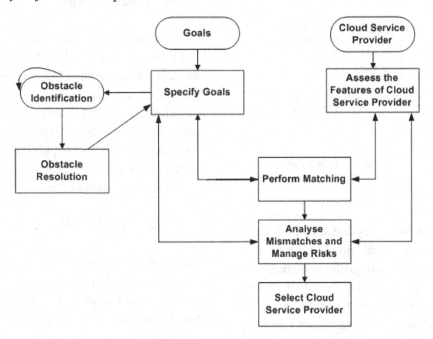

cloud adoption. An obstacle from the perspective of a cloud user can be defined as any hindrance in achieving any goal or the desired properties as set out by the cloud user. Obstacles obstruct the goal such that when the obstacle is true then the goal may not be achieved (Lamsweerde, Leiter, 2000). Suppose a social networking website hosted on cloud wants 24/7 availability. If there is a power outage at the data center of the cloud service provider then the service may not be available and hence power outage will be an obstacle in achieving the goal of 24/7 availability.

We are briefly describing the steps involved in the lifecycle shown in Figure 1. For details read (Zardari, Bahsoon, 2011).

Acquire and Specify Goals

Requirements act as criteria to evaluate cloud service providers. The goals can be divided into three categories (i) strategic or business goals, (ii) high level or core goals, (iii) and low level or operational goals. Strategic goals are concerned with the survival of the enterprise/business. As-

sume that University of Birmingham (UoB) wants to outsource its email services to the cloud in order to reduce cost by 20% in next five years; this is the strategic/business goal of UoB. High Level goals are nothing but core goals described in requirements engineering phase for cloud adoption. Suppose UoB wants that the cloud should be able to handle 500 users during the peak time and provide high level of security; these are high-level goals to be achieved. Operational goals can be encryption of data, password protection, and backup mechanisms etc. Sometimes, operational goals are required to be assessed and evaluated against high level core goals in certain cases. See Figure 2.

We will have to define the acceptance level for each goal as these cannot be completely met; instead they are satisfied to a certain degree within acceptable limits (Mylopoulos et al, 1992). The acceptance interval ranges from target level i.e. the optimum value that users consider to be fully satisfied, to the worst level, i.e. the lowest value of the acceptable interval in which the goal starts to be considered unsatisfied. The goals need

Figure 2. Goal categories

to be prioritized once they are specified, users have to engage in an extensive prioritization process in order to distinguish core goals (i.e. critical needs that should always be satisfied) from desirable goals (i.e. the ones that could be traded off). Section 8 describes the prioritization process for goals.

Obstacle Identification

During the Specify Goals phase obstacles are generated. The obstacles can be recursively refined. Obstacles are identified from the goal graph. It is suggested that obstacles be identified from the terminal goals that are assigned to agents. It is essential that the set of identified obstacles is complete for every goal (at least for high-priority goals). To resolve obstacles we would like to identify as many obstacles as possible for the goals- particularly for high-priority goals. A set of obstacles $O_1, \ldots, O_n$ is complete for goal G if the following condition is true:

$$\{\neg O_1, \ldots, \neg O_n\} \models G$$

This condition means that if none of the identified obstacles occur than the goal is satisfied. Figure 3 and Figure 4 show the obstacles identified from the case study.

Obstacle Resolution

Obstacle resolution tactics are applied to resolve the identified obstacles. The selection of a specific obstacle resolution tactic depends on the likelihood of the obstacle occurrence and the impact of such occurrence. The goal/obstacle loop may terminate once the obstacle that remain are thought to be acceptable without applying any resolution tactics. Table 2 shows some obstacle resolution tactics in the process of cloud adoption.

Cloud Service Provider

Once the generic goals have been defined the search for potential cloud service provider will start. At initial stage goals are kept generic so that the search for a cloud service provider is not limited by unnecessary constraints. At initial phase of cloud service provider identification it should be ensured whether the cloud satisfies the critical goal; total cost of ownership match the available budget, reputation of service provider with other users is compared and that the service provider is willing to participate in collaborative partnership etc.

Perform Matching

This phase involves gathering sufficient information about the cloud service provider and its services in order to assign the satisfaction scores to operational goals. Based on the results of matching the evaluation team can aggregate individual satisfaction score (i.e. how the cloud satisfies each operational goal) into global satisfaction scores (i.e. how the cloud satisfies the set of operational goals). Therefore, it is possible to compare cloud service providers and then, inform the decision making process. The matching process involves analysis of cloud service provider satisfaction and further discussion with users to determine whether or not a particular cloud sufficiently satisfies their needs. The matching of a particu-

Figure 3. Goal tree of obstacles to achieve security in an Indus Cloud

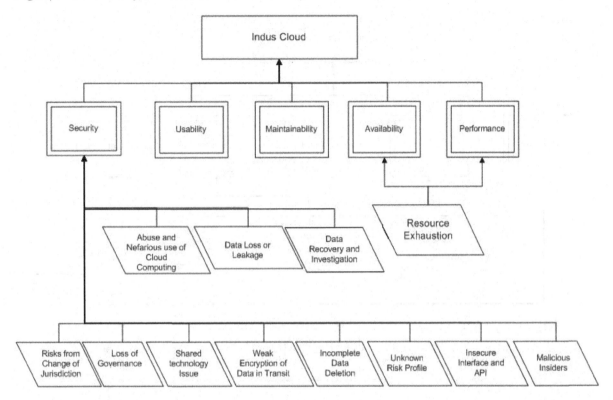

lar cloud is considered satisfactory if the cloud satisfies the operational goals within acceptable range. The information regarding features and service provisions of different clouds can be accessed through various sources like cloud white papers, SLAs, available benchmarks, the Internet, reviews, evaluations and recommendations of users, experiences etc. After looking at the features provided by the cloud service providers, the user may come up with new set of requirements that were not identified during the initial step. The examination of the cloud service providers' features is a better technique to refine and understand how high-level requirements of the stakeholders can be actually satisfied. As cloud services and SLAs are designed to satisfy the generic requirements of the market, some users' requirements may not be satisfied and therefore users should be prepared to engage in extensive process of requirements prioritisation and negotiation.

Analyse Mismatches and Manage Risks

A systematic approach is needed for the evaluation team to understand the effects of mismatches, analyse conflicts between goals, explore tradeoffs and manage risks. In the context of cloud service provider's selection, risks are defined as unacceptable outcomes, generally caused as a result of conflicting goals, mismatches and obstacles. Given that mismatches represent non-adherence of cloud to operational goals and conflict arise when satisfying one goal damages the satisfaction of another goal, we deduce that risks arise when the loss caused by unsatisfied goal is intolerable. A fundamental issue in handling mismatches is the capacity to systematically structure tradeoffs. The tradeoffs analysis forms the basis of risk management strategy. The objectives of risk management strategy are to understand and handle risk events prior to their conversion to threats. Risk

Figure 4. Portion of the goal tree for Smart Bank

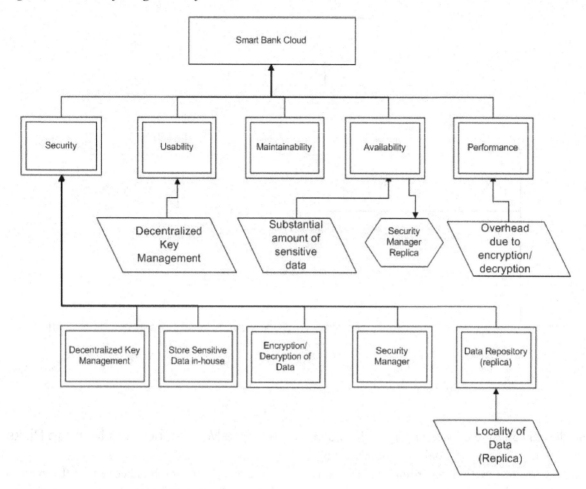

Table 2. Obstacle resolution tactics for cloud adoption

Category	Short Description	Obstacle Resolution Tactic	Example
Obstacle Prevention	Avoid the obstacle	**Tactic1:** Add another goal to prevent obstacle **Tactic2:** Improve/Negotiate SLA.	Figure 5 shows a goal which cannot be achieved if the data is stored outside home country. Figure 7 and Figure 8 show the resolution technique for such obstacles.
Cloud Service Substitution	Assign the responsibility of obstructed goal to another cloud	**Tactic3:** Transfer goal to another cloud **Tactic4:** Split goal among multiple clouds	Figure 9 show the obstacle and Figure 10 shows obstacle resolution by using tactic 3 Figure 11 show the obstacle resolution using tactic 4.
Goal Weakening	Weaken the obstructed goal specification	**Tactic 5:** Weaken goal objective function Relax requirements Relax the degree of satisfaction	Figure 12 shows the obstacle resolution using tactic 5.

management helps in successfully selecting and integrating the chosen cloud service provider. Risk management process has three steps: risk identification, risk analysis and risk mitigation. Risk mitigation action may cover options such as: change goals, negotiate cloud services features, or choose other alternatives. There is no one solution for all the risks; therefore, decision for the best risk mitigation strategy relies on the judgments and experience of the evaluation team.

Cloud Service Provider Selection

The ultimate objective of this phase is to choose the "optimal cloud." By optimal selection we mean that the selected cloud not necessarily needs to be optimal but satisfying. A satisfying cloud is the one that sufficiently satisfies the set of goals defined by stakeholders, where as an optimal cloud aims to maximize the satisfaction of goals at any cost. Factors to assess the worthiness of each cloud service provider for selection are value, cost, and risk. Cost represents the monetary investment, time and effort. The overall merit of a cloud based system is the combined measure of the value, cost, and risk. Value refers to ascertaining level of happiness of the stakeholders if a given alternative successfully satisfies the desired goals. Notably this is related to the priority stakeholders have assigned to goals. The risk is assessed using goal mismatches, conflicting goals and involves risk scenario elements.

6. CASE STUDY

We have modelled two perspectives (the cloud service provider and cloud user) of a case study. Figure 3 and Figure 4 show the goal tree of the obstacles that have been identified the case study. For the purpose of this case study we have adopted the following conventions. Double edged rectangles show the goals, parallelograms are

the obstacles in achieving some of the goals and hexagons represent an agent. An AND-refinement is represented by an arrow with a small circle connecting the subgoals contributing to the parent goal. An OR-refinement is graphically represented by multiple arrows pointing to the same goal.

The objective of modelling two different perspectives of a case study is to show obstacles at the service providers' and the user level. Cloud service provider may have claimed about high security in their cloud but a close look at their whitepapers revealed that the risks associated with the adoption of such cloud are imminent. After looking at the Indus Web Services Customer Agreement and Indus white papers we identified many risks associated with adoption of Indus cloud. For the purpose of simplicity we have not modelled all the risks identified. The goal graph of the Indus informs users of the possible risks that may occur due to adoption of this cloud. The goal tree of Smart Bank helps us in introducing some obstacle resolution tactics which may mitigate the risks associated with adopting the wrong cloud service provider.

6.1 Goal Tree of Indus

Figure 3 shows the goal tree of Indus cloud. Many obstacles were identified to achieve security while migrating to the Indus cloud. The goal tree of Indus cloud informs users of the potential risks that are involved with Indus cloud adoption.

6.2 Smart Bank Goal Tree

Recently a cloud architecture evaluation method was proposed by Faniyi et al in (Faniyi et al, 2011). A case study of a Smart bank was presented where the bank decides to adopt cloud services to deliver a robust, scalable and on-demand service provisioning for the risk management aspect of its business. The architecture proposed was evaluated using Architectural Tradeoffs Analysis Method

(ATAM) (Clements et al, 2001) incorporating dynamic analysis via implied scenario generation and was named as ATMIS.

Smart Bank policies prohibit some of the sensitive data from being hosted on any server outside its country of operation. As cloud acts as a black box and the user has little or no knowledge about the location of the data centre; this pose a threat to Smart Bank's contents. SLA clauses often make no mention of any sub-contracting of data centres. Data from Linode, a leading Cloud service Provider was unavailable to the users for about 20 minutes due to a power outage at Hurricane Electric which owns the data centre where Linode stores data (CloudHarmony, 2011). The outage at Hurricane Electric was completely outside the control of Linode. Such sub-contracting poses a grave threat to Smart Bank's policies. See Figure 5.

Goal 1

Goal Achieve [Store Sensitive Data in home country]

Category Security

Definition Store Sensitive data in the country of operation.

---

7. RESOLVING OBSTACLES IN THE PROCESS OF CLOUD ADOPTION

By Looking at both the perspectives of the case study i.e. Indus (see Section 6.1) and Smart Bank (see Section 6.2) we will try to map the requirements of the user with the features of Indus. We are proposing some concrete and abstract obstacle resolution tactics which could help the user in minimizing the risks associated with cloud adoption. Table 2 shows the obstacle resolution tactics. Some of the obstacles cannot be fully resolved. We can set the priority of resolving the obstacles by quantifying the value of the obstacles. Every obstacle has a value. The value of an obstacle is the product of the likelihood of the obstacle occurrence and the consequence of that obstacle. As obstacles lead to risks therefore they should be quantified in order to know the damage that may be caused due to the resulting risks.

$$V(O) = L(O) * C(O) \qquad (1)$$

where $L(O)$ is the likelihood that obstacle O will occur, $C(O)$ is the cost/consequence, and $V(O)$ is the value of obstacle O. For simplicity we will rate each on 1 to 4 scales. The larger the number

Figure 5. Obstacle for achieving goal 1

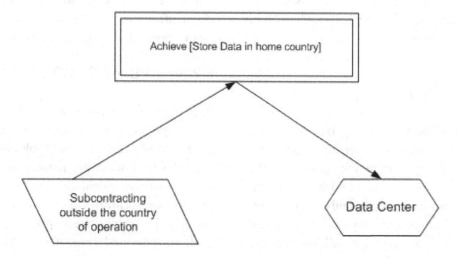

the larger would be the consequence or likelihood. Priority for resolving the obstacle can be established by using the matrix shown in Figure 6. Equation 1 is based on Boehm et al equation for quantifying the risks in a software development process (Boehm, DeMarco, 1997).

It may be possible that the obstacle resolution for a particular obstacle is more expensive than the value of the damage that may be caused due to the obstacle itself. Some obstacle may be resolved to a certain degree but may not be fully resolved. Table 2 defines some obstacle resolution tactics in the process of cloud adoption.

7.1 Obstacle Prevention

Obstacle prevention strategy resolves the obstacle by adding a new goal. By adding a new goal obstacle occurrence can be avoided.

Tactic 1: Goal tree of Indus revealed an obstacle of resource exhaustion. The same obstacle was identified in Smart Bank case study where the sensitive information is stored in-house. If the amount of sensitive information is significant than we have to move sensitive

Figure 6. Matrix for quantifying the value of obstacles

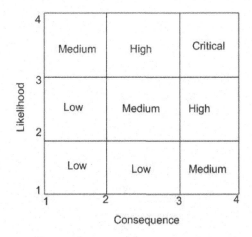

data to the cloud. Smart Bank can store the sensitive data in the cloud in encrypted form using Trusted Platform Module (TPM) (Santos et al, 2009). Using TPM is a new goal which has been added to the system for avoiding the obstacle. This will prevent Smart Bank from the maintenance of data repository in-house. See Figure 7.

Tactic 2: Let's take Linode example where the data centre has been subcontracted to Hurricane Electric. In this situation if Smart Bank wants to exploit the services of Linode then the SLA should clearly state that the data center is not owned by Linode. SLA should also mention the location of the data center as Smart Bank does not want its data to be stored outside its country of operation. This will allow the user to make decision by keeping their requirements satisfied. Negotiation of SLA is another goal which has been added to the goal tree to prevent the obstacle shown in Figure 5. See Figure 8 for the resolution to this obstacle and Figure 9 for the goal tree of this tactic.

7.2 Cloud Service Substitution

Tactic 3: Smart Bank wants its system to be available 24/7. We assume that Bank also wants to scale up when there is increased traffic and scale down when the demand is low. Nallur et al have proposed a self-optimising architecture (Nallur et al, 2009) where the website can scale up and scale down according to the traffic. Assume that when the traffic is low the website is using cloud C1 and when the traffic is high the website starts using cloud C2. This strategy resolves the obstacle of non-availability of the website when the traffic is high. Smart Bank can sign up to the services of different clouds for different time. See Figure 10.

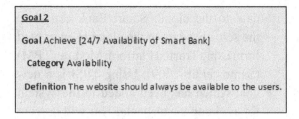

Goal 2

Goal Achieve [24/7 Availability of Smart Bank]

Category Availability

Definition The website should always be available to the users.

Tactic 4: This tactic consists of splitting a goal assigned into subgoals, so that every subgoal can be assigned to a different cloud to satisfy it. Application of this tactic may lead to the

introduction of some new clouds to satisfy the subgoals. As web services hosted on the cloud evolve with the passage of time, their requirements evolve accordingly. Smart Bank is a new bank with fewer customers. With the passage of time the bank will become more popular and it will be critical for Smart Bank to be highly stable, secure and available. Downtime of Smart Bank is unacceptable to its customers. Such web applications which have become popular

Figure 7. Obstacle resolution tactic1

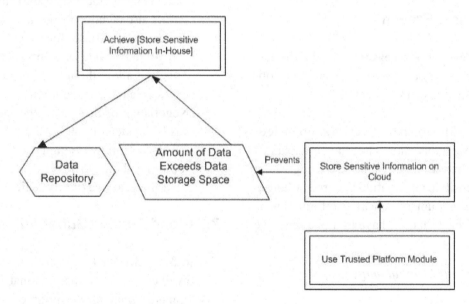

Figure 8. Obstacle resolution tactic 2

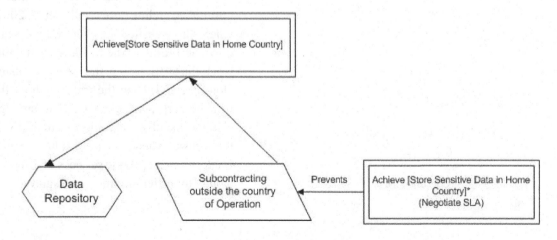

Figure 9. Goal tree of tactic 2

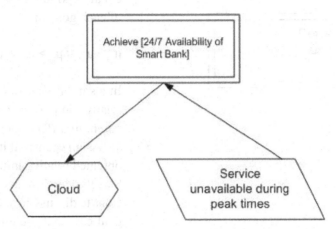

Figure 10. Obstacle resolution tactic 3

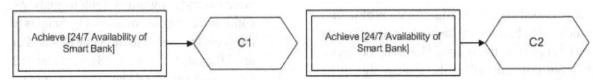

among the users need to adapt their architecture with the growing demand. Assume that the data centre D1 was used by Smart Bank but as the demand grew Smart Bank has to lease another data centre to avoid any chances of unavailability to the user. The SLA can be negotiated to lease another data centre from a cloud different than the current one so that data centres D1 and D2 are owned by two different cloud service providers. See Figure 11.

Figure 11. Obstacle resolution tactic 4

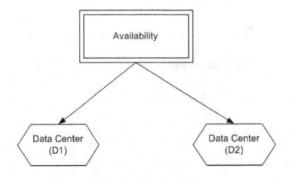

7.3 Goal Weakening

Tactic 5: This tactic involves weakening the goal definition or the degree of satisfaction. As an example UoB wants the response time for its email service to be 10 seconds but agrees to settle for 12 seconds if the cloud service provider C1 is unable to guarantee a response time of 10 seconds. The satisfaction degree of the goal was relaxed to avoid the elimination of a potential cloud service provider for service provision. See Figure 12.

8. GOAL PRIORITIZATION

Goal prioritization is a core activity for resolving the obstacles in the requirements engineering process for cloud adoption. Stakeholders engage in extensive prioritization process to distinguish core goals (i.e. critical goals that should always be satisfied) from the desirable goals (i.e. goals that

Figure 12. Obstacle resolution tactic 5

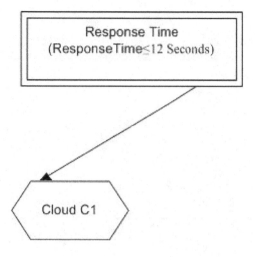

can be traded off). There might be some obstacles which could be avoided due to their significantly lower impact on the system. However, obstacles that can critically affect the system should be resolved with high priority. In the goal prioritization process goals are assigned weights according to the stakeholders' preferences. We describe an approach which helps in prioritizing the goals and obstacles. The highest level of goal refinement tree is level 0; the next level of subgoals is level 1 and so on. We assign the weights to goals in each level, so that the sum of the weights of goals in each level is 1.

Step 1: Obtain the relative importance of the goals. Consider the goal tree of smart bank. In level 1 we have five goals g_1, g_2, g_3, g_4, g_5 and now we want to know their relative value. Rank the importance of each goal. Smart Bank prefers security over everything else. After comparing and obtaining the relative importance of the level 1 goals, we have that:

$$g_1 > g_4 \approx g_5 > g_3 > g_2$$

This implies that g_1 is the most important goal followed by g_4 and g_5 (g_4 and g_5 are of equal importance), g_3, and g_2. The weight μ of each goal is:

$$\mu_{g1} > \mu_{g4} \approx \mu_{g5} > \mu_{g3} > \mu_{g2}$$

In a similar way stakeholders compare the relative importance of goals of the same parent in different levels.

Step 2: Assign each goal its weight based on the obtained relative importance.

Stakeholders' engage in brain storming sessions to discuss how the satisfaction of each goal can contribute to the achievement of strategic objectives. These sessions lead to an agreement among stakeholders about their priorities and assigning weights to goals. We continue the process of assigning weights to the goals belonging to the same parent. For level 0 goals (see Figure 13) we assign 0.3 to g_1 as security was deemed most important by the stakeholders. Since g_4 and g_5 have an equal importance therefore they have been assigned the same weight. The weights have been assigned to the goals keeping in view their relative importance.

Step 3: Obtain composed weights for offspring goals.

The final weight of the goal is called a composed weight. Composed weight is the product of the weight of each goal with the weights of all the parent goals. We can obtain the composed weight for the obstacles $\neg g_2$, $\neg g_4$, $\neg g_5$ and $\neg g_{1.5}$, so that:

$$\mu g_2 = 0.1$$

$$\mu g_0 = 1$$

$$\omega g_2 = \mu g_2 \times \mu g_0$$

$$\omega g_2 = 0.1 \times 1 = 0.1$$

Figure 13. Goal prioritization: goal weights and composed weights

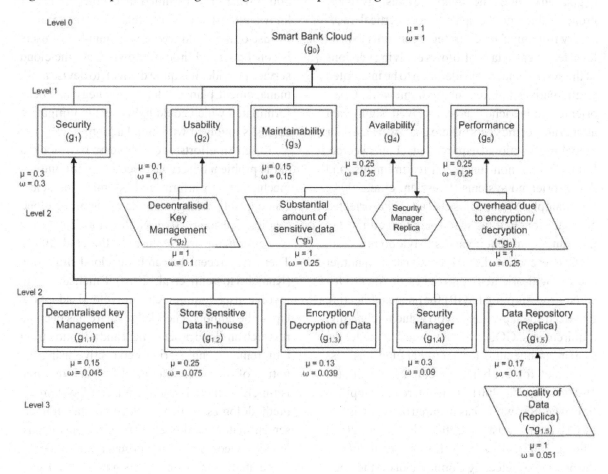

Now calculating the composed weight ω for obstacle $\neg g_2$:

$$\omega\neg g_2 = \mu\neg g_2 \times \mu g_2 \times \mu g_0$$

$$\omega\neg g_2 = 1 \times 0.1 \times 1 = 0.1$$

Similarly the composed weights for other obstacles can be calculated:

$$\omega \neg g_4 = 0.25$$

$$\omega \neg g_5 = 0.25$$

$$\omega \neg g_{1.5} = 0.051$$

This technique of prioritizing goals by comparing the offspring of the same parent allow decision makers to reason about the importance of a particular goal in comparison to other goals. The calculated composed weight helps in prioritizing the obstacles. The greater the value of composed weight the higher would be the priority of the obstacle/goal. The prioritized list of obstacles provides the basis for the obstacle resolution phase.

9. RELATED WORK

A comprehensive use of goal-oriented requirements engineering can be found in Lamsweerde (2001). Requirements are represented in the form of goals in GORE. The advantage of using this approach is that a goal graph provides vertical traceability from high-level strategic concerns to low-level technical details; it allows evolving versions of the system under consideration to be integrated as alternatives into one single framework. Goal-oriented approaches have received significant attention over the years, where goals were used for modelling functional requirements (Lamsweerde, Letier, 2004), non-functional requirements, and Agent-oriented systems (Bresciani et al, 2004). For example, Mylopoulos et al used goal oriented approach for eliciting, specifying and refining the non-functional requirements (Mylopoulos et al, 1992; Bresciani et al, 2004) demonstrates another use of Goal-oriented approaches in Agent Oriented Programming (AOP) for open architecture that need to change and evolve due to changing requirements. GORE was also used to model the system architecture to meet changing business goals and for evolving systems (Anton, Potts, 1998; Gross, Yu, 2001). One interesting application of GORE, which has inspired our work is that of (Alves, Finkelstein, 2002; Alves et al, 2005; Chung, 2002), where GORE was used to inform the process of selecting Commercial off the Shelf (CotS) products matching user's requirements. Though the fundamental use of GORE exhibits resemblance with that of (Alves, Finkelstein, 2002; Alves et al, 2005; Chung, Cooper, 2002) the problem of cloud adoption is by far more challenging as we are dealing with "open loop" systems, with dynamic, unbounded and elastic scale where continuous service evolution is the norm. Due to continuous evolution of the cloud there may be numerous obstacles for adopting cloud services.(Lamsweerde, Leiter, 2000) present a detailed view of handling obstacles in goal-oriented requirements engineering.

There is a well cited work in software risk management (Boehm, DeMarco, 1997; Boehm, 1991). Most of the work carried out in this field is related to software projects (Fairley, 1994; Schmidt et al, 2001) where it is assumed that project manager knows almost everything related to the system. In case of the cloud where large number of users is concerned and little is known about the cloud service provider it is quite difficult to devise a risk management plan. So far, no strategy has been formulated which could help users in mitigating the risks involved with cloud adoption.

Research efforts over the years have looked at the problem of service discovery with runtime mechanisms to inform and optimize the selection e.g. self-managed applications in the cloud (Nallur, Bahsoon, 2010; Nallur et al, 2009) and self-optimizing architecture (Nallur et al, 2009). There is a recent research on cloud migration (Khajeh-Hosseini et al, 2010) which does not involve user requirements for cloud adoption. Up to the authors' knowledge, there has been no research on cloud procurement and adoption from requirements engineering perspective using the notion of obstacles. The need for such research is timely as there is complete lack of systematic methodologies, which could help stakeholders screen, match, negotiate their requirements against cloud services' provision and manage the tradeoffs associated with matches/mismatches of users' requirements and mitigating risks.

10. DISCUSSION AND FUTURE WORK

Cloud computing has gained popularity among businesses in recent years. Users are as excited as nervous about using the cloud. They are excited as most of the services provided by the cloud are low cost and readily available. At the same time, in spite of many promises by the cloud service providers, users remain much concerned about the general risk associated with the adoption of the cloud such as security and privacy of the data held, processed and exploited. We have proposed a framework which would help in addressing the genuine concerns of the cloud users. We looked at the case study of a cloud service provider and found that there were indeed many risks associated with cloud adoption. We advocated the necessity of a systematic methodology, for cloud adoption. The methodology can help the users in refining their requirements and negotiating with the cloud service provider while using goal oriented approach for our research. Our approach will help the users to identify the conflicts between the requirements and to reduce them. There might be certain obstacles involved in achieving some goals. Obstacles can be any hindrance in achieving any goal or the undesired properties (Potts, 1995). Obstacle analysis needs to be done in the initial phase of requirements engineering i.e. at the goal level (Lamsweerde, Leiter, 2000). Obstacles can also be regarded as expression of risks. We have proposed obstacle resolution tactics for cloud adoption process inspired from Axel et al's work (Lamsweerde, Leiter, 1998). Up till now no work has modelled the obstacles for cloud adoption process. We have also defined a framework for prioritizing user requirements. The framework is based on utility theory. Prioritizing the requirements help users to resolve the most critical obstacles first and to achieve goals that are most important. We intend to complement our methodology by using economic-driven approaches for evaluating the cost effectiveness of the decisions and the tradeoffs concerned. As the cloud services keep evolving it is imperative for the user to adapt to the changes made in the cloud. A requirements engineering framework could help users in elaborating and specifying user requirements and later matching it to the cloud service providers' features. Such dynamic selection of cloud with respect to user requirements is challenging but is outside the scope of this paper.

11. CONCLUSION

We have defined the steps involved in the requirements engineering phase for cloud adoption. This paper contributes a lifecycle which is an extension of our previous work (Zardari, Bahsoon, 2011). The lifecycle could help in making a framework for cloud adoption. We have used goal oriented approach for eliciting and modelling the requirements of the user. We have presented a systematic guidance for the identification and evaluation of cloud service providers. The evaluation process concludes in the selection of potentially best cloud service provider available. Key phase of the method is the matching phase where mismatches between the requirements and cloud service providers' features are identified. The analysis of the mismatches may inform the existence of risks. Our approach advocates risk mitigation in early stages of cloud adoption. We have proposed a number of abstract and concrete obstacle resolution tactics. The approach also tries to manage the tradeoffs involved with cloud adoption. The Service Level Agreements presently are too static and non-negotiable. The SLAs do not address the individual needs of every user. This framework would help the cloud service provider and the user to negotiate their requirements and cloud features. It would help making SLAs that are specifically designed for a particular organization. We have also defined a requirement prioritization technique based on utility theory for prioritizing user requirements.

REFERENCES

Alves, C., & Finkelstein, A. (2002). *Challenges in COTS decision-making: A goal-driven requirements engineering perspective.* Paper presented at the 14th International Conference on Software Engineering and Knowledge Engineering.

Alves, C., Franch, X., Carvallo, J. P., & Finkelstein, A. (2005). Lecture Notes in Computer Science: *Vol. 3412. Using goals and quality models to support the matching analysis during COTS selection* (pp. 146–156). doi:10.1007/978-3-540-30587-3_25

Amburst, M., Fox, A., Griffith, R., Joseph, A. D., Katz, R. H., & Konwinski, A. … Zaharia, M. (2009). *Above the clouds: A Berkley view of cloud computing.* Technical Report UCB/EECS-2009-28.

Amburst, M., Fox, A., Griffith, R., Joseph, A. D., Katz, R., & Konwinski, A. (2010). A view of cloud computing. *Communications of the ACM, 53*(4), 50–58. doi:10.1145/1721654.1721672

Anton, A. I. (1996). *Goal-based requirements analysis.* Paper presented at the Second IEEE International Conference on Requirements Engineering, Colorado Springs, USA.

Anton, A. I., McCracken, W. M., & Potts, C. (1994). *Goal decomposition and scenario analysis in business process reengineering.* Paper presented at the 6th International Conference on Advanced Information System Engineering.

Anton, A. I., & Potts, C. (1998). *The use of goals to surface requirements for evolving systems.* Paper presented at the 20th International Conference on Software Engineering.

Biggs, S., & Vidalis, S. (2009). *Cloud computing: The impact on digital forensic investigations.* Paper presented at the International Conference for Internet Technology and Secured Transactions, London.

Boehm, B. W. (1981). *Software engineering economics.* Prentice-Hall.

Boehm, B. W. (1991). Software risk management: Principles and practices. *IEEE Software, 8*(1), 32–41. doi:10.1109/52.62930

Boehm, B. W., & DeMarco, T. (1997). *Software risk management* (pp. 17–19). IEEE Software.

Bresciani, P., Perini, A., Giorgini, P., Giunchiglia, F., & Mylopoulos, J. (2004). Tropos: An agent-oriented software development methodology. *Autonomous Agents and Multi-Agent Systems, 8*(3), 203–236. doi:10.1023/B:AGNT.0000018806.20944.ef

Buyya, R., Yeo, C. H., & Venugopal, S. (2008). *Market oriented cloud computing: Vision, Hype, and reality for delivering it services as computing utilities.* Paper presented at The 10th IEEE International Conference on High Performance Computing and Communication.

Chung, L., & Cooper, K. (2002). *A knowledge-based COTS-aware requirements engineering approach.* Paper presented at the 14th International Conference on Software Engineering and Knowledge Engineering.

Clements, P., Kazman, R., & Klein, M. (2001). *Evaluating software architectures: Methods and case studies.* ISBN-13: 978-0-201-70482-2

CloudHarmony. (2011). *Do SLA really matter? A 1 year case study of 38 cloud services.* Retrieved from http://cloudharmony.com/b/2011/01/do-slas-really-matter-1-year-case-study.html

Fairley, R. (1994). Risk management for software projects. *IEEE Software, 11*(3), 57–67. doi:10.1109/52.281716

Faniyi, F., Bahsoon, R., Evans, A., & Kazman, R. (2011). *Evaluating security of architectures in unpredictable environments: A case for Cloud.* Paper presented at the 9th Working IEEE/IFIP Conference on Software Architecture.

Goscinski, A., & Brock, M. (2010). Toward dynamic and attribute based publication, discovery and selection for cloud computing. *Future Generation Computer Systems*, *26*, 947–970. doi:10.1016/j.future.2010.03.009

Gottfrid, D. (2007, January 11). Protrated super-computing fun! *The New York Times*.

Gross, D., & Yu, E. (2001). *Evolving system architecture to meet changing business goals: An agent and goal-oriented approach*. Paper presented at the Fifth IEEE International Symposium on Requirements Engineering.

IBM. (2008). *IBM perspective on cloud computing*. Retrieved from ftp://ftp.software.ibm.com/software/tivoli/brochures/IBM_Perspective_on_Cloud_Computing.pdf

Khajeh-Hosseini, A., Greenwood, D., & Sommerville, I. (2010). *Cloud migration: A case study of migrating an enterprise IT system to IaaS*. Paper presented at the 3rd International Conference on Cloud Computing.

Lamsweerde, A. V. (2001). *Goal-oriented requirements engineering: A guided tour*. Paper presented at the 5th IEEE International Symposium on Requirements Engineering, Toronto

Lamsweerde, A. V. (2004). *Goal-oriented requirements engineering: A roundtrip from research to practice*. Paper presented at the 12th IEEE International Requirements Engineering Conference, Kyoto.

Lamsweerde, A. V., Darimont, R., & Letier, E. (1998). Managing conflicts in goal-driven requirements engineering. *IEEE Transactions on Software Engineering*, *24*(11), 908–926. doi:10.1109/32.730542

Lamsweerde, A. V., & Leiter, E. (1998). *Integrating obstacles in goal-driven requirements engineering*. Paper presented at the 20th International Conference on Software Engineering, Kyoto.

Lamsweerde, A. V., & Leiter, E. (2000). Handling obstacles in goal-oriented requirements engineering. *IEEE Transactions on Software Engineering*, *26*(10), 978–1005. doi:10.1109/32.879820

Lamsweerde, A. V., & Letier, E. (2004). Lecture Notes in Computer Science: *Vol. 2941. From object orientation to goal orientation: A paradigm shift for requirements engineering* (pp. 153–166). doi:10.1007/978-3-540-24626-8_23

Miller, M. (2008). *Cloud computing: Web based applications that change the way you work and collaborate online*. Que Publishing.

Mylopoulos, J., Chung, L., & Nixon, B. (1992). Representing and using nonfuntional requirements: A process oriented approach. *IEEE Transactions on Software Engineering*, *18*(6), 483–497. doi:10.1109/32.142871

Nallur, V., & Bahsoon, R. (2010). *Design of a market-based mechanism for quality attributes tradeoff of services in the cloud*. Paper presented at the 2010 ACM Symposium on Applied Computing.

Nallur, V., Bahsoon, R., & Yao, X. (2009). *Self-optimizing architecture for ensuring quality attributes in the cloud*. Paper presented at the 2009 IEEE/IFIP WICSA/ECSA.

Nuseibeh, B., & Easterbrook, S. (2000). *Requirements engineering: A roadmap*. Paper presented at the The Future of Software Engineering.

Potts, C. (1995). *Using schematic scenarios to understand user needs*. Paper presented at the of 1st Conference on Designing Interactive Systems: Processes, Methods and Techniques.

Santos, N., Gummadi, K. P., & Rodrigues, R. (2009). *Towards trusted cloud computing*. Paper presented at the 2009 Conference on Hot Topics in Cloud Computing.

Schmidt, R., Lyytinen, K., Keil, M., & Cule, P. (2001). Identifying software project risks: An international Delphi study. *Journal of Management Information Systems, 17*(4), 5–36.

Zardari, S., & Bahsoon, R. (2011). *Cloud adoption: A goal-oriented requirements engineering approach*. Paper presented at the IEEE/ACM International Workshop on Cloud Software Engineering, The ACM/IEEE 33rd International Conference on Software Engineering, Hawaii, USA.

Zave, P. (1997). Classification of research efforts in requirements engineering. *ACM Computing Surveys, 29*(4), 315–321. doi:10.1145/267580.267581

Compilation of References

Abrahamsson, P., Babar, M. A., & Kruchten, P. (2010). Agility and architecture: Can they coexist? *IEEE Software, 27*(2), 16–22. doi:10.1109/MS.2010.36

Ackoff, R. (1999). *Ackoff's best: His classic writings on management*. Marblehead, MA: John Wiley & Sons Publishing.

Agile Alliance. (2001). *Manifesto for agile software development*. Retrieved January 10, 2012, from http://agilemanifesto.org

Aier, S., & Winter, R. (2009). Virtual decoupling for IT/business alignment- Conceptual foundations, architecture design and implementation example. *Business and Information Systems Engineering, 2*, 1–13.

Akenine, D. (2008). A study of architect roles by IASA Sweden. *Architecture Journal, 15*. Retrieved September 1, 2011, from http://msdn.microsoft.com/en-us/architecture/cc505968

Alebrahim, A., Hatebur, D., & Heisel, M. (2011). A method to derive software architectures from quality requirements. In T. D. Thu & K. Leung (Eds.), *Proceedings of the 18th Asia-Pacific Software Engineering Conference (APSEC)* (pp. 322–330). IEEE Computer Society.

Alexander, C. (1979). *A timeless way of building*. New York, NY: Oxford University Press.

Alexander, I., & Robertson, S. (2004). Understanding project sociology by modeling stakeholders. *IEEE Software, 21*(1), 23–27. doi:10.1109/MS.2004.1259199

Alfred, C. (2005). Product strategy and architecture. *Microsoft Architecture Journal, 5*, 33–39.

Alfred, C. (2010). Multiple-context systems: A new frontier in architecture. *Microsoft Architecture Journal, 23*, 26–31.

Ali Babar, M., Dingsøyr, T., Lago, P., & van Vliet, H. (2009). *Software architecture knowledge management: Theory and practice*. Springer-Verlag. doi:10.1007/978-3-642-02374-3

Alspaugh, T. A., Asuncion, H. A., & Scacchi, W. (2009). Intellectual property rights for heterogeneously licensed systems. In *Proceedings 17th International Requirements Engineering Conference (RE09)*, Atlanta, GA, 24-33, September 2009.

Alspaugh, T. A., Asuncion, H. A., & Scacchi, W. (2011). Presenting software license conflicts through argumentation. In *Proceedings 23rd International Conference on Software Engineering and Knowledge Engineering (SEKE'11)*.

Alspaugh, T. A., & Antón, A. I. (2007). Scenario support for effective requirement. *Information and Software Technology, 50*(3), 198–220. doi:10.1016/j.infsof.2006.12.003

Alspaugh, T. A., Scacchi, W., & Asuncion, H. A. (2010). Software licenses in context: The challenge of heterogeneously licenses systems. *Journal of the Association for Information Systems, 11*(11), 730–755.

Alves, C., & Finkelstein, A. (2002). *Challenges in COTS decision-making: A goal-driven requirements engineering perspective*. Paper presented at the 14th International Conference on Software Engineering and Knowledge Engineering.

Alves, C., Franch, X., Carvallo, J. P., & Finkelstein, A. (2005). Lecture Notes in Computer Science: *Vol. 3412. Using goals and quality models to support the matching analysis during COTS selection* (pp. 146–156). doi:10.1007/978-3-540-30587-3_25

Ambler, S. (2009). *Agile model driven development (AMDD): The key to scaling agile software development.* Essay available online.

Ambler, S., Nalbone, J., & Vizdos, M. (2009). *The enterprise unified process: Extending the rational unified process*. Prentice Hall.

Amburst, M., Fox, A., Griffith, R., Joseph, A. D., Katz, R. H., & Konwinski, A. ... Zaharia, M. (2009). *Above the clouds: A Berkley view of cloud computing*. Technical Report UCB/EECS-2009-28.

Amburst, M., Fox, A., Griffith, R., Joseph, A. D., Katz, R., & Konwinski, A. (2010). A view of cloud computing. *Communications of the ACM*, *53*(4), 50–58. doi:10.1145/1721654.1721672

Anton, A. I. (1996). *Goal-based requirements analysis*. Paper presented at the Second IEEE International Conference on Requirements Engineering, Colorado Springs, USA.

Anton, A. I., & Potts, C. (1998). *The use of goals to surface requirements for evolving systems*. Paper presented at the 20th International Conference on Software Engineering.

Anton, A. I., McCracken, W. M., & Potts, C. (1994). *Goal decomposition and scenario analysis in business process reengineering*. Paper presented at the 6th International Conference on Advanced Information System Engineering.

Asuncion, H. (2008). Towards practical software traceability. In *Companion of the 30th International Conference on Software Engineering*, (pp. 1023-1026). Leipzig, Germany.

Asuncion, H. U., & Taylor, R. N. (2012). Automated techniques for capturing custom traceability links across heterogeneous artifacts. In *Software and Systems Traceability* (pp. 129–146). Springer-Verlag. doi:10.1007/978-1-4471-2239-5_6

Atkinson, C., Bostan, P., Brenner, D., Falcone, G., & Gutheil, M. (2008). Lecture Notes in Computer Science: *Vol. 5153. Modeling components and component-based systems in KobrA* (pp. 54–84). The Common Component Modelling Example. doi:10.1007/978-3-540-85289-6_4

Auer, S., Riechert, T., & Fähnrich, K.-P. (2006). SoftWiki – Agiles Requirements-Engineering für Softwareprojekte mit einer großen Anzahl verteilter Stakeholder. In Meißner, K., & Engelien, M. (Eds.), *Workshop Gemeinschaften in Neuen Medien (GeNeMe)* (pp. 97–108).

Axelsson, J. (2010). Towards a process maturity model for evolutionary architecting of embedded system product lines. In *Proceedings 4th European Conference on Software Architecture*, Volume 2.

Babar, M. A. (2009). An exploratory study of architectural practices and challenges in using agile software development approaches. In *Proceedings of the European Conference on Software Architecture (ICSA/ECSA 2009)*, (pp. 81-90). IEEE.

Babar, M. A., & Gorton, I. (2009). Software architecture review: The state of practice. *IEEE Computer*, July (pp. 26-32).

Babar, M. A., Ihme, T., & Pikkarainen, M. (2009). An industrial case of exploiting product line architectures in agile software development. In *SPLC '09 – Proceedings of the 13th International Software Product Line Conference*, (pp. 171-179). Pittsburgh, PA: Carnegie Mellon University.

Bachmann, F., & Merson, P. (2005). *Experience using the web-based tool wiki for architecture documentation*. Technical Note CMU.

Bahsoon, R. (2003). Evaluating software architectures for stability: A real options approach. In *Proceedings of the 25th International Conference on Software Engineering (doctoral symposium)*.

Barroca, L., Fiadeiro, J. L., Jackson, M., Laney, R. C., & Nuseibeh, B. (2004). Problem frames: A case for coordination. In *Coordination Models and Languages, Proceedings 6th International Conference Coordination* (pp. 5-19).

Baskerville, R., Pries-Heje, J., & Madsen, S. (2010). Post-agility: What follows a decade of agility? *Information and Software Technology*, *53*(5), 543–555. doi:10.1016/j.infsof.2010.10.010

Bass, L., Clements, P., Kazman, R., & Klein, M. (2008). Evaluating the software architecture competence of organizations. In *Proceedings 7th Working IEEE/IFIP Conference on Software Architecture* (pp. 249-252).

Bass, L., Clements, P., & Kazman, R. (2003). *Software architecture in practice* (2nd ed.). Addison Wesley.

BAWG. (2011). *Business architecture overview.* Retrieved August 5, 2011, from http://bawg.omg.org/.

BAWG. (2011). *Business architecture working group.* Retrieved August 5, 2011, from http://bawg.omg.org/business architecture overview.htm

Becker, S., Koziolek, H., & Reussner, R. (2009). The Palladio component model for model driven performance prediction. *Journal of Systems and Software*, *82*, 3-22. Retrieved from http://dx.doi.org/10.1016/j.jss.2008.03.066

Beck, K. (2002). *Test driven development: By example.* Boston, MA: Addison-Wesley Professional.

Bentley, P. J., & Wakefield, J. P. (1997). Finding acceptable solutions in the pareto-optimal range using multiobjective genetic algorithms. In Chawdhry, P. K., Roy, R., & Pant, R. K. (Eds.), *Soft computing in engineering design and manufacturing* (pp. 231–240). Springer Verlag London Limited. doi:10.1007/978-1-4471-0427-8_25

Bertrand, P., Darimont, R., Delor, E., Massonet, P., & van Lamsweerde, A. (1998). GRAIL/KAOS: An environment for goal driven requirements engineering. In *ICSE'98 - 20th International Conference on Software Engineering.*

Biggs, S., & Vidalis, S. (2009). *Cloud computing: The impact on digital forensic investigations.* Paper presented at the International Conference for Internet Technology and Secured Transactions, London.

Bleistein, S. J., Cox, K., & Verner, J. (2006, Mar). Validating strategic alignment of organizational IT requirements using goal modeling and problem diagrams. *Journal of Systems and Software*, *79*(3), 362–378. doi:10.1016/j.jss.2005.04.033

Boardman, J., & Sauser, B. (2008). *Systems thinking: Coping with 21st century problems.* CRC Press. doi:10.1201/9781420054927

Boden, A., Nett, B., & Wulf, V. (2007). Coordination practices in distributed software development of small enterprises. *Second IEEE International Conference on Global Software Engineering*, (pp. 235–246).

Boehm, B. W. (1981). *Software engineering economics.* Prentice-Hall.

Boehm, B. W. (1991). Software risk management: Principles and practices. *IEEE Software*, *8*(1), 32–41. doi:10.1109/52.62930

Boehm, B. W., & DeMarco, T. (1997). *Software risk management* (pp. 17–19). IEEE Software.

Boehm, B., & Ross, R. (1989). Theory W: Software project management: Principles and examples. *IEEE Transactions on Software Engineering*, *15*(7), 902–916. doi:10.1109/32.29489

Bonnema, M. (2008). *FunKey architecting - An integrated approach to system architecting using functions, key drivers and system budgets.* Doctoral dissertation, University of Twente, the Netherlands.

Booch, G. (2009). *AoT presentation.* IBM internal.

Booth, D., Haas, H., McCabe, F., Newcomer, E., Champion, M., Ferris, C., & Orchard, D. (2004). *Web services architecture.* Retrieved September 15, 2011, from http://www.w3.org/TR/ws-arch/

Borches, D. (2010). *A3 architecture overviews; A tool for effective communication in product evolution.* Doctoral dissertation, University of Twente, the Netherlands.

Brandes, U. (2001). A faster algorithm for betweenness centrality. *The Journal of Mathematical Sociology*, *25*(2), 163–177. doi:10.1080/0022250X.2001.9990249

Brandes, U. (2008). On variants of shortest-path betweenness centrality and their generic computation. *Social Networks*, *30*(2), 136–145. doi:10.1016/j.socnet.2007.11.001

Breaux, T. D., & Anton, A. I. (2008). Analyzing regulatory rules for privacy and security requirements. *IEEE Transactions on Software Engineering*, *34*(1), 5–20. doi:10.1109/TSE.2007.70746

Bresciani, P., Perini, A., Giorgini, P., Giunchiglia, F., & Mylopoulos, J. (2004). Tropos: An agent-oriented software development methodology. *Autonomous Agents and Multi-Agent Systems, 8*(3), 203–236. doi:10.1023/B:AGNT.0000018806.20944.ef

Bresciani, P., Perini, A., Giorgini, P., Giunchiglia, F., & Mylopoulos, J. (2004). Tropos: An agent-oriented software development methodology. *Autonomous Agents and Multi-Agent Systems, 8*(3), 203–236. doi:10.1023/B:AGNT.0000018806.20944.ef

Brim, L., Černá, I., Vařeková, P., & Zimmerova, B. (2005). Component-interaction automata as a verification-oriented component-based system specification. *SIGSOFT Software Engineering Notes, 31*.

Brooks, F. (1987). No silver bullet. *IEEE Computer, 20*(4), 10–19. doi:10.1109/MC.1987.1663532

Brooks, F. (1995). *The mythical man-month: Essays on software engineering, (2nd anniversary edition)*. Boston, MA: Addison-Wesley Professional.

Brown, N., Nord, R., & Ozkaya, I. (2011). *Strategic management of technical debt*. WICSA 2011 Tutorial.

Brown, W. J., Malveau, R. C., McCormick, H. W., & Thomas, S. W. Theresa Hudson (Ed.) (2000). *Anti-patterns in project management*. New York, NY: John Wiley & Sons.

Broy, M. (1995). Advanced component interface specification. In T. Ito & A. Yonezawa (Eds.), *Theory and Practice of Parallel Programming* (Vol. 907, pp. 369–392). *Lecture Notes in Computer Science* Berlin, Germany: Springer. Retrieved from. doi:10.1007/BFb0026580doi:10.1007/BFb0026580

Broy, M. (2000). Algebraic specification of reactive systems. *Theoretical Computer Science, 239*(1), 3–40. doi:10.1016/S0304-3975(99)00212-1doi:10.1016/S0304-3975(99)00212-1

Broy, M., Krüger, I. H., Pretschner, A., & Salzmann, C. (2007). Engineering automotive software. *Proceedings of the IEEE, 95*(2), 356–373. doi:10.1109/JPROC.2006.888386

Bruneton, E., Coupaye, T., Leclercq, M., Quema, V., & Stefani, J.-B. (2004). An open component model and its support in Java. In I. Crnkovic, J. A. Stafford, H. W. Schmidt, & K. Wallnau (Eds.), *Component-Based Software Engineering* (Vol. 3054, pp. 7–22). *Lecture Notes in Computer Science* Berlin, Germany: Springer. doi:10.1007/978-3-540-24774-6_3doi:10.1007/978-3-540-24774-6_3

Bu, W., Tang, A., & Han, J. (2009). An analysis of decision-centric architectural design approaches. *Proceedings of the 2009 ICSE Workshop on Sharing and Reusing Architectural Knowledge*, ICSE (pp. 33-40).

Buschmann, F., Henney, K., & Schmidt, D. (2007). *Pattern-oriented software, Vol. 4 – A language for distributed computing*. Wiley.

Business Process Model and Notation (BPMN). (2011). Retrieved January 29, 2012, from http://www.omg.org/spec/BPMN/2.0/

Buyya, R., Yeo, C. H., & Venugopal, S. (2008). *Market oriented cloud computing: Vision, Hype, and reality for delivering it services as computing utilities*. Paper presented at The 10th IEEE International Conference on High Performance Computing and Communication.

Cameron, B. (2007). *Capability maps anchor business complexity*. Forrester Research. Retrieved January 8, 2012, from http://www.forrester.com/rb/Research/capability_maps_anchor_business_complexity/q/id/43049/t/

Chaki, S., Diaz-Pace, S., Garlan, D., Gurfinkel, A., & Ozkaya, I. (2009). Towards engineered architecture evolution. In *Proceedings ICSE Workshop on Modeling of Software Engineering*.

Charfi, A., Gamatié, A., Honoré, A., Dekeyser, J. L., & Abid, M. (2008). Validation de modèles dans un cadre d'IDM dédié à la conception de systèmes sur puce. In *4èmes Jounées sur L'ingénierie Dirigée par les Modèles (IDM 08)*.

Chatha, K. A., Ajaefobi, J. O., & Weston, R. H. (2007). Enriched multi-process modelling in support of lifecycle engineering of business processes. *International Journal of Production Research, 45*(1), 103–141. doi:10.1080/00207540600607150

Cheng, B. H. C., & Atlee, J. M. (2007). Research directions in requirements engineering. *Proceedings of the Conference on the Future of Software Engineering*, (pp. 285-303).

Choi, S., & Scacchi, W. (1990). Extracting and restructuring the design of large systems. *IEEE Software, 7*(1), 66–71. doi:10.1109/52.43051

Choppy, C., & Heisel, M. (2003). Use of patterns in formal development: Systematic transition from problems to architectural designs. In *Recent Trends in Algebraic Development Techniques, 16th WADT, Selected Papers* (pp. 205–220). Springer Verlag.

Choppy, C., & Reggio, G. (2006). Requirements capture and specification for enterprise applications: A UML based attempt. In J. Han & M. Staples (Eds.), *Proc of the Australian Software Engineering Conference (ASWEC 2006), IEEE* (p. 19-28).

Choppy, C., Hatebur, D., & Heisel, M. (2005). Architectural patterns for problem frames. *IEE Proceedings – Software, Special Issue on Relating Software Requirements and Architectures, 152*(4), 198–208.

Choppy, C., Hatebur, D., & Heisel, M. (2006). Component composition through architectural patterns for problem frames. In *Proc. XIII Asia Pacific Software Engineering Conference (APSEC)* (pp. 27–34). IEEE.

Choppy, C., Hatebur, D., & Heisel, M. (2011). Systematic architectural design based on problem patterns. In Avgeriou, P., Grundy, J., Hall, J., Lago, P., & Mistrik, I. (Eds.), *Relating software requirements and architectures* (pp. 133–159). Springer. doi:10.1007/978-3-642-21001-3_9

Choppy, C., & Heisel, M. (2004). Une approche à base de "patrons" pour la spécification et le développement de systèmes d'information. In *Proceedings Approches Formelles dans L'assistance au Développement de Logiciels* (pp. 61–76). AFADL.

Choppy, C., & Reggio, G. (2005). A UML-based approach for problem frame oriented software development. *Journal of Information and Software Technology, 47*, 929–954. doi:10.1016/j.infsof.2005.08.006

Christensen, J. H. (2009). Using RESTful web-services and cloud computing to create next generation mobile applications. In *Proceedings of the 24th ACM SIGPLAN Conference Companion on Object Oriented Programming Systems Languages and Applications (OOPSLA '09)* (pp. 627-633). New York, NY: ACM.

Chung, L., & Cooper, K. (2002). *A knowledge-based COTS-aware requirements engineering approach.* Paper presented at the 14th International Conference on Software Engineering and Knowledge Engineering.

Cleland-Huang, J., & Mobasher, B. (2008). Using data mining and recommender systems to scale up the requirements process. *Proceedings of the 2nd International Workshop on Ultra-Large-Scale Software-Intensive Systems*, (pp. 3-6).

Clements, P., Kazman, R., & Klein, M. (2001). *Evaluating software architectures: Methods and case studies.* ISBN-13: 978-0-201-70482-2

Clements, P., Kazman, R., Klein, M., Devesh, D., Reddy, S., & Verma, P. (2007). The duties, skills, and knowledge of software architects. In *Proceedings of the 6th Working IEEE/IFIP Conference on Software Architecture* (pp. 44-47).

Clements, P., & Northrup, L. (2001). *Software product lines: Practices and patterns.* Boston, MA: Addison-Wesley.

CloudHarmony. (2011). *Do SLA really matter? A 1 year case study of 38 cloud services.* Retrieved from http://cloudharmony.com/b/2011/01/do-slas-really-matter-1-year-case-study.html

Cockburn, A. (2006). *Agile software development: The cooperative game* (2nd ed.). Addison-Wesley.

Conway, M. (1968). How do committees invent? *Datamation*, April.

Coplien, J., & Bjørnvig, G. (2010). *Lean architecture for agile software development.* Wiley.

Crnkovic, I., & Larsson, M. (2002). *Building reliable component-based software systems.*

Cullen, A. (2010). *Sample business capability map: Insurance*. Forrester Research. Retrieved January 8, 2012 from http://www.forrester.com/rb/Research/sample_business_capability_map_insurance/q/id/56540/t/2

Cullen, A. (2010). *Using business capability maps to guide IT investment governance*. Forrester Research. Retrieved January 8, 2012, from http://www.forrester.com/rb/Research/using_business_capability_maps_to_guide_it/q/id/56376/t/2

Cunningham, W. (1995). *Portland pattern repository: WikiWikiWeb*. Retrieved August 11, 2011, from http://c2.com/cgi-bin/wiki

Damian, D., Marczak, S., & Kwan, I. (2007). Collaboration patterns and the impact of distance on awareness in requirements-centred social networks. *Proceedings of the 15th IEEE International Conference on Requirements Engineering (RE)*, (pp. 59-68).

Dashofy, E., Asuncion, H., Hendrickson, S. A., Suryanarayana, G., Georgas, J. C., & Taylor, R. N. ArchStudio 4: An architecture-based meta-modeling environment. In *28th International Conference on Software Engineering (ICSE '07), Companion Volume*, (pp. 67–68). 20–26 May 2007.

Dashofy, E. M., Hoek, A. d., & Taylor, R. N. (2005). A comprehensive approach for the development of modular software architecture description languages. *ACM Transactions on Software Engineering and Methodology, 14*(2), 199–245. doi:10.1145/1061254.1061258

de Boor, R., & van Vliet, H. (2008). On the similarity between requirements and architecture. *Journal of Systems and Software, 82*, 544–550. doi:10.1016/j.jss.2008.11.185

Dengler, F., & Happel, H. J. (2010). Collaborative modeling with semantic mediawiki. In *Proceedings of the 6th International Symposium on Wikis and Open Collaboration*. Gdansk, Poland: ACM.

Dengler, F., Lamparter, S., Hefke, M., & Abecker, A. (2009). Collaborative process development using semantic MediaWiki. *Proceedings of the 5th Conf. of Professional Knowledge Management*, Solothurn, Switzerland, (pp. 97-107).

Department of Defense. (1996). *Technical architecture framework for information management (Vol. 1)*.

Department of Defense. (2010). *The DoDAF architecture framework*, Version 2.02, 2010. Retrieved from http://cio-nii.defense.gov/sites/dodaf20/index.html

Dersten, S., Fröberg, J., Axelsson, J., & Land, R. (2010). Analysis of the business effects of software architecture refactoring in an automotive development organization. In *Proceedings of the 36th EUROMICRO Conference on Software Engineering and Advanced Applications*.

Dorst, K., & Cross, N. (2001). Creativity in the design process: Co-evolution of problem-solution. *Design Studies, 22*, 425–437. doi:10.1016/S0142-694X(01)00009-6

Eeles, P., & Cripps, P. (2010). *The process of software architecting*. Addison-Wesley.

Ehrig, H., Orejas, F., Braatz, B., Klein, M., & Piirainen, M. (2002). A generic component framework for system modeling. In R. D. Kutsche & H. Weber (Eds.), *FASE* (pp. 33–48). Berlin, Germany: Springer. doi:10.1007/3-540-45923-5_3doi:10.1007/3-540-45923-5_3

Ellison, R. J., & Moore, A. P. (2003). *Trustworthy refinement through intrusion-aware design (TRIAD)*. Technical Report, CMU/SEI-2003-TR-002, March 2003.

Eloranta, V.-P. (2011). *Scrum and architecture work survey – Interview questions*. Retrieved, January 10, 2012, from http://www.cs.tut.fi/~elorantv/interview_questions.html

Erder, M., & Pureur, P. (2006). Transitional architectures for enterprise evolution. *IT Professional*, (May-June): 10–17. doi:10.1109/MITP.2006.77

EssentialProjectTeam. (2010). *Essential meta-model*. Retrieved August 8, 2011, from http://www.enterprise-architecture.org/about/35-essential-meta-model

Estefan, J. A. (2007). *Survey of candidate model-based engineering (MBSE): Methodologies Rev A*. INCOSE MBSE Focus Group. Retrieved July 11, 2011, from www.omgsysml.org/MBSE_Methodology_Survey_RevA.pdf

Evans, E. (2003). *Domain-driven design: Tackling complexity in the heart of software*. Boston, MA: Addison-Wesley.

Fairbanks, G. (2011). *Architecture Haiku*. WICSA 2011 tutorial. Retrieved from http://rhinoresearch.com/files/Haiku-tutorial-2011-06-24-final.pdf

Fairley, R. (1994). Risk management for software projects. *IEEE Software, 11*(3), 57–67. doi:10.1109/52.281716

Faniyi, F., Bahsoon, R., Evans, A., & Kazman, R. (2011). *Evaluating security of architectures in unpredictable environments: A case for Cloud.* Paper presented at the 9th Working IEEE/IFIP Conference on Software Architecture.

Feldt, K. (2007). *Programming Firefox: Building rich internet applications with XUL.* Sebastopol, CA: O'Reilly Press.

Fielding, R. T. (2000). *Architectural styles and the design of network-based software architectures.* Ph.D. dissertation, University of California, Irvine. Retrieved September 15, 2011, from http://www.ics.uci.edu/fielding/pubs/dissertation/top.htm

Fielding, R., & Taylor, R. N. (2002). Principled design of the modern web architecture. *ACM Transactions on Internet Technology, 2*(2), 115–150. doi:10.1145/514183.514185

Filipe, J. K. (2002). A logic-based formalization for component specification. *Journal of Object Technology, 1*(3), 231–248. doi:10.5381/jot.2002.1.3.a13doi:10.5381/jot.2002.1.3.a13

Finkelstein, A., Harman, M., Mansouri, S. A., Ren, J., & Zhang, Y. (2009). A search based approach to fairness analysis in requirement assignments to aid negotiation, mediation and decision making. *Requirements Engineering Journal, 14*(4), 231–245. doi:10.1007/s00766-009-0075-y

Fisher, R., Ury, W., & Patton, B. (1991). *Getting to yes: Negotiating agreement without giving in* (2nd ed.). New York, NY: Penguin Books.

Fontana, R., Kuhn, B. M., Molgen, E., et al. (2008). *A legal issues primer for open source and free software projects.* Software Freedom Law Center, Version 1.5.1. Retrieved from http://www.softwarefreedom.org/resources/2008/foss-primer.pdf

Fowler, M. (2002). *Patterns of enterprise application architecture.* Boston, MA: Addison-Wesley.

Fowler, M. (2003). Who needs an architect? *IEEE Software, 20*(5), 11–13. doi:10.1109/MS.2003.1231144

Fowler, M. (2003). *Patterns of enterprise application architecture.* Addison Wesley.

Fowler, M. (2003). Who needs an architect? *IEEE Software, 20*(5). doi:10.1109/MS.2003.1231144

Fricke, E., Schulz, A., Wehlitz, A., & Negele, H. (2000). A generic approach to implement information-based system development. *Proceedings INCOSE 2000,* Minneapolis. Retrieved from www.gfse.de/se/pubs/downloads/Info_based_SD_INC2000.pdf

Garlan, D., Barnes, J. M., Schmerl, B., & Celiku, O. (2009). Evolution styles: Foundations and tools support for software architecture evolution. In *Proceeding Joint Working IEEE/IFIP Conference on Software Architecture 2009 & European Conference on Software Architecture* (pp. 131-140).

Garland, D., & Shaw, M. (1994). An introduction to software architecture (pp. 1-39). Carnegie Mellon University Technical Report, CMU-CS-94-166.

Gause, D. C., & Weinberg, G. M. (1989). *Exploring requirements: Quality before design.* Dorset House Publishing Company, Inc.

Geurts, G., & Geelhoed, A. (2004). Business process decomposition and service identification using communication patterns. *Mirosoft Architecture Journal, 1,* 18–27.

Gilb, T. (2005). *Competitive engineering: A handbook for systems engineering, requirements engineering, and software engineering using pLanguage.* London, UK: Elsevier Butterworth-Heinemann.

Glinz, M., & Wieringa, R. J. (2007). Guest editors' introduction: Stakeholders in requirements engineering. *IEEE Software, 24*(2), 18–20. doi:10.1109/MS.2007.42

Gokhale, A. (2010). *Increasing effectiveness of the Zachman framework using the Balanced Scorecard.* Unpublished Master's thesis, Purdue University, Indiana

Goldberg, D. E. (1989). *Genetic algorithms in search, optimization, and machine learning.* Addison-wesley.

Goscinski, A., & Brock, M. (2010). Toward dynamic and attribute based publication, discovery and selection for cloud computing. *Future Generation Computer Systems, 26,* 947–970. doi:10.1016/j.future.2010.03.009

Gottfrid, D. (2007, January 11). Protrated supercomputing fun! *The New York Times.*

Grassi, V., Mirandola, R., & Sabetta, A. (2007). Filling the gap between design and performance/ reliability models of component-based systems: A model-driven approach. *Journal of Systems and Software, 80*(4), 528–558. doi:10.1016/j.jss.2006.07.023

Greenfield, J., Short, K., Cook, S., & Kent, S. (2004). *Software factories: Assembling applications with patterns, models, frameworks, and tools.* Indianapolis, IN: Wiley.

Greer, D., & Ruhe, G. (2004). Software release planning: An evolutionary and iterative approach. *Information and Software Technology, 46*(4), 243–253. doi:10.1016/j.infsof.2003.07.002

Grimm, K. (2003). Software technology in an automotive company – Major challenges. In *Proceedings of the 25th International Conference on Software Engineering* (pp. 498-503).

Gross, D., & Yu, E. (2001). *Evolving system architecture to meet changing business goals: An agent and goal-oriented approach.* Paper presented at the Fifth IEEE International Symposium on Requirements Engineering.

Gustavsson, H., & Axelsson, J. (2008). Evaluating flexibility in embedded automotive product lines using real options. In *Proceedings of the 12th International Software Product Line Conference* (pp. 235-242).

Gustavsson, H., & Axelsson, J. (2010). *Improving the system architecting process through the use of lean tools.* Paper presented at the Portland International Conference on Management of Engineering and Technology, Phuket, Thailand.

Hacklinger, F. (2004). Java\A - Taking components into Java. In W. Dosch & N. Debnath (Eds.), *Proceedings of the 13th ISCA Conference, Intelligent and Adaptive Systems and Software Engineering.*

Haischt, D., & Georg, F. (2010). *Get me approved, please! Lizenzkompatibilitaet von Open-Source Komponenten. Objektspektrum, Sonderbeilage Agilitaet, Winter 2010.* SIGS Datacom.

Hall, J. G., Jackson, M., Laney, R. C., Nuseibeh, B., & Rapanotti, L. (2002, 9-13 September). Relating software requirements and architectures using problem frames. In *Proceedings of IEEE International Requirements Engineering Conference (RE'02).* Essen, Germany.

Hamberg, R., & Verriet, J. (Eds.). (2011). *Automation in warehouse development.* Dordrecht, The Netherlands: Springer.

Happel, H.-J., & Seedorf, S. (2006). Applications of ontologies in software engineering. *Proceedings of Workshop on Sematic Web Enabled Software Engineering* (SWESE) at ISWC 2006, Athens, Georgia, November 5-9.

Happel, H.-J., & Seedorf, S. (2007). Ontobrowse: A semantic wiki for sharing knowledge about software architectures. *Proceedings of the 19th International Conference on Software Engineering and Knowledge Engineering (SEKE)*, Boston, USA, July 9-11, (pp. 506-512).

Harman, M. (2007). *The current state and future of search based software engineering.* Paper presented at the Future of Software Engineering Conference (FoSE), Minneapolis, USA.

Hatebur, D., & Heisel, M. (2009). Deriving software architectures from problem descriptions. In *Software Engineering 2009 – Workshop Band* (pp. 383–302). GI.

Hatebur, D., & Heisel, M. (2010). Making pattern- and model-based software development more rigorous. In J. S. Dong & H. Zhu (Eds.), *Proceedings of International Conference on Formal Engineering Methods (ICFEM)* (LNCS Vol. 6447, pp. 253–269). Springer.

Heemels, M., & Muller, G. (Eds.). (2007). *Boderc: Model-based design of high-tech systems.* Eindhoven, The Netherlands: Embedded Systems Institute.

Heisel, M., & Hatebur, D. (2005). A model-based development process for embedded systems. In T. Klein, B. Rumpe, & B. Schätz (Eds.), *Proceedings of the Workshop on Model-Based Development of Embedded Systems.* Technical University of Braunschweig. Retrieved from http://www.sse.cs.tu-bs.de/publications/MBEES-Tagungsband.pdf

Henderson, J. C., & Venkatraman, N. (1993). Strategic alignment: Leveraging information technology for transforming organizations. *IBM Systems Journal, 32*, 472–484. doi:10.1147/sj.382.0472doi:10.1147/sj.382.0472

Herzum, P., & Sims, O. (1998). *The business component approach.* OOPSLA'98, Business Object Workshop IV.

Hildenbrand, T. (2008). *Improving traceability in distributed collaborative software development - A design science approach.* Frankfurt, Germany: Peter Lang Verlag.

Hitchins, D. K. (2003). *Advanced systems thinking, engineering and management.* Artech House.

Hoare, C. A. R., & Jifeng, H. (1998). *Foundations of component-based systems.*

Hofmeister, C., Kruchten, P., Nord, R. L., Obbink, H., Ran, A., & America, P. (2005). Generalizing a model of software architecture design from five industrial approaches. In *Proceedings 5ᵗʰ IEEE/IFIP Conference on Software Architecture* (pp. 77-88).

Hofmeister, C., Nord, R. L., & Soni, D. (1999). Describing software architecture with UML. In *Proceedings of the First Working IFIP Conference on Software Architecture* (pp. 145–160). Kluwer Academic Publishers.

Hofmeister, C., & Kruchten, P., Nord, Obbink, J. H., Ran, A., & America, P. (2007). A general model of software architecture design derived from five industrial approaches. *Journal of Systems and Software, 80*(1), 106–126. doi:10.1016/j.jss.2006.05.024

Hohfeld, W. N. (1913). Some fundamental legal conceptions as applied in judicial reasoning. *The Yale Law Journal, 23*(1), 16–59. doi:10.2307/785533

Hohpe, G., & Woolf, B. (2004). *Enterprise integration patterns.* Addison Wesley.

Hole, E., & Muller, G. (2006). *Architectural descriptions and models.* White Paper Resulting from Architecture Forum Meeting. Retrieved July 12, 2011, from http://www.architectingforum.org/whitepapers/SAF_WhitePaper_2006_2.pdf

Hoorn, J. F., Farenhorst, R., Lago, P., & van Vliet, H. (2011). The lonesome architect. *Journal of Systems and Software, 84*(9), 1424–1435. doi:10.1016/j.jss.2010.11.909

Huo, M., Verner, J., Zhu, L., & Babar, M. A. (2004). Software quality and agile methods. In *Proceedings of the COMPSAC 2004.* IEEE Computer Society.

Hussain, T., Balakrishnan, R., & Viswanathan, A. (2009). Semantic wiki aided business process specification. *Proceedings of the 18th International Conference on World Wide Web (WWW'09),* (pp. 1135-1136). New York, NY: ACM.

IASA. (2011). *Architecture roles.* Retrieved 28 September, 2011, from http://www.iasaglobal.org/iasa/Roles.asp

IBM. (2008). *IBM perspective on cloud computing.* Retrieved from ftp://ftp.software.ibm.com/software/tivoli/brochures/IBM_Perspective_on_Cloud_Computing.pdf

IBM. (2009). *Unified method framework: Work product description ARC 0513 (Architectural Decisions).* IBM Corporation.

IEEE. (1995). *Software, 12*(6).

IEEE. (2000). *IEEE standard 1471-2000, recommended practice for architectural description of software-intensive systems.*

Inoki, M., & Fukazawa, Y. (2007). Software product line evolution method based on kaizen approach. In *Proceedings of the ACM Symposium on Applied Computing* (pp. 1207-1214).

Isham, M. (2008). Agile architecture is possible – You first have to believe! In *Proceedings of Agile 2008 conference,* (pp. 484-489). IEEE Computer Society.

ISO. (2007). *ISO/IEC 42010:2007: Systems and software engineering -- Recommended practice for architectural description of software-intensive systems.*

ISO. IEC 42010 CD1. (2010). *Systems and software engineering –Architectural description,* draft. Retrieved August 30, 2011, from http://www.iso-architecture.org/ieee-1471/docs/ISO-IEC-IEEE-latest-draft-42010.pdf

ISO. IEC 42010. (2007). *Systems and software engineering: Architectural description.* International Standards Organization.

ISO/IEC/IEEE. 42010. (2011). *Systems and software engineering — Architecture description.* Retrieved from http://www.iso-architecture.org/ieee-1471/

Jackson, M., & Zave, P. (1995). Deriving specifications from requirements: an example. In *Proceedings of 17th International Conference on Software Engineering* (pp. 15–24). ACM Press.

Jackson, M. (2001). *Problem frames: Analyzing and Structuring Software Development Problems*. Addison-Wesley.

Jansen, A., & Bosch, J. (2005). Software architecture as a set of architectural design decisions. *Proceedings of the 5th Working IEEE/IFIP Conference on Software Architecture*, (pp. 109-120). IEEE Software.

Jansen, A., Bosch, J., & Avgeriou, P. (2008). Documenting after the fact: Recovering architectural design decisions. *Journal of Systems and Software, 81*(4), 536–557. doi:10.1016/j.jss.2007.08.025

Jifeng, H., Li, X., & Liu, Z. (2005). *Component-based software engineering -The need to link methods and their theories*. The United Nations University.

Jifeng, H., Li, X., & Liu, Z. (2005). *rCOS: A refinement calculus for object systems*. The United Nations University.

Jifeng, H., Liu, Z., & Li, X. (2005). *Reactive components*. The United Nations University.

Jifeng, H., Liu, Z., & Xiaoshan, L. (2003). *Contract-oriented component software development*. The United Nations University.

Julisch, K., Suter, C., Woitalla, T., & Zimmermann, O. (2011). Compliance by design – Bridging the chasm between auditors and IT architects. *Computers & Security, 30*(6-7). doi:10.1016/j.cose.2011.03.005

Kaisler, S. H., Armour, F., & Valivullah, M. (2005). Enterprise architecting: Critical problems. In *Proceedings of the 38th Hawaii International Conference on Systems Sciences*.

Kamath, S. (2011). Capabilities and features: Linking business and application architectures - I. *International Conference on Information Science and Applications*, (pp. 1-7). Retrieved from doi:http://doi.ieeecomputersociety.org/10.1109/ICISA.2011.5772351

Kaplan, R. S., & Norton, D. P. (1996). Using the Balanced Scorecard as a strategic management system. *Harvard Business Review*, (January-February): 76.

Kazman, R., Asundi, J., & Klein, M. (2001). Quantifying the costs and benefits of architectural decisions. In *Proceedings 23rd International Conference on Software Engineering* (pp. 297-306).

Kazman, R., Bass, L., Abowd, G., & Webb, M. (1994). SAAM: A method for analyzing properties of software architecture. In *Proceedings of the 16th International Conference on Software Engineering*, (pp. 81-90).

Kazman, R., Klein, M., & Clements, P. (2000). *ATAM: Method for architecture evaluation*. Software Engineering Institute Technical Report, CMU/SEI-2000-TR-004, Pittsburgh, PA.

Kazman, R., Klein, M., Barbacci, M., Longstaff, T., Lipson, H., & Carriere, J. (1998). The architecture tradeoff analysis method. In *Proceeding 4th IEEE International Conference on Engineering of Complex Computer Systems* (pp. 68-78).

Kazman, R., & Carrière, J. (1999). Playing detective: Reconstructing software architecture from available evidence. *Journal of Automated Software Engineering, 6*(2), 107–138. doi:10.1023/A:1008781513258

Kepner, C., & Tregoe, B. (1981). *The new rational manager*. Princeton, NJ: Princeton Research Press.

Khajeh-Hosseini, A., Greenwood, D., & Sommerville, I. (2010). *Cloud migration: A case study of migrating an enterprise IT system to IaaS*. Paper presented at the 3rd International Conference on Cloud Computing.

Kneuper, R. (2008). *CMMI: Improving software and systems development processes using capability maturity model integration (CMMI-Dev)*. Rocky Nook.

Koehler, J., Gschwind, T., Kuster, J., Volzer, H., & Zimmermann, O. (2011). Towards a compiler for business-IT systems- A vision statement complemented with a research agenda. In Z. Huzar & M. Koci (Eds.), *Springer* (*Vol. 4980*). *Lecture Notes in Computer Science*.

Korherr, B. (2008). *Business process modeling – Languages, goals, and variabilities*. PhD thesis, Vienna University of Technology.

Korhonen, K. (2010). Evaluating the effect of agile methods on software defect data and defect reporting practices - A case study. In *Proceedings of the 7th International Conference on the Quality of Information and Communications Technology*, (pp. 35–43). IEEE Computer Society.

Koschmider, A., & Mevius, M. (2005). *A Petri Net based Approach for process model driven deduction of BPEL code*. OTM Confederated International Conferences, Agia Napa, Cyprus.

Koziolek, H., Happe, J., & Becker, S. (2006). Parameter dependent performance specification of software components. In *Proceedings of the Second International Conference on Quality of Software Architectures (QoSA2006), Lecture Notes in Computer Science, vol. 4214*. Berlin, Germany: Springer-Verlag.

Krafzig, D., Banke, K., & Slama, D. (2005). *Enterprise SOA*. Prentice Hall.

Krogmann, K., Kuperberg, M., & Reussner, R. (2010). Using genetic search for reverse engineering of parametric behaviour models for performance prediction. *IEEE Transactions on Software Engineering, 36*(6), 865–877. doi:10.1109/TSE.2010.69

Krötzsch, M., Vrandecic, D., & Völkel, M. (2006). Semantic Mediawiki. *Proceedings of 5th International Semantic Web Conference (ISWC06)*, (pp. 935-942).

Krötzsch, M., Vrandecic, D., Völkel, M., Haller, H., & Studer, R. (2007). Semantic Wikipedia. *Journal of Web Semantics, 5*(4), 251–261. doi:10.1016/j.websem.2007.09.001

Kruchten, P. (2004). An ontology of architectural design decisions. In J. Bosch (Ed.), *Proceedings of the 2nd Groningen Workshop on Software Variability Management*, Groningen, NL, (pp. 54-61).

Kruchten, P., Lago, P., & van Vliet, H. (2006). Building up and reasoning about architectural knowledge. *Proceedings of QoSA 2006, LNCS 4214*, (pp. 43-58). Springer.

Kruchten, P. (2003). *The rational unified process: An introduction*. Addison-Wesley.

Kruchten, P. (2008). What do software architects really do? *Journal of Software and Systems, 81*, 2413–2416. doi:10.1016/j.jss.2008.08.025

Kruchten, P. (2010). Software architecture and agile software development: A clash of two cultures? *Proceedings of ICSE, 2010*, 497–498. Cape Town, South Africa: ACM.

Kruger, C., & Cross, N. (2006). Solution driven versus problem driven design: Strategies and outcomes. *Design Studies, 27*, 527–548. doi:10.1016/j.destud.2006.01.001

Kuhl, F., Weatherly, R., & Dahmann, J. (2000). *Creating computer simulation systems: An introduction to the high level architecture*. Upper Saddle River, NJ: Prentice-Hall PTR.

Küster, J. M., Völzer, H., & Zimmermann, O. (2011). Managing artifacts with a viewpoint-realization level matrix. In Avgeriou, P., Grundy, J., Hall, J. G., Lago, P., & Mistrik, I. (Eds.), *Relating requirements and architectures*. Springer-Verlag. doi:10.1007/978-3-642-21001-3_15

Lamsweerde, A. V. (2001). *Goal-oriented requirements engineering: A guided tour*. Paper presented at the 5th IEEE International Symposium on Requirements Engineering, Toronto

Lamsweerde, A. V. (2004). *Goal-oriented requirements engineering: A roundtrip from research to practice*. Paper presented at the 12th IEEE International Requirements Engineering Conference, Kyoto.

Lamsweerde, A. V., & Leiter, E. (1998). *Integrating obstacles in goal-driven requirements engineering*. Paper presented at the 20th International Conference on Software Engineering, Kyoto.

Lamsweerde, A. V., Darimont, R., & Letier, E. (1998). Managing conflicts in goal-driven requirements engineering. *IEEE Transactions on Software Engineering, 24*(11), 908–926. doi:10.1109/32.730542

Lamsweerde, A. V., & Leiter, E. (2000). Handling obstacles in goal-oriented requirements engineering. *IEEE Transactions on Software Engineering, 26*(10), 978–1005. doi:10.1109/32.879820

Lamsweerde, A. V., & Letier, E. (2004). Lecture Notes in Computer Science: *Vol. 2941. From object orientation to goal orientation: A paradigm shift for requirements engineering* (pp. 153–166). doi:10.1007/978-3-540-24626-8_23

Landre, E., Wesenberg, H., & Rønneberg, H. (2006). *Architectural improvement by use of strategic level domain-driven design.* OOPSLA Companion. doi:10.1145/1176617.1176728

Lane, J., & Valerdi, R. (2010). Accelerating system of systems engineering understanding and optimization through lean enterprise principles. *4th Annual IEEE Systems Conference* (pp. 196-201). San Diego, CA: IEEE Systems.

Lavazza, L., & Bianco, V. D. (2006). Combining problem frames and UML in the description of software requirements. *Fundamental Approaches to Software Engineering, LNCS 3922.*

Lavazza, L., & Bianco, V. D. (2008, February). Enhancing problem frames with scenarios and histories in UML-based software development. *Expert Systems - The Journal of Knowledge Engineering, 25*(1).

Lawson, H. (2010). *A journey through the systems landscape.*

Lentz, J. L., & Bleizeffer, T. M. (2007). *IT ecosystems: Evolved complexity and unintelligent design.* In CHIMIT 2007, Cambridge, MA, USA

Leymann, F., & Roller, D. (200). *Production workflow – Concepts and techniques.* Prentice Hall.

Lim, S. L. (2010). *Social networks and collaborative filtering for large-scale requirements elicitation.* PhD Thesis, University of New South Wales, Australia.

Lim, S. L., & Bentley, P. J. (2011). Evolving relationships between social networks and stakeholder involvement in software projects. *Proceedings of the Genetic and Evolutionary Computation Conference (GECCO),* (pp. 1899-1906).

Lim, S. L., Damian, D., & Finkelstein, A. (2011). StakeSource2.0: using social networks of stakeholders to identify and prioritise requirements. *Proceedings of the 33rd International Conference on Software Engineering (ICSE),* (pp. 1022-1024).

Lim, S. L., Quercia, D., & Finkelstein, A. (2010). StakeNet: Using social networks to analyse the stakeholders of large-scale software projects. *Proceedings of the 32nd International Conference on Software Engineering (ICSE) -Vol. 1,* (pp. 295-304).

Lim, S. L., & Finkelstein, A. (2011). StakeRare: Using social networks and collaborative filtering for large-scale requirements elicitation. *IEEE Transactions on Software Engineering, 38*(3), 707–735. doi:10.1109/TSE.2011.36

Liu, Z., Jifeng, H., & Li, X. (2004). *Component-oriented development of component software.* Macau: The United Nations University.

Liu, Y., Wang, Q., Zhuang, M., & Zhu, Y. (2008). Re-engineering legacy systems with RESTful web service. *Proceedings of COMPSAC, 08,* 785–790.

Lopez-Fernandez, L., Robles, G., & Gonzalez-Barahona, J. M. (2004). Applying social network analysis to the information in CVS repositories. *Proceedings of the International Workshop on Mining Software Repositories (MSR),* (pp. 101-105).

Louridas, P. (2006). Using wikis in software development. *Software, 23,* 88–91. doi:10.1109/MS.2006.62

Lu, R. (2005). Towards a mathematical theory of knowledge—Categorical analysis of knowledge. *Journal of Computer Science and Technology, 20*(6), 751–757. doi:10.1007/s11390-005-0751-4doi:10.1007/s11390-005-0751-4

Maalej, W., Happel, H. J., & Seedorf, S. (2010). Applications of ontologies in collaborative software development. In I. Mistrík, J. Grundy, A.V.D. Hoek, & J. Whitehead (Eds.), *Collaborative software engineering.* Berlin, Germany: Springer.

MacLane, S. (1998). *Categories for the working mathematician: Graduate texts in mathematics* (2nd ed., Vol. 5). Springer-Verlag.

Maier, M. (1998). Architecting principles for systems-of-systems. *Systems Engineering, 1*(4), 267–284. doi:10.1002/(SICI)1520-6858(1998)1:4<267::AID-SYS3>3.0.CO;2-D

Maier, M., & Rechtin, E. (2009). *The art of systems architecting* (3rd ed.). Boca Raton, FL: CRC Press.

Marshall, S., & Mitchell, G. (2004). Applying SPICE to e-learning: An e-learning maturity model? In *ACE '04: Proceedings of the Sixth Conference on Australasian Computing Education,* (pp. 185-191). Dunedin, New Zealand.

Mascitelli, R. (2006). *The lean product development guidebook: Everything your design team needs to improve efficiency and slash time to market.*

Matthes, F., Neubert, C., & Steinhoff, A. (2009). *A. federated application lifecycle management based on an open web architecture.* Karlsruhe, Germany: Workshop Design for Future – Langlebige Softwaresysteme, GI-Arbeitskreis Langlebige Softwaresysteme (L2S2).

McDavid, D. W. (1999). A standard for business architecture description. *IBM Systems Journal, 38,* 12–31. doi:10.1147/sj.381.0012doi:10.1147/sj.381.0012

McManus, J., & Wood-Harper, D. (2008). *A study in project failure.* Retrieved February 5, 2012, from http://www.bcs.org/content/ConWebDoc/19584

Medvidovic, N., & Taylor, R. N. (2000). A classification and comparison framework for software architecture description languages. *IEEE Transactions on Software Engineering, 26,* 70–93. doi:10.1109/32.825767doi:10.1109/32.825767

Medvidovic, N., Dashofy, E. M., & Taylor, R. N. (2007). Moving architectural description from under the technology lamppost. *Information and Software Technology, 49,* 12–31. doi:10.1016/j.infsof.2006.08.006doi:10.1016/j.infsof.2006.08.006

Medvidovic, N., Rosenblum, D. S., & Taylor, R. N. (1999). A language and environment for architecture-based software development and evolution. In *Proceedings 21st International Conference Software Engineering (ICSE '99)* (pp. 44-53). Los Angeles, CA: IEEE Computer Society.

Meneely, A., Williams, L., Snipes, W., & Osborne, J. (2008). Predicting failures with developer networks and social network analysis. *Proceedings of the 16th International Symposium on the Foundations of Software Engineering (FSE),* (pp. 13-23).

Meng, S., & Aichernig, B. K. (2002). *Component-based coalgebraic specification and verification in RSL.* The United Nations University.

Meyers, B. C., & Obendorf, P. (2001). *Managing software acquisition: Open systems and COTS products.* New York, NY: Addison-Wesley.

Miksovic, C., & Zimmermann, O. (2011) Architecturally significant requirements, reference architecture and metamodel for knowledge management in information technology services. *Proceedings of IEEE/IFIP WICSA 2011.*

Miller, M. (2008). *Cloud computing: Web based applications that change the way you work and collaborate online.* Que Publishing.

Muller, G. (2004). *CAFCR: A multi-view method for embedded systems architecting; Balancing genericity and specificity.* PhD thesis, University of Delft. Retrieved from http://www.gaudisite.nl/ThesisBook.pdf

Muller, G. (2007). *System modeling and analysis: A practical approach.* Retrieved February 7, 2012, from http://www.gaudisite.nl/SystemModelingAndAnalysisBook.pdf

Muller, G. (2011). *Systems architecting: A business perspective.* CRC Press.

Mylopoulos, J., Chung, L., & Nixon, B. (1992). Representing and using nonfuntional requirements: A process oriented approach. *IEEE Transactions on Software Engineering, 18*(6), 483–497. doi:10.1109/32.142871

Nallur, V., & Bahsoon, R. (2010). *Design of a market-based mechanism for quality attributes tradeoff of services in the cloud.* Paper presented at the 2010 ACM Symposium on Applied Computing.

Nallur, V., Bahsoon, R., & Yao, X. (2009). *Self-optimizing architecture for ensuring quality attributes in the cloud.* Paper presented at the 2009 IEEE/IFIP WICSA/ECSA.

Nelson, L., & Churchill, E. F. (2006). Repurposing: Techniques for reuse and integration of interactive services. *Proceedings 2006 IEEE International Conference Information Reuse and Integration.*

Nelson, M., Cowan, D., & Alencar, P. (2001). Geographic problem frames. In *Fifth IEEE International Symposium on Requirements Engineering* (pp. 306–307).

Nierstrasz, O., & Achermann, F. (2003). A calculus for modeling software components. In F. S. de Boer, M. M. Bonsangue, S. Graf, & W.-P. de Roever (Eds.), *Formal methods for components and objects, LNCS 2852.* Springer. doi:10.1007/978-3-540-39656-7_14doi:10.1007/978-3-540-39656-7_14

Nord, R. L., & Tomayko, J. E. (2006). Software architecture-centric methods and agile development. *IEEE Software, 23*(2), 47–53. doi:10.1109/MS.2006.54

Northrop, L. M. (2002). SEI's software product line tenets. *IEEE Software,* (July-August): 32–40. doi:10.1109/MS.2002.1020285

Nuseibeh, B., & Easterbrook, S. (2000). *Requirements engineering: A roadmap.* Paper presented at the The Future of Software Engineering.

Oasis WS-BPEL TC. (2011). *Web services business process execution language, version 2.0.* Retrieved May 23, 2011, from http://docs.oasis-open.org/wsbpel/2.0/OS/wsbpel-v2.0-OS.html

Object Management Group (OMG). (2006). *UML profile for modeling and analysis of real-time and embedded systems (MARTE)* RFP (realtime/05-02-06). Retrieved from http://www.omg.org/cgi-bin/doc?realtime/2005-2-6

OpenGroup. (2007). *The open group architecture framework (TOGAF) version 8.1.1,* enterprise edition. Retrieved August 5, 2011, from http://www.opengroup.org/

OpenGroup. (2009). *Archimate 1.0 specification.* Retrieved August 5, 2011, from http://www.opengroup.org/

OSI. (2011). *The open source initiative.* Retrieved from http://www.opensource.org/

Padberg, J. (2002). Integration of categorical frameworks: Rule-based refinement and hierarchical composition for components. *Applied Categorical Structures,* 333–364.

Padberg, J., & Ehrig, H. (2006). Petri net modules in the transformation-based component framework. *Journal of Logic and Algebraic Programming, 67*(1-2), 198–225. doi:10.1016/j.jlap.2005.09.007doi:10.1016/j.jlap.2005.09.007

Page, L., Brin, S., Motwani, R., & Winograd, T. (1999). *The pagerank citation ranking: Bringing order to the Web.* Stanford InfoLab.

Pahl, C. (2001). *Components, contracts, and connectors for the unified modeling language.* FME, LNCS 2021 (pp. 259–277). Berlin, Germany: Springer.

Papazoglou, M., & van den Heuvel, W.-J. (2007, October). Business process development lifecycle methodology. *Communications of the ACM, 50*(10). doi:10.1145/1290958.1290966

Pautasso, C., Zimmermann, O., & Leymann, F. (2008). RESTful web services vs. Big web services: Making the right architectural decision. *Proceedings of WWW, 2008,* 805–814. ACM. doi:10.1145/1367497.1367606

Pernstål, J., Magazinovic, A., & Öhman, P. (2008). A multiple case study investigating the interaction between manufacturing and development organizations in automotive software engineering. In *Proceedings of the Second ACM-IEEE International Symposium on Empirical Software Engineering and Measurement* (pp. 12-21).

Plasil, F., Balek, D., & Janecek, R. (1998). SOFA/DCUP: Architecture for component trading and dynamic updating. *Fourth International Conference on Configurable Distributed Systems* (pp. 43–52). IEEE CS Press.

Ploesser, K., Recker, J., & Rosemann, M. (2008). Towards a classification and lifecycle of business process change. In *Proceedings of 9th Workshop on Business Process Modeling, Development and Support (BPMDS '08): Business Process Life-Cycle: Design, Deployment, Operation & Evaluation,* Montpellier, France.

Poppendieck, M., & Poppendieck, T. (2003). *Lean software development: An agile toolkit.* Addison-Wesley.

Poppendieck, M., & Poppendieck, T. (2006). *Implementing lean software development from concept to cash.* Addison-Wesley.

Potts, C. (1995). *Using schematic scenarios to understand user needs.* Paper presented at the of 1st Conference on Designing Interactive Systems: Processes, Methods and Techniques.

Potts, C. (1993). Software-engineering research revisited. *IEEE Software, 10*(5), 19–28. doi:10.1109/52.232392

Pugh, S. (1981). Concept selection: A method that works. In V. Hubka (Ed.), *Review of Design Methodology: Proceedings International Conference on Engineering Design,* Rome, (pp. 497–506). Zürich, Switzerland: Heurista.

Ramesh, B., & Jarke, M. (1999). Toward reference models for requirements traceability. *IEEE Transactions on Software Engineering, 27*(1), 58–93. doi:10.1109/32.895989

Ran, A., & Kuusela, J. (1996). Design decision trees. *Proceedings of 8th International Workshop on Software Specification and Design, International Workshop on Software Specifications & Design,* (pp. 172-175). IEEE Computer Society.

Rapanotti, L., Hall, J. G., Jackson, M., & Nuseibeh, B. (2004, 6-10 September). Architecture driven problem decomposition. In *Proceedings of 12th IEEE International Requirements Engineering Conference (RE'04).* Kyoto, Japan.

Rawsthorne, D. (2007). *Collabnet Scrum and agile blog: Sprint zero.* Retrieved, August 30, 2011, from http://blogs.danube.com/sprint-zero?q=blog/dan_rawsthorne/sprint_zero

Reisig, W. (1985). *Petri Nets: An introduction. EATCS: Monographs on Theoretical Computer Science (Vol. 4).* Springer-Verlag.

Reussner, R., Becker, S., Burger, E., Happe, J., Hauck, M., Koziolek, A., et al. (2011). *The Palladio component model.* Technical report, Karlsruhe, Germany.

Richardson, I., Avram, G., Deshpande, S., & Casey, V. (2008). Having a foot on each shore –Bridging global software development in the case of SMEs. *IEEE International Conference on Global Software Engineering,* (pp. 13–22).

Richardson, L., & Ruby, S. (2007). *RESTful web services.* O'Reilly Media.

Rosen, L. (2005). *Open source licensing: Software freedom and intellectual property law.* Upper Saddle River, NJ: Prentice-Hall PTR. Retrieved from http://www.rosenlaw.com/oslbook.htm

Rozanski, N., & Woods, E. (2005). *Software systems architecture: Working with stakeholders using viewpoints and perspectives.* Addison-Wesley.

Sangiovanni-Vincentelli, A., & Di Natale, M. (2007). Embedded system design for automotive applications. *IEEE Computer,* October (pp. 42-51).

Santos, N., Gummadi, K. P., & Rodrigues, R. (2009). *Towards trusted cloud computing.* Paper presented at the 2009 Conference on Hot Topics in Cloud Computing.

Scacchi, W. (2007). Free/open source software development: Recent research results and emerging opportunities. *Proceedings of European Software Engineering Conference and ACM SIGSOFT Symposium on the Foundations of Software Engineering,* Dubrovnik, Croatia, (pp. 459-468).

Scacchi, W., & Alspaugh, T. A. (2008). Emerging issues in the acquisition of open source software within the U.S. Department of Defense. *Proceedings 5th Annual Acquisition Research Symposium,* Vol. 1, (pp. 230-244). NPS-AM-08-036, Naval Postgraduate School, Monterey, CA

Scacchi, W. (2002). Understanding the requirements for developing open source software systems. *IEE Proceedings. Software, 149*(1), 24–39, February. doi:10.1049/ip-sen:20020202

Schaffert, S., Bischof, D., Bürger, T., Gruber, A., & Hilzensauer, W. (2006). *Learning with Semantic Wikis.* First Workshop SemWiki2006 – From Wiki to Semantics, co-located with the 3rd Annual European Semantic Web Conference (ESWC), Budva, Montenegro.

Schaffert, S., Bry, F., Baumeister, J., & Kiesel, M. (2007). Semantic Wiki. *Informatik Spektrum, 30*(6), 434–439. doi:10.1007/s00287-007-0195-z

Scheer, A., Thomas, O., & Adam, O. (2005). Process modeling using event-driven process chains. In Dumas, M., van der Aalst, W. M., & ter Hofstede, A. H. (Eds.), *Process-aware information systems: Bridging people and software through process technology.* Hoboken, NJ: John Wiley & Sons. doi:10.1002/0471741442.ch6

Schmidt, D. C. (2006). Model-driven engineering. *IEEE Computer, 39*(2). Retrieved July 11, 2011, from http://www.cs.wustl.edu/~schmidt/PDF/GEI.pdf

Schmidt, R., Lyytinen, K., Keil, M., & Cule, P. (2001). Identifying software project risks: An international Delphi study. *Journal of Management Information Systems, 17*(4), 5–36.

Schneider, K. (2011). Focusing spontaneous feedback to support system evolution. In *Proceedings of the IEEE 19th International Requirements Engineering Conference (RE '11)* (pp. 165-174).

Schneider, K., Meyer, S., Peters, M., & Schliephacke, F. Mörschbach & J., Aguirre, L. (2010). Feedback in context: Supporting the evolution of IT-ecosystems. In M. Ali Babar, M. Vierimaa, & M. Oivo (Eds.), *Proceedings of the 11th International Conference on Product-Focused Software Process Improvement (PROFES 2010)* (pp. 191-205). Berlin, Germany: Springer-Verlag.

Schönthaler, F., Vossen, G., Oberweis, A., & Karle, T. (2012). *Business processes for business communities: Modeling languages, methods, tools*. Springer-Verlag.

Schougaard, K., Hansen, K., & Christensen, H. (2008) Sa@work: A field study of software architecture and software quality at work. In *Proceedings of the 15ᵗʰ Asia-Pacific Software Engineering Conference APSEC 2008*, (pp. 411-418). IEEE.

Schreiner, S. (2011). Modeling RESTful applications. In C. Pautasso & E. Wilde (Eds.), *Proceedings of the Second International Workshop on RESTful Design (WS-REST '11)* (pp. 15-21). New York, NY: ACM.

Schwaber, K. (1995). Scrum development process. *Proceedings of OOPSLA'95 Workshop on Business Object Design and Implementation*.

Scott, J. (2010). *The anatomy of a capability map*. Forrester Research. Retrieved January 8, 2012, from http://www.forrester.com/rb/Research/anatomy_of_capability_map/q/id/55972/t/2

Scott, J. (2010). *Building capability maps for business-IT alignment*. Forrester Research. Retrieved January 8, 2012, from http://www.forrester.com/rb/Research/building_capability_maps_for_business-it_alignment/q/id/56405/t/2

Scott, J. (2000). Social network analysis: A handbook. *Sage (Atlanta, Ga.)*.

Scrum Pattern Community. (2011). *Published patterns*. Retrieved August 10, 2011, from http://sites.google.com/a/scrumplop.org/published-patterns/

Scrum.org. (2012). *Scrum extension library*. Retrieved, January 2, 2012, from http://www.scrum.org/scrum-extensions/

Seaman, C. B. (2010). Qualitative methods in empirical studies of software engineering. *IEEE Software*, *27*(2), 16–22.

SEI. (2006). *CMMI for development*, Version 1.2. Software Engineering Institute, Technical Report CMU/SEI-2006-TR-008.

Senge, P. (1990). *The fifth discipline: The art & practice of the learning organization*.

Sessions, R. (2007). *A comparison of the top four enterprise-architecture methodologies*. Retrieved August 2, 2011, from http://msdn.microsoft.com/en-us/library/bb466232.asp

Sessions, r. (2009). *The it complexity crisis: danger and opportunity*. Retrieved September 3, 2011, from http://www.objectwatch.com/whitepapers/ITComplexity-WhitePaper.pdf

Sharp, H., Galal, G. H., & Finkelstein, A. (1999). Stakeholder identification in the requirements engineering process. *Proceedings of the Database & Expert System Applications Workshop (DEXA)*, (pp. 387–391).

Shaw, M., & Garlan, D. (1996). *Software architecture: Perspectives on an emerging discipline*. Prentice Hall.

Smith, P. G., & Reinertsen, D. G. (1995). *Developing products in half the time: New rules, new tools*. New York, NY: John Wiley.

Software Engineering Institute. (2011). *Software product lines*. Retrieved October 30, 2011, from http://www.sei.cmu.edu/productlines/

Sommerville, I. (1995). *Software engineering* (5th ed.). Addison Wesley.

Sommerville, I., & Sawyer, P. (2003). *Requirements engineering: A good practice guide*. Wiley.

Sondhi, R. (1999). *Total strategy*. Airworthy Publications International Ltd.

Sowa, J. F., & Zachman, J. A. (1992). Extending and formalizing the framework for information systems architecture. *IBM Systems Journal*, *31*(3), 590–616. doi:10.1147/sj.313.0590

St. Laurent, A. M. (2004). *Understanding open source and free software licensing*. Sebastopol, CA: O'Reilly Press.

Stafford, J. A., & Wolf, A. L. (2001). Software architecture. In G. T. Heinman & W. T. Council (Eds.), *Component-based software engineering* (pp. 371–387). Addison Wesley.

Sutherland, J. (2008). *Nokia test: Where did it come from?* Retrieved November 19, 2011 from http://scrum.jeffsutherland.com/2008/08/nokia-test-where-did-it-come-from.html

Sutherland, J. (2010). *Scrumbut test aka the Nokia test.* Retrieved November 19, 2011, from http://jeffsutherland.com/scrumbutttest.pdf

Sutherland, J. (n.d.). *Scrum blog.* Retrieved from http://scrum.jeffsutherland.com/

Sutherland, J., & Schwaber, K. (2011). *The Scrum guide – The definitive guide to Scrum: The rules of the game.* Retrieved September 9, 2011, from http://www.scrum.org/storage/scrumguides/Scrum_Guide.pdf

Sutton, T., & Osterweil, L. J. (1997). The design of a next-generation process language. In *Software Engineering – ESEC/FSE'97 (Vol. 1301)*. Lecture Notes in Computer ScienceBerlin, Germany: Springer. doi:10.1007/3-540-63531-9_12

SWEBOK. (2004). *The software engineering body of knowledge* (Abran, A., Moore, J., Borque, P., & Dupuis, R., Eds.). Los Alamitos, CA: IEEE Computer Society.

Szyperski, C. (2002). *Component software: Beyond object-oriented programming.* Addison-Wesley.

Tang, A., Aleti, A., Burge, J., & van Vliet, H. (2010). What makes software design effective. *Design Studies, 31*, 614–640. doi:10.1016/j.destud.2010.09.004

Tang, A., Han, J., & Vasa, R. (2009). Software architecture design reasoning: A case for improved methodology support. *IEEE Software, 26*, 43–49. doi:10.1109/MS.2009.46

Taylor, R., Medvidovic, N., & Dashofy, E. (2010). *Software architecture: Foundations, theory and practice.* Hoboken, NJ: John Wiley and Sons.

The Open Group. (2009). *The Open Group architecture framework*, Version 9. Retrieved from http://www.opengroup.org/togaf

The Open Group. (2010). *Cloud buyers' decision tree.* Poppendieck, M., & Poppendieck, T. (2003). *Lean software development: An agile toolkit.* Addison Wesley.

Thum, C., Schwind, M., & Schader, M. (2009). *SLIM—A lightweight environment for synchronous collaborative modeling.* ACM/IEEE 12th International Conference on Model Driven Engineering Languages and Systems (MoDELS'09), Denver, USA; October 04-10.

Tian, C., Ding, W., Cao, R., & Lee, J. (2006). *Business componentization: A principle for enterprise architecture design.* IBM.

Tilkov, S. (2011). *REST und HTTP: Einsatz der Architektur des Web für Integrationsszenarien* (2nd ed.). Dpunkt Verlag.

Tonella, P., Susi, A., & Palma, F. (2010). Using interactive GA for requirements prioritization. *Proceedings of the 2nd Symposium on Search Based Software Engineering (SSBSE)*, (pp. 57-66).

Tyree, J., & Ackerman, A. (2002). Architecture decisions: Demystifying architecture. *IEEE Software, 22*(2), 19–27. doi:10.1109/MS.2005.27

UML Revision Task Force. (2009, February). *OMG unified modeling language: Superstructure.* Retrieved from http://www.omg.org/docs/formal/09-02-02.pdf

UML Revision Task Force. (2010, February). *Object constraint language specification.*

van der Linden, F., Schmidt, K., & Rommes, E. (2007). *Software product lines in action: The best industrial practice in product line engineering.* Berlin, Germany: Springer.

van Lamsweerde, A. (2009). *Requirements engineering: From system goals to UML models to software specifications.* John Wiley & Sons, Inc. doi:10.1109/ICSE.2003.1201266

van't Wout, J., Waage, M., & Hartman, H. Stahlecker & M., Hofman, A. (2010). *The integrated architecture framework explained: Why, what, how.* Springer, Yi Qun, P. (2009). *IBM's ITA & ITS profession.* Retrieved September 1, 2011, from http://www.kingdee.com/news/subject/09togaf/pdf/wuzhifan.pdf

Ven, K., & Mannaert, H. (2008). Challenges and strategies in the use of open source software by independent software vendors. *Information and Software Technology*, *50*, 991–1002. doi:10.1016/j.infsof.2007.09.001

VersionOne. (2009). *4th annual state of agile survey*. Retrieved December 30, 2011, from http://www.versionone.com/pdf/2009_State_of_Agile_Development_Survey_Results.pdf

VersionOne. (2010). *5th annual state of agile survey*. Retrieved December 30, 2011, from http://www.versionone.com/pdf/2010_State_of_Agile_Development_Survey_Results.pdf

Versteeg, G., & Bouwman, H. (2006). Business architecture: A new paradigm to relate business strategy to ICT. *Information Systems Frontiers*, *8*, 91–102. doi:10.1007/s10796-006-7973-zdoi:10.1007/s10796-006-7973-z

Vickers, B. (2004). Architecting a software architect. In *Proceedings Aerospace Conference 2004*, Big Sky, MT, USA, 6-13 March 2004. Piscataway, NJ: IEEE.

Waldo, J., Wyant, J., Wolrath, A., & Kendall, S. (1994). *A note on distributed computing*. Sun Microsystems Laboratories Inc., SMLI TR-94-29, 1994. Retrieved July 9, 2011, from http://citeseerx.ist.psu.edu/viewdoc/download?doi=10.1.1.48.7969&rep=rep1&type=pdf

Wallin, P., & Axelsson, J. (2008). A case study of issues related to automotive E/E system architecture development. In *Proceedings of the 15th IEEE International Conference on Engineering of Computer Based Systems* (pp. 87-95).

Wallin, P., Johnsson, S., & Axelsson, J. (2009). Issues related to development of E/E product line architectures in heavy vehicles. In *Proceedings of the 42nd Hawaii International Conference on System Sciences*.

Wallin, P., Larsson, S., Fröberg, J., & Axelsson, J. (2012). Problems and their mitigation in system and software architecting. *Information and Software Technology*, *54*(7). doi:10.1016/j.infsof.2012.01.004

Ward, A. C., Liker, J. K., Cristiano, J. J., & Sobek, D. K. II. (1995). The second Toyota paradox: How delaying decisions can make better cars faster. *Sloan Management Review*, *36*(3), 43–61.

Warmer, J., & Kleppe, A. (2003). *The object constraint language 2.0: Getting your models ready for MDA* (2nd ed.). Pearson Education.

Webber, J., Parastatidis, S., & Robinson, I. (2010). *REST in practice: Hypermedia and systems architecture*. O'Reilly Media.

Weerawarana, S., Curbera, F., Leymann, F., Storey, T., & Ferguson, D. F. (2005). *Web services platform architecture*. Prentice Hall.

Weill, P. (2007). *Innovating with information systems*. Presented at 6th e-Business Conference, Barcelona, Spain, 27th March 2007. Retrieved January 5, 2012, from http://www.iese.edu/en/files/6_29338.pdf

Wesenberg, H., Landre, E., & Rønneberg, H. (2006). *Using domain-driven design to evaluate commercial off-the-shelf software*. OOPSLA Companion. Retrieved from http://dblp.uni-trier.de/db/conf/oopsla/oopsla2006c.html - Wesenberg

Wetzstein, B., Ma, Z., Filipowska, A., Kaczmarek, M., Bhiri, S., & Losada, S. … Cicurel, L. (2007). Semantic business process management: A lifecycle based requirements analysis. In *Proceedings of Workshops on Semantic Business Process and Product Lifecycle Management (SBPM 2007) at the 4th European Semantic Web Conference (ESWC 2007)*, Innsbruck, Austria.

Woicik R. et al. (2006). *Attribute driven design*. Technical Report, CMU/SEI-2006-TR-023, November 2006.

Wojcik, R., Bachmann, F., Bass, L., Clements, P., Merson, P., & Nord, R. (2006). *Attribute-driven design (ADD) (Version 2.0)*. Software Engineering Institute.

Wolf, T., Schroter, A., Damian, D., & Nguyen, T. (2009). Predicting build failures using social network analysis on developer communication. *Proceedings of the 31st International Conference on Software Engineering (ICSE)*, (pp. 1-11).

Woods, E. (2011, June). Industrial architectural assessment using TARA. In *Proceedings 9th Working IEEE Conference on Software Architecture, WICSA 2011*, Colorado, USA, 20–24 June 2011. Piscataway, NJ: IEEE Computer Society Press.

Yu, E. (1997). Towards modelling and reasoning support for early-phase requirements engineering. In *Proceedings of the 3rd IEEE International Symposium on Requirements Engineering* (pp. 226 – 235).

Zachman, J. A. (1987). A framework for information system architecture. *IBM Systems Journal, 26*(3), 276–292. doi:10.1147/sj.263.0276doi:10.1147/sj.263.0276

Zardari, S., & Bahsoon, R. (2011). *Cloud adoption: A goal-oriented requirements engineering approach.* Paper presented at the IEEE/ACM International Workshop on Cloud Software Engineering, The ACM/IEEE 33rd International Conference on Software Engineering, Hawaii, USA.

Zave, P. (1997). Classification of research efforts in requirements engineering. *ACM Computing Surveys, 29*(4), 315–321. doi:10.1145/267580.267581

Zdun U., Hentrich C., & Dustdar, S. (2007). Modeling process-driven and service-oriented architectures using patterns and pattern primitives. *ACM Transactions on the Web, 1*(3).

Zhan, N., Kang, E., & Liu, Z. (2010). Component publications and compositions. In A. Butterfield (Ed.), *Unifying Theories of Programming* (*Vol. 5713,* pp. 238–257). *Lecture Notes in Computer Science* Berlin, Germany: Springer. doi:10.1007/978-3-642-14521-6_14doi:10.1007/978-3-642-14521-6_14

Zhang, Y. (2010). *Multi-objective search-based requirements selection and optimisation.* PhD Thesis, King's College London.

Zimmermann, O. (2009). *An architectural decision modeling framework for service-oriented architecture design.* PhD Thesis, University of Stuttgart.

Zimmermann, O., Schuster, N., & Eeles, P. (2008). *Modeling and sharing architectural decisions, Part 1: Concepts.* IBM developerWorks.

Zimmermann, T., & Nagappan, N. (2008). Predicting defects using network analysis on dependency graphs. *Proceedings of the 30th International Conference on Software Engineering (ICSE),* (pp. 531-540).

Zimmermann, O. (2011). Architectural decisions as reusable design assets. *IEEE Software, 28*(1), 64–69. doi:10.1109/MS.2011.3

Zimmermann, O., Koehler, J., Leymann, F., Polley, R., & Schuster, N. (2009). Managing architectural decision models with dependency relations, integrity constraints, and production rules. *The Journal of Systems and Software and Services, 82*(8).

Zimmermann, O., Tomlinson, M., & Peuser, S. (2003). *Perspectives on web services: Applying SOAP, WSDL, and UDDI to real-world projects.* Springer Professional Computing.

About the Contributors

Ivan Mistrík is an independent researcher in software-intensive systems engineering. He is a computer scientist who is interested in system and software engineering (SE/SWE) and in system and software architecture (SA/SWA), in particular: life cycle system/software engineering, requirements engineering, relating software requirements and architectures, knowledge management in software development, rationale-based software development, aligning enterprise/system/software architectures, value-based software engineering, agile software architectures, and collaborative system/software engineering. He has more than forty years' experience in the field of computer systems engineering as an information systems developer, R&D leader, SE/SA research analyst, educator in computer sciences, and ICT management consultant. In the past 40 years, he has been primarily working at various R&D institutions in USA and Germany and has done consulting on a variety of large international projects sponsored by ESA, EU, NASA, NATO, and UN. He has also taught university-level computer sciences courses in software engineering, software architecture, distributed information systems, and human-computer interaction. He is the author or co-author of more than 90 articles and papers in international journals, conferences, books and workshops, most recently a chapter "Capture of Software Requirements and Rationale through Collaborative Software Development," a paper "Knowledge Management in the Global Software Engineering Environment," and a paper "Architectural Knowledge Management in Global Software Development." He has also written over 120 technical reports and presented over 70 scientific/technical talks. He has served in many program committees and panels of reputable international conferences and organized a number of scientific workshops, most recently two workshops on Knowledge Engineering in Global Software and Development at International Conference on Global Software Engineering 2009 and 2010 and IEEE International Workshop on the Future of Software Engineering for/in the Cloud (FoSEC) held in conjunction with IEEE Cloud 2011.

Antony Tang is an Associate Professor in Swinburne University of Technology's Faculty of Information and Computer Technology. His research interests include software architecture design reasoning, software development processes, and knowledge engineering. He spent over 20 years in the software industry before becoming a researcher. He received his Bachelor degrees in Computer Science and Commerce from the University of Melbourne and his PhD degree in Information Technology from the Swinburne University of Technology.

Rami Bahsoon is a Lecturer in Software Engineering at the University of Birmingham. He holds a PhD in Software Engineering from UCL for his research in architectural evaluation using real options. He had also read for MBA in technology strategy, dynamics, and new communications industry in London Business School. He is currently leading a software engineering in and for the cloud interest group, where he is currently supervising seven PhD students on the topic. He has published in the area of cloud software engineering, economics-driven software engineering, relating between non-functional requirements and software architectures, software maintenance and evolution, and regression testing. He acted as a co-chair for the IEEE Workshop on Software Architectural and Mobility, affiliated with International Conference on Software Engineering (ICSE), the IEEE Workshop Towards Stable and Adaptable Software Architectures; the IEEE Intl. Workshop on Software Stability at Work, and the OOPSLA Workshop on Unified Data Mining Engine. He is a guest editor for a special issue on the future of software engineering in/for the cloud with the *Journal of Systems and Software*. He is a reviewer for various journals, conferences, and workshops in software engineering.

Judith A. Stafford is a Senior Lecturer on the faculty of the Department of Computer Science at Tufts University in Medford, Massachusetts. She is also a visiting scientist at the Software Engineering Institute at Carnegie Mellon University, Pittsburgh, Pennsylvania and is a member of the International Foundations of Information Processing Working Group on Software Architecture (IFIP WG2.10), IEEE Computer Society, and ACM SigSoft. Dr. Stafford's research focuses on software architecture and component based-software engineering, more specifically documenting software architecture and using software architecture as a base for quality analysis of component-based systems. She has co-authored a book on documenting software architectures, several book chapters on component-based software engineering and software architecture. She was co-founded the International Federation of Component-Based Systems and Software Architecture (CompArch), and has chaired conferences and program committees on these subjects. Dr. Stafford serves as Software Engineering Area Editor on the editorial board for the *Journal of System Architecture*, edited several journal special issues of *IEEE Software* and the *Journal of Software and Systems*, and published numerous articles in these areas.

* * *

Charlie Alfred has 30 years of experience as a Software Engineer, working in a wide range of application areas including: medical devices, semiconductor control systems, electronic payment systems, realtime options trading, and workflow management. He is a leader in the development of software architecture formulation and evaluation methods and has published several journal articles and white papers in these areas. Architecture challenges and value models are two of his innovative contributions in this area. In addition, he has extensive experience in distributed architectures, relational and object database management systems, object-oriented design and programming, design patterns, real-time control systems, and multi-threaded techniques.

Thomas A. Alspaugh is a project scientist at the Institute for Software Research, University of California, Irvine, where he was on the faculty from 2002-2008. From 2008-2011 he served as an adjunct faculty member in Computer Science at Georgetown University. His research interests are in software engineering, requirements, and licensing. Before completing his Ph.D. in 2002 at North Carolina State University, he worked as a software developer, team lead, and manager in industry, and as a computer scientist at the Naval Research Laboratory on the Software Cost Reduction (A-7) project.

Hazeline U. Asuncion is an Assistant Professor at the Computing and Software Systems Program, University of Washington, Bothell. She was previously a Postdoctoral Researcher at the Institute for Software Research at the University of California, Irvine. She has worked in the industry in a variety of roles: as a software engineer at Unisys Corporation, and as a traceability engineer at Wonderware Corporation where she designed a successful in-house traceability system. Her research emphasis is on traceability and she has developed a novel software traceability approach that automatically links distributed and heterogeneous information.

Jakob Axelsson received an M.Sc. in Computer Science in 1993 and a Ph.D. in Computer Systems in 1997, both from Linköping University in Sweden. He has been with Volvo Technology, Carlstedt Research & Technology, and Volvo Car Corporation, all in Gothenburg, Sweden. He is currently director of Software and Systems Engineering Research at the Swedish Institute of Computer Science (SICS) in Kista, Sweden. He is also Professor in Computer Science at Mälardalen University in Västerås, Sweden. Prof. Axelsson is author or co-author of about 60 papers, and received the best paper award at the IEEE Conference on Engineering of Computer-Based Systems in 2008. His current research interests are in the area of system architecture and development processes for embedded systems. Prof. Axelsson is a certified 6 Sigma Black Belt and a Senior Member of IEEE.

Stefanie Betz received her Diploma in Information Engineering and Management from Universität Karlsruhe. She is currently a senior researcher at the Software Engineering Lab, Blekinge Institute of Technology, Sweden. Before, she worked as a scientific coworker at the Institute of Applied Informatics and Formal Description Methods (AIFB), Karlsruhe Institute for Technology (KIT). She spent the autumn 2009 as an invited visiting researcher at the Enterprise Simulation Laboratory SimLab, Aalto University, Finland. Her research interests are in (global) software engineering, process management, and risk management. She is a member of ACM and German Informatics Society.

Erik Burger studied computer science at Universität Karlsruhe from 2002-2008. He wrote his Diploma Thesis at SAP AG, Walldorf, where he was employed as a working student in the MOIN (modeling infrastructure) project. Since 2009, he has been a PhD student in the Software Design and Quality group of Prof. Ralf Reussner at Karlsruhe Institute of Technology (KIT). His research is focused on model-driven software development and view-based modeling techniques. He is head of the sub-project "Quality prediction and assurance" in the GlobaliSE project, a research contract of the state of Baden-Württemberg which is funded by the Landesstiftung Baden-Württemberg gGmbH.

Christine Choppy has been a full Professor in Informatics at Université Paris 13 within LIPN (Informatics Laboratory) at Institut Galilée (Faculty of Science) since 1998. She was Head of Department from 2004 to 2009, and is currently Vice-Dean for International affairs at Institut Galilée (Faculty of Science). She was Vice-President of Informatics Europe till 2011, and was previously President of Specif, the French "academics in informatics" association. She is a member of IFIP WG1.3 Foundations of System Specification. She was previously Professor in Informatics at Université of Nantes with the Informatics Laboratory at Faculty of Science, and Assistant Professor at Université Paris 11 with the Informatics Laboratory at Faculty of Science. Her research topics are formal specifications and modelling.

Alexander Eckert is pursuing a Master's degree in Information Engineering and Management at the Karlsruhe Institute of Technology (KIT). In 2011, he completed his Bachelor's thesis, where he examined the expressive power and suitability for defining typical access control models of the "Access Definition and Query Language" (ADQL) authorization service, which was part of the European research project "WeKnowIt." He is interested in distributed systems, data analysis, and business process engineering. Since April 2011, Alexander is working as a Student Assistant at FZI Research Center for Information Technology in the GlobaliSE project.

Veli-Pekka Eloranta is a Researcher at the Department of Software Systems, Tampere University of Technology. He has worked four years with the software architectures and agile methods. His research focuses on software architectures, lean architecting practices, agile methods, architecture evaluations, design patterns and pattern languages. He has been an active person in pattern community and served in program committees of several PLoP conferences. In general, he is a passionate researcher and aims to closely collaborate with the industry in his research.

Funmilade Faniyi holds a BSc (Hons) degree in Computer Science (First class). He received the MSc degree in Advanced Computer Science from the University of Birmingham, United Kingdom, in 2010. He is currently working towards a PhD degree in Computer Science in the same university. Prior to PhD studies, he worked as a software engineer for financial and software consulting firms for over four years, leading the deployment of enterprise software systems. His main research interests include economics-inspired software engineering, design and evaluation of software architectures, especially for large-scale and self-adaptive systems.

Mark Harman is a Professor of Software Engineering at the Department of Computer Science, University College London, where he is the director of the Centre for Research on Evolution Search and Testing (CREST). His research interests are in the areas of search-based software engineering, program slicing, source code analysis, model transformation, software testing, and requirements engineering. Before joining University College London, he was the head of the Software Engineering Group and Professor of Software Engineering and at the Department of Computer Science, King's College London.

Denis Hatebur is a PhD student at University Duisburg-Essen in Germany and since 2004 he is the CEO of ITESYS Institut für technische Systeme GmbH in Dortmund/Germany. He worked in different industrial engineering projects as a consultancy. In these projects he was responsible for specification and testing parts. His research interest is the dependability engineering considering requirements engineering, architectural design and testing. In this field he has authored numerous reviewed conference and workshop papers. He holds a Diploma degree in Information Technology from University of Applied Science in Dortmund/Germany and a Master degree in Computer Engineering from University Duisburg-Essen.

Maritta Heisel is a full Professor for Software Engineering at the University of Duisburg-Essen, Germany. Her research interests include the development of dependable software, pattern- and component-based software development, software architecture, and software evolution. She is particularly interested in incorporating security considerations into software development processes and in integrating the development of safe and secure software. She co-authored more than 70 refereed publications, including monographs, book chapters, journals and conference papers. She is member of various program committees and served as reviewer for a number of journals and conferences. Moreover, she is a member of the European Workshop on Industrial Computer Systems Reliability, Safety and Security (EWICS).

Suresh Kamath holds a Bachelor's degree in Engineering, Masters in Industrial Management and Engineering, and a PhD in Machine Scheduling Research. Has twenty five years of experience in information technology and consulting areas. Experience in IT spans several industries: manufacturing, telecommunications, insurance, software products, and services. The experience involved performing in several roles such as managing software development teams, architecting software solutions, and as developer of specialized applications: manufacturing optimization, data warehouse solutions for banking, data mining in telecommunications etc. In consulting area the experience includes CMM Process Capability, Business Process Re-engineering, IT Strategy (IT divisional level). He has published several papers in the area of machine scheduling and architecture.

Kai Koskimies is a Professor of Software Engineering at the Department of Software Systems, Tampere University of Technology, Finland since 1999. Before that he has worked at Nokia Research Center as a Project Manager and at University of Tampere as a Professor. He has led research projects on software modeling tools, pattern-based software development tools, automated software architecture design, and software architecture evaluation. His current research interests are agile software architecting and architectural self-adaptation.

Soo Ling Lim is a Research Associate at the Department of Computer Science, University College London. Her research interests are in the area of requirements engineering, specifically in the areas of stakeholder analysis, requirements elicitation, prioritisation, and modelling and requirements change management. In 2011, she received a PhD from the School of Computer Science and Engineering, the University of New South Wales in Sydney, Australia. Before her PhD, she worked as an SAP consultant at the Computer Sciences Corporation and as a software engineer at CIC Secure in Australia.

Christoph Miksovic is a Senior IT Architect and Senior Software Engineer at IBM Research in Zurich, Switzerland. His focus areas are decision modeling for architectural decisions and strategic outsourcing, mobile computing, and business analytics. Prior to joining IBM Research, he was a solution architect at IBM Global Business Services working for clients in various industries on application development, application integration, and enterprise architecture consulting projects. Mr. Miksovic holds an M.Sc. (Dipl. Ing.) from the Swiss Federal Institute of Technology. He is an Open Group Master Certified IT Architect, IBM Certified IT Architect, TOGAF Certified, and a Certified Scrum Master.

Gerrit Muller, originally from The Netherlands, received his Master's degree in Physics from the University of Amsterdam in 1979. He worked from 1980 until 1997 at Philips Medical Systems as a system architect, followed by two years at ASML as a manager of systems engineering, returning to Philips (Research) in 1999. Since 2003 he has worked as a senior research fellow at the Embedded Systems Institute in Eindhoven, focusing on developing system architecture methods and the education of new system architects, receiving his doctorate in 2004. In January 2008, he became a full professor of systems engineering at Buskerud University College in Kongsberg, Norway. He continues to work as a senior research fellow at the Embedded Systems Institute in Eindhoven in a part-time position.

Khrystyna Nordheimer studied Information Systems at the University of Mannheim with focus on object-oriented programming, informatics, insurance management, and statistics. In her diploma thesis, she developed a distributed version of the Metropolis-Hastings-Algorithm and implemented it in a grid environment. Since April 2009 she has been working as Research Assistant at the Chair in Information Systems III at the University of Mannheim. She is currently involved in the GlobaliSE project funded by the Ministry of Science, Research, and the Arts of Baden-Württemberg and Landesstiftung Baden-Württemberg foundation, which explores the development of flexible business software by using global resources.

Andreas Oberweis is full Professor for Applied Informatics at the Karlsruhe Institute of Technology (KIT). Since 2004 he is also Director at the FZI Research Center for Information Technology Karlsruhe. He received a Doctoral Degree in Informatics from Universitaet Mannheim in 1990 and a Habilitation Degree in Applied Informatics from Universitaet Karlsruhe in 1995. From 1995 to 2003 he was Professor for Information Systems Development at Goethe-Universitaet Frankfurt/Main. His research and teaching interests are in the field of business process engineering and information systems development. He is co-founder of PROMATIS software GmbH in Ettlingen (1990).

Gianna Regio is an Associate Professor in Computer Science at University of Genova since 1992; before she was working as Researcher in the same university. She actively took part in many research projects, national and international, and has co-organized many international workshops and conferences. The research activity has been centered around the following topics: Software development methods; Formal specification and modelling of concurrent systems; Semantics of programming languages. In particular she has developed: specification methods for concurrent systems based on the use of formal techniques; visual notations derived from formal specifications; formal techniques supporting the use of Java; techniques for making "precise" UML; and rigorous software development methods based on UML.

Ralf Reussner is a full Professor of Software Engineering at the Karlsruhe Institute of Technology KIT since 2006. He holds the Chair of Software Design and Quality and is Director at the FZI Research Center for Information Technology Karlsruhe. His main research areas are software architecture, quantitative prediction models for software quality, in particular performance, but also reliability and maintainability. In particular, Prof. Reussner is interested in investigating the impact of design decisions on the quality of software. Therefore, his research group developed "Palladio," an architectural modeling language and a simulator for predicting software performance and reliability. Prior to his position in Karlsruhe, he was an Emmy-Noether Research Group leader and Juniorprofessor for Software Engineering at the University of Oldenburg, Germany, and scientific leader at the OFFIS institute in Oldenburg. He is editor of the German Handbook on Software Architecture and elected member of the presidial board of the GI.

Nick Rozanski is a Software Architect at a major international investment bank and has been working in the software engineering field for over 30 years. His professional interests include the role and practice of software architecture, information management, quality assurance and application integration; he is co-author of the book "Software Systems Architecture: Working with Stakeholders Using Viewpoints and Perspectives," published by Addison Wesley.

Walt Scacchi is a senior research scientist and research faculty member at the Institute for Software Research, University of California, Irvine. He received a Ph.D. in Information and Computer Science from UC Irvine in 1981. From 1981-1998, he was on the faculty at the University of Southern California. In 1999, he joined the Institute for Software Research at UC Irvine. He has published more than 150 research papers, and has directed 60 externally funded research projects. Last, in 2012, he serves as General Co-Chair of the 8th IFIP International Conference on Open Source Systems (OSS2012).

Kurt Schneider studied Computer Science and received a Doctoral degree in Software Engineering. He was a postdoctoral researcher at the Center for Life Long Learning and Design at the University of Colorado at Boulder, USA. In 1996-2003, he was a researcher and project manager at the DaimlerChrysler Research Center, Ulm, Germany. He is now a full Professor of Software Engineering at Leibniz Universität Hannover, Germany. His research interests include requirements engineering and techniques that enable people to contribute to and benefit from software.

Stefan Seedorf is a researcher at University of Mannheim and the founder of a computer firm. As part of his Doctoral degree he worked on ontologies and knowledge-based systems to support the software development life-cycle. He has several years' experience as project manager in different research projects. His main interests include semantic technologies, social software, and E-Commerce.

Angelo Susi is a Researcher at the Software Engineering Unit of the Fondazione Bruno Kessler in Trento, Italy. His research interests include requirements engineering, agent-oriented and goal-oriented software engineering methodologies, software testing, case-based reasoning and machine learning. He received a M.S. degree in Computer Science Engineering from the University of Roma "La Sapienza" in Italy. In 2000, he joined the Institute for Scientific and Technological Research in Trento, Italy, as a full time Researcher.

Christian Thum is a Researcher at University of Mannheim and founder. Prior to founding the collaborative web solutions startup "synchronite" he worked in the GlobaliSE research project. In his Doctoral thesis he proposed a new architecture for real-time collaboration on the web. His interests include software engineering, collaborative technologies, and web development.

Ralf Trunko studied Industrial Engineering (with specialization in computer sciences and operations research) at the Universitaet Karlsruhe. After his academic studies, he started a conferral of a Doctorate at the Institute of Applied Informatics and Formal Description Methods (AIFB) of the Universitaet Karlsruhe in the area applied informatics with the topic "context-aware exception handling in business processes."

In 2009, he changed from university to FZI Research Center for Information Technology Karlsruhe and received his doctor's degree in May 2011. Currently, he is department manager within the research area "Software Engineering" at FZI and project leader of the German research project "GlobaliSE."

Tristan Wehrmaker is a Researcher and Doctoral student at the Software Engineering Group of Prof. Dr. Kurt Schneider at Leibniz Universität Hannover, Germany. He received his Master's degree in Computer Science in 2009. His Master's thesis dealt with the interoperability and integration of social media services in the Web 2.0. Tristan's research interests include model-driven development of mobile and web applications. Primarily he uses domain specific languages to describe the concepts of an application independently of concrete technical implementation and constraints of a specific platform.

Eoin Woods is a lead software architect within the equities technology group of a major international investment bank, and has been working in the software engineering field for over 20 years. His main technical interests are software architecture, distributed systems, computer security, and data management; he is co-author of the book "Software Systems Architecture: Working with Stakeholders Using Viewpoints and Perspectives," published by Addison Wesley.

Shehnila Zardari is a PhD student at the School of Computer Science, the University of Birmingham. She has been supervised by Dr. Rami Bahsoon since August 2010. Her PhD investigation is aimed at developing a goal-oriented requirements engineering framework for reasoning about cloud adoption. Her research interests include cloud software architectures, requirements engineering, and risk management. Currently, she is Assistant Professor in the Department of Computer Science and Information Technology, NED University of Engineering and Technology, Pakistan (2009- to date). Shehnila holds a Master's of Engineering (Communication Systems and Networks) and Bachelor's of Engineering (Software Engineering) in 2006 from Mehran University of Engineering and Technology, Pakistan.

Olaf Zimmermann is a Senior Principal Scientist at ABB Corporate Research in Switzerland. His areas of interest include Web-based application and integration architectures, SOA design, and architectural knowledge management. Until January 2012, Olaf was a research staff member and executive IT architect at IBM Research, investigating the role of architectural decisions in the design process. Prior to that, Olaf worked as a solution architect and consultant, helping international clients in multiple industries build enterprise-scale SOA/Web services and Java Enterprise Edition solutions on professional services projects. In the beginning of his career, Olaf was a scientific consultant and developer in the IBM European Networking Center (ENC) in Heidelberg, Germany, focusing on industry-specific middleware frameworks for systems and network management. Olaf is a certified The Open Group Distinguished (Chief/Lead) IT Architect and a member of the Advisory Board of IEEE Software. He is an author of Perspectives on Web Services (Springer, 2003) and contributed to IBM Redbooks such as Web Services Wizardry with WebSphere Studio Application Developer, the first one on Eclipse and Web services (2001). Olaf received a PhD in Computer Science from the University of Stuttgart in 2009 and a "Diplom-Informatiker" (MS) degree in Computer Science from the Technical University in Braunschweig (1993).

Index